Sh'ma
From *The Book of Blessings*

Marcia Falk

שְׁמַע, יִשְׂרָאֵל –
לָאֱלֹהוּת אַלְפֵּי פָּנִים,
מְלָא עוֹלָם שְׁכִינָתָה,
רִבּוּי פָּנֶיהָ אֶחָד.

Sh'ma, yisra'eyl—
la'elohut alfey panim,
m'lo olam sh'khinatah,
ribuy panéha ehad.

Hear, O Israel—
The divine abounds everywhere
and dwells in everything;
the many are One.

Wrestling with Zion

Wrestling with Zion

*Progressive Jewish-American Responses
to the Israeli-Palestinian Conflict*

Edited and with an Introduction by
Tony Kushner and Alisa Solomon

Grove Press
New York

"Sh'ma" and "Birkat Shalom, Blessing of Peace" by Marcia Falk. Excerpted from *The Book of Blessings: New Jewish Prayers for Daily Life, the Sabbath, and the New Moon Festival* (Harper, 1996; Beacon, 1999) copyright © 1996 by Marcia Lee Falk. Used by permission of the author.

"Morning News" by Marilyn Hacker. From *Desesperanto* by Marilyn Hacker. Copyright © 2003 by Marilyn Hacker.

"Separating Spiritual and Political, He Pays a Price" (copyright © 2002 by The New York Times Co.) and "A Skeptic About Wars Intended to Stamp Out Evil" (copyright © 2003 by The New York Times Co.) by Chris Hedges. Reprinted with permission.

"Rescuing Private Lynch, Forgetting Rachel Corrie" by Naomi Klein. Published May 2003, copyright © Naomi Klein. "Sharon, LePen, and Anti-Semitism" by Naomi Klein. Published April 2002, copyright Naomi Klein.

"Deal Breakers," by Michael Massing. *The American Prospect*, vol. 13 no. 5, March 11, 2002.

"The Fundamental Truth" from *The Art of Blessing the Day* by Marge Piercy, copyright © 1999 by Middlemarsh, Inc. Used by permission of Alfred A. Knopf, a division of Random House, Inc.

"Imman Square Incantation" and "Immature Song" by Robert Pinsky. "Imman Square Incantation" was originally published in *Ploughshares*. "Immature Song" was originally published in *The Threepenny Review*.

"Living with the Holocaust" by Sara Roy. Copyright © 2002 by Institute for Palestine Studies; Reprinted from *Journal of Palestine Studies:* Vol. 32 No. 1 Issue: Autumn 2002 pp. 5-12.

"Prayer" from *Days of Wonder: New and Selected Poems* by Grace Schulman. Copyright © 2002 by Grace Schulman. Reproduced by permission of Houghton Mifflin Company. All rights reserved.

"Dislocated Identities: Reflections of an Arab-Jew" by Ella Shohat. Originally published: *Movement Research: Performance Journal* #5 (Fall-Winter, 1992) p.8.

"Intifada Diptych" by Alisa Solomon was first published in a special issue of the *Michigan Quarterly Review*, edited by Sara Blair and Jonathan Freedman, on the theme of "Jewish in America," vol. XLI, no. 4, Fall 2002, pp. 634-650.

"If We Really Care about Israel: Breira and the Limits of Dissent" by Michael Staub. Portions of this essay appeared in different form in *Torn at the Roots: The Crisis of Jewish Liberalism in Postwar America*. Copyright © 2002 Columbia University Press. Reprinted with the permission of the publisher.

Published simultaneously in Canada

Library of Congress Cataloging-in-Publication Data
Wrestling with Zion : progressive Jewish-American responses to the

Israeli-Palestinian conflict / edited and with an introduction by Tony Kushner and Alisa Solomon.
    p. cm.
  ISBN 978-0-8021-4015-9
    1. Israel and the diaspora.   2. Zionism—Public opinion.   3. Arab-Israeli conflict—Public opinion.   4. Israel—Foreign public opinion, American.
5. Public opinion—United States.   6. Jews—United States—Attitudes toward Israel.   I. Kushner, Tony.   II. Solomon, Alisa, 1956–
DS 132.W74 2003
956.9405'4—dc22   2003061787

Grove Press
an imprint of Grove Atlantic
154 West 14th Street
New York, NY 10011

Distributed by Publishers Group West

groveatlantic.com

Contents

SECTION TWO: The Contemporary Crisis—Analytical Perspectives

Acknowledgments

The editors wish to thank Eric Price and Brando Skyhorse at Grove/Atlantic for their immediate and unflagging support for this project. Antonia Grilikhes-Lasky provided invaluable assistance in every aspect of the book's assemblage.

Our contributors' generosity, courage, talent, intelligence, and their passion for peace and justice inspire us. As always we are grateful beyond words to our partners, Mark Harris and Marilyn Kleinberg Neimark.

And we'd like to dedicate our work in assembling this book to the people of Palestine, the people of Israel, and the people of the United States, with hope for justice and peace in our immediate, mutual, interdependent futures.

Wrestling with Zion: An Introduction

Tony Kushner and Alisa Solomon

The second intifada is in its third year. Between September 2000 and the date of our writing this introduction, more than 23,000 Palestinians and nearly 6,000 Israelis have been seriously injured. More than 2,400 Palestinians and more than 800 Israelis have died. The Bush administration announced early on its intention to remove the United States from the business of brokering a Mideast peace agreement, and until recently it has stuck to that decision, in spite of catastrophically escalating violence and suffering. A few months ago, the administration, compelled by the need to curry favor with the Muslim world after the U.S. invasion and occupation of Iraq, changed its course, offering a "Road Map" to peace. Predictably, this late and lopsided attempt is already faltering.

A peaceful resolution to this increasingly bloody conflict is a critically necessary outcome of global importance entirely disproportionate to the size of the contested area or the number of people directly involved. There are embattled areas elsewhere, other "low-level" "dirty" wars, perhaps not many of a duration equal to this, but some far more costly in terms of human life (at least as is measured by fatality statistics). No single explanation of the meaning of the Mideast conflict, no single reading of its etiology or its current trends and tendencies, is sufficient to explain the central position it occupies in the world's attention, its iconic and geopolitical significance. The tragic dimensions and persistence of this struggle are fed by many sources: the strategic value of the terrain; clashing theologies and nationalist aspirations; imperialism past and present; the genocidal legacies of colonialism and Holocaust, racism and anti-Semitism; formations of postcolonial power imbalances, unequal development, petrochemical exploitation. And, to borrow from Walter Benjamin, driving on both sides there is the hope for a better future for grandchildren and perhaps even more potent, the memory of murdered ancestors.

The complexities are overwhelming, as they always are in political and territorial disputes stemming from long, vexed histories. Uncertainties and ambiguities multiply each time arms are taken up, bullets fired, bombs detonated. An understandable temptation upon confronting this conflict, especially for people living thousands of miles from the actual carnage, is to leave rigorous analysis, studied, disciplined comprehension, and finally policy itself to the experts, the diplomats, the soldiers, and the leadership of the nations and would-be nations involved. There is a temptation to fall back on instinct, on tribal loyalties of various kinds—ethnic, religious, ideological—to guide us in shaping our sense of why this disaster has befallen the people of the region, how the situation might be sorted out, and where, in all this farrago of contradictory reportage and mutual accusation, we might locate justice and a real hope for peace. Debilitating emotions—a shudder of horror, the depression that follows heartbreak, the fear of worse to come—reinforce in many of us the desire to surrender reason, ethical principle, and even our own agency, our power to act, to affect the path toward peace.

The daunting complexity of the situation must be given its due. Books must be read, news accounts scrutinized critically, easy blame refused, sentimentality and melodrama eschewed. But at the same time, the reflex to wave away discomforting facts by asserting that "the situation is too complicated" must also be avoided. For at its heart, this is a grim and miserable story, stark in its simplicity.

The founding of the state of Israel required the dispossession of an indigenous group, the Palestinians. This is unignorable reality, obscured by but not dissolved in preexisting and subsequent claims made by, or acts of inhumanity committed by, both sides, long before and long after Israel's formal declaration as a state. Tracking through a forest of competing identities and histories of persecution and oppression, one must adhere to this simple fact or else one's moral compass loses its true north and ceases to function: The founding of the state of Israel required the dispossession of a sizable indigenous population. This is only to say that the violence inherent in the building of any nation-state was present at the creation of Israel. Scholars, historians, and human rights workers and peace activists in Israel join with much of the rest of the planet in a near-universal recognition of Palestinian dispossession and dislocation, the subsequent gruesome reality for the Palestinian people, the insurmountable obstacle posed to any peace process by the existence of Israeli settlements in and around every West Bank town and in the Gaza Strip, and the fatal illogic of a policy that makes the peace process hostage to suicide bombers.

Jews have a long history of suffering the dreadful consequences of willed forgetting, self-interested misremembering, statistical and historical manipulations for the purpose of covering up horrific crimes. Even today there is a widespread eagerness to erase Jewish history, against which Jews and all people of conscience remain appropriately and passionately vigilant. Hence the Jewish historian Yosef Hayim Yerushalmi's dictum, "the antonym of forgetting is not remembering, but justice."

On April 15, 2002, a quarter-page ad appeared in the *New York Times*. It was entitled "To Our Fellow Americans" and it detailed what its sponsors clearly felt to be urgent, self-evident truths:

> We affirm our love for the State of Israel, the hope of the Jewish people. Our gratitude goes out to the citizen-soldiers of Israel who protect one another from their would-be destroyers. We embrace the resolve of the Israeli citizens who suffer ongoing merciless terror in their streets, buses, restaurants, and synagogues.

We declare that it is past time for the governments and leaders of all Arab and Muslim nations to recognize—unconditionally and unequivocally—The State of Israel, a democracy that has flourished honorably for fifty-four years despite repeated Arab attempts to annihilate it. We justly expect Arab and Muslim countries, as members of the family of nations and claimants of numerous lands and extensive territories, to respect the sovereign right of the Jewish people to its one historic homeland.

We invite all people of conscience to join us in condemning the murderous suicide attacks on our fellow Jews in Israel, and in asserting the incontrovertible necessity of self-defense in a war that Israel neither sought nor initiated—a war begun eighteen months ago by the Palestinian leadership as an attack upon constructive diplomacy. Civilization chooses the credo of life, not the worship of death.

We confirm our confidence in the President's adherence to principle, and our gratitude to our fellow Americans for their recognition of Israel's bravery and resiliency. Confronting the storm of Islamist terrorism that assaulted these shores on September 11, 2001, we are reminded that the State of Israel has been the fighting front line of democracy since its founding in 1948. In this hour of peril and anguish, we call upon the continuing support of America for our Israeli allies.

The list of signatories to this declaration could not have been more illustrious, including some of the most prominent names in Jewish-American literature and intellectual life: Robert Alter, Saul Bellow, Harold Bloom, Allegra Goodman, Jerome Groopman, Mark Helprin, Neal Kozodoy, David Mamet, Leonard Michaels, Cynthia Ozick, Martin Peretz, Norman Podhoretz, Chaim Potok, Elie Wiesel, Leon Wieseltier, and Ruth Wisse.

In March 2002, before the ad appeared, a series of sixteen bombs, most of them carried by suicide bombers, had killed 100 Israeli citizens. Israel's response to this slaughter, Operation Defensive Shield, was to reoccupy the West Bank and the Gaza Strip.

Rage and grief over the deaths of so many Israelis must have been a catalyst for the decision by these prominent Jewish Americans to make public their absolute and uncritical support of Israel, and their demand that the world understand Israel's military response as nothing more than self-defense in a war against a murderous foe.

It is remarkable that these eminent people decided that a successful defense of Israel's actions must feature a refusal to let slip one syllable of concern for the non-Jewish, non-Israeli civilians caught up in the carnage, or even to mention that these people exist. The word "Palestinian" does not appear at any point in the declaration. It is useful, as we note this silence, to remember what was happening to Palestinian civilians in the occupied territories, reported around the world, while these Jewish-American leaders composed their ad copy.

At the commencement of Operation Defensive Shield, the major cities of the West Bank, Ramallah, Tulkarm, Qalqilya, Bethlehem, Nablus, and the Jenin refugee camp were attacked by Israeli troops, tanks, helicopter gunships, and rocket fire. According to the report of the Secretary General of the United Nations, "Israeli Defence Forces declared the cities they had entered 'special closed military areas,' imposing restrictions on, and at times completely barring, the movement of international personnel, including at times humanitarian and medical personnel as well as human rights monitors and journalists. As a result of these restrictions on movement, including the round-the-clock curfews that lasted with periodic liftings throughout the incursions, the civilian populations of the cities suffered severe hardships, compounded in some places by the extensive fighting that occurred during the operation. As was the case with the first wave of incursions from 27 February to 14 March described above, during Operation Defensive Shield, in many instances, IDF made use of heavy weaponry in Palestinian civilian areas."

Fifty percent of the civilian population of Palestinian cities, it should be noted, are under the age of fifteen. According to the Secretary General's report, one million Palestinians lived under a one-week curfew. More than 200,000 remained under curfew for a longer period, without appropriate access to medical supplies or attention. More than 7,000 Palestinians were arrested; 1,500 were held for extended periods without legal representation in conditions that violated the Geneva conventions. Groups providing medical aid were refused entrance into some of the hardest-hit areas; ambulances reportedly came under fire by the IDF. The ancient center of Nablus was bombed and heavily damaged. The siege at Jenin refugee camp provoked worldwide outrage. The attack on Palestinian National Authority buildings in Ramallah, including those outside Arafat's compound, caused monumental damage to the informational base of Palestinian society, including the extensive destruction of banking and educational records. The IDF admitted that Israeli soldiers had engaged in looting. More than 2,800 refugee housing units were damaged and 878 homes were demolished, leaving more than 17,000 people homeless or in need of shelter rehabilitation. Eleven Palestinian schools were destroyed, fifty were damaged, nine were vandalized, fifteen were used as military outposts and another fifteen schools were used as mass arrest and detention centers. The Secretary General notes that the principal economic result of the occupation was "a near-complete cessation of all productive activity in the main West Bank centers of manufacturing, construction, commerce and private and public services"—all this in cities where the poverty rate, before Operation Defensive Shield began, had risen to 45 percent. Widespread malnutrition was reported. "While it is difficult to ascertain with precision the magnitude of the socio-economic effects of the incursions, available preliminary information indicates a sharp intensification of the hardships faced by the population," the report asserts.

Human Rights Watch, Amnesty International, and the International Commission of Jurists issued a joint statement from Jerusalem on April 7, 2002. As the United Nations had done, the groups deplored the use of suicide bombs against Israeli civilians: "Such deliberate attacks on civilians are absolutely prohibited by international humanitarian law. These actions tarnish the Palestinian cause and will not at all help the situation—they only increase the fear and mistrust of ordinary Israelis as well as adding to the suffering in the region." The groups also noted that IDF abuses "raise not simply humanitarian issues: they are serious violations of international humanitarian law."

One indication of the savagery of Operation Defensive Shield is given in these statistics, reported by B'Tselem, the Israeli human rights organization: There were ninety-nine Palestinian intifada-related fatalities for January through February 2002; for March 2002 the number was 238; in April there were 247 Palestinian fatalities.

None of this mattered enough to the people who wrote and paid for the ad that appeared in the *Times* to merit a mention. Not a word of acknowledgment, much less regret or sorrow, could be spared for the Palestinians. Their terrible suffering seems only to have inspired the eminent writers and scholars who published this ad to make a tactical decision—to obliterate any trace of the other side in their description of the conflict.

That the word "Palestinian" cannot occur at any point in their declaration is more than a sign of how polarized discourse around the conflict has become. It also reveals how desperately a certain version of "love for the State of Israel" requires nothing less than the disappearance of Palestinians, at least figuratively (and for some, who openly advocate transfer, even literally). To name these unmentionables alongside an accounting of the sufferings of Israeli Jews quickly earns the charge of drawing a "moral equivalency" between those deemed to be acting in careful, innocent self-defense and those regarded as acting with unwarrantable, bloodthirsty abandon. One hardly justifies suicide bombings by pointing out that there's also no "equivalence" between a dispossessed people resisting a thirty-six-year-old occupation and a massive military machine enforcing that repressive occupation, nor by noting that IDF attacks on civilians are themselves sometimes far less than careful or innocent. (Take the official policy of house demolitions, for example. Or Chris Hedges's report in *Harper's* magazine that he observed soldiers taunt Palestinian boys into throwing stones and then open fire.)

To avoid facing up to such atrocity, to sustain the refusal of any Israeli share in culpability, Zionism has produced a long, shameful, and debilitating history of denial—one warned of as far back as the earliest stages of the movement by one of its fathers, Ahad Ha'am. Its grim and ruthless logic underlies the ad in the *Times* and similar pronouncements, and it goes like this: The Palestinians cannot be mentioned for they do not exist. There are no such people. They are an invention of the Arabs to provide a pretext for destroying Israel, a pretext for "a second Holocaust." They are Hashemite Jordanians; let Jordan take them. They are an invention of anti-Semites; they are the latest fad of the left. There were not 1.2 million of them living in British Mandate Palestine before

1946. There were only 600,000; there were 250,000; there were fewer than that. They sold their land, and they stole their land. They have no culture and no history; they are death-obsessed; their children are crazy with hate; they have refused great kindness from their enemies; for their own sufferings they have only themselves to blame. Accounts of Israeli attacks on them, such as the one above, are propaganda, the result of falsified, unbalanced information, a lack of sympathy for the sufferings of Israelis, and anti-Semitism. And modern Israel is the Jewish patrimony; it was given to us by God.

Now, horribly, the refusal to see Palestinians is being manifest in concrete, barbed wire, and electronic sensors: in the so-called "security fence" the Sharon government is building within the West Bank—twenty-four feet high, surrounded by moats and studded with guard towers. Behind it, writes Meron Rappaport in the Israeli daily *Yediot Ahronot,* unfold "thousands of personal tragedies which are entirely invisible to the Israeli public."

Justified in the name of security, the wall, on the contrary, will more likely provoke more animosity and violence as its building results in the expropriation of yet more Palestinian land and as it cuts off entire communities from external connection and livelihood. A once-thriving market town of 45,000, Qalqilya, for one, has already been utterly surrounded by the wall, with a single entrance that is controlled by IDF soldiers. They alone determine which goods, medicines, vehicles, and people can pass in or out. According to B'Tselem, the wall's northern section alone "will likely infringe the human rights of more than 210,000 Palestinians residing in sixty-seven villages, towns and cities." The World Bank—hardly a bastion of radicalism—warns that the wall will "isolate, fragment, and in some cases impoverish those affected by its construction."

Encountering new, desperate, and deadly Palestinian resistance, failing utterly to comprehend realities of Palestinian life, or cynically exploiting those realities to provoke a state of crisis as cover for settlement building and unending occupation, the current government has brought its country to a time in which Israelis die in far greater numbers from Palestinian attacks than under any previous government. Ariel Sharon's mad, bloody dream of Greater Israel, which he and his comrades of the radical Israeli right have pursued for decades, has led to a situation recently characterized by Avrum Burg, former chair of the Knesset, as "a scaffolding of corruption, [resting] on foundations of oppression and injustice. . . . It turns out that the 2,000-year struggle for Jewish survival comes down to a state of settlements, run by an amoral clique of lawbreakers who are deaf both to their citizens and to their enemies. A state lacking justice," Burg declares, "cannot survive."

Palestinians continue to die in numbers wildly disproportionate to Israeli fatalities—three or four or five times more Palestinians dead every month. Newly ghettoized by the wall, they watch as the possibility of a Palestinian state, of escape from poverty and occupation for future generations, hope of escape from refugee camps, hope for redress of past wrongs and a future life of dignity and possibility, recedes beyond a vanishing point on the nether horizon.

The authors of the *New York Times* ad fail to express the merest concern for a civilian population under such fearsome duress (perhaps the signatories were too busy "confirm[ing]" their "confidence" in George W. Bush's "adherence to principle"). They fail to recognize even the existence of the Palestinian people. In this way they recapitulate the rhetoric of the Sharon government and the callousness behind its policies. Their declaration is presumed to represent Jewish-American opinion as regards the crisis. But for Jewish Americans in general, the complex questions raised by the state of Israel and our relationship to it do not begin nor will they end with Sharon. The depth of this questioning is alluded to, though barely sounded, by the writers of the *Times* statement: "We affirm our love for the State of Israel, the hope of the Jewish people."

Since almost all of the signers are Jews who have lived privileged, if not downright blessed, existences in the United States, beneficiaries of citizenship in a secular pluralist democracy, each a lucky inheritor of the remarkable success of the Jewish community in America, rooted in early traditions of tolerance and in the broad protection the Constitution extends to minorities, a series of questions, upon encountering this bold assertion, naturally comes to mind: Why is Israel the "hope of the Jewish people"? In what sense is "hope" meant? In what sense "the Jewish people"? If one doesn't feel hopeful, looking at Israel, facing not only the Palestinian problem but also, within its own borders, the formidable question of defining itself as both a Jewish state (with a more rapidly growing Israeli-Arab population) and a democracy (with an ever more politically powerful Jewish fundamentalist bloc); or if one feels more hopeful, even feels more hope for Jews, contemplating Jewish active participation in the American democratic project; if Israel is not one's "hope," is one therefore not a Jew?

One of us is a professor, journalist, and theater critic who has traveled extensively in Israel and the occupied territories, writing about the situation there for more than fifteen years. One of us is a playwright who has traveled to Israel twice, to the occupied territories once, and who has written about these issues on occasion, in a few essays and lectures. One of us is a lesbian, the other a gay man. We are both Jewish, strongly identifying as such, each in her or his way. And we are both American citizens, each with our own complicated and powerful connection to that identity. Our shared anger, bewilderment, grief, and occasional despair over the Palestinian-Israeli conflict was the original basis of an ongoing conversation that has grown into a cherished friendship. If a theater critic and a playwright can become dear friends and comrades, surely there is hope for peace in the Mideast.

In the summer and fall of 2002 as our conversations intensified, we felt we'd like to read additional analytical, historical, personal, and creative responses to the situation by other progressive Jews and we agreed such responses needed to be gathered—and so we decided to gather them. In the ensuing months, we sent a letter to some sixty Jewish-American writers. It read (with occasional variation) as follows:

Dear _____,

We're writing to invite you to participate in an anthology of essays and
other writings we are editing for Grove Press, which will bring together
works by Jewish-American poets, essayists, journalists, academics, novelists, and playwrights representing the spectrum of dissenting views regarding
Zionism, Israel, and American and Jewish-American involvement in the
current crisis in the Mideast.

We believe that there's an urgent need for a book of this kind. As the
Israeli-Palestinian conflict escalates, and casualties and violence on both
sides mount, a dangerous illusion persists that the Jewish-American community speaks with a single voice, expressing universal, uncritical support
for the policies of the Sharon government. A widespread but relatively recent
conflation of Judaism and Jewish identity with Israel and Israeli nationalist identity has done a grave disservice to the heterogeneity of Jewish thought,
to the centuries-old Jewish traditions of lively dispute and rigorous, un-
apologetic skeptical inquiry. As a consequence of this artificial flattening
and deadening of discourse, enforced by rage and even violence, the vital
connection between Jewish culture and the struggle for social and economic justice is coming apart. And, of course, because American foreign
policy has a tidal effect on the politics of the region, the Jewish-American
community can play a pivotal role in the pursuit of a just and lasting peace.
We hope this book will help liberate American voices of negotiation for
the end of the occupation, for justice for the Palestinians, for peace and
security for both nations.

We hope, too, that this anthology will open up, from many different
angles, questions that increasingly—and dangerously—go unexamined in
the Jewish-American mainstream: What is at the heart of the connection
between Israel and American Jews? Why should we have a connection (or
not)? What is Israel's role in shaping Jewish-American identities? Is it good
for the Jews?

We expect to gather a number of progressive perspectives on the subject, including anti-Zionist, Zionist, and ambivalent critics of the occupation, and to include historical analyses, journalistic investigations, poetry,
and even a prophetic harangue or two.

We encouraged contributors to write about *American* relationships to Israel—
historical, political, personal—for that, we felt, was what needed to be interrogated here and what we could uniquely offer. But we had no idea what sort of
response we were likely to get. The response we got is the book that follows.

It's not comprehensive. There are many other writers and activists who could
have been included, and doubtless there are issues that aren't addressed or are
addressed insufficiently. Although each contribution makes specific and unique
points, inevitably some points are returned to, some almost obsessively, mostly
from one contribution to another, but sometimes within a single piece of writ-

ing. The stakes are high, the fight is unavoidably ugly, and family, kindred, the *mishpokheh* is involved. And so articulation is hard, and so those who attempt it feel a keen need to say everything.

We make no apologies for anything contradictory, or for anything expressed. We have not tried to forge a movement or codify an orthodoxy of opinion. Indeed, as it's turned out, some contributors may even find themselves feeling uncomfortable to discover certain other writers' arguments alongside their own in this volume. We've invited a plurality, convened an assemblage of smart, engaged, and talented people, to join in debate over an issue of the greatest moment. Though we do not think that Jews can—or should—"own" the movement for peace and justice in Israel/Palestine, we believe in the value of Jewish voices raised in dissent. We believe that when the Jewish community is presented an image of itself as monolithic, bound up in a chain, a mythified unanimity, when it is told to be wary of *emet,* of truth, that life-giving word, it grows strange to itself, alienated from an essential source of its political, philosophical, ethical, spiritual richness. We hope you'll find, as we have, that vitality, exuberant imagination, compassion, daring, anger, and real moral courage that are identifiably Jewish manifest in abundance in these pages.

That the road map Bush has presented—outrageously asymmetrical in terms of what is being asked versus what is being offered, with absurd power given to the rejectionists on both sides—is already failing is no surprise; but the reappearance of something called a peace process in which Palestinians and Israelis are engaged, with the critical participation of the United States, is a beginning, if only a flimsy and dubious one. Its continuation is critical. More encouraging, there remain, resolute, daring, and principled Israeli and Palestinian activists working for a just and lasting peace despite being ostracized by their communities, ground down by the Sisyphean task, beleaguered by the many obstacles in the way.

Here is a book of Jewish-American argument for that just and lasting peace, for the deconstruction of that which stands in the way and for the construction of a viable future for all people in the region, Palestinian and Israeli. The nature of our connection, as Jewish Americans, to the land, the people, the conflict, is interrogated in these essays and poems. The connection is both loosened and strengthened, de-mythified, de-fetishized, considered as a dynamic problematic, as is only appropriate to the consideration of a living bond. Nothing is concluded here, but perhaps this book may join with and contribute to the movement for peace and justice that boldly persists and that speedily, in our day, must prevail.

Tony Kushner
Alisa Solomon
New York
September 1, 2003

Section One

Zionism and
Its Discontents—
Historical Documents

What We've Always Known:
A Century's Sample of Dissenting Voices
Marilyn Kleinberg Neimark

In recent months, as violence between Israeli Jews and Palestinians raged, the range of dissent tolerated within the American Jewish community once again narrowed. Before expressing criticism, one is expected to assert one's love and support of Israel as a Jewish state. And then, if a critic is allowed a place at the table, it is certainly at the foot. There are few still alive who remember a time when, even among Zionists, debate flourished and the nature of Jewish settlement in Palestine was still a question. We want to present in this section the voices of dissenters over the course of the Zionist century, beginning with selections from Ahad Ha'am's report on his first visit to Palestine in 1891 and ending in 1982 with Henry Schwarzschild's impassioned resignation from the board of the journal *Sh'ma*.

Today, any American Jew who would dare to express the views so freely articulated in the pieces that follow would be drummed out of the community as a traitor, an Israel-basher, a self-hating Jew. It is therefore striking to note that most of these writers positioned themselves within Zionism and, despite their views, remained respected members of the Jewish community—albeit always criticized and, particularly after World War II, often marginalized. Despite the "Jewish-American" designation in this book's title, several of the excerpts presented here are from writers who were neither American by birth nor by domicile (Judah Magnes and I. F. Stone are the only ones born in the United States; Hannah Arendt and Albert Einstein lived out their lives in the United States). We include them to demonstrate the lucidity, directness and moral force of critical voices that are nowadays a neglected part of Jewish history. (It's unimaginable that any of these writings would today find their way into the curriculum of a standard American Hebrew school.) Occasionally, their words disappoint, reflecting the colonialist and racist attitudes of the authors' times. But most often they remind us that the trajectory of the conflict that is roiling Palestine and Israel today was clear from the very beginning for those who would only see it.

Ahad Ha'am ("One of the People") was born Asher Ginsberg in the Russian Ukraine in 1856; he died in 1927 in Tel Aviv. A Hebrew essayist, he argued that "Zionism could not solve the 'problem of the Jews'—their economic, social and political plight—but it could solve 'the problem of Judaism,' i.e., assimilation" by "fostering a secular Jewish culture based on Jewish national consciousness and the renewal of Hebrew as a means of assuring the continuity of Jewish creativity." For Ahad Ha'am the Jewish community in Palestine would "serve as a 'spiritual center' nourishing Jewish life in the Diaspora."[1]

Ahad Ha'am made his first trip to Palestine in 1891. The trip was prompted by concern that the Jaffa members of the semi-secret elite order, Bnei Moshe, were mishandling land purchases for prospective immigrants and contributing to soaring land prices. Ahad Ha'am's reputation as Zionism's major internal critic has its roots in this essay,[2] found in *Kol Kitve Ahad Ha'am* (The Jerusalem Publishing House, 1953).

A Truth from Eretz Yisrael
Translated by Hilla Dayan

. . . We who live abroad are accustomed to believe that almost all Eretz Yisrael is now uninhabited desert and whoever wishes can buy land there as he pleases. But this is not true. It is very difficult to find in the land [*ha'aretz*] cultivated fields that are not used for planting. Only those sand fields or stone mountains that would require the investment of hard labor and great expense to make them good for planting remain uncultivated and that's because the Arabs do not like working too much in the present for a distant future. Therefore, it is very difficult to find good land for cattle and not only peasants, but also rich landowners, are not selling good land so easily. . . .

We who live abroad are accustomed to believing that the Arabs are all wild desert people who, like donkeys, neither see nor understand what is happening around them. But this is a grave mistake. The Arab, like all the Semites, is sharp minded and shrewd. All the townships of Syria and Eretz Yisrael are full of Arab merchants who know how to exploit the masses and keep track of everyone with whom they deal—the same as in Europe. The Arabs, especially the urban elite, see and understand what we are doing and what we wish to do on the land, but they keep quiet and pretend not to notice anything. For now, they do not consider our actions as presenting a future danger to them. They therefore do their best to exploit us, to benefit from the newly arrived guests as much as they can and yet, in their hearts, they laugh at us. The peasants are happy when a Jewish colony is formed among them because they get better wages for their work and get richer and richer every year, as experience has shown us. The big

1. Paul R. Mendes-Flohr and Jehuda Reinharz, editors, *The Jew in the Modern World: A Documentary History*, New York: Oxford University Press, 1980, p. 432.

2. Steven J. Zipperstein, *Elusive Prophet: Ahad Ha'am and the Origins of Zionism*, Berkeley: University of California Press, 1993.

landowners also have no problem accepting us because we pay them, for stone and sand land, amounts they would never have dreamed of getting before. But, if the time comes that our people's life in Eretz Yisrael will develop to a point where we are taking their place, either slightly or significantly, the natives are not going to just step aside so easily. . . .

If we have this ambition to settle in a new country and radically change our way of life and we truly want to achieve our goals, then we can't ignore the fact that ahead of us is a great war and this war is going to need significant preparation. . . .

The only one good thing about all our actions—the purchase of land—is failing because of disorder and lack of unity. He who sees how land is bought and sold in Eretz Yisrael these days never saw such a detestable and despised competition in his life. All the mongering between the shopkeepers and the petty merchants in one of those Jewish ghettos is nothing but justice and truth considering the state of affairs in Eretz Yisrael. Three months ago, when I was there, there were only two speculating companies (those who buy big chunks of land to sell them piece by piece), and even then we realized that future land speculation would be a problem for the *Yishuv*. Shortly after, the number of speculating companies grew alarmingly, and before I left there were already six . . . and some of the newcomers, to our shame, describe themselves as "future colonialists.". . .

It is not our way to learn nothing for the future from the past. We must surely learn, from both our past and present history, how careful we must be not to provoke the anger of the native people by doing them wrong, how we should be cautious in our dealings with a foreign people among whom we returned to live, to handle these people with love and respect and, needless to say, with justice and good judgment. And what do our brothers do? Exactly the opposite! They were slaves in their diasporas, and suddenly they find themselves with unlimited freedom, wild freedom that only a country like Turkey can offer. This sudden change has planted despotic tendencies in their hearts, as always happens to former slaves ['*eved ki yimlokh*]. They deal with the Arabs with hostility and cruelty, trespass unjustly, beat them shamefully for no sufficient reason, and even boast about their actions. There is no one to stop the flood and put an end to this despicable and dangerous tendency. Our brothers indeed were right when they said that the Arab only respects he who exhibits bravery and courage. But when these people feel that the law is on their rival's side and, even more so, if they are right to think their rival's actions are unjust and oppressive, then, even if they are silent and endlessly reserved, they keep their anger in their hearts. And these people will be revengeful like no other. . . .

If only we would have in Eretz Yisrael good, honest and healthy people, hard workers who live off their labor in peace and order. Such people would not have initially created hatred among the natives because they would not have provoked them and trespassed their borders. Even if eventually their jealousy would have turned into hate, it wouldn't have mattered because by then our brothers would have been able to strengthen their hold on the land by sheer numbers, their large and rich estates, their unity and their organized way of life. [But as long as things continue the way they are, with uncontrolled land speculation,] the society that I envision, if my dream is not just a false notion, this society will have to begin to create itself in the midst of fuss, noisiness and panic, and will have to face the prospects of both internal and external war . . .

Judah L. Magnes was an American Reform rabbi, born in San Francisco in 1877, whose charisma, intelligence, and social connections quickly catapulted him to leadership positions in the American Jewish community. An early Zionist, Magnes resigned from the American branch of the movement in 1915 because according to Rabbi Arthur Hertzberg, "neither a Jewish state nor Jewish mass political action, but his religious version of Ahad Ha-Amism—careful colonization and spiritual rebirth—seemed to him to be the meaning of Zionism."[3] In 1917, as the United States moved toward war, Magnes "[t]o the consternation of friends and the community at large . . . took up the causes of pacifism, civil liberties, and anti-imperialism."[4] Magnes moved to Palestine in 1922, where he served as chancellor and then first president of the Hebrew University in Jerusalem from 1925 until his death. In Palestine and in Washington, D.C., Magnes was a forceful advocate for a binational state and Arab-Jewish reconciliation. At the time of his death, in late 1948, he was arguing for an Arab-Jewish confederation.

In the following letters to Chaim Weizmann[5] and Felix Warburg,[6] Magnes clearly articulates his views regarding Jewish policy in Palestine and relations

3. Arthur Hertzberg, editor, *The Zionist Idea: A Historical Analysis and Reader*, New York: Atheneum, 1959, p. 442.

4. Arthur A. Goren, editor, *Dissenter in Zion: From the Writings of Judah L. Magnes*, Cambridge, MA: Harvard University Press, 1982.

5. Chaim Weizmann was arguably the leading Zionist of the first half of the twentieth century. He led the negotiations that in 1917 resulted in the Balfour Declaration, the British government's statement that it viewed "with favour the establishment in Palestine of a national home for the Jewish people . . . it being clearly understood that nothing shall be done which may prejudice the civil and religious rights of existing non-Jewish communities in Palestine or the rights and political status of Jews in any other country." (Paul R. Mendes-Flohr and Jehuda Reinharz, 1980, p. 458.)

6. Felix Warburg was a successful banker and philanthropist who, like Magnes, was committed to the development of Palestine as a cultural and religious center for world Jewry. He was instrumental in the founding of the Jewish Agency, initially a joint venture between Zionists and non-Zionists.

between Jews and Arabs. "The present situation" Magnes refers to was a series of attacks by Arab rioters on Jews throughout Palestine (including massacres in Hebron and Safad). Within one week 133 Jews and 116 Arabs were dead and hundreds wounded.[7]

These letters are found in *Dissenter in Zion: From the Writings of Judah L. Magnes* edited by Arthur A. Goren.

To Chaim Weizmann
London

Zurich, September 7, 1929

Dear Dr. Weizmann,

You asked me over the telephone last night to write you my views on the present situation. I wanted to have a long talk with you, and for that reason had been trying to get in touch with you for several days. Writing is a poor substitute for an oral exchange of opinions, and I shall try to be brief.

I think that the time has come when the Jewish policy as to Palestine must be very clear, and that now only one of two policies is possible. Either the logical policy outlined by Jabotinsky in a letter in the *Times* which came today, basing our Jewish life in Palestine on militarism and imperialism; or a pacific policy that treats as entirely secondary such things as a "Jewish State" or a Jewish majority, or even "The Jewish National Home," and as primary the development of a Jewish spiritual, educational, moral and religious center in Palestine. The first policy has to deal primarily with politics, governments, declarations, propaganda and bayonets, and only secondarily with the Jews, and last of all with the Arabs; whereas the pacific policy has to deal first of all with the Jews, and then with the Arabs, and only incidentally with governments and all the rest.

The imperialist, military and political policy is based upon mass immigration of Jews and the creation (forcible if necessary) of a Jewish majority, no matter how much this oppresses the Arabs meanwhile, or deprives them of their rights. In this kind of policy the end always justifies the means. The policy, on the other hand, of developing a Jewish spiritual Center does not depend upon mass immigration, a Jewish majority, a Jewish State, or upon depriving the Arabs (or the Jews) of their political rights for a generation or a day; but on the contrary, is desirous of having Palestine become a country of two nations and three religions, all of them having equal rights and none of them having special privileges; a country where nation-

---

7. Benny Morris, *Righteous Victims: A History of the Zionist-Arab Conflict 1881–2001*, New York: Vintage Books, 2001.

alism is but the basis of internationalism, where the population is pacifistic and disarmed—in short, the Holy Land.

The one policy may be termed that of militarist, imperialist, political Zionism; the other that of pacific, international, spiritual Zionism; and if some authorities will not choose to call the latter idea Zionism, then let it be called the Love of Zion, or the Return to Zion, or any other name that you will.

We have been toying with the words "Jewish State," "majority," "Jewish Palestine," "politics," "Balfour Declaration," etc., long enough. It is time that we came down to realities. We have passed resolutions concerning cooperation with the Arabs, but we have done very little seriously to carry them out.

I do not say that this is easy of achievement nor do I absolutely know that it is possible. The Palestine Arabs are unhappily still half savage, and their leaders are almost all small men. But this policy of cooperation is certainly more possible and more hopeful of achievement than building up a Jewish Home (National or otherwise) on bayonets and oppression. Moreover, a Jewish Home in Palestine built up on bayonets and oppression is not worth having, even though it succeed, whereas the very attempt to build it up peacefully, cooperatively, with understanding, education, and good will, is worth a great deal, even though the attempt should fail.

The question is, do we want to conquer Palestine now as Joshua did in his day—with fire and sword? Or do we want to take cognizance of Jewish religious development since Joshua—our Prophets, Psalmists and Rabbis, and repeat the words: "Not by might, and not by violence, but by my spirit, saith the Lord." The question is, can any country be entered, colonized, and built up pacifistically, and can we Jews do that in the Holy Land? If we can not (and I do not say that we can rise to these heights), I for my part have lost half my interest in the enterprise. If we can not even attempt this, I should much rather see this eternal people without such a "National Home," with the wanderer's staff in hand and forming new ghettos among the peoples of the world.

As you know, these are not new views on my part. I was read out of the Zionist Organization of America in 1915 because among other things, I contended that the Jews should ask for no special privileges in Palestine, but should be content with equal rights. When the Balfour Declaration was issued and the Mandate signed, I did not rejoice. I wrote two modest newspaper articles and delivered a speech (which is printed) in the sense of the views as given above. When you and Felix Warburg and I were discussing matters in Palestine, you with your usual keenness referred to me as believing Zionist policy was altogether too political. I have, as you also know, done what little I could to help bring about a united front for Palestine ever since the beginning, and I must confess that I had hoped that the non-Zionist members of the Agency might give the whole movement a non-political, non-imperialist turn. But your great persuasiveness has carried them with you on the political issues also, and it was mainly on this account that I could not accept the invitation to participate in the Agency. It is also for this reason that I have resolutely tried to keep the University entirely distinct from the political organization.

All these years I have kept silent, not wishing to obtrude what appeared to me my minority views, and I had thought that by devoting myself wholly and without deflection to the University, I could make a contribution to my kind of Zionism. But I cannot keep silent for Zion's sake in these tragic days, and I want to do what little I can to give voice to the views to which I have been trying hitherto to give expression through work alone.

You said you would want to convey my views to the meeting of the Actions Committee, and you are at liberty to read them this letter if you think it worthwhile.

I am sending a copy of this letter to Felix Warburg.

I sympathize with you in the fearful burden you now have to bear, and I can only pray that you may be led to walk in the right path.

Yours truly, JLM

To Felix Warburg
New York

Paris, September 13, 1929

Dear Felix,

I am enclosing a copy of a letter I wrote to Doctor Weizmann on September 7th. I have had no answer as yet. From this you will get my general point of view. You will see from this probably more clearly than I could make clear to you before, why I could not join with you in the Agency. You may have thought that there was too much of the personal element in it. There is, of course, in everything. But my attitude is based on something much deeper, as you have doubtless felt, but as I doubtless have been unsuccessful in conveying to you.

I have, I regret to say, no confidence whatever that Doctor Weizmann and his associates understand the situation today any better than they have before. They may pass peace resolutions and agree to White Papers and lots of other things out of political necessity, but not out of inner conviction. Unless the whole aim of Zionism is changed, there will never be peace. Maybe there can be no peace anyway, but in that event the Jewish People would have added a glorious instead of a disgraceful page to its history.

Palestine does not belong to the Jews and it does not belong to the Arabs, nor to Judaism or Christianity or Islam. It belongs to all of them together; it is the Holy Land. If the Arabs want an Arab national state in Palestine, it is as much or as little to be defended as if the Jews want a Jewish national state there. We must once and for all give up the idea of a "Jewish Palestine" in the sense that a Jewish Palestine is to exclude and do away with an Arab Palestine. This is the historic fact, and Palestine is nothing if it is not history. If a Jewish national home in Palestine is compatible with an Arab national home there, well and good, but if it is not, the name makes very little difference. The fact is that nothing there is possible unless Jews and Arabs work together in peace for the benefit of their common Holy Land. It must be our endeavor first to convince ourselves and then to convince others that Jews and Arabs, Moslems, Christians, and Jews have each as much right there, no more and no less, than the other: equal rights and equal privileges and equal duties. That is practically quite sufficient for all purposes of the Jewish religion, and it is the sole ethical basis of our claims there. Judaism did not begin with Zionism, and if Zionism is ethically not in accord with Judaism, so much the worse for Zionism.

I must say that I have been amazed that not one official Jewish voice has been lifted in sympathy with such slain and injured Moslems or Christians who may have been innocent; that no money was earmarked for their injured. Of course, the Arabs were the aggressors and the most bloodthirsty. Do I also have to be shouting that? But do you not know that we, too, have had our preachers of hate and disseminators of lies, our armed youth, our provocative processions, our unforgivable stupidity in our handling of the Western Wall incidents since last Yom Kippur, making out of what should have been a police incident an international political issue? Politics, statesmanship, hobnobbing with the masters of empire, using high-sounding phrases instead of disciplining and purifying our community and trying to understand and make terms with our neighbors.

Is it conceivable that responsible men should at this moment of all moments make additional demands for increased immigration, etc., a "blue-white book" instead of the White Book which they signed with more than Jesuitical reservations? Is it conceivable that among all the official Zionist demands and proposals there is not the faintest hint that a Jewish-Arab understanding, a peace conference if you will, is more important than anything else? Of course life must be protected by the Mandatory Power—that is the most elemental of considerations. Of course the bureaucracies of Jerusalem (British and Jewish) have not done their simplest duty and should be investigated without flinching. Of course the guilty—Arabs, British, Jews—should be punished. But he who takes it all out in this and in making chauvinistic demands is no better than were the war mongers in 1914 and 1917. The situation is essentially the same; each side talks of the other's *Alleinschuld* [sole blame] and of war *a la victoire integrale* [for total victory], whereas they should be thinking also of their own sins and of ways of stopping the war and of living at peace. And if the Arabs are not capable of this, we Jews must be, else we are false to our spiritual heritage and give the lie to our much-vaunted higher civilization. If I were as religious a man as I should like to be, I should say that this was God's testing of His People. Can we be humble and courageous and intelligent enough to make this testing into a source of blessing?

You may ask me for a practical program. There are practical programs long since worked out on paper. But what is the good of them if the whole spirit and aim of those officially charged with carrying them out are such as to make these programs only a necessary evil for them or a burden or a lie? . . .

Martin Buber was born in Vienna in 1878. A theologian and philosopher, he was also "a political radical, a humanist socialist actively committed to a fundamental economic and political reconstruction of society as well as to the pursuit of international peace and fraternity."[8] Buber joined the Zionist movement in 1898 and for a few months worked as the editor of *Die Welt,* Zionism's official publication. But he soon broke with Theodore Herzl and aligned himself with Zionism's more cultural and spiritual, rather than political, movement.[9] Buber moved to Palestine in 1939 and held the chair in social philosophy at Hebrew University until he retired in 1951. He died in 1965.

In April 1936 the Arabs launched a revolt against the British occupation. In May 1939, in what the Zionist movement regarded as an act of treachery, the British issued a White Paper that imposed severe limitations on the purchase of land by Jews, limited Jewish immigration to 75,000 over five years (after which all immigrants would require Arab agreement), and proposed an independent Palestine "in which Arabs and Jews share in government."[10] The *Yishuv* (the Jewish settlers in Palestine) held angry demonstrations and their underground organization, the Irgun, initiated an outburst of Jewish attacks, including sabotage, murder, and deliberate bombing of civilians. The following essay first appeared in the newspaper *Davar* on June 5, 1939; it is found in *A Land of Two Peoples: Martin Buber on Jews and Arabs,* edited by Paul R. Mendes-Flohr.

Our Pseudo-Samsons

Apparently there are young men in the *Yishuv* who fancy themselves to be contemporary Samsons. It seems they regard the placing of mines in

8. Paul R. Mendes-Flohr, editor, *A Land of Two Peoples: Martin Buber on Jews and Arabs,* New York: Oxford University Press, 1983, p. 3.

9. Paul R. Mendes-Flohr, 1983, p. 451.

10. Benny Morris, 2001, p. 158; Paul R. Mendes-Flohr and Jehuda Reinharz, 1980, pp. 466–469.

the path of vehicles bearing innocent, defenseless non-Jews or attacking the homes of innocent, defenseless non-Jews as similar to Samson's exploits. They tell youths in the street that the time has come to act as Samson did; and if those youths want to be contemporary Samsons, all they have to do is learn from the speakers. It goes without saying that they find plenty of children who like listening to such things.

How is this to be explained? When we returned to our land after many hundreds of years, we behaved as though the land were empty of inhabitants—no, even worse—as though the people we saw didn't affect us, as though we didn't have to deal with them, that is, as if they didn't see us. But they did see us. They saw us, not with the same clarity with which we would have seen them had we been the veteran denizens of the land and another people came to settle in it in ever-increasing numbers; not with the same but with sufficient clarity, clarity that naturally only increased from year to year. We didn't pay any attention to this development. We didn't say to ourselves that there is only one way to forestall the results of this ever-increasing clarity of vision: to form a serious partnership with that people, to involve them earnestly in our building of the land, and to give them a share in our labor and in the fruits of our labor. We did not wish to believe those among us who sounded the warning.

Meanwhile, in any case, in the arena of world politics where we were suddenly needed, we had received the promise of protection for our undertaking [in Palestine] from one great power, a promise that the League of Nations had, as it were, confirmed. Wasn't that enough for us? We didn't say to ourselves that, in the world of politics in which we have lived for twenty-five years or more now, such promises are valid only as long as the political situation created by them exists unchanged and that we should prepare ourselves for the hour of change, bound to come sooner or later, with a different sort of guarantee: instead of a declaration—reality, the reality of a shared undertaking and of common interests with our neighbors in the Land. But we didn't want to believe those among us who sounded the warning. . . . And to whoever pointed to the growing Arab national movement, we responded that there was no need to take it into account—or that we would assuredly prevail. Therefore everything has happened as it did. Jewish terrorist gangs have perpetrated acts that our youth regard as Samson-like deeds. Perhaps there were those among the terrorists who saw themselves as contemporary Samsons, that is, if they knew anything of Samson. The question of whom they regard as the contemporary Philistines invading the country, the British or the Jews, requires no reply. I assume they mean both. I don't believe that there is a single person among us who sees these murderers as Samsons. Why? Because the Samsons of old fought face to face against a well-armed group that outnumbered them; because terrorism is not legitimate warfare. We refuse to regard them as heroes, but rather as madmen. I do not mean by that, however, madman in the heroic sense, i.e., a man thought to be mad but in reality a hero; no, I mean by madman someone who really has lost his wits, a real fool.

And our attitude to the Arabs? Almost all of us knew how to distinguish between the [Arab] terrorists and the Arab people. But there's no hope that the Arabs will be able to distinguish between our thugs and the Jewish people, for very long. And then how shall we arrive at an understanding with the Arabs? It is true that there are those among us who consider such an understanding unnecessary and even harmful; but only politicians of illusion such as they—who only know how to replace one old, broken illusion with another, equally ephemeral—only they could imagine that our *Yishuv* will exist forever without understanding and cooperation with the Arabs. At this critical hour, whoever encourages eruptions of blind violence, endangers the very existence of the *Yishuv*. Everything that has been built with such great labor and such great sacrifice, stone after stone, may be destroyed wholesale in the chaos to which these imagined Samsons lead us. Every blow they believe they strike at our enemies, strikes us. They deal in suicide; and not Samson's kind of suicide—he who killed three thousand Philistines as he died—but the destruction of everything cultivated by generations of dedicated, self-sacrificing *halutzim* [pioneers]. We have no right to commit this kind of suicide. "Thou shalt not murder" it is written. He who murders as these self-styled Samsons do, murders his own people.

Herein lies the foulest and most fraudulent deception of all: that it is possible to achieve redemption through sin, if the sin is at all intended from the beginning to redeem. If the people justifies the murder, identifies with the perpetrators, and thus accepts responsibility for the sin as its own, we will bequeath to our children not a free and pure land but a thieves' den to live in and raise their children in.

The order of the day is the whole *Yishuv*'s battle against the White Paper. The White Paper not only belittles the demand for our people's survival and for the continued development of our work here, it ignores the interests of this country and the kind of peace needed here. What is needed is orderly, well-coordinated, and responsible opposition. This sort of opposition should not be expressed as the Arabs have expressed theirs or as the Irish have theirs. (Those among us who admire Irish terrorism forget that there are only two sides involved—apart from Ulster—in the Irish question, while there are three in ours.) The fact is that in this country, we, unlike the Irish, face the opposition of a majority population supported to a greater or lesser degree by 230 million Muslims. This fact reveals the fond comparison with the Irish to be just so much drivel. (By the way, Ireland did not achieve independence because of terror tactics, tactics that Lord Balfour among others fought most successfully, but because of England's sophisticated policy, the new imperialism of the "round table" that seeks centralized control through decentralization.) In our battle we must do anything to cut our ties with England, since that will be an obstacle to any future agreement with the Arabs and will endanger the *Yishuv*'s survival. We must continue to do whatever is required for the growth and flowering of our settlement work, nothing more and nothing less. As before, the ploughshare must remain our only weapon, the ploughshare without fear. We need fearless hoers of the soil and not throwers of bombs. We need leaders to guide us in our work, leaders who know what they want and how to achieve it; we do not need disturbers of the peace—what they disturb is our work.

Hannah Arendt, historian and social and political philosopher, was born in Germany in 1906 and fled to the United States in 1941. Her *Origins of Totalitarianism*, published in 1951, established her as a major political thinker. The following brief excerpt is from a lengthy essay, "Zionism Reconsidered," that appeared in *The Menorah Journal* in Autumn 1945.

In her essay Arendt is responding to the unanimous adoption by American Zionists (confirmed in 1945 by the World Zionist Organization) of the demand for a "free and democratic Jewish Commonwealth . . . [which] shall embrace the whole of Palestine, undivided and undiminished." She continues:

Zionism Reconsidered

. . . [T]he Revisionist[11] program, so long bitterly repudiated, has proved finally victorious. The Atlantic City Resolution goes even a step further than the Biltmore Program (1942), in which the Jewish minority had granted minority rights to the Arab majority. This time the Arabs were simply not mentioned in the resolution, which obviously leaves them the choice between voluntary emigration or second-class citizenship. It seems to admit that only opportunist reasons had previously prevented the Zionist movement from stating its final aims. These aims now appear to be completely identical with those of the extremists as far as the future political constitution of Palestine is concerned. It is a deadly blow to those Jewish parties in Palestine itself that have tirelessly preached the necessity of an understanding between the Arab and the Jewish peoples. On the other hand, it will considerably strengthen the majority under the leadership of Ben-Gurion, which, through the pressure of major injustices in Palestine and the terrible catastrophes in Europe, have turned more than ever nationalistic.

Why "general" Zionists should still quarrel officially with Revisionists is hard to understand, unless it be that the former do not quite believe in the fulfillment of their demands but think it wise to demand the maximum as the base for future compromises, while the latter are serious, honest

11. See below, the letter to the editor, signed by Arendt and others, published in *The New York Times*, December 4, 1948.

and intransigent in their nationalism. The general Zionists, furthermore, have set their hopes on the help of the Big Powers, while the Revisionists seem pretty much decided to take matters into their own hands. Foolish and unrealistic as it may be, it will bring the Revisionists many new adherents from among the most honest and most idealistic elements of Jewry.

In any case, the significant development lies in the unanimous adherence of all Zionist parties to the ultimate aim, the very discussion of which was still tabooed during the 1930s . . .

Nationalism is bad enough when it trusts in nothing but the rude force of the nation. A nationalism that necessarily and admittedly totally depends upon the force of a foreign nation is certainly worse. This is the threatened fate of Jewish nationalism and of the proposed Jewish State, surrounded inevitably by Arab states and Arab peoples. Even a Jewish majority in Palestine—nay, even a transfer of all Palestine Arabs, which is openly demanded by Revisionists—would not substantially change a situation in which Jews must either ask protection from an outside power against their neighbors or effect a working agreement with the neighbors.

If such an agreement is not brought about, there is the imminent danger that, through their need and willingness to accept any power in the Mediterranean basin which might assure their existence, Jewish interests will clash with those of all other Mediterranean peoples; so that, instead of one "tragic conflict" we shall face tomorrow as many insoluble conflicts as there are Mediterranean nations. For these nations, bound to demand a *mare nostrum* shared only by those who have settled territories along its shores, must in the long run oppose any outside—that is, interfering—power creating or holding a sphere of interest. These outside powers, however powerful at the moment, certainly cannot afford to antagonize the Arabs, one of the most numerous peoples of the Mediterranean basin. If, in the present situation, the powers should be willing to help the establishment of a Jewish homestead, they could do so only on the basis of a broad understanding that takes into account the whole region and the needs of all its peoples. On the other hand, the Zionists, if they continue to ignore the Mediterranean peoples and watch out only for the big far-away powers, will appear only as their tools, the agents of foreign and hostile interests. Jews who know their own history should be aware that such a state of affairs will inevitably lead to a new wave of Jew-hatred; the antisemitism of tomorrow will assert that Jews not only profiteered from the presence of the foreign big powers in that region but had actually plotted it and hence are guilty of the consequences. . . .

Leo Baeck was born in Germany in 1875. Rabbi, scholar and Holocaust survivor, Baeck moved to London in 1945, where he became the president of the World Union for Progressive Judaism. He died in 1956.
Albert Einstein, born in Germany in 1879, was one of the world's greatest physicists and an activist for the cause of world peace. Awarded the Nobel Prize in 1921,

he became a U.S. citizen in 1940 and was associated with the Institute for Advanced Study at Princeton University until his death in 1955.

The first letter to the editor was published in *The New York Times*, April 12, 1948. Einstein and Arendt, but not Baeck, were also among other prominent signers of the second letter to the editor, published in *The New York Times* on December 4, 1948.

Letters to *The New York Times*
April 12, 1948

Palestine Cooperation
Appeal Made to Jews to Work for Goal of Common Welfare

Of the writers of the following letter, one is a rabbi, an important religious personality in Jewish life, having been the spiritual head of the German Jews, who was put in a concentration camp under the Nazis. The other is the world-famous scientist, now living in this country, best known for his theory of relativity.

To the Editor of The New York Times:

Both Arab and Jewish extremists are today recklessly pushing Palestine into a futile war. While believing in the defense of legitimate claims, these extremists on each side play into each other's hands. In this reign of terror the needs and desires of the common man in Palestine are being ignored.

We believe that in such a situation of national conflict it is vitally important that each group and particularly its leaders uphold standards of morality and reason in their own ranks rather than confine themselves to accuse their opponents of the violation of these standards. Hence we feel it to be our duty to declare emphatically that we do not condone methods of terrorism and of fanatical nationalism any more if practiced by Jews than if practiced by Arabs. We hope that responsible Arabs will appeal to their people as we do to the Jews.

Were war to occur, the peace would still leave the necessity of the two people working together, unless one of the other were exterminated or enslaved. Short of such a calamity, a decisive victory by either would yield a corroding bitterness. Common sense dictates joint efforts to prevent war and to foster cooperation now.

Opposition to Terror

Jewish-Arab cooperation has been for many years the aim of far-sighted Jewish groups opposed to any form of terror. Recently a declaration of such a group was published in the American press under the dateline Jerusalem, March 28, 1948, to which we want to draw attention. We quote here some of the key sentences:

"An understanding between the two peoples is possible, despite the constant refrain that Jewish and Arab aspirations are irreconcilable. The claims of their extremists are indeed irreconcilable, but the common Jew and the common

Arab are not extremists. They yearn for the opportunity of building up their common country, the Holy Land, through labor and cooperation."

The signers of the statement represent various groups in Palestine Jewry. Besides Dr. Magnes, the chairman, those who signed were Dr. Martin Buber, Professor of Jewish Philosophy at Hebrew University; Dr. David Senator, administrator of the university; Dr. Kurt Wilhelm, rabbi of Emeth Ve'Emunah, liberal congregation in Jerusalem; Simon Shereshevsky, a surgeon, who belongs to the Mizrachi Zionist religious group, and Isaac Motho of the Spanish Jewish community.

Those who signed this declaration represent at the moment only a minority. However, besides the fact that they speak for a much wider circle of inarticulate people, they speak in the name of principles which have been the most significant contributions of the Jewish people to humanity.

We appeal to the Jews in this country and in Palestine not to permit themselves to be driven into a mood of despair or false heroism which eventually results in suicidal measures. While such a mood is undoubtedly understandable as a reaction to the wanton destruction of six million Jewish lives in the last decade, it is nevertheless destructive morally as well as practically.

We believe that any constructive solution is possible only if it is based on the concern for the welfare and cooperation of both Jews and Arabs in Palestine. We believe that it is the unquestionable right of the Jewish community in Palestine to protect its life and work, and that Jewish immigration into Palestine must be permitted to the optimal degree.

The undersigned plead with all Jews to focus on the one important goal: the survival and permanent development of the Jewish settlement in Palestine on a peaceful and democratic basis, the single one which secures its future in accordance with the fundamental spiritual and moral principles inherent in the Jewish tradition and essential for Jewish hope.

Leo Baeck
Albert Einstein
New York, April 12, 1948

Letter to *The New York Times*
December 4, 1948

New Palestine Party
Visit of Menachem Begin and Aims of Political Movement Discussed

To the Editor of The New York Times:

Among the most disturbing political phenomena of our time is the emergence in the newly created state of Israel of the "Freedom Party" (*Tnuat Haherut*), a

political party closely akin in its organization, methods, political philosophy and
social appeal to the Nazi and Fascist parties. It was formed out of the membership and following of the former Irgun Zvai Leumi, a terrorist, right-wing, chau-
vinist organization in Palestine.

The current visit of Menachem Begin, leader of this party, to the United States
is obviously calculated to give the impression of American support for his party
in the coming Israeli elections, and to cement political ties with conservative
Zionist elements in the United States. Several Americans of national repute have
lent their names to welcome his visit. It is inconceivable that those who oppose
fascism throughout the world, if correctly informed as to Mr. Begin's political
record and perspectives, could add their names and support to the movement
he represents.

Before irreparable damage is done by way of financial contributions, public
manifestations in Begin's behalf, and the creation in Palestine of the impression that a large segment of America supports Fascist elements in Israel, the
American public must be informed as to the record and objectives of Mr. Begin
and his movement.

The public avowals of Begin's party are no guide whatever to its actual character. Today they speak of freedom, democracy and anti-imperialism, whereas
until recently they openly preached the doctrine of the Fascist state. It is in its
actions that the terrorist party betrays its real character; from its past actions
we can judge what it may be expected to do in the future.

Attack on Arab Village

A shocking example was their behavior in the Arab village of Deir Yassin.
This village, off the main roads and surrounded by Jewish lands, had taken
no part in the war, and had even fought off Arab bands who wanted to use
the village as their base. On April 9 (*The New York Times*), terrorist bands attacked this peaceful village, which was not a military objective in the fighting, killed most of its inhabitants—240 men, women and children—and kept
a few of them alive to parade as captives through the streets of Jerusalem. Most
of the Jewish community was horrified at the deed, and the Jewish Agency
sent a telegram of apology to King Abdullah of Trans-Jordan. But the terrorists, far from being ashamed of their act, were proud of this massacre, publicized it widely, and invited all the foreign correspondents present in the country
to view the heaped corpses and the general havoc at Deir Yassin.

The Deir Yassin incident exemplifies the character and actions of the Freedom Party.

Within the Jewish community they have preached an admixture of ultrana-
tionalism, religious mysticism, and racial superiority. Like other Fascist parties
they have been used to break strikes, and have themselves pressed for the destruction of free trade unions. In their stead they have proposed corporate unions
on the Italian Fascist model.

During the last years of sporadic anti-British violence, the IZL and Stern
groups inaugurated a reign of terror in the Palestine Jewish community. Teach-

ers were beaten up for speaking against them, adults were shot for not letting their children join them. By gangster methods, beatings, window-smashing, and wide-spread robberies, the terrorists intimidated the population and exacted a heavy tribute.

The people of the Freedom Party have had no part in the constructive achievements in Palestine. They have reclaimed no land, built no settlements, and only detracted from the Jewish defense activity. Their much-publicized immigration endeavors were minute, and devoted mainly to bringing in Fascist compatriots.

Discrepancies Seen

The discrepancies between the bold claims now being made by Begin and his party, and their record of past performance in Palestine bear the imprint of no ordinary political party. This is the unmistakable stamp of a Fascist party for whom terrorism (against Jews, Arabs, and British alike), and misrepresentation are means, and a "Leader State" is the goal.

In the light of the foregoing considerations, it is imperative that the truth about Mr. Begin and his movement be made known in this country. It is all the more tragic that the top leadership of American Zionism has refused to campaign against Begin's efforts, or even to expose to its own constituents the dangers to Israel from support to Begin.

The undersigned therefore take this means of publicly presenting a few salient facts concerning Begin and his party; and of urging all concerned not to support this latest manifestation of fascism.

ISIDORE ABRAMOWITZ, HANNAH ARENDT, ABRAHAM BRICK, RABBI JESSURUN
  CARDOZO, ALBERT EINSTEIN, HERMAN EISEN, M.D., HAYIM FINEMAN,
  M. GALLEN, M.D., H.H. HARRIS, ZELIG S. HARRIS, SIDNEY HOOK, FRED
  KARUSH, BRURIA KAUFMAN, IRMA L. LINDHEIM, NACHMAN MAJSEL, SEYMOUR
  MELMAN, MYER D. MENDELSON, M.D., HARRY M. ORLINSKY, SAMUEL PITLICK,
  FRITZ ROHRLICH, LOUIS P. ROCKER, RUTH SAGER, ITZHAK SANKOWSKY, I.J.
  SCHOENBERG, SAMUEL SHUMAN, M. ZINGER, IRMA WOLPE, STEFAN WOLPE.
                                                   New York, Dec. 2, 1948

Isaac Deutscher was a Marxist historian, born in Poland in 1907. In 1939 he fled to England, where he was on the staff of *The Economist* and *The Observer* and authored highly regarded biographies of Stalin and Trotsky. This essay, "Israel's Spiritual Climate," was originally published in *The Reporter*, April–May 1954; it is found in *The Non-Jewish Jew and Other Essays*, edited and with an introduction by Tamara Deutscher (London: Oxford University Press, 1968.)

Israel's Spiritual Climate

. . . Israelis who have known me as an anti-Zionist of long standing are curious to hear what I think about Zionism. I have, of course, long since abandoned my anti-Zionism, which was based on a confidence in the European labour movement, or more broadly, in European society and civilization, which that society and civilization have not justified. If, instead of arguing against Zionism in the 1920s and 1930s I had urged European Jews to go to Palestine, I might have helped to save some of the lives that were later extinguished in Hitler's gas chambers . . .

Even now, however, I am not a Zionist; and I have repeatedly said so in public and in private. The Israelis accept this with unexpected tolerance but seem bewildered: "How is it possible *not* to embrace Zionism?" they ask, "if one recognizes the State of Israel as an historic necessity?"

What a difficult and painful question to answer!

From a burning or sinking ship people jump no matter where—on to a lifeboat, a raft, or a float. The jumping is for them an "historic necessity"; and the raft is in a sense the basis of their whole existence. But does it follow that the jumping should be made into a programme, or that one should take a raft-State as the basis of a political orientation? (I hope that Israelis or Zionists who happen to read this will not misunderstand the expression "raft-State." It describes the precariousness of Israel, but is not meant to belittle Israel's constructive achievement.)

To my mind it is just another Jewish tragedy that the world has driven the Jew to seek safety in a nation-state in the middle of this century when the nation-state is falling into decay.

Through several centuries every progressive development in the life of Western nations was bound up with the formation and growth of the nation-state or with the movement for the nation-state. The Jew was not connected with that movement and did not benefit from it. He remained shut up in his synagogue and in his religious loyalties while Western man subordinated religious to national loyalties and found his stature with his nation rather than within his Church. Only now, when man no longer grows in stature within the nation and when he can find himself anew only within some supranational community, has the Jew found his Nation and his State. What a melancholy anachronism! . . .

The state of Israel has had explosives—the grievances of hundreds of thousands of displaced Arabs—built into its very foundations. One cannot in fairness blame the Jews for this. People pursued by a monster and running to save their lives cannot help injuring those who are in the way and cannot help trampling over their property. The Jews feel that the injury they have done to the Arabs is child's play compared with their own tragedy. This is true enough, but it does not prevent the Arabs from smarting under their grievance and craving revenge. To the Israelis Palestine is and never ceased to be Jewish. To the Arabs the Jews are and will for long remain invaders and intruders.

As long as a solution to the problem is sought in nationalist terms both Arab and Jew are condemned to move within a vicious circle of hatred and revenge. Arabs murder Jewish mothers and children. Jews stage the Kibiya massacre. The Arabs are only waiting for a turn in Middle East affairs which will allow them to crush Israel; in the meantime they watch intently for any false step Israel may make. Israel's hope is that the Arab states will forever remain as backward, indolent, corrupt and friendless as they were during the Arab-Jewish war; for otherwise the Israelis, even if their numbers were trebled, could not hold their ground against forty million Arabs. Each side sees its own security and prosperity in the insecurity, destitution and distress of the other.

There seems to be no immediate way out of this predicament. In the long run a way out may be found beyond the nation-state, perhaps within the broader framework of a Middle East federation. Israel might then play among the Arab states a role as modest as are its numbers and as great as are its intellectual and spiritual resources. This idea, I am told, is beginning to gain ground among younger politicians and political thinkers; but it is not likely to gain much ground in the near future. The Jews are still too deeply intoxicated with their newly acquired nation-state and the Arabs are too fully obsessed with their grievance to look very far ahead. Any supranational organization, like a Middle East federation, is sheer *Zukunftsmusik* to both. But sometimes it is only the music of the future to which it is worth listening.

I. F. Stone, journalist and newspaper publisher, was born Isidore Feinstein in 1907 in Philadelphia. Stone edited *The Nation* from 1940 to 1946 and founded *I. F. Stone's Weekly* in 1953. He was a vigorous opponent of the Cold War and McCarthyism.

In June 1967, *Les Temps Modernes*, Paris, published a collection of essays by Israeli and Arab contributors: "Le conflit israéli-arabe." The special issue of the journal was inspired by Jean-Paul Sartre and edited by Claude Lanzmann. Stone reviewed the collection in an essay titled "Holy War," which appeared in *The New York Review of Books* August 3, 1967. In the review Stone focused primarily on the views of the contributors. But in selecting the following excerpts I've chosen to focus on Stone's personal reflections:

Holy War

Stripped of propaganda and sentiment, the Palestine problem is, simply, the struggle of two different peoples for the same strip of land. For the Jews, the establishment of Israel was a Return, with all the mystical significance the capital R implies. For the Arabs it was another invasion. This has led to three wars between them in twenty years. Each has been a victory for the Jews. With each victory the size of Israel has grown. So has the number of Arab homeless.

Now to find a solution which will satisfy both peoples is like trying to square a circle. In the language of mathematics, the aspirations of the Jews and the Arabs are incommensurable. Their conflicting ambitions cannot be fitted into the confines of any ethical system which transcends the tribalistic. This is what frustrates the benevolent outsider, anxious to satisfy both peoples. . . .

The experiences from which M. Sartre draws his emotional ties [to both Jews, through the Resistance, and Arabs, through the struggle for Algerian independence] are irrelevant to this new struggle. Both sides draw from them conclusions which must horrify the man of rational tradition and universalist ideals. The bulk of the Jews and the Israelis draw from the Hitler period the conviction that, in this world, when threatened one must be prepared to kill or be killed. The Arabs draw from the Algerian conflict the conviction that, even in dealing with so rational and civilized a people as the French, liberation was made possible only by resorting to the gun and the knife. Both Israelis and Arabs in other words feel that only force can assure justice. In this they agree, and this sets them on a collision course. For the Jews believe justice requires the recognition of Israel as a fact; for the Arabs, to recognize the fact is to acquiesce in the wrong done them by the conquest of Palestine. If God as some now say is dead, He no doubt died of trying to find an equitable solution to the Arab-Jewish problem. . . .

There is a good deal of simplistic sophistry in the Zionist case. The whole earth would have to be reshuffled if claims 2,000 years old to *irredento* were suddenly to be allowed. Zionism from its beginning tried to gain its aims by offering to serve as outpost in the Arab world for one of the great empires. Herzl sought to win first the Sultan and then the Kaiser by such arguments. Considerations of imperial strategy finally won the Balfour Declaration from Britain. The fact that the Jewish community in Palestine afterward fought the British is no more evidence of its not being a colonial implantation than similar wars of British colonists against the mother country from the American Revolution to Rhodesia. In the case of Palestine, as of other such struggles, the Mother Country was assailed because it showed more concern for the native majority than was palatable to the colonist minority. The argument that the [Arab] refugees ran away "voluntarily" or because their leaders urged them to do so until after the fighting was over not only rests on a myth but is irrelevant. Have refugees no right to return? Have German Jews no right to recover their properties because they fled? . . .

The effort to equate the expulsion of the Arabs from Palestine with the new Jewish immigration out of the Arab countries is not so simple nor so equitable as it is made to appear in Zionist propaganda. The Palestinian Arabs feel about this "swap" as German Jews would if denied restitution on the grounds that they have been "swapped" for German refugees from the Sudetenland. In a sanely conceived settlement, some allowance should equitably be made for Jewish properties left behind in Arab countries. What is objectionable in the simplified version of the question is the idea that Palestinian Arabs whom Israel didn't want should have no objection to being "exchanged" for Arab Jews it did want. One uprooting cannot morally be equated with the other.

A certain moral imbecility marks all ethnocentric movements. The Others are always either less than human, and thus their interests may be ignored, or more than human, and therefore so dangerous that it is right to destroy them. The latter is the underlying pan-Arab attitude toward the Jews; the former is Zionism's basic attitude toward the Arabs . . . For the Zionists the Arab was the Invisible Man. Psychologically he was not there. Achad Ha-Am, the Russian Jew who became a great Hebrew philosopher, tried to draw attention as early as 1891 to the fact that Palestine was not an empty territory and that this posed problems. But as little attention was paid to him as was later accorded his successors in "spiritual Zionism," men like Buber and Judah Magnes who tried to preach, *Ichud*, "unity," i.e., with the Arabs. Of all the formulas with which Zionism comforted itself none was more false and more enduring than Israel Zangwill's phrase about "a land without people for a people without a land."[12] Buber related that Max Nordau, hearing for the first time that there was an Arab population in Palestine, ran to Herzl crying, "I didn't know that—but then we are committing an injustice.". . .

When Israel's Defense Minister, Moshe Dayan, was on *Face the Nation*, June 11, after Israel's latest victories, this colloquy occurred.

SIDNEY GRUSON (*New York Times*): Is there any possible way that Israel could absorb the huge number of Arabs whose territory it has gained control of now?

GEN. DAYAN: Economically we can; but I think that is not in accord with our aims in the future. It would turn Israel into either a bi-national or poly-Arab-Jewish state instead of the Jewish state, and we want to have a Jewish state. We can absorb them, but then it won't be the same country.

MR. GRUSON: And it is necessary in your opinion to maintain this as a Jewish state and purely a Jewish state?

12. Although Zangwill was one of Herzl's early supporters, he eventually opposed establishing a Jewish state in Palestine and favored, instead, accepting Britain's offer to settle the Jews in Uganda. In 1904, in a speech in New York, he said: "There is, however, a difficulty from which the Zionist dares not avert his eyes, though rarely likes to face it. Palestine proper has already its inhabitants. The pashalik of Jerusalem is already twice as thickly populated as the United States, having fifty-two souls to every square mile and not 25 percent of them Jews; so we must be prepared either to drive out by the sword the tribes in possession as our forefathers did, or to grapple with the problem of a large alien population, mostly Mohammedan." (Israel Zangwill, *The Voice of Jerusalem*, London: William Heinemann, 1920, p. 88, quoted in Hani A. Faris, "Israel Zangwill's Challenge to Zionism," *Journal of Palestine Studies*, Spring 1975, p. 85.)

GEN. DAYAN: Absolutely—absolutely. We want a Jewish state like the
French have a French state.

This must deeply disturb the thoughtful Jewish reader. Ferdinand and
Isabel[la] in expelling the Jews and Moors from Spain were in the same
way saying they wanted a Spain as "Spanish" (i.e., Christian) as France was
French. It is not hard to recall more recent parallels.

It is a pity the editors of *Les Temps Modernes* didn't widen their symposium to include a Jewish as distinct from an Israeli point of view. For Israel is creating a kind of schizophrenia in world Jewry. In the outside world
the welfare of Jewry depends on the maintenance of secular, non-racial
pluralistic societies. In Israel, Jewry finds itself defending a society in which
mixed marriages cannot be legalized, in which non-Jews have a lesser status
than Jews, and in which the ideal is racial and exclusionist. Jews must fight
elsewhere for their very security and existence—against principles and practices they find themselves defending in Israel. . . .

Another Arab contributor from Israel, Ibrahim Shabath . . . relates a
recent conversation with Ben Gurion. "You must know," Ben Gurion told
him, "that Israel is the country of the Jews and only of the Jews. Every Arab
who lives here has the same rights as any minority citizen in any country
of the world, but he must admit the fact that he lives in a Jewish country."
The implications must chill Jews in the outside world.

And in a footnote Stone comments: "It may help Jewry and Israel to understand that the way to a fraternal life with the Arabs inside and outside Israel
must begin with the eradication of the prejudices that greet the Oriental and
Arabic-speaking Jews in Israel who now make up over half the population of
the country. The bias against the Arab extends to a bias against the Jews from
the Arab countries. In this, as in so many other respects, Israel presents in minia-
ture all the problems of the outside world. Were the rest of the planet to disappear, Israel could regenerate from itself—as from a new Ark—all the bigotries,
follies, and feuds of a vanished mankind (as well as some of its most splendid
accomplishments)."

Henry Schwarzschild was born in Berlin, Germany, in 1926 and arrived with
his family in the United States in 1939, after celebrating his bar mitzvah in the
shadow of Kristallnacht. His experience with Nazism imprinted on him a lifelong passion for political liberty. He worked in the South during the sixties,
against the death penalty (he directed the ACLU's capital punishment project
and was a major architect and head of the New York office of the National Coalition to Abolish the Death Penalty), and on behalf of peace between Israelis
and Palestinians. "Jews," he once said, "are defined by neither doctrine nor credo.
We are defined by *task*. That task is to redeem the world through justice . . .
Even the unbelievers among us are never so Jewish as when they reject social

apathy and confront the desperate needs of their brothers and sisters, here and now, in our own city, our own state, our own country, not because our well-being depends on it, but because Judaism does." He died in 1996.

On Withdrawing from *Sh'ma*

This is my resignation from the Editorial Advisory Board of *Sh'ma*.

The contributions from me that you have published over the years have been few in number and less than earth-shaking in import, and you are therefore not deprived of a great editorial asset. In any case, my resignation has almost nothing to do with my relationship to *Sh'ma* as such. It is the consequence of a very much superordinated reorientation by me of my relationship to the Jewish community in the largest sense. Let me explain as best I can.

For a generation now, I have been deeply troubled by the chauvinistic assumptions and repressive effects of Israeli nationalism. I have experienced the War on Lebanon of the past few weeks as a turning point in Jewish history and consciousness exceeded in importance perhaps only by the End of the Second Commonwealth and the Holocaust. I have resisted the inference for over thirty years, but the War on Lebanon has now made clear to me that the resumption of political power by the Jewish people after two thousand years of diaspora has been a tragedy of historical dimensions. The State of Israel has demanded recognition as the modern political incarnation of the Jewish people. To grant that is to betray the Jewish tradition.

The State of Israel and its supporters have probably been right all along in arguing that political power comes at the price of the normal detritus of the nation state, such as Jewish criminals, prostitutes, and generals. They may also be right in asserting that the War on Lebanon is the sort of thing a Jewish state has to do to survive. I am not disposed to await the outcome of debates by politicians and theologians on whether the threat from the Palestine Liberation Organization was sufficiently clear and present to justify the killing of so many Lebanese and Palestinian men, women, and children, or only so many. I will not avoid an unambiguous response to the Israeli army's turning West Beirut into another Warsaw Ghetto.

I now conclude and avow that the price of a Jewish state is, to me, Jewishly unacceptable and that the existence of this (or any similar) Jewish ethnic-religious nation state is a Jewish, i.e. a human and moral, disaster and violates every remaining value for which Judaism and Jews might exist in history. The lethal military triumphalism and corrosive racism that inheres in the State and in its supporters (both there and here) are profoundly abhorrent to me. So is the message that now goes forth to the nations of the world that the Jewish people claim the right to impose a holocaust on others in order to preserve its State.

For several decades, I have supported those minority forces in and for the State that wanted to salvage the values of peace and social justice that the Jewish tradition commands. The "blitzkrieg" in Lebanon, terrifying and Teutonic in its ruthlessness, shows how vain those hopes have been.

I now renounce the State of Israel, disavow any political connection or emotional obligation to it, and declare myself its enemy. I retain, of course, the same deep concern for its inhabitants, Jewish, Arab, and other, that I hold for all humankind.

I remain a member of the Jewish people—indeed, I have no other inner identity. But the State of Israel has now also triumphed over the Jewish people and its history, for the time being at least. I deem it possible that the State, morally bankrupted and mortally endangered by its victories, will prove essential to the survival of the Jewish people and that it may likely take the Jewish people with it to eventual extinction. Yet I believe that the death of the Jewish people would not be inherently more tragic than the death of the Palestinian people that Israel and its supporters evidently seek or at least accept as the cost of the "security" of the State of Israel. The price of the millennial survival of the Jewish people has been high; I did not think the point was to make others pay it. That moral scandal intolerably assaults the accumulated values of Jewish history and tradition.

If those be the places where the State of Israel chooses to stand, I cannot stand with it. I therefore resign all connections with Jewish political and public institutions that will not radically oppose the State and its claim to Jewish legitimacy. *Sh'ma* is one of those.

Morning News

Marilyn Hacker

Spring wafts up the smell of bus exhaust, of bread
and fried potatoes, tips green on the branches,
but it's old news: arrogance, ignorance, war.
A cinder-block wall shared by two houses
is new rubble. On one side was a kitchen
sink and a cupboard, on the other was
a bed, a bookshelf, three framed photographs.

Glass is shattered across the photographs;
two half-circles of hardened pocket-bread
sit on the cupboard. There provisionally was
shelter, a plastic truck under the branches
of a fig-tree. A knife flashed in the kitchen,
merely dicing garlic. Engines of war
move inexorably towards certain houses

while citizens sit safe in other houses
reading the newspaper, whose photographs
give sanitized excuses for the war.
There are innumerable kinds of bread
brought up from bakeries, baked in the kitchen:
the date, the latitude, tell which one was
dropped by a child beneath the bloodied branches.

The uncontrolled and multifurcate branches
of possibility infiltrate houses'
walls, windowframes, ceilings. Where there was
a tower, a town: ash and burnt wires, a graph
on a distant computer screen. Elsewhere, a kitchen
table's setting gapes, where children bred
to branch into new lives were culled for war.

Who wore this starched smocked cotton dress? Who wore
this jersey blazoned for the local branch
of the district soccer team? Who left this black bread
and this flat gold bread in their abandoned houses?
Whose father begged for mercy in the kitchen?

Whose memory will frame the photograph
and use the memory for what it was

never meant for by this girl, that old man, who was
caught on a ball-field, near a window: war,
exhorted through the grief a photograph
revives (or was the team a covert branch
of a banned group; were maps drawn in the kitchen,
a bomb thrust in a hollowed loaf of bread?).
What did the old men pray for in their houses

of prayer, the teachers teach in schoolhouses
between blackouts and blasts, when each word was
flensed by new censure, books exchanged for bread,
both hostage to the happenstance of war?
Sometimes the only schoolroom is a kitchen.
Outside the window, black strokes on a graph
of broken glass, birds line up on bare branches.

"This letter curves, this one spreads its branches
like friends holding hands outside their houses."
Was the lesson stopped by gunfire, was
there panic, silence, does a torn photograph
still gather children in the teacher's kitchen?
Are they there meticulously learning war-
time lessons with the signs for house, book, bread?

Section Two

The Contemporary Crisis—Analytical Perspectives

The United States–Israeli Alliance

Joel Beinin

The United States was not always an unreserved supporter of Israel. In the late 1940s and early 1950s many State Department and Pentagon officials saw the Arab states as more important allies than Israel because their primary interest in the Middle East was oil and, consequently, Saudi Arabia. The current U.S.-Israeli alliance began to take shape in the mid-1960s and was consolidated after the Arab-Israeli War of 1967. It is primarily a product of cold war geo-strategic considerations, not the power of the "pro-Israel" lobby. The strong presence of Jews in the Democratic Party, the electoral clout of the lobby, and, in recent years, the aggressive pro-Israelism of evangelical Protestants and the arms industry have, however, provided an important domestic base of support for this alliance.

The Eisenhower administration opposed Israel's activist politico-military doctrine, which entailed rejecting several secret diplomatic overtures of the Arab states and massive retaliations for violations of Israel's borders by Palestinian infiltrators, most of whom were unarmed. After Secretary of State Dulles's trip to the Middle East in 1953 to investigate rising Arab-Israeli tensions, U.S. economic assistance loans were suspended for several months. When Israel, in alliance with Britain and France, invaded and occupied the Gaza Strip and Sinai Peninsula in 1956, President Eisenhower ordered Israel to withdraw. Although this was days before the presidential election, Eisenhower was not constrained by concern about "pro-Israel" voters, who were marginal for the Republican Party. Eisenhower's main concerns were keeping Britain and France from recolonizing the Middle East and maintaining good relations with anti-communist Arab regimes. Consequently, from 1953 to 1967 France was Israel's most important political and military ally based on their common interests in opposing Egyptian president Gamal Abdel Nasser.

The Eisenhower administration responded to the rise of Nasserist pan-Arabism by enunciating the Eisenhower doctrine, which portrayed Egypt as a country controlled by international communism. Successive administrations increasingly perceived the Arab-Israeli conflict as a local front in the global cold war. This implied closer relations with Israel and deterioration of relations with the surrounding Arab states.

Tensions between Egypt and the United States combined with the prominent role of liberal Jews in the Democratic Party inclined the Kennedy and Johnson administrations toward a more pro-Israel policy than that of the Eisenhower administration. Kennedy attempted simultaneously to improve relations with Egypt and Israel by dispatching the Johnson mission: a secret effort to resolve the Palestinian refugee problem. As part of his effort to win Israeli compliance to the Johnson plan, Kennedy offered to sell Israel Hawk anti-aircraft missiles in 1962. Israel took the missiles and then rejected the Johnson plan. This was the first time the United States supplied a major weapons system to Israel. President Johnson had a tendency to view the Arab-Israeli conflict as analogous to the nineteenth-century Texas-Mexican conflict. Relations with Egypt deteriorated sharply during the Johnson years. Egypt supported army officers who overthrew the Saudi-backed Zaydi Imam of Yemen in 1962. During the subsequent civil war of 1962–67 the United States supported the Saudis while Egypt supported the officers. Washington saw this as a regional proxy war. The intensification of the Vietnam War with the bombing of the North in 1965 led to closer Soviet ties to Egypt and Syria. A coup from within the ruling Ba'th Party radicalized the Syrian regime in 1966.

This was the context for the supply of the first U.S. offensive weapons system to Israel—the A4 Skyhawk jet deal approved in 1965. Intelligence links between the United States and Israel were also enhanced in 1960s. Meir Amit, chief of Israel's Mossad, visited Washington on the eve of the 1967 war and got a green light for Israel's preemptive attack on Egypt and Syria from CIA and Pentagon officials.[1]

Formation of the U.S.-Israel Strategic Alliance, 1967–73

Following the 1967 war an unnamed State Department official remarked, "Israel has probably done more for the United States in the Middle East in relation to money and effort than any of our so-called allies elsewhere around the globe since the end of the Second World War. In the Far East we can get almost no one to help us in Vietnam. Here the Israelis won the war single-handedly, have taken us off the hook, and have served our interest as well as theirs."[2]

As this comment suggests, U.S.-Israeli ties grew closer partly in response to U.S. difficulties in Vietnam. In the fall of 1968 the United States sold Phantom jets to Israel, the first time this weapon was offered to a non-NATO ally. Israel received these jet fighters even before the South Vietnamese air force did.

The new American military relationship with Israel was an expression of the Nixon Doctrine, which crystallized in late 1969 and early 1970. Facing impending defeat in Vietnam, President Nixon and National Security Advisor Henry Kissinger decided that the United States would no longer send troops to fight everywhere in the third world. Instead, arms and training would be supplied to "regional influentials" who would maintain a pro-American order. In the Eastern Mediterranean Israel was the chosen ally. In the Persian Gulf Iran and Saudi Arabia were the "two pillars" of U.S. security policy.

1. William Quandt, *Peace Process: American Diplomacy and the Arab-Israeli Conflict* (Berkeley: University of California Press, 2001), pp. 23ff calls it a "yellow light." For Israel, as long as it was not a strong red light, the effect was the same.

2. *U.S. News and World Report*, June 19, 1967.

The U.S.-Israeli relationship was consolidated by the September 1970 Palestinian-Jordanian civil war. Armed groups of the PLO challenged King Hussein's control over the country. Jordan responded with a massive crackdown on the Palestinians. Israel threatened to bomb a column of Syrian tanks preparing to invade Jordan and support the Palestinians. The tanks did not deploy due to the Israeli threat and internal dissension in the Syrian leadership. Hence, the Hashemite throne was saved and the PLO was expelled from Jordan. According to William Quandt, former National Security Council Middle East advisor under presidents Ford and Carter, as a result of that crisis Nixon, Kissinger and the foreign policy makers in Washington came to see the U.S.-Israeli relationship "as the key to combating Soviet influence in the Arab world and attaining regional stability."[3]

The articulation of the Nixon Doctrine and the consolidation of the U.S.-Israeli military alliance led to a sharp jump in U.S. military sales to Israel. From 1968 to 1970 the total was $140 million. From 1971 to 1973 this increased to $1.2 billion. After 1971 the U.S. government replaced world Jewry as Israel's largest donor and the leading source of unilateral capital transfers. Military aid to Israel took another qualitative leap after the 1973 war, when Israel once again proved its efficacy in defeating what Washington regarded as the Soviet client states of Egypt and Syria. Aid totaled $2.57 billion in 1974, including, for the first time, an outright military grant of $1.5 billion.

The qualitative change in the U.S.-Israeli relationship in the early 1970s did not occur without a debate in foreign policy-making circles. Secretary of State William Rogers advocated an "even-handed" approach to the Arab-Israeli conflict based on his view that the conflict had regional components independent of the cold war. National Security Advisor Henry Kissinger saw the Middle East as subordinate to his understanding of the global balance of power. This did tend to reduce the Middle East to a regional front in the cold war. Kissinger prevailed, and he ultimately replaced Rogers as secretary of state. Kissinger saw the radical Arab nationalist regimes of Egypt, Syria, Libya, Iraq, and the PLO as vehicles for expansion of Soviet influence. Therefore, the United States should support Israel. There was no point in pressing Israel to be more accommodating toward the Arabs because Israel was "our asset."

One very negative consequence of this policy was the U.S. and Israeli response to the mission of UN envoy, Gunner Jarring, who visited the Middle East in February 1971. Recently installed Egyptian president Anwar al-Sadat told Jarring he was willing to sign a peace agreement with Israel in exchange for Israeli evacuation of all Egyptian territories occupied in the 1967 war—the same terms that the two parties were to agree on in their 1979 peace treaty. Because Israel wanted to annex the eastern coast of the Sinai Peninsula down to Sharm al-Shaykh, Prime Minister Golda Meir rejected the Egyptian offer. Kissinger did not press Israel to

3. William Quandt, *Decade of Decisions: American Policy towards the Arab-Israeli Conflict, 1967–1976* (Berkeley: University of California Press, 1977), p. 106.

respond positively to Egypt. Israel's successful defeat of radical Arab nationalism in the form of Ba'thism and Nasserism in 1967, its intervention to save the Jordanian regime in 1970, and the Israeli-Iranian alliance against Iraq, which involved encouraging a rebellion of Iraqi Kurds in the early 1970s, "proved" that supporting Israel was a successful policy within the framework of Kissinger's globalist outlook. Any U.S. pressure on Israel would ultimately benefit the Soviet Union. Israel's failure to respond to Egypt's offer led directly to the 1973 Arab-Israeli War.

Step-by-Step Diplomacy and the Deepening U.S.-Israeli Alliance

By the end of the 1973 war the Israeli Labor Party had already made clear (in the Allon Plan of July 1967 and the Galili Document of 1973) that it rejected the concept of returning all or almost all of the territories occupied in 1967 in exchange for peace. Israel thus departed from the understanding of most of world opinion, which regarded both UN Security Council resolution 242, which marked the end of the 1967 war, and UN Security Council resolution 338, which marked the end of the 1973 war, as requiring this. There were, by this time, more than fifty Jewish settlements in the territories Israel occupied in 1967. Therefore, negotiations after the 1973 war could not proceed on the basis of seeking a comprehensive settlement based on the "land for peace" formula unless the United States was prepared to pressure Israel to acquiesce, which Kissinger was unwilling to do.

The unsustainable military situation at the end of the war—the Israeli and Egyptian armies were intertwined with each other—facilitated the negotiation of limited disengagement of forces agreements. Kissinger's intensive shuttle diplomacy produced a series of such agreements between Israel and Egypt and Israel and Syria, which resulted in Israeli withdrawal from small slivers of territory captured in 1967. Israel refused to consider such an agreement with Jordan, which did not participate in the 1973 war. Israel was very reluctant to agree to the second disengagement of forces agreement with Egypt, which left Egypt in full control of the Suez Canal and required Israel to pull back behind the strategic mountain passes in the Sinai Peninsula. Kissinger pressured Israel's Prime Minister Yitzhak Rabin and Foreign Minister Shimon Peres to accept the agreement, saying, "This is a real tragedy. We've attempted to reconcile our support for you with our other interests in the Middle East [i.e., oil], so that you wouldn't have to make your decisions all at once. If we wanted the 1967 borders we could do it with all of world opinion and considerable domestic opinion behind us. *Our strategy was designed to protect you from this.* [Emphasis added.] We've avoided drawing up an overall plan for a global settlement."[4]

Kissinger finally secured Israel's agreement to the second disengagement agreement with Egypt on September 4, 1975, with an extra $2 billion in U.S. aid and

4. Quoted in Nadav Safran, *Israel: The Embattled Ally* (Cambridge: Harvard University Press, 1981), pp. 546–47.

the promise that the United States would not negotiate with the Palestine Liberation Organization unless it recognized Israel's right to exist, renounced terrorism, and accepted UN Security Council resolution 242. Kissinger made this commitment after the leading body of the PLO, the Palestine National Council, adopted a resolution suggesting it might be open to the possibility of a two-state solution to the Palestinian-Israeli conflict in 1974. Israel regarded such a solution as a grave threat. In December 1975, when the Knesset passed a resolution opposing PLO participation in any peace negotiations, Prime Minister Rabin announced, "If Israel agrees to negotiate with any Palestinian element this will provide a basis for creating a third state between Israel and Jordan. But Israel will never accept such a state. I repeat firmly, clearly, categorically: it will not be created."[5]

Thus, by the mid-1970s a U.S.-Israeli alliance was consolidated on the basis of enhanced U.S. military aid to Israel, rejection of the creation of a Palestinian state in the West Bank and the Gaza Strip, and rejection of negotiations with the PLO.

From Kissinger to Camp David

The difficulty of achieving the second Sinai disengagement agreement between Israel and Egypt and the high diplomatic and financial price the United States paid to get it indicated that Kissinger's step-by-step approach and avoidance of a comprehensive settlement to the Arab-Israeli conflict had reached its limits. The rising power of OPEC throughout the 1970s increased the urgency of achieving Arab-Israeli peace. On the eve of the 1976 presidential election campaign, a group of foreign policy elites released a Report on Prospects for Peace in the Middle East, published by the Brookings Institution, then a Democratic Party–oriented think tank. The report advocated comprehensive solution on basis of UN Security Council resolution 242 plus a vaguely defined Palestinian entity. This was a belated endorsement of Rogers's approach to the conflict in contrast to Kissinger's approach.

Several signers of the report entered the Carter administration, including National Security Advisor Zbigniew Brzezinski and National Security Council Middle East staffer William Quandt. Hence, the Brookings report was adopted as policy by the early Carter administration. The Soviet Union also accepted this approach, and a joint U.S.-Soviet statement was issued on October 1, 1977, envisioning a peace conference at Geneva sponsored by the two superpowers with all the parties present.

Israel and Egypt colluded in undermining this initiative. In November, Egyptian President Anwar Sadat dramatically announced his willingness to travel to

---

5. *Ma'ariv*, Dec. 5, 1975. Quoted in Noam Chomsky, *The Fateful Triangle: The United States, Israel and the Palestinians* (Boston: South End Press, 1983), p. 70.

Jerusalem to negotiate peace with Israel. The offer stunned world opinion and surprised the Carter administration. But the Egyptian overture had been previously agreed on in secret Israeli- Egyptian talks in Morocco. Sadat's trip to Jerusalem; the September 1978 Camp David summit of Jimmy Carter, Sadat, and Israeli Prime Minister Menachem Begin; and the Egyptian-Israeli peace treaty signed on March 26, 1979 sidelined the possibility of a comprehensive settlement initially envisioned by the Brookings report and the Carter administration.

The Camp David accords included a framework for an Egyptian-Israeli peace treaty and a framework for peace in the Middle East, that is, a settlement of the Palestinian-Israeli conflict. The framework for peace in the Middle East was based on the concept of establishing a five-year interim period during which the West Bank and the Gaza Strip would be governed by an autonomous Palestinian authority. The Israeli army would at least partially withdraw from the occupied territories. After the interim period the final status of the territories would be determined.

There was no explicit link between the two frameworks. Hence the basis for a separate peace between Egypt and Israel that would leave the Palestinian-Israeli conflict unresolved was established. The Egyptian-Israeli element of the Camp David accords was, albeit with great difficulty, implemented. Consequently, Egypt became a strategic ally of the United States in the Middle East. Since the signing of the treaty, Israel and Egypt have been the number one and two recipients of U.S. foreign aid. Egypt's allotment is roughly two-thirds what Israel receives and is currently approximately $1.3 billion in military aid and $700 million in economic assistance annually.

Almost as soon as the Camp David agreements were finalized, Israel began to undermine the framework for peace in the Middle East. Begin claimed that the concept of the "legitimate rights of the Palestinian people" applied only to residents of the West Bank and the Gaza Strip, not to the refugees. President Carter believed that Begin had agreed to freeze settlement expansion until the autonomy negotiations were completed with the Palestinians, but Begin claimed he had agreed to a freeze for only three months. Begin further argued that the concept of autonomy applied only to the people living in the West Bank and the Gaza Strip, not to the territories themselves. Israel would, therefore, continue to control the territories and assert its claim to sovereignty at the end of the five-year interim period.

Global Reach of the Strategic Alliance

Once they were out of office, both Zbigniew Brzezinski and Jimmy Carter wrote that Begin had reneged on the commitments they believed he made at Camp David.[6] Why didn't the Carter administration press Israel to live up to its under-

6. Brzezinski stated, "Begin himself has walked away from what he committed himself to—full autonomy. He has said autonomy for the people, not the territory or

standing of the Camp David accords? The fall of the Shah of Iran in January–February 1979 meant the collapse of the Nixon Doctrine in the Persian Gulf. The United States needed to move quickly to rebuild the structure of its military power in the region. As *New York Times* military correspondent Drew Middleton wrote, "A new power structure in the Middle East could evolve from the Israeli-Egyptian peace treaty in which Israel and a rearmed Egypt, both supported by expanded U.S. military involvement and arms deliveries, would more than balance Syria, Iraq and Libya, the principal Soviet clients, and the Palestine Liberation Organization."[7] Similarly *The Washington Post* reported: "U.S. officials concede privately that the administration lowered the priority it had put on getting Israeli commitments on the Palestine problem because of a new sense of urgency that Carter felt about getting the Egyptian-Israeli treaty as a way to stem the tide of reverses for his administration [i.e., Iran]."[8]

The Soviet invasion of Afghanistan in December 1979 made it even more unlikely that the Carter administration would press for fulfillment of what it understood to be Israel's Camp David commitments. Entering a new cold war, the Carter administration reverted to the Kissingerian view of Israel as a U.S. strategic asset. That view was explicitly embraced by Ronald Reagan during the 1980 presidential campaign and trumpeted repeatedly once he won office.

The Reagan administration built closer ties with Israel on the basis of Secretary of State Alexander Haig's vision of an anti-Soviet "strategic consensus" in the Middle East. Reversing declared U.S. policy since 1967, at his first press conference President Reagan declared that Israeli settlements in the West Bank and the Gaza Strip are "not illegal."[9] Reagan's replacement of the Carter administration's foreign policy orientation around "human rights" with an orientation toward "anti-terrorism" enhanced the already entrenched U.S. antipathy to the PLO.

Israel understood the signals coming from Washington and responded with much more aggressive behavior throughout the Arab world. In June 1981 it bombed Iraq's nuclear reactor. In July 1981 it carried out a massive air raid in downtown Beirut. In December 1981 the Knesset applied Israeli law to (that is, all but formally annexed) the Golan Heights and confirmed the annexation of East Jerusalem first announced in 1967. All of this was a prelude to Israel's invasion of Lebanon in June 1982.

According to Jimmy Carter, high Israeli officials received a "green light" from Washington to invade Lebanon.[10] In light of the prevailing neo–cold war

---

autonomy administratively but not legislatively. . . . We thought we had an agreement on no more settlements until negotiations with the Palestinians and Begin reinterpreted that as meaning no more settlements until negotiations with the Egyptians on the peace treaty." *New York Times*, March 20, 1982. Jimmy Carter, *Keeping Faith: Memoirs of a President* (New York: Bantam Books, 1982), pp. 405–406.

7. *New York Times*, March 27, 1979.
8. *Washington Post*, March 26, 1979.
9. *New York Times*, February 3, 1981.
10. *Washington Post*, August 21, 1982.

approach to the Middle East in Washington, the PLO and the Syrian troops in Lebanon were viewed as Soviet surrogates, and it was legitimate to attack them.[11] The United States learned of Israel's plan to invade Lebanon as early as December 1981. In an interview with Israeli TV on June 16, 1982, Ariel Sharon, then Israel's minister of defense, acknowledged, "I would not say we have surprised the Americans." Israel's ambassador to the United States, Moshe Arens, told the army radio station that he was not surprised by the modest U.S. reaction to Israel's invasion. "It would have been difficult for us to have been surprised because for many months a lot of work was being done here," he said.[12]

In the late 1970s and 1980s the U.S.-Israeli alliance expanded its ambit far beyond the Middle East. By 1981 Israel had become the seventh largest arms exporter in the world.[13] Its principal customers included the U.S. client states of El Salvador, Guatemala, and Nicaragua—all of them engaged in repressing popular insurgencies. Chile under Augusto Pinochet and the Argentinian junta were other important purchasers of Israeli weaponry. Israel had an extensive commercial and arms development relationship with South Africa. In 1979 Israel and South Africa jointly detonated a nuclear device. Iran under the Shah was an ally of Israel. Its notorious secret police, the Savak, received Israeli training. After the Iranian revolution, Israel served as an intermediary in the fiasco known as the Iran-Contra scandal. U.S. weapons were sold to Iran and the profits were used, in violation of explicit legislation, to fund the Nicaraguan rebels against the Sandinista government.

In all these relationships, as well as others in Africa and Asia, Israel performed surrogate tasks for the United States, enhancing its value as a "strategic asset."[14] In 1983 the Reagan administration signed a memorandum of strategic cooperation with Israel, renewing an agreement that had been signed on November 30, 1981, and suspended because of Israel's annexation of Jerusalem and the Golan Heights. The June 1985 Free Trade Agreement institutionalized the U.S.-Israeli relationship. All U.S. aid was converted to outright grants that were not linked to any specific project, as is the case with U.S. aid to all other countries.

The Alliance after the Cold War

The demise of the Soviet Union and the U.S. supremacy in the Middle East achieved by the first Gulf War made it possible for the administration of President Bush

---

11. See Robert Tucker's "Lebanon: The Case for the War," *Commentary*, October 1982, pp. 19–30 for an explication of this logic.

12. Galei Tzahal, Israeli Army Radio, June 14, 1982.

13. *New York Times*, March 15, 1981.

14. Israel Shahak, *Israel's Global Role: Weapons for Repression* (Belmont, MA: Association of Arab-American University Graduates, 1982); Jane Hunter, *Israeli Foreign Policy: South Africa and Central America* (Boston: South End Press, 1987).

the elder to adopt a policy toward the Arab-Israeli conflict free of cold war considerations. Secretary of State James Baker III dragged Israel kicking and screaming to the Madrid conference of October 1991—the first time all the parties to the Arab-Israeli conflict met face to face. But Baker accepted the veto of Israeli Prime Minister Yitzhak Shamir on the participation of Palestinians from Jerusalem and the diaspora as well as those openly identified with the PLO, despite the fact that in November 1988 the Palestine National Council, the supreme body of the PLO, had recognized Israel and resolved to abandon armed struggle.

The Madrid conference marked a critical point in the U.S.-Israeli relationship when it sometimes became unclear which was the senior party in the alliance. On the one hand Bush and Baker seemed to understand that no resolution of the Palestinian-Israeli conflict would be possible without considerable pressure from the United States. President Bush disregarded Israel's supporters in Congress in September 1991 by postponing for 120 days consideration of Israel's request for $10 billion in loan guarantees in order to press Shamir into coming to Madrid. Baker had already made his general views known when he addressed the annual conference of the American Israel Public Affairs Committee in 1989 and urged Israel to "lay aside, once and for all, the unrealistic vision of a greater Israel," halt settlement construction, and reach out to the Palestinians "as neighbors who deserve political rights."[15]

On the other hand, the Bush administration could not muster the political resolve to exercise consistently the necessary pressure on Israel. In part, this was because several of the administration's key Middle East policy personnel in the State Department and the National Security Council were associates of the Washington Institute for Near East Policy (WINEP), the leading pro-Israel think tank. The Bush administration backed away from confrontations with congressional supporters of Israel over a proposal to cut U.S. foreign aid by 5 percent to the five largest recipients, including Israel, and over the president's reminder that East Jerusalem is occupied territory and should not be used to house Soviet Jewish refugees.[16] The Bush administration suspended the dialogue it began with the PLO following a raid by a minor PLO faction on Israel's coast in June 1990. In addition to some degree of fear from the "pro-Israel" lobby and its congressional supporters, the stance of the first Bush administration reflected its discomfort with the PLO—an armed, popular, third world nationalist movement that had been supported by the Soviet bloc and other countries not in favor in Washington.

The Clinton administration, which was awash with WINEP associates, was even less successful in pursuing an "even-handed" policy. The president and his advi-

15. Kathleen Christison, *Perceptions of Palestine: Their Influence on U.S. Middle East Policy* (Berkeley: University of California Press, 1999), p. 256.

16. Naseer Aruri, "U.S. Policy toward the Arab-Israeli Conflict," in Hooshang Amirahmadi (ed.), *The United States and the Middle East: A Search for New Approaches* (Albany: SUNY Press, 1993), pp. 115–16.

sors were warm "supporters of Israel." Throughout the era of the Oslo Declaration of Principles and the subsequent negotiations between Israel and the PLO they failed to grasp that Israel's expansion of settlements and construction of a network of bypass roads disrupting the territorial contiguity of the West Bank, and its continued closures of the Palestinian population, would undermine the chances of reaching a final status agreement between Israel and the PLO.[17] President Clinton was genuinely surprised at the failure of the July 2000 Camp David summit, for which he blamed Yasser Arafat, despite a prior promise not to do so. It was not until December that Clinton proclaimed that he "understood" the Palestinians' point of view on the issues in dispute. By that time it was too late to stop the Palestinian intifada, which broke out following Ariel Sharon's September 28 visit to the Temple Mount/Noble Sanctuary in Jerusalem and destroyed the Oslo process.

Several factors have influenced U.S. policy on the Arab-Israeli conflict and the shaping of the U.S.-Israeli alliance. There has been sympathy for Israel as the moral legatee of the victims of the Nazi mass murder of European Jewry. Liberals and progressives have been attracted to Israel by institutions like the kibbutzim (which are now in terminal crisis). There is a Western cultural antipathy toward Arabs and Muslims exemplified by the Crusades, whose imagery remains powerful in the minds of many Christians and Muslims. The Zionist lobby, whose flagship organization is the American Israel Public Affairs Committee (AIPAC), exercises considerable power over Congress through its massive campaign contributions. The arms industry, which contributes twice the amount of money to congressional campaigns as does AIPAC, enthusiastically supports military aid to Israel (on which it receives a kickback in the form of contracts and profits). Evangelical Protestants, who have become the strongest popular element in the social base of the Republican Party, are closely tied to the most right-wing elements in Israeli society.

The single most important factor shaping the U.S.-Israeli relationship over the last thirty years has been the geo-strategic interest of the United States as perceived by Washington policy makers. Israel has protected the flank of the Persian Gulf—the repository of two-thirds of the world's known petroleum reserves—and threatened to topple or punish any Arab regime that undermined the secure supply of oil at a reasonable price. It has also been willing to do Washington's bidding in a wide range of foreign adventures. No Arab state as presently constituted can reliably serve as a replacement for these functions. After the 1991 Gulf War such geo-strategic considerations were reduced. But twenty years of momentum and a thick network of relations had been established. A powerful coalition comprised of the Zionist lobby, evangelical Protestants, and arms makers now constitutes a significant domestic constraint on those who might seek to alter U.S. policy toward Israel.

17. Robert Malley, Hussein Agha, "Camp David: The Tragedy of Errors," *The New York Review of Books*, August 9, 2001, *http://www.nybooks.com/articles/14380.*

Deal Breakers

Michael Massing

Jews remain one of the most liberal groups in American society. And although concern about Israel's security has pushed some of them to the right, the majority have supported the peace process, including the efforts of President Clinton late in his term to bring about an agreement with the Palestinians. During and since those years, however, the two Jewish organizations with the most influence on foreign policy have had leaders who are far more conservative and hard-line than are most American Jews.

One of those groups is the American Israel Public Affairs Committee. Long regarded as the most effective foreign-policy lobby in Washington, AIPAC has an annual budget of $19.5 million, a staff of 130, and 60,000 members. Those members constitute a powerful grass-roots network that can be activated almost instantly to press Congress to take this action or that.

The other major group, the Conference of Presidents of Major American Jewish Organizations, is less well known. Made up of the heads of fifty-one Jewish organizations, the Presidents Conference is meant to reflect the broad spectrum of opinion among America's 6.1 million Jews. By charter, it is supposed to act only when there is a consensus among its members. In practice, however, the organization is run largely by one man, Malcolm Hoenlein, who has tilted it decisively to the right on critical issues involving Israel in recent years.

This is sensitive territory. On the streets of Cairo, Beirut, and Tehran, vendors hawk anti-Semitic pamphlets claiming that a small cabal of Zionists runs the world. Among Arab elites, it's an article of faith that the "Jewish lobby" dictates U.S. policy toward the Middle East. In fact, that policy reflects an array of factors, including America's dependence on foreign oil, its fight against Islamic terrorism, its efforts to contain Iraq and Iran, and the fact that Israel is the one and only democracy in the region. What's more, American Jews, in seeking to influence U.S. policy in the area, are simply exercising their rights as American citizens to organize politically and press their interests.

Unfortunately, those who are most adept at this do not necessarily represent the broad range of Jewish views on the subject. At a time when Palestinian terror bombings grow more horrific daily and Israeli military action in the occupied territories grows steadily harsher, the bias in political representation has complicated negotiations and reduced the likelihood that the United States will be able to mediate the conflict successfully.

According to public-opinion polls, most American Jews support a more active U.S. role in the Middle East. In the late 1990s, as negotiations were taking place between Israel and the Palestinians, polls showed that more than 80 percent of American Jews wanted the United States to apply pressure on both sides to help bring about a settlement. Since September 11 and since the rash of attacks on Israeli civilians, American Jews have become more hawkish, but even now they decisively support efforts to draw the two sides together. An October 2001 survey sponsored in part by the New York–based *Jewish Week* found that 85 percent of American Jews believe it is important for the United States to become more involved in ending the violence between Israelis and Palestinians and in moving the parties back to the negotiating table. Another 73 percent said that they believe it's in Israel's interest for the United States to serve as a "credible and effective facilitator" of the peace process, even if that means occasional disagreements between Washington and Jerusalem.

"Most American Jews vote in favor of Oslo," says J. J. Goldberg, the editor of the *Forward,* citing polls conducted by his paper. He adds, however, that Jews who identify themselves as doves feel much less strongly about Israel than those who identify themselves as hawks. "Jewish liberals give to the Sierra Fund," Goldberg says. "Jewish conservatives are Jewish all the time. That's the whole ball game. It's not what six million American Jews feel is best—it's what fifty Jewish organizations feel is best." More precisely, it's what two Jewish organizations feel is best.

The Conference of Presidents of Major American Jewish Organizations was founded, oddly enough, at the suggestion of John Foster Dulles. Not known as a friend of the Jews, Dwight Eisenhower's secretary of state grew tired of being approached by so many different Jewish leaders and suggested that they form one organization to represent them. They did. Created in 1956, the conference was led by one man, Yehuda Hellman, for its first thirty years and under him it remained a relatively sleepy organization.

In 1986, however, Hellman suddenly died, and Malcolm Hoenlein took his place. A product of an Orthodox Jewish family in Philadelphia, Hoenlein (pronounced HONE-line) graduated from the University of Pennsylvania and came to New York in 1971 to work on behalf of Soviet Jewry. Five years later, he was named head of the Jewish Community Relations Council of New York, an umbrella group of Jewish organizations that he helped build into a powerful force. When the job at the Presidents Conference became vacant, Hoenlein was named to fill it.

Aside from its letterhead, Hoenlein found, the conference had few assets. But what a letterhead it was. Virtually every organization of influence in the Jewish community was on it, so that when the conference spoke, it did so with great authority. And Hoenlein moved quickly to assert it. Impassioned, energetic, and dynamic, he used his impressive knowledge of the Middle East to pry open doors at the National Security Council, the State Department, and the Pentagon. Not a day went by that Hoenlein wasn't on the phone to an assistant secretary of state, a White House adviser, an ambassador, or a congressman, extracting information from one, doling it out to another, cajoling and maneuvering key players to tilt U.S. policy in Israel's direction. To boost the conference's influence abroad, Hoenlein began taking his board on annual trips to Israel and one other country. Those other nations have included Turkey, Bahrain, Egypt, Jordan, Russia, and Uzbekistan. Everywhere, the delegations have been received by heads of state and foreign ministers.

Today, the conference employs a staff of only six and has an annual budget of less than a million dollars, but its clout belies its modest size. The *Forward*, which every year publishes a list of the fifty most influential Jews, this year ranked Hoenlein first. "The most influential private citizen in American foreign policy-making," a former high-ranking U.S. diplomat was quoted as saying of him.

In wielding that influence, Hoenlein is supposed to reflect the broad consensus within the conference. And, when there actually is a consensus, he gives it an effective voice. It's when there's not that the trouble begins. The problem in part reflects how the conference is organized. Of the group's fifty-one members, the two largest are the Union of American Hebrew Congregations and the United Synagogue of Conservative Judaism. The former represents America's 1.5 million Reform Jews and their 900 synagogues; the latter, America's 1.5 million Conservative Jews and their 760 synagogues. Both of these groups are generally liberal in outlook and supportive of the peace process in the Middle East. Each gets one vote on the board. By contrast, the Orthodox Union—the organized arm of Orthodox Judaism—represents 600,000 Jews and 800 congregations. Nonetheless, it, too, gets one vote. So do a host of smaller organizations, such as Agudath Israel of America, the Zionist Organization of America, and American Friends of Likud—all of them conservative and unenthusiastic about the peace process. The smaller conservative groups in the conference decisively outnumber the larger liberal ones and so can neutralize their influence. And that leaves considerable discretion in the hands of Malcolm Hoenlein.

As to how he uses it, Hoenlein insists that he is scrupulously evenhanded. "I'm not an ideologue," he told me in an interview at the conference's modest suite of offices on Third Avenue in midtown Manhattan. "I devote myself to the security of the Jewish state." A balding, bespectacled fifty-seven-year-old who speaks with crisp self-assurance, Hoenlein added: "People have said we're too close to Rabin, to Barak, to Sharon, to Bibi. But we have to be in the center. I was and am close to Al Gore and the Clintons, but I've formed a real relation with George Bush, too."

Hoenlein's statements, however, reflect a viewpoint closer to Sharon's than Barak's. "Jews," he noted, "have a right to live in Judea and Samaria, part of the ancient Jewish homeland—just as they have a right to live in Paris or Washington." The catchphrase "Judea and Samaria" is a biblically inspired reference that Likud Party supporters use to justify the presence of Jewish settlers on the West Bank. Hoenlein, in fact, has long been involved with the settlers' movement. For several years in the mid-1990s, he served as an associate chairman for the annual fundraising dinners held in New York for Bet El, a militant settlement near Ramallah that actively worked to scuttle the peace process by provoking confrontations with neighboring Palestinians.

Such activities have fed the impression among some conference members that Hoenlein has given the group a strong conservative tilt. The organization "has been much more outspoken and forceful in supporting governments of the right than those of the left," says Rabbi Eric Yoffie, the president of the Union of American Hebrew Congregations. "I feel strongly that during the Rabin and Barak years the conference simply did not demonstrate the same kind of energy and aggressive support for the policies of the Israeli government that it did during the [Yitzhak] Shamir and Netanyahu years."

Adding to the impression of partisanship are the individuals who've been selected to serve as the conference chair. Candidates for the two-year position are put forward by a nominating committee that is appointed by the outgoing chairperson in consultation with Hoenlein; the final decision is made by the full board. In 1999 one of the nominees was Ronald Lauder, the billionaire heir of the Estée Lauder cosmetics company. A former U.S. ambassador to Austria in the Reagan administration, Lauder had donated millions of dollars to Jewish causes over the years. Politically, however, he seemed out of step with most American Jews; in 1989, while seeking the Republican nomination for mayor of New York, he ran to the right of Rudolph Giuliani. And, on Israeli issues, he was a vocal Likudnik, with long-standing ties to Netanyahu. While Lauder was seeking the conference chair, the Jewish press carried reports that he had helped bankroll Netanyahu's campaign for prime minister. Such foreign contributions are illegal under Israeli law; Lauder denied the reports, but that did little to mollify his opponents. But Lauder had one key asset: He was widely believed to be Hoenlein's choice, and in the end he was duly elected.

While in office, Lauder realized his critics' worst fears. The flash point was a rally scheduled for Jerusalem in January 2001 to express opposition to the idea of sharing sovereignty over that city with the Palestinians. Organized in part by Natan Sharansky's Yisrael Ba'aliya Party, the rally was widely viewed as a right-wing protest against the Barak government and its efforts to forge a peace agreement with the Palestinians. At a meeting of the conference board called to discuss whether to endorse the event, Sharansky was invited to present his views; the Barak government wasn't. Several members of the board, including Eric Yoffie, spoke out strongly against participating. Various Orthodox groups and other conservatives expressed their support. In the end, seventeen board members voted in favor of participating and ten voted against—hardly the consensus required for conference action.

Nonetheless, Lauder decided to attend—as a private citizen, he said. At the rally, which attracted more than 100,000 people, Lauder was introduced as the chairman of the Presidents Conference, and in his speech he said he was expressing the feelings of the "millions of Jews" who felt that Jerusalem must never be divided. Lauder's presence was widely seen as constituting conference endorsement of the rally and its goals. Rabbi Yoffie and his allies on the board were so upset that a special meeting was called to discuss the issue, and at it a new policy was adopted prohibiting the chairman from speaking out on issues when not explicitly authorized to do so.

Such developments have raised deep concerns among some about how the conference is run. "The real work is done behind the scenes, involving a handful of people," Yoffie says. Several years ago, he observes, the Reform representatives on the board got together to try to make the conference more representative; among other things, they pushed for the creation of an executive committee that could supervise the staff's work. But the effort collapsed. Today, Yoffie says, he rarely attends board meetings. "They're useless," he maintains. "Many of the small groups are extremely conservative, and that creates an atmosphere at meetings. You try to make points, but nobody's interested." Overall, he complains, "We're rarely consulted on anything."

In recent months, the conference has enjoyed relative calm. With Israel under attack, most American Jews have united behind the country, and even Hoenlein's detractors believe that the conference has done a good job of communicating their concerns. But when the issue of peace negotiations with the Palestinians again rises to the fore, as it inevitably will, the conference's tilt, and its lack of representativeness, will no doubt resurface as a serious issue.

The activities of the American Israel Public Affairs Committee have raised similar concerns. AIPAC and the Presidents Conference work together closely; all of the members of the conference, in fact, sit on AIPAC's executive committee (which is distinct from its board of directors). The two organizations follow a clear division of labor, however: Whereas the conference focuses on the executive branch of the U.S. government, AIPAC concentrates on Congress. Its staff, which occupies two floors of a nondescript office building near Capitol Hill, includes registered lobbyists and a crack research team that tracks legislation, investigates issues, and keeps a detailed record of how each member of Congress votes on every issue of importance to Israel. Periodically, when matters of importance arise, the staff issues a pithy "talking points" report that updates AIPAC members and urges them to action. In virtually every congressional district, meanwhile, AIPAC has a group of prominent citizens it can mobilize if an individual senator or representative needs stroking.

Most important of all, AIPAC distributes money. Lots of it. It does this not as an organization—despite its name, AIPAC is not a political action committee—but through its members. The scale of their giving can be glimpsed at the Web site of the Federal Election Commission (www.fec.gov), where contributions are listed by individual. Between 1997 and 2001, the forty-six members of AIPAC's board together gave well in excess of $3 million, or more than $70,000 apiece. At least seven gave more than $100,000, and one—David Steiner, a New Jersey real-estate developer—gave more than $1 million. (Much of this funding goes to political parties and other "soft money" recipients who are not subject to federal election donation limits.)

And that's just the board. Many of AIPAC's 60,000 members contribute funds as well, in sums ranging from a hundred dollars to hundreds of thousands of dollars. Much of this money is distributed through a network of pro-Israel PACs. Often, when an individual candidate is favored, these PACs will organize multiple fundraisers in different parts of the country. Consider the case of Tom Daschle. When, as a four-term congressman, Daschle first ran for the Senate, in 1986, his opponent was considered no friend of Israel. Daschle's own record was not particularly distinguished on matters Israeli, but AIPAC and other Jewish groups, intent on nurturing him, helped organize a round of fundraisers in different locales. In the end, say former AIPAC officials, these events netted Daschle roughly one-quarter of the $2 million he spent on the campaign. Daschle has received similar amounts in subsequent races. And as he's ascended the Democratic ladder in the Senate, his votes on the Middle East have reliably reflected AIPAC's perspective. Similarly, when Trent Lott was rising in the House under Newt Gingrich, AIPAC assigned some if its wealthy southern members to cultivate him. The Mississippian became a strong supporter of Israel, and he remains so as Senate minority leader.

There are many others like them. An examination of AIPAC giving on the FEC Web site turns up many of the same recipient names from across the political spectrum: Joseph Biden, Christopher Bond, Barbara Boxer, Hillary Clinton, Susan Collins, Dianne Feinstein, Charles Grassley, Tom Harkin, Dennis Hastert, James Jeffords, Trent Lott, Nita Lowey, Mitch McConnell, Patty Murray, Charles Schumer, and so on. In all, hundreds of members on both sides of the aisle receive substantial pro-Israel contributions. This giving packs all the more punch because of the lack of a counterweight by pro-Arab and pro-Muslim PACs. As a result of such lopsided giving, says William Quandt, a member of the National Security Council in the Nixon and Carter administrations, "Seventy to 80 percent of all members of Congress will go along with whatever they think AIPAC wants."

What AIPAC wants, meanwhile, is determined by its board of directors. And directors are selected on the basis of how much money they give, not how well they represent AIPAC's members. "If you want to be a player at AIPAC, you have to be a significant giver both to AIPAC and to politicians," says Douglas Bloomfield, a former legislative director at AIPAC. Accordingly, AIPAC's board is thick with corporate lawyers, Wall Street investors, business executives, and heirs to family fortunes. Within the board itself, power is concentrated among an extremely wealthy subgroup made up of past AIPAC presidents.

During the 1980s, when AIPAC was establishing its reputation, policy was effectively set by four ex-presidents: Robert Asher, a lighting-fixtures dealer in Chicago; Edward Levy, a building-supplies executive in Detroit; Mayer "Bubba" Mitchell, a scrap-metal dealer in Mobile, Alabama; and Larry Weinberg, a real-estate broker in Los Angeles (and a former owner of the Portland Trailblazers). Asher, Levy, and Mitchell were stalwart Republicans who raised huge sums for that party; Weinberg was a Scoop Jackson Democrat. Regardless of party affiliation, the Gang of Four, as they are known, were all committed to a strong Israel, and while Shamir was prime minister, say current and former AIPAC officials, the organization acted more or less as an arm of the Israeli government. Among other things, AIPAC was instrumental in securing for Israel an annual aid package of nearly $3 billion, making Israel the largest recipient of U.S. largesse in the world.

In 1992, after becoming prime minister, Yitzhak Rabin visited Washington, met with AIPAC, and upbraided the group for its coziness with Likud. No longer, he said, would AIPAC act as Jerusalem's representative in Washington. The AIPAC board, deciding it needed a leader with ready access to both the Democrats in Washington and the Labor Party in Jerusalem, found its man in Steven Grossman, a stationery executive in Massachusetts who had served as that state's Democratic Party chair. (Grossman has also been a financial supporter of this magazine.)[1] During his four years as AIPAC's president, Grossman remained on excellent terms with both Clinton and Rabin. In 1993, after Rabin signed the Oslo peace accords and shook hands with Yasir Arafat in the White House Rose Garden, Grossman coaxed from his board a unanimous declaration of support.

But, according to former AIPAC officials, the Gang of Four was not enthusiastic, and, in contrast to the bullish statements AIPAC had issued on behalf of the Likud government, its board remained largely silent on Rabin's peace initiative. Then in 1995, the board, showing its true feelings, took up an issue calculated to impede Rabin's efforts: the location of the U.S. embassy in Israel. Jerusalem was Israel's capital, but the United States—like all but a handful of nations—had its embassy in Tel Aviv because of Jerusalem's contested status. According to Oslo, talks on the city's final disposition were to begin in May 1996 and conclude three years later. But AIPAC was not willing to wait. Flexing its muscle in Congress, it got 93 of 100 senators to sign a letter urging the administration to move the embassy by 1999, regardless of what happened in the negotiations. Going further, it got Republican Senator Bob Dole, who was preparing to run for president against Bill Clinton, to introduce a bill that would make the transfer mandatory by that year.

The Clinton administration opposed the bill, asserting that it would damage the peace process. So did the Rabin government. Members of Likud, by contrast, were jubilant. In a tribute to AIPAC's influence in Congress, both houses passed the Jerusalem Embassy Act by wide margins, and Clinton let it become law without signing it. The measure included a waiver allowing the president to suspend the transfer of the embassy if national security warranted, and it was duly invoked, so no move occurred. But by inflaming Arab opinion, the bill complicated the efforts to implement Oslo—and that, of course, was AIPAC's goal.

Since 1996, when Steve Grossman stepped down, AIPAC has had three presidents: Melvin Dow, a Houston attorney; Lonny Kaplan, a New Jersey insurance executive; and Tim Wuliger, a Cleveland investor. Together with ex-presidents Asher, Levy, Mitchell, and Weinberg, this group holds the real power on the board, according to current and former staffers. And while most of the recent presidents have been Democrats, all share the Gang of Four's unyielding stance

---

1. *The American Prospect,* where this essay first appeared.

on Israel. These board members, in turn, work closely with a handful of AIPAC staff members, including Howard Kohr, the executive director, and Steven Rosen, the head of research. Whether Democrat or Republican, liberal or conservative, all members of this policy-making core subscribe to one main principle: that there should be "no daylight" between the government of Israel and that of the United States.

While Clinton and Barak were in office, AIPAC's influence was limited; with both leaders committed to the peace process, the organization often found itself on the sidelines. But, with the election of George W. Bush and Ariel Sharon, AIPAC is back on the front line. That has been especially true since September 11. In waging its war on terrorism, the Bush administration has come under strong pressure from European and Arab leaders to push more aggressively for peace in the Middle East. For Israel and the Palestinians to return to the negotiating table, it's widely believed, the United States must get tough with both Sharon and Arafat, demanding not only that the Palestinians cease their terrorist attacks but also that the Israelis ease their tough policies in the occupied territories.

AIPAC, however, has pressed the administration to crack down on Arafat— and to leave Sharon alone. In November 2001, for example, it got Senators Christopher Bond of Missouri, a Republican, and Charles Schumer of New York, a Democrat, to circulate a letter praising President Bush for refusing to meet with Arafat and urging him not to restrain Israel from retaliating against Palestinian violence; eighty-nine senators signed it.

Meanwhile, as Secretary of State Colin Powell was preparing to announce a new peace initiative with retired U.S. Marine General Anthony Zinni serving as a special envoy, AIPAC was seeking to torpedo it. AIPAC's main vehicle was a "talking points" memo sent to its members in the field urging them to meet with their congressional representatives and press them to keep the administration off Israel's back. Titled "America-Israel Standing Together," the memo provided members a point-by-point agenda to follow in their meetings. "We are concerned about recent subtle shifts in the administration's policies toward Israel," it stated. While the United States is "actively seeking to eradicate bin Laden and his terrorist network," it added, the administration has "routinely criticized Israel for taking actions to defend itself from terrorists Arafat refused to arrest." The memo went on to note concern over the "poor timing" of the administration's statements in support of a Palestinian state and over the pressure Washington was applying to Israel "to negotiate with Arafat before he fulfills his commitments to combat terrorism."

The memo, says a former AIPAC official, was part of "an aggressive campaign to get AIPAC members to call on their congressmen to put pressure on the administration not to send Zinni to the region. Their emphasis was clearly to try to minimize any effort by the administration to say Israel must exercise restraint."

Any suggestion that AIPAC tilts against peace, or toward Likud, draws strong denials from the organization. "People who assert that have a political motive," says a senior AIPAC staff member who asked not to be identified. "There are fewer conservatives at AIPAC than there are in Israel." Israel, he added, "has a permanent dilemma: Should it take a risk for peace? Honest people can differ. The only way to resolve the matter is through the democratic process—and the people of Israel have a robust democracy." Nonetheless, AIPAC's activities over the years—its cozy ties with the Shamir government, its support for moving the U.S. embassy to Jerusalem, its efforts to keep Washington from leaning too hard on Sharon—leave the unmistakable impression that it, like the Presidents Conference, does not want to see the United States become too involved in pushing for peace in the Middle East.

That President Bush did speak in favor of a Palestinian state shows that these groups do not always get what they want. Furthermore, the United States has clear strategic and ideological reasons for supporting Israel and would no doubt do so regardless of any pressure from the Jewish community. The Bush administration's determination to stamp out global terrorism has given it added reasons for working closely with Israel. Israel's status as the one true democracy in the Middle East further cements its ties to Washington.

Still, AIPAC and the Presidents Conference have kept the United States from taking steps that many believe are essential if peace is ever to come to the region. The issue of settlements illustrates the point. Under both Labor and Likud governments, Israel has continued to expand and entrench its outposts in the occupied territories, a policy that has been a constant irritant in the Arab world. As the supplier of billions of dollars of aid to Israel every year, the United States could exercise some leverage on this issue. Yet it rarely uses it, and these organizations deserve much of the credit—or blame. "We could privately and publicly make clear to Sharon that settlement activity has to stop, and spell out the consequences if it doesn't," says William Quandt. "We shouldn't be subsidizing with U.S. taxpayers' money policies that we see as detrimental to peace, such as the building of settlements."

Certain elements in the American Jewish community do support a more robust U.S. role in the peace process. One is the Israel Policy Forum, founded in 1993. With financial backing from moguls like Norman Lear, David Geffen, and Michael Medavoy, the IPF has managed to establish itself as an alternative voice to AIPAC and the Presidents Conference. Last fall, for instance, as AIPAC was trying to keep the Bush administration from leaning too hard on Sharon, the IPF got fifty Jewish leaders to sign a letter praising the president for seeking new peace negotiations. Jonathan Jacoby, the IPF's founding executive vice president, who is currently a consultant to the group, says: "It's a fundamental mistake to think, as some American Jews still do, that America's special relationship with Israel is in conflict with America's role as an honest broker. The only thing the IPF stands for is that America has to play both these roles." The IPF has managed to forge close ties with many influential members of Congress, but, lacking a formal membership and a strong fundraising apparatus, it cannot match the influence of AIPAC and the conference.

And that's unfortunate. For the IPF's position seems more in line with that of the American Jewish mainstream—and with what many Middle East specialists believe is necessary if the violence in the region is to end. With Israelis and Palestinians killing one another in an ever-escalating cycle of revenge and retaliation, only strong intervention by the United States seems capable of stopping it. But as long as groups like AIPAC and the Presidents Conference continue to be controlled by a small, unrepresentative core, such a role for Washington seems out of the question.

Israel and the Media:
An Acquired Taste

Seth Ackerman

It's hard to think of a foreign country that enjoys a special relationship with the American media quite like Israel's.

In the waning days of the first Intifada, one could watch CBS's Dan Rather and ABC's Peter Jennings team up to entertain an all-star gala tribute for departing Israeli consul-general Uri Savir—complete with a comic skit performed by a pair of *New York Times* reporters, emceed by a popular New York news anchor, and capped by a send-off rendition of "New York, New York" rewritten specially for the occasion ("You'll be remembered here / By friends who hold you dear / Good luck, Ambassador Savir!") [Melman, 362].

Thomas Friedman, the unofficial dean of American foreign affairs journalism, has written of growing up "as a Jew who was raised on all the stories, all the folk songs, and all the myths about Israel"—as well as of his anguish in reporting on the 1982 Sabra-Shatila massacre, a story that pained him so much to write that at one point he asked his editor to assign the story to someone else [Diamond, 44].

On any American newsstand, a reader will find major national magazines owned and run by a pillar of the Israel lobby (Mort Zuckerman's *U.S. News & World Report*, the New York *Daily News* and, until recently, *The Atlantic*); a leading American Zionist intellectual (Martin Peretz's *New Republic*); and a media mogul whose politics are probably to the right of any Israeli government in memory (Rupert Murdoch's *New York Post* and *Weekly Standard*).

What explains the extraordinary alignment of so many prominent American media figures with Israel? And does it necessarily mean the media themselves are pro-Israel?

A little history is in order. The American journalism establishment doesn't exist in a vacuum. It is tied umbilically to a whole constellation of politicians, lobbyists, business interests, diplomats, Washington wise men and fixers who collectively create the conventional wisdom of an era. Today it's often forgotten that in Israel's early years conventional wisdom was not so favorably disposed to the Jewish State. Elite opinion in the 1940s and early 1950s, although sympathetic to the plight of Jewish refugees, viewed fervent support for Israel as the clamoring of an unruly ethnic special-interest minority—one with a suspiciously leftist tinge.

American Jews in those Cold War years were seen as liberals and leftists. Israel was a "socialist democracy" and the Soviet Union had backed its creation in 1948. That year, the leftist anti-Cold War presidential candidate Henry Wallace denounced President Truman, who haltingly arrived at a decision to support the new state, for his insufficient commitment to the Zionist cause.

American Jewish organizations, staunchly assimilationist and craving respectability, winced at such publicity. They were usually anti-Zionist. The largest and most influential of them, the American Jewish Committee, came around to endorsing a Jewish state only at the last minute, and then only reluctantly [Novick].

Those Jews who did try to lobby for Israel did not get very far in the Eisenhower years. One group of Zionists who visited the White House in 1953 to enlist the administration's support were treated instead to a lecture from the general: "He pointed to a map of the world and indicated to them the great Arab land bridge astride these three continents. He told them in no uncertain terms that whoever had the friendship of the people of this land bridge would in any worldwide conflict have the advantage" [Rev. Edward L. R. Elson, National Presbyterian Church in Washington D.C., quoted in Ben-Zvi]. (At the same time, active political sympathy—or even awareness—of the Palestinian cause was almost unknown in that era, limited to a handful of missionaries and Arabists.)

In such a climate, it is not surprising that the country's leading newspaper, the *New York Times,* owned by an old respectable Jewish family, was decidedly cool to Zionism. Like Adolph Ochs, the family patriarch, Arthur Hays Sulzberger, the publisher of the *Times* in those years, was opposed to a Jewish state. "If what you say is so," he once told a Zionist classmate at Columbia who extolled Jewish nationalism, "I will resign from the Jewish people." In the early 1940s, Sulzberger helped found the anti-Zionist American Council for Judaism [Grose, 226].

Even as late as the early 1960s, former *Times* reporter Ben Franklin recalls observing what he termed "the Jewish craziness": "I saw two copy boys begin to do their 'Jew-Arab count' . . . One would scan the paragraphs of Middle East or Israeli news stories and then read off the numbers for the other copy boy to record on a sheet of paper: 'Jew. Arab. Arab. Jew. Jew. Arab.'" The editors demanded equal space by the end of the week "or else a bell would go off, like a smoke alarm" [Diamond, 43].

In the 1960s, conventional wisdom changed. A new view of Israel had quietly been evolving in Washington officialdom in the years since the 1956 Suez crisis. Radical Arab nationalism was gathering strength in the Middle East and Israel was increasingly seen as a vital counterweight. Before the crisis, Eisenhower officials like Vice President Richard Nixon would privately grumble that "we were in the present jam because the past administration had always dealt with the area from a political standpoint and had tried to meet the wishes of the Zionists" [Ben-Zvi, 35].

But as the influence of Egypt's Nasser spread—menacingly, in Washington's eyes—a new type of thinking emerged: "If we choose to combat radical Arab nationalism and to hold Persian Gulf oil by force if necessary, a logical corollary would be to support Israel as the only strong pro-West power left in the Near East," Eisenhower asserted at a 1958 National Security Council meeting. In that year of crisis in the Middle East, when it seemed as if Jordan's monarchy might fall to radical forces allied to Nasser, John Foster Dulles for the first time looked to Israel as a valuable deterrent: "What was important was what the [Egyptians] thought the Israelis would do. If [they] thought the Israelis would touch off a big war, it was doubtful if [they] would want Jordan" [Ben-Zvi, 81].

The changing view of Israel filtered into the perceptions of the news media. As Vietnam dragged on and Third World liberation movements challenged American power on every continent, editors, opinion makers, columnists, and pundits absorbed a newfound admiring regard for the Jewish State: It was now a bulwark of Western values and interests, a battering ram against Third World radicalism, a strategic asset. In the media, the Six-Day War of 1967 was the turning point. E. Clifton Daniel, then managing editor of the *New York Times*, has said that the paper's final rejection of "Ochs's anti-Zionism" came with the 1967 war: "The war was a critical point in [Punch Sulzberger's] thinking. Here was Jewish nationalism on the rise; there was a need for the *Times* to change and it did" [Diamond, 43].

And so did the rest of the media. In the 1970s and 1980s, as the new conventional wisdom hardened, prominent media figures became closely aligned with Israel's cause. In 1991, Lally Weymouth, daughter of *Washington Post* publisher Katharine Graham, began writing a fiercely pro-Israel reporting column for the paper and its sister magazine *Newsweek* [Alterman, 149]. In 1992, CBS anchor Dan Rather, CBS board member Henry Kissinger, and CBS Middle East analyst Fouad Ajami were the featured guests at a $250-a-plate fundraiser for the Jerusalem Foundation, a Zionist group devoted to increasing the Jewish population of Jerusalem. Rather warned of an "Arab population explosion" threatening Jerusalem. Kissinger offered his own bon mot: "I tend to agree with Fouad—you can't really believe anything an Arab says" [*Boston Globe*, 8/6/92]. At the *Times*, A. M. Rosenthal, a ferociously hawkish Zionist, took the helm as executive editor in 1977, where he stayed through the early 1990s.

But if there was a media bias on the Arab-Israeli issue, it was a bias not so much toward Israel as in favor of a Washington establishment that had long ago decided that Israel was good for American power. By the time the current Intifada broke out in September 2000, the media's sympathies were not in doubt. In the first weeks of the crisis, newspaper editorials lined up overwhelmingly behind Israel. An October 2000 study by the Anti-Defamation League (ADL), which often accuses the media of anti-Israel bias, found that editorials displayed "overwhelming support and sympathy for Israel's position" [ADL, 10/24/2000].

Examining forty-three major papers, the ADL found that thirty-six expressed either "out-and-out support" for Israel or what the organization called "even-handed" commentary. Only seven papers voiced what the group described as "support for the Palestinian cause" or "focused blame on Israeli officials." In reality, media attitudes were even more monolithic. To be sure, opinion was somewhat divided over who was more to blame for derailing Israeli Prime Minister Ehud Barak's courageous and steadfast march toward peace: Was it the malign cunning of Yassir Arafat or Ariel Sharon's "unhelpful visit" to the Temple

Mount? Most papers settled on the first interpretation. (Commentaries that mentioned Sharon were deemed "pro-Palestinian" by the ADL.)

But central elements of the crisis were almost totally exempt from editorial criticism: Barak himself, who had been building settlements at a faster pace than his Likudist predecessor; the Clinton administration, which had tolerated and subsidized Israel's occupation while claiming the mantle of "honest broker"; and the entire U.S.- driven Oslo negotiating process, which had in effect served to protect Israel from its international obligations. The pro-Washington bias of the media's coverage could not have been clearer.

For reporters trying to explain the sudden outbreak of fighting in the Middle East, the word "occupation" had become almost taboo. Even the designation "occupied territories," once routine, had all but disappeared by the end of the Oslo period. In the early 1990s "occupied territories" showed up in hundreds of Associated Press articles each year—699 in 1992 and 731 in 1993. Nearly a third of all articles mentioning Palestinians used the term. By the end of the decade, the number of appearances had dwindled to a few dozen. In the nine months leading up to the Intifada, barely 1 percent of such articles mentioned the dreaded phrase.

On the three networks' evening news broadcasts—*ABC World News Tonight, NBC Nightly News,* and *CBS Evening News*—the West Bank or Gaza were mentioned in 437 news stories in the year after fighting began. Of those, only 34 used the word "occupied," "occupation," or any other variation. Thus, incredibly, more than 90 percent of network TV reporting on the occupied territories failed to report that the territories are occupied. Tellingly, while Israel's occupation was mentioned in almost three-fifths of the news stories in the *London Independent* that year, it was omitted from more than two-thirds of the stories in the *New York Times.*

As the violence has dragged on, day-to-day reporting has settled into a familiar routine. The almost daily killings of Palestinians in the occupied territories typically receive scant coverage—that is, until a suicide bombing in Israel "shatters the calm." The bombing and its Israeli victims then dominate headlines for a few days, along with the Israeli army's subsequent "retaliation" against Palestinian targets. (About 80 percent of the references to "retaliation" in network news reporting from the Middle East refer to Israeli attacks; Palestinian attacks are rarely described that way—9 percent—even though both sides obviously claim to be "retaliating"—[FAIR Action Alert, "In U.S. Media, Palestinians Attack, Israel Retaliates," 4/4/02].) Soon, coverage of the violence dies down, to be followed by another "lull in the violence" (during which Palestinians are again quietly killed on an almost daily basis). The cycle begins again with another suicide bombing.

The result is that Palestinian deaths are simply much less likely to be covered than Israeli deaths. In the first six months of 2001, National Public Radio reported on the killings of 62 Israelis and 51 Palestinians. In the same period, 77 Israelis and 148 Palestinians died in the conflict. In other words, there was an 81 percent likelihood that an Israeli death would be reported on NPR, but only a 34 percent likelihood that a Palestinian death would be. The pattern can't be explained by "innocent" victims getting more coverage: Palestinian kids who died were less likely to be covered than Palestinian adults (20 percent versus 38 percent); and Palestinian security officials were more likely to have their deaths reported than Palestinian civilians (72 percent versus 22 percent). The pattern was reversed in the case of Israelis: kids got more coverage than adults (89 percent versus 78 percent) and civilians got more coverage than soldiers (84 percent versus 69 percent) [*Extra!* "The Illusion of Balance," Seth Ackerman, 11–12/01].

No issue better epitomizes the media's deference to Washington conventional wisdom than the myth of "the Generous Offer." After the collapse of the Camp David peace talks in July 2000, all it took was a public statement from President Clinton blaming Arafat for the failure, and a new consensus was born: The post-September violence was Arafat's fault. Israel had made him an astonishingly generous offer at Camp David and he had stubbornly turned it down. With stunning near-unanimity, the pundit class adopted Clinton's accusation as a rallying cry. Israel had "offered extraordinary concessions" (Michael Kelly), "far-reaching concessions" (*Boston Globe*), "unprecedented concessions" (E. J. Dionne). Israel's "generous peace terms" (*L.A. Times* editorial) constituted "the most far-reaching offer ever" (*Chicago Tribune* editorial) to create a Palestinian state. In short, Camp David was "an unprecedented concession" to the Palestinians (*Time*) [Kelly—WP 3/13/02; BG 12/30/01; Dionne—WP 12/4/01; LAT—editorial, 3/15/02; Trib—editorial 6/6/01; *Time* 12/15/00].

But due to "Arafat's recalcitrance" (*L.A. Times* editorial) and "Palestinian rejectionism" (Mortimer Zuckerman), "Arafat walked away from generous Israeli peacemaking proposals without even making a counteroffer" (Salon.com). Yes, Arafat "walked away without making a counteroffer" (Samuel G. Freedman). Israel "offered peace terms more generous than ever before and Arafat did not even make a counteroffer" (*Chicago Sun-Times* editorial). In case the point wasn't clear: "At Camp David, Ehud Barak offered the Palestinians an astonishingly generous peace with dignity and statehood. Arafat not only turned it down, he refused to make a counteroffer!" (Charles Krauthammer) [LAT 4/9/02; *US News* 3/22/02; *Salon* 3/8/01; Freedman, *USA Today*, 6/18/01; CST 11/10/00; Krauthammer, *Seattle Times*, 10/16/00].

The implications of the new consensus were obvious: There was nothing Israel could do to make peace with the Palestinians. The Israeli army's deadly attacks in the occupied territories could be seen purely as self-defense against Palestinian aggression motivated by little more than blind hatred.

To understand what actually happened at Camp David, it's necessary to know that for many years the PLO has officially called for a two-state solution in which Israel would keep the 78 percent of "Mandate Palestine" (as Britain's former protectorate was called) that it has controlled since 1948, and a Palestinian state would be formed on the remaining 22 percent that Israel has occupied since the 1967 war (the West Bank, the Gaza Strip and East Jerusalem). Israel would withdraw completely from those lands, return to the pre-1967 borders and a resolution to the problem of the Palestinian refugees who were forced to flee their homes in 1948 would be negotiated between the two sides. Then, in exchange, the Palestinians would agree to recognize Israel [PLO Stockholm Declaration, 12/7/88; PLO Negotiations Department website, *www.nad-plo.org*].

Although some people describe Israel's Camp David proposal as practically a return to the 1967 borders, it was far from that. Under the plan, Israel would have withdrawn completely from the small Gaza Strip. But it would annex carefully selected and highly valuable sections of the West Bank—while retaining "security control" over other parts—that would have made it impossible for the Palestinians to travel or trade freely within their own state without the permission of the Israeli government. The annexations and security arrangements would divide the West Bank into three disconnected cantons. In exchange for taking fertile West Bank lands that happen to contain most of the region's scarce water aquifers, Israel offered to give up a piece of its own territory in the Negev Desert—about one-tenth the size of the land it would annex—including a former toxic waste dump. [For all discussion of Camp David details: *Political Science Quarterly*, 6/22/01; *New York Times*, 7/26/01; Report on Israeli Settlement in the Occupied Territories, 9/10/00; Robert Malley, *New York Review of Books*, 8/9/01.]

Because of the geographic placement of Israel's proposed West Bank annexations, Palestinians living in their new "independent state" would be forced to cross Israeli territory every time they traveled or shipped goods from one section of the West Bank to another, and Israel could close those routes at will. Israel would also retain a network of so-called "bypass roads" that would crisscross the Palestinian state while remaining sovereign Israeli territory, further dividing the West Bank.

Israel was also to have kept "security control" for an indefinite period of time over the Jordan Valley, the strip of territory that forms the border between the West Bank and neighboring Jordan. Palestine would not have free access to its own international borders with Jordan and Egypt—putting Palestinian trade, and therefore its economy, at the mercy of the Israeli military.

None of this was by accident. As Barak's chief negotiator Shlomo Ben-Ami, a fervent supporter of the Oslo process, had written: "In practice, the Oslo agreements were founded on a neo-colonialist basis, on a life of dependence of one on the other forever" [Ben-Ami, *A Place for All*, Hakibbutz Hameuchad, 1998; cited by Efraim Davidi, "Globalization and Economy in the Middle East," *Palestine-Israel Journal* VII.1&2, 2000]. Had Arafat agreed to these arrangements, the Palestinians would have permanently locked in place many of the worst aspects of the very occupation they were trying to bring to an end. For at Camp David, Israel also demanded that Arafat sign an "end-of-conflict" agreement stating that the decades-old war between Israel and the Palestinians was over and waiving all further claims against Israel.

The summit meeting ended on July 25, 2000. At that point, according to conventional wisdom, Arafat's "response to the Camp David proposals was not a counteroffer but an assault" (*Oregonian* editorial). "Arafat figured he could push one more time to get one more batch of concessions. The talks collapsed. Violence erupted again" (E. J. Dionne). He "used the uprising to obtain through violence . . . what he couldn't get at the Camp David bargaining table" (*Chicago Sun-Times*) [Oregon edit, 8/15/01; Dionne—WP, 12/4/01; CST 12/21/01].

But the Intifada actually did not start for another two months. In the meantime, there was relative calm in the occupied territories. During this period of quiet, the two sides continued negotiating behind closed doors.

Meanwhile, life for the Palestinian population under Israeli occupation went on as usual. On July 28, Prime Minister Barak announced that Israel had no plans to withdraw from the town of Abu Dis, as it had pledged to do in the 1995 Oslo II agreement [Israel Wire 7/28/00]. In August and early September, Israel announced new construction on Jewish-only settlements in Efrat and Har Adar, while the Israeli statistics bureau reported that settlement building had increased 81 percent in the first quarter of 2000. Two Palestinian houses were demolished in East Jerusalem, and Arab residents of Sur Bahir and Suwahara received expropriation notices; their houses lay in the path of a planned Jewish-only highway [Report on Israeli Settlement in the Occupied Territories, 11–12/00].

The Intifada began on September 29, 2000, when Israeli troops opened fire on unarmed Palestinian rock-throwers at Al-Aqsa Mosque in Jerusalem, killing four and wounding over 200 [State Department human rights report for Israel, 2/01]. Demonstrations spread throughout the territories. Barak and Arafat, having both staked their domestic reputations on their ability to win a negotiated peace from the other side, now felt politically threatened by the violence.

In January 2001, they resumed formal negotiations at Taba, Egypt. The Taba talks are one of the most significant and least remembered events of the "peace process." While Camp David was mentioned in conjunction with Israel thirty-five times on broadcast network news shows in early 2002, Taba came up only four times—never on any of the nightly newscasts. In February 2002, Israel's leading newspaper, *Ha'aretz*, published for the first time the text of the European Union's official notes of the Taba talks [2/14/02], which were confirmed in their essential points by negotiators from both sides.

"Anyone who reads the European Union account of the Taba talks," *Ha'aretz* noted in its introduction, "will find it hard to believe that only 13 months ago, Israel and the Palestinians were so close to a peace agreement." At Taba, Israel dropped its demand to control Palestine's borders and the Jordan Valley. The Palestinians, for the first time, made detailed counterproposals—in other words, counteroffers—showing which changes to the 1967 borders they would be willing to accept. The Israeli map that has emerged from the talks shows a fully contiguous West Bank, though with a very narrow middle and a strange gerrymandered western border to accommodate annexed settlements.

In the end, however, all this proved too much for Israel's Labor prime minister. On January 28, Barak unilaterally broke off the negotiations. "The pressure of Israeli public opinion against the talks could not be resisted," Ben-Ami said [*New York Times*, 7/26/01].

In February 2001, Ariel Sharon was elected prime minister of Israel. Sharon made his position on the negotiations crystal clear. "You know, it's not by accident that the settlements are located where they are" [*Ha'aretz* 4/12/01], he said in an interview a few months after his election: "They safeguard the cradle of the Jewish people's birth and also provide strategic depth which is vital to our existence.

"The settlements were established according to the conception that, come what may, we have to hold the western security area [of the West Bank], which is adjacent to the Green Line, and the eastern security area along the Jordan River and the roads linking the two. And Jerusalem, of course. And the hill aquifer. Nothing has changed with respect to any of those things. The importance of the security areas has not diminished, it may even have increased. So I see no reason for evacuating any settlements."

Meanwhile, Ehud Barak repudiated his own positions at Taba, and now speaks pointedly of the need for a negotiated settlement "based on the principles presented at Camp David" [NYT op-ed, 4/14/02]. In March 2002, the countries of the Arab League—from moderate Jordan to hard-line Iraq—unanimously agreed on a Saudi peace plan centering on full peace, recognition and normalization of relations with Israel in exchange for a complete Israeli withdrawal to the 1967 borders as well as a "just resolution" to the refugee issue. Palestinian negotiator Nabil Sha'ath declared himself "delighted" with the plan. "The proposal constitutes the best terms of reference for our political struggle," he told the *Jordan Times* [3/28/02]. Ariel Sharon responded by declaring that "a return to the 1967 borders will destroy Israel" [NYT, 5/4/02].

In a commentary on the Arab plan, *Ha'aretz*'s Bradley Burston noted [2/27/02] that the offer was "forcing Israel to confront peace terms it has quietly feared for decades."

Works Cited

Alterman, Eric. *Sound and Fury: The Washington Punditocracy and the Collapse of American Politics.* HarperCollins, New York: 1992.

Ben-Zvi, Abraham. *Decade of Transition: Eisenhower, Kennedy, and the Origins of the American-Israeli Alliance.* Columbia University Press, New York: 1998.

Diamond, Edwin. *Behind the Times: Inside the New York Times.* Villard Books, New York: 1993.

Frankel, Max. *The Times of My Life and My Life With the Times.* Random House, New York: 1992.

Grose, Peter. *Israel in the Mind of America.* Knopf, New York: 1983.

Melman, Yossi and Dan Raviv. *Friends in Deed: Inside the U.S.-Israel Alliance.* Hyperion Press, New York: 1994.

Novick, Peter. *The Holocaust in American Life.* Houghton Mifflin, Boston: 1999.

Rescuing Private Lynch, Forgetting Rachel Corrie

Naomi Klein

Jessica Lynch and Rachel Corrie could have passed for sisters. Two all-American blondes, two destinies forever changed in a Middle East war zone. Private Jessica Lynch, the soldier, was born in Palestine, West Virginia. Rachel Corrie, the activist, died in Israeli-occupied Palestine. Corrie was four years older than nineteen-year-old Lynch. Her body was crushed by an Israeli bulldozer in Gaza seven days before Lynch was taken into Iraqi custody on March 23. Before she went to Iraq, Lynch organized a pen pal program with a local kindergarten. Before Corrie left for Gaza, she organized a pen pal program between kids in her hometown of Olympia, Washington, and children in Rafah.

Lynch went to Iraq as a soldier loyal to her government. In the words of West Virginia Senator Jay Rockefeller, "she approached the prospect of combat with determination rather than fear." Corrie went to Gaza to oppose the actions of her government. As a U.S. citizen, she believed she had a special responsibility to defend Palestinians against U.S.-built weapons, purchased with U.S. aid to Israel. In letters home, she vividly described how fresh water was being diverted from Gaza to Israeli settlements, how death was more normal than life. "This is what we pay for here," she wrote.

Unlike Lynch, Corrie did not go to Gaza to engage in combat—she went to try to thwart it. Along with her fellow members of the International Solidarity Movement (ISM), she believed that the Israeli military's incursions could be slowed by the presence of highly visible "internationals." The killing of Palestinian civilians may have become commonplace, the thinking went, but Israel doesn't want the diplomatic or media scandals that would come if it killed a U.S. college student. In a way, Corrie was harnessing the very thing that she disliked most about her country—the belief that American lives are worth more than any others—and trying to use it to save a few Palestinian homes from demolition.

Believing her fluorescent orange jacket would serve as armor, that her bullhorn could repel bullets, Corrie stood in front of bulldozers, slept beside water wells, and escorted children to school. If suicide bombers turn their bodies into weapons of death, Corrie turned hers into the opposite: a weapon of life, a "human shield." When that Israeli bulldozer driver looked at Corrie's orange jacket and pressed the accelerator, her strategy failed. It turns out that the lives of some U.S. citizens—even beautiful, young, white women—are valued more than others. And nothing demonstrates this more starkly than the opposing responses to Rachel Corrie and Private Jessica Lynch.

When the Pentagon announced Lynch's successful rescue, she became an overnight hero, complete with "America loves Jessica" fridge magnets, stickers, T-shirts, mugs, country songs, and an NBC made-for-TV movie. According to White House spokesman Ari Fleisher, President George W. Bush was "full of joy for Jessica Lynch." Lynch's rescue, we were told, was a testament to a core American value: as Senator Rockefeller put it in a speech to the Senate, "We take care of our people." Do they?

Corrie's death, which made the papers for two days and then virtually disappeared, has met with almost total official silence, despite the fact that eyewitnesses claim it was a deliberate act. President Bush has said nothing about a U.S. citizen killed by a U.S.-made bulldozer bought with U.S. tax dollars. A U.S. congressional resolution demanding an independent inquiry into Corrie's death has been buried in committee, leaving the Israeli military's investigation—which conveniently cleared itself of any wrong doing—as the only official probe. The ISM says that this non-response has sent a clear, and dangerous, signal. According to Olivia Jackson, a twenty-five-year-old British citizen still in Rafah, "after Rachel was killed, [the Israeli military] waited for the response from the American government and the response was pathetic. They have realized that they can get away with it and it has encouraged them to keep on going." First there was Brian Avery, a twenty-four-year-old citizen shot in the face on April 5. Then Tom Hurndall, a British ISM activist shot in the head and left brain-dead on April 11. Next was James Miller, the British cameraman shot dead while wearing a vest that said "TV." In all of these cases, eyewitnesses say the shooters were Israeli soldiers.

There is something else that Jessica Lynch and Rachel Corrie have in common: both of their stories have been distorted by a military for its own purposes. According to the official story, Lynch was captured in a bloody gun battle, mistreated by sadistic Iraqi doctors, then rescued in another storm of bullets by heroic Navy SEALs. In the past weeks, another version has emerged. The doctors who treated Lynch found no evidence of battle wounds, and donated their own blood to save her life. Most embarrassing of all, witnesses have told the BBC that those daring Navy SEALs already knew there were no Iraqi fighters left in the area when they stormed the hospital. But while Lynch's story has been distorted to make its protagonists appear more heroic, Corrie's story has been posthumously twisted to make her, and her fellow ISM activists, appear sinister.

For months, the Israeli military had been looking for an excuse to get rid of the ISM "troublemakers." It found it in Asif Mohammed Hanif and Omar Khan Sharif, the two British suicide bombers. It turns out that they had attended a memorial to Rachel Corrie in Rafah, a fact the Israeli military has seized on to link the ISM to terrorism. Members of ISM point out that the memorial was open to the public, and that they knew nothing of the British visitors' intentions. As an organization, the ISM is explicitly opposed to the targeting of civilians, whether by Israeli bulldozers or Palestinian bombers. Furthermore, many ISMers believe that their work may reduce terrorist incidents by demonstrating that there are ways to resist occupation other than the nihilistic revenge offered by suicide bombing. No matter. In the past two weeks, half a dozen ISM activists have been arrested, several deported, and the organization's offices have been raided. The crackdown is now spreading to all "internationals," meaning there are fewer and fewer people in the occupied territories to either witness the ongoing abuses or assist the victims.

On Monday (May 22, 2003), the United Nations special coordinator for the Middle East Peace Process told the Security Council that dozens of UN aid workers had been prevented from getting in and out of Gaza, calling it a violation of "Israel's international humanitarian law obligations." On June 5 there will be an international day of action for Palestinian rights. One of the key demands is for the UN to send an international monitoring force into the occupied territories. Until that happens, many are determined to continue Corrie's work, despite the risks. Over forty students at her former college, Evergreen State in Olympia, have already signed up to go to Gaza with the ISM this summer. So who is a hero? During the attack on Iraq, some of Corrie's friends e-mailed her picture to MSNBC asking that it be included on the station's "wall of heroes," along with Jessica Lynch. The network didn't comply, but Corrie is being honored in other ways. Her family has received more than 10,000 letters of support, communities across the country have organized powerful memorials, and children all over the occupied territories are being named Rachel. It's not a made-for-TV kind of tribute, but perhaps that's for the best.

The Chosen: Ideological Roots of the U.S.-Israeli Special Relationship

Daniel Lazare

British politicians like to talk about their special relationship with Washington, but it should be obvious by now that the real special relationship is not between the United States and the United Kingdom, but between the United States and Israel. When George W. Bush sits down with Tony Blair, he encounters a politician who is still a liberal of sorts, even if he has managed to fit himself to the U.S. war drive. But when he sits down with Ariel Sharon, he encounters a lifelong warrior who was battling "terrorists" back when Washington still believed in the fine art of negotiation. Where Blair made it clear immediately after the fall of Baghdad that he would not countenance an extension of hostilities to Syria, Sharon, it is plain, would welcome anything the United States might do to terminate Syria's support for Hizbollah in Southern Lebanon. Where Blair believes in war to accomplish certain ends, Sharon believes in war without end against an enemy that will never entirely go away. Where Blair still sees war as an exceptional state of affairs, Sharon, who has spent virtually his entire life in combat with the Palestinians, sees it as normal and even healthy, which, it is now apparent, is the way Bush sees it, too.

But the fact that the two countries find themselves in combat against a common foe is not the only thing that draws them together. In addition, they are both shaped by certain common underlying principles, the most important of which can be summed up in a single word: chosenness.

Chosenness, of course, means a sense not only of being special, but of being consecrated or dedicated to some higher purpose. While one may set goals for oneself, an individual or nation can only be said to be chosen if it is by some higher authority or force. In the case of Israel, the origins of a national sense of chosenness would seem to be clear. Since the Hebrew Bible repeatedly speaks of the Jews as entering into a special covenant with God, the concept of a chosen people appears to be an example of an idea transmitted directly by the Jewish religion to the Jewish state. But this would be a gross simplification. While the concept of chosenness is indeed central to some 2,000 years of rabbinic Judaism, equally central is the renunciation of political power. Indeed, the two are linked. If the Jews are chosen, as the rabbis long taught, it was not to joust with other nations in the political realm of the here-and-now, but to give up power until some distant end-time when they could at last take revenge on their enemies. They had to forgo earthly power so as to wield heavenly power in some future apocalypse.

What changed this was not Zionism so much as the Holocaust. Prior to World War II, Zionists largely agreed with the rabbinate as to the trade-off between chosenness and political power, the difference being that the Zionists were more than happy to renounce the latter in order to exercise the former. The purpose of a Jewish state was not to exalt the Jews above all other nations, but to normalize them so that they could take their place as equals in the international community. The goal was not a Jewish state better than that of, say, the Irish or Poles, but one essentially the same. Despite the strained relations between the orthodox and the largely secular nationalists, the two camps had more in common than either cared to admit.

The Holocaust, however, destroyed this underlying symmetry once and for all. "In every generation there arises one that seeks to destroy us"—so Jews had declared during countless Passover seders. Grim as this sounds, it actually reflects a certain complacency: they may seek to destroy us, it suggests, but our presence is proof that they never succeed. But Nazism, in large measure, did succeed. Instead of the old oppression redux, it was an entirely new phenomenon that managed to exterminate the greater part of European Jewry. Its "success," consequently, added new meaning to the concept of chosenness. If Jews had been chosen, it was as victims of an unprecedented crime against humanity. As such, they were also chosen to take extraordinary measures to see to it that such an event never happened again. Their nearly total destruction had also been their liberation, in a sense, from having to obey the usual strictures governing the international community. Where other nations were expected to conform to certain norms, Jews, thanks to the horrifying ordeal they had just undergone, were exempt.

To be sure, this idea did not spring fully formed out of the Holocaust. Rather, it took decades to grow to maturity. Immediately following World War II, Chaim Weizmann clearly had in mind the old goal of normal Jewish nationhood when he told Harry Truman that what Zionists were seeking was "a secular state . . . based on sound democratic foundations with political machinery and constitutions on the pattern of those in the United States and Western Europe."[1] But once independence was achieved, normalcy was never quite within reach. The simple task of writing a constitution, for instance, the sine qua non of a modern democratic state, proved unexpectedly difficult. Liberals and Laborites favored something along West European lines, a document that would enshrine popular sovereignty, safeguard civil liberties, and set forth goals having to do with insuring justice, providing for the common defense, promoting the general welfare, etc. But it soon became evident that the new Israeli government was not of the people, by the people, and for the people who lived within its bound-

---

1. Michael T. Benson, *Harry S. Truman and the Founding of Israel* (Westport, CT.: Praeger, 1997), p. 121.

aries, but of, by, and for only a certain portion thereof, namely the Jews. Moreover, not only did the new government purport to represent Jews within its territory, but it also claimed to speak on behalf of Jews outside it as well. Where in a normal democracy the citizenry and the constituent power are one and the same, in Israel they only partially overlapped. There was also the question of popular versus divine sovereignty—whether the new state would serve the people (or, rather, a portion) or whether it would serve God. A draft proposal tried to please both secularists and the orthodox by calling for a modern democratic state that would nonetheless be guided by "the basic principles of Jewish Law."[2] Predictably, it wound up pleasing neither. In the end, Ben Gurion threw up his hands and chose to do without.

A similar problem arose in response to the issue of who, exactly, the Jews were that the new state was supposed to represent. Were they to be defined religiously or ethnically? Rather than further widen the breach between the secular and the orthodox, the Knesset abandoned the traditional matrilineal standard and opted for one developed by the Nazis, of all people, on the not-unreasonable grounds that if a single Jewish grandparent was enough to get one shipped off to Auschwitz, it was enough to obtain entry into the new Jewish state. Unable to define themselves, Israeli Jews relied on their enemies to define them instead.

Decisions like these may have satisfied no one other than American-style liberals who believe that democratic politics are of necessity pragmatic and ad hoc. But in fact they were not decisions at all, merely ideological vacuums that subsequent events would eventually fill. The Six-Day War proved to be the turning point. For a moment, the euphoria unleashed by Israel's stunning victory made bitter arguments over "who's a Jew" seem old hat. Who cared whether Jews defined themselves ethnically or religiously now that they had proven themselves militarily against the combined forces of Egypt, Syria, and Jordan? Ultimately, though, the war's effect was the opposite. Instead of defusing such arguments, it intensified them. Why had the Jews prevailed? In the eyes of the Zionist right, the answer was obvious.

The Jews had prevailed not only because they were better armed, better organized, and better led, but because they were Jews, which is to say a people possessed of a certain spark, a certain animating genius, that allowed them to prevail against their enemies. Whether this spark was racial, religious, or both was unknown; the important thing was that it existed. The concept of a Jewish state underwent a quasi-Hegelian twist. Rather than merely a state of the Jews, it was now a state of Jewishness, a state dedicated to the growth and development of a certain Jewish genius. As with German nationalism in the late nineteenth century, the more Jewishness was idealized, the more it was seen as a distinguishing characteristic setting off the Jewish nation from the world at large. Given the immense influence of the orthodox rabbinate, a sense of national

2. Bernard Avishai, *The Tragedy of Zionism: How Its Revolutionary Past Haunts Israeli Democracy* (New York: Helios Press, 2002), pp. 185–86.

distinctiveness inevitably led to a renewed feeling of having been chosen by a higher authority for some super-national goal. Instead of a state like any other, Israel saw itself as a state unlike any other. The greater its isolation due to its policies in the occupied territories, the greater the conviction that Israel should stand alone against the mob. Its loneliness was a sign of its moral exaltation.

This, in a nutshell, explains why the messianic right in Israel is powerful far beyond its numbers. If the point ever came to make peace with the Palestinians, Israel, presumably, could dismantle the settlements in the occupied territories and shake off the far-right movement behind them like a bug. After all, what is a movement whose hard-core numbers only in the tens of thousands against some four million Jews living in pre-1967 Israel? But the settlers' movement is more than just a group of individuals. Rather, it represents a nationalist ideal increasingly important to the Israeli polity as a whole. It has become a key mobilizing force. It is the cutting edge on which Zionism has come to depend.

The American sense of chosenness, by contrast, is rooted in the Anglo-American politics of the seventeenth and eighteenth centuries. As historians like J. G. A. Pocock, Lawrence Stone, J. R. Jones, and others have pointed out, the more the trans-Atlantic English-speaking community grew from roughly the 1620s on, the more polarized it became. On one side was a "Court" party centered in London that was composed not just of the monarchy, but also of the aristocracy, the church prelates, the Bank of England, the City of London, plus ruthless Whig powerbrokers like Sir Robert Walpole, England's first prime minister. On the other side was a "Country" opposition composed of small burghers, the rural gentry, American colonists, and various nonconformist Protestant sects. The kulturkampf between the two was every bit as bitter as that between American liberals and conservatives today. Where the Court was foppish and "citified," the Country saw itself as rural and homespun. Where the Court was imperialistic, the Country was wary of foreign entanglements. Where the Court believed in centralization, the Country believed that political power should be broken up. Where the Court was cool and calculating as it picked its way through the minefield of European big-power politics, the Country, true to its low-church origins, was passionate and messianic. "Give me liberty or give me death," was the quintessential Country cry. Patriots would prevail not by entering into sordid alliances with corrupt foreign princes, but by standing for something that was pure, morally exalted, and divinely blessed.

We can see in this complex latticework of religious and political beliefs the first stirrings of what would eventually be known as the American Way. Although the Americans succeeded in hammering out a written constitution not long after independence, they wrestled with, and ultimately ducked, many of the same problems that would later beset the Israelis. At first glance, for instance, the U.S. Constitution would seem to be crystal clear in its embrace of popular sovereignty. Rather than God or manifest destiny, the Preamble invokes only "We the people of the United States" as the sole constituent power. The Constitution, the Preamble seems to state, is something that the people have created themselves in order to advance their rule and "secure the blessings of liberty." As unambiguous as that seems, however, the rest of the document proceeds to muddy the waters. By repeatedly referring to certain "persons" held in slavery, it suggests that not all the people are sovereign, only a fragment.[3]

While the Preamble seems to acknowledge the power of a sovereign people both to make constitutions and to break them—in ordaining and establishing a new constitution, "we the people" were implicitly overturning an old one, the Articles of Confederation of 1781—Article V, the amending clause, severely limits the people's ability to change so much as a comma. By requiring approval by two-thirds of each house of Congress plus three-fourths of the states for any alteration, no matter how minute, it gave tiny minorities effective veto power over any and all constitutional reform. The people would be able to modify their plan of government only with great difficulty, if at all.[4]

The people totally control their government except when they don't. For all its homespun republicanism, the Country was, in the final analysis, an eighteenth-century ideology and therefore no closer to modern democratic theory of the nineteenth and twentieth centuries than the Court. It was leery of popular power, which it saw as indistinguishable from the mob, and, while extolling morality and virtue, saw them not as qualities arising from the people, but as something that would have to be imposed on them from without. A true republican was not part of the crowd, but a figure off by himself, disdainful of parties and the mob, lonely and austere (a role George Washington played to the hilt). Since the Country was opposed to concentrated power, it was opposed to the Hobbesian concept of sovereignty as supreme power emanating from a single source, be it the people, Parliament, or the crown. Rather, the Country preferred to see power checked, balanced, and separated into myriad pieces, while it preferred to think of sovereignty as something diffuse, multi-layered, and beholden to an authority higher than itself. To a degree, it was up to a fixed and sacred Constitution to exercise that higher authority. But in as fervently Protestant a country as the United States, a mere piece of parchment would not do the trick. Something animate was required, which is to say God.

Thus, sovereignty in American political theory "rests, of course, with the people," as Robert Bellah put it in a landmark essay on civil religion,[5] "but implicitly, and often explicitly, the ultimate sovereignty has been attributed to God." This is not the abstract "creator" of the Deists, but the active, vengeful God of low-church Protestantism, a God who doesn't set the universe in motion and then withdraws, but an Old Testament Jehovah who is constantly letting loose "the fateful lightning of His terrible swift sword." God blesses the people with liberty; a free people,

3. See Article I, sections 2 and 9, as well as Article IV, section 2.

4. In today's United States, the three-fourths rule means that just thirteen states representing as little as 5 percent of the population can block any change sought by the remaining 95 percent.

5. Robert N. Bellah, "Civil Religion in America," *Daedalus*, Spring 1967.

in turn, is one that is free to do His will. A free people is thus chosen. From the first days of the republic, according to Bellah, God was seen as "actively interested and involved in history, with a special concern for America," while the United States was seen as a second Israel: "Europe is Egypt; America, the promised land," a place where "God has led his people to establish a new sort of social order that shall be a light unto all the nations."

But what happens when two chosen peoples collide? Even though many of them thought of their country as a new Israel—*because* they thought of their country as a new Israel—Americans might just as easily have viewed a new Jewish national movement with hostility. As Secretary of State Robert Lansing warned his boss Woodrow Wilson in December 1917, "Many Christian sects and individuals would undoubtedly resent turning the Holy Land over to the absolute control of a race credited with the death of Christ."[6] True, but then Palestine was far away and the Zionist movement seemed to be loyal to Anglo-American values, which meant that Americans could afford to look upon Zionism as something distant and unthreatening, a force for civilization in a benighted land, a fulfillment of the Gospels rather than their undoing. Wilson, consequently, brushed aside Lansing's advice and embraced the new movement unreservedly. As he told Rabbi Stephen Wise, "I am a son of the manse, son of a Presbyterian clergyman, and therefore I am with you completely and am proud to think that I may in some degree help you to rebuild Palestine."[7]

This is not to say that important political sectors did not remain leery of a Jewish state. Franklin D. Roosevelt, for one, played his cards close to his vest, especially toward the close of World War II when he was concerned with cultivating good relations with the Saudis. But Truman represented a return to nativist American Zionism. Much more of a Midwestern isolationist (prior to Pearl Harbor, he said he would be happy to see the Nazis and Soviets kill each other off), he was born into Confederate stock in Missouri and brought up reading the Bible. As a result, he thought of democracy in classic American terms as not something the people create for themselves, but something handed down from on high. As he put it in 1948, "Democracy is a matter of faith—faith in the soul of man—a faith in human beings. . . . Without faith, the people would perish." Americans were not free by virtue of their own efforts, he argued on another occasion, but because they are blessed:

Divine Providence has played a great part in our history. I have the feeling that God has created us and brought us to our present position of power and strength for some great purpose. It is not given to us to know fully what that purpose is. But I think we may be sure of one thing. And that is that our country is intended to do all it can, in cooperating with other nations, to help create peace and preserve peace in the world. It is given

6. Benson, *Harry S. Truman,* p. 16.
7. Ibid., p. 19.

to us to defend the spiritual values—the moral code—against the vast forces of evil that seek to destroy them.

Finally, because America was chosen, it was its duty to help another chosen people as well. As Clark Clifford recalled, Truman was "a real student of the Bible . . . [who] felt that there was an obligation and a commitment made in the Old Testament that one day the Jews would have a homeland, and that appealed to him a great deal." When, following his retirement, Truman heard himself praised as one who had helped create the State of Israel, he erupted: "What do you mean, helped create? I am Cyrus, I am Cyrus"—Cyrus, of course, being the Persian king who freed the Jews from the Babylonian captivity and allowed them to rebuild the temple in Jerusalem.[8]

But where Truman insisted that faith was the essence of democracy, he was merely revealing how premodern his politics actually were. Although Bellah tried to put the best liberal spin on it that he could, "civil religion" has served to narrow American politics by subjecting them to the most backward religious prejudices. Instead of opening their eyes, it fairly forced Americans to view events in the Middle East through the prism of the Old Testament. As a consequence, they either ignored the non-Jewish population in Palestine or viewed it with contempt. FDR was typical in this regard. "What about the Arabs?" he remarked at one point to Chaim Weizmann. "Can't that be settled with a little baksheesh?" To Henry Morgenthau Jr., he suggested putting "barbed wire around Palestine" and moving the Arabs out as the Jews moved in.[9]

Which brings us once again to George W. Bush and Ariel Sharon. The difference between today's Republican Party and that of previous decades is that the new GOP is dominated by a kind of American civil religion in extremis in which divine sovereignty looms so large over the polity that popular sovereignty has all but faded to zero. As Michael Lind notes in his provocative new study, *Made in Texas,* former Vice President Dan Quayle joined the audience at a conservative conference in Florida in 1994 in reciting an eerily theocratic version of the Pledge of Allegiance: "I pledge allegiance to the Christian flag, and to the Savior for whose Kingdom it stands. One Savior, crucified, risen, and coming again, with life and liberty for all who believe." More recently, House majority whip Tom DeLay has assured a group of Texas Baptists that God was using him to promote "a biblical worldview" in American politics. For his part, George W. Bush, who starts each day kneeling in prayer and reading the Bible, believes that "[t]he true strength of America lies in the fact that we are a faithful America by and large." Instead of democracy, in other words, its strength lies in the people's obedience to a higher authority.[10] Indeed, it was the GOP's conviction that higher

8. Ibid., pp. 34, 35, 189.
9. Ibid., pp. 20–21.
10. Michael Lind, *Made in Texas: George W. Bush and the Southern Takeover of American Politics* (New York: Basic Books, 2003), pp. 109–11.

authority trumped anything as trivial as a popular election that stood it in such good stead in the Battle of Florida in November–December 2000. "I believe God wants me to be president," Bush reportedly once remarked. So did the Supreme Court, the Republican-controlled Florida state legislature, and the electoral college, which, as far as the GOP was concerned, was all that mattered.[11]

According to Lind, Bush's foreign policy rests on three pillars: unilateralism, pre-emptive warfare, and an ever-closer alliance with the Sharon government.[12] All derive from an increasingly extreme notion of America as the new Israel. A people chosen by God, for example, is not one to feel bound by man-made rules and regulations. Accordingly, Bush feels free to abrogate treaties, turn his back on the UN, and disregard international law. A president who, in the wake of September 11, privately spoke of being chosen to lead by the grace of God, obviously needs no one's say-so to attack whatever "evil-doer" that at the moment happens to strike his fancy.[13]

As for America's relations with the Sharon government, Lind argues that the Republican Party has been effectively captured from two angles by pro-Likud neocons like Deputy Secretary of Defense Paul Wolfowitz on the one hand and by Christian fundamentalists like Jerry Falwell, recipient of the Israeli government's Jabotinsky Award in 1981, on the other. The "Christian Zionism" of today's fundamentalists is essentially a revved-up version of the nativist Zionism of Woodrow Wilson and Harry S. Truman. Where Wilson and Truman were merely sympathetic to Zionist aspirations, Falwell and others like him believe that Christians must do everything they can to facilitate the return of the Jews to the Holy Land so as to hasten the Second Coming. What was once a fringe movement is now mainstream.

In 2002, Christian fundamentalists launched an "adopt-a-settlement" program in the occupied territories, while, a few years earlier, John Hagee, a pastor in San Antonio, Texas, announced that his congregation would give $1 million to Israel to settle Russian Jews in Jerusalem and the West Bank. When told that the United States formally regards the West Bank settlements as illegal, Hagee replied: "I am a Bible scholar and theologian and from my perspective, the law of God transcends the law of the United States government and the U.S. State Department." In April 2002, Tom DeLay declared that "Judea and Samaria" belonged to Israel, while House Majority Leader Dick Armey told a TV interviewer that he would be "content to have Israel grab the entire West Bank." "Well, where do you put the Palestinian state," the interviewer promptly replied, "in Norway?" Armey's answer: "I happen to believe the Palestinians should leave."[14]

11. Lee McAuliffe Rambo, "Bush Believes He Is Leading a Holy War," *The Atlanta Journal and Constitution*, Apr. 21, 2003, p. 15A.

12. Lind, *Made in Texas*, pp. 135–36.

13. Michael Duffy, "Marching Alone," *Time*, Sept. 9, 2002, p. 40.

14. Lind, *Made in Texas*, p. 148.

In his campaign autobiography, Bush told of a junket to Israel that he once made in the company of four Christian governors and "several Jewish-American friends." As he recounted: "It was an overwhelming feeling to stand in the spot [at the Sea of Galilee] where the most famous speech in the history of the world was delivered, the spot where Jesus outlined the character and conduct of a believer and gave to his disciples and the world the beatitudes, the golden rule, and the Lord's Prayer." Subsequently, Bush told of how one member of the group held hands underwater in the Sea of Galilee with a Jewish friend and prayed. Out of the first man's mouth came a hymn that he remembered from childhood:

Now is the time approaching,
By prophets long foretold,
When all shall dwell together,
One Shepherd and one fold.
Now Jew and gentile meeting,
From many a distant shore,
Around an altar kneeling,
One common Lord adore.[15]

It was the perfect Apocalyptic vision of the Jew and Gentile laying aside their differences with the coming of the Lord. For a fundamentalist like Bush, the coming together of Jew and gentile and of Israel and the United States are much the same thing. Christian Zionism and Jewish Zionism have combined to create an international alliance superseding anything that NATO or the UN has to offer. As Noam Chomsky might put it, the United States and Israel have discovered that they have something in common, namely a mutual contempt for international law. But as both an orthodox rabbi and Christian fundamentalist might reply, Israel and America are not contemptuous of international law, but beholden to divine law handed down from above. Instead of rebellious, they see themselves as obedient to a force that trumps international democracy. They believe they have been chosen to impose their will on the world whether the international community likes it or not.

15. Ibid., p. 157.

"Globalize the Intifada"

Esther Kaplan

It's fair to say I come from the old school of Jewish activism on Palestine. Though varying sharply on questions of loyalty or disloyalty to the state of Israel, activists of this sort—participating in organizations from Breira in the 1970s to New Jewish Agenda, the International Jewish Peace Union, the Road to Peace and Women in Black in the 1980s and early '90s, along with countless local and ad hoc efforts in their mold—shared a few common assumptions and strategies. Roughly, they sought to support and create audiences for the Israeli left, to educate and mobilize the American Jewish community against the occupation, to bring Israelis and Palestinians into dialogue, and to promote both negotiations and the validity of the PLO as a negotiating partner. This work was rooted in a few central if not always fully articulated ideas: that American Jewish dissent was influential among Palestinians and Israelis; that there was something inherently valuable in Jews and Palestinians working together, side by side; that moving the American Jewish community to oppose the occupation was not only possible, but an essential step in moving the U.S. government stance on the Israel/Palestine conflict.

Much of this activism navigated under the star of identity politics, the idea that American Palestinians and Jews had a special stake in the conflict and were uniquely situated to intervene. Donna Nevel, a coordinator of 1989's landmark Road to Peace conference, which brought together PLO members and members of the Israeli Knesset for the first time in the United States, recalls that "it was just assumed that the American delegation would be composed of their Jewish and Palestinian counterparts." Many activists felt personally implicated by Israel's transgressions and were motivated in part by a deep urge to redeem the Jewish community. Elissa Sampson, a longtime activist with the IJPU, recalls in almost spiritual terms that "even if you felt like the work you were doing was going nowhere, you felt at least some Palestinians out there would know that not all Jews agreed, and that these were footsteps that other Jews could pass over in the future." Unlike the mainstream media, which tended to paint a picture of an ancient tribal conflict between two sides with competing land claims, these activists typically avoided a rhetoric of parity and strongly opposed settlements and occupation. But they still tended to speak of a "peace movement" to resolve a "conflict" between "two peoples," as in the common slogan, "Two peoples, two states."

Traces of this model may be found even in newer, more militant formations such as New York City's Jews Against the Occupation and Washington, D.C.'s Jews for Peace in Palestine and Israel, whose mission statement reads in part,

"We believe that as Jews outside of Israel, we have both a right and obligation to speak out."

In the past few years, these assumptions and strategies, even this emotional tone, have begun to seem anachronistic. New emotional and political currents are coursing through the stateside struggle for Palestinian rights. The International Solidarity Movement, founded in 2001, has attracted thousands of activists to the West Bank and Gaza to disrupt the occupation and bear witness to its brutality. Only a quarter of the participants are Jewish or Arab. The U.S. Campaign Against the Occupation, founded in 2002, has a multiracial steering committee and an outreach plan to target churches and African American communities; a major project is to push unions and city councils to divest from Israel bonds. SUSTAIN, founded in late 2000 to stop U.S. aid to Israel, now has seventeen chapters across the country, including in cities far from Jewish or Arab population clusters, such as New Orleans and Gainesville, Florida. A campus divestment movement, with extremely diverse leadership, has emerged at Berkeley, Michigan, Ohio, Princeton, Harvard and several other campuses; their most recent conference, in late 2002, attracted some 500 students.

As these new campaigns emerge, activists in nearly every significant sector are taking up the Palestinian cause: San Francisco's Global Exchange, a nerve center of the antiglobalization movement, has launched an Israel divestment project. The Bay Area's Labor Committee for Peace and Justice sponsored a tour for Palestinian trade unionists. New York City activists from racial justice groups such as the Prison Moratorium Project and the Puerto Rican independence group ProLibertad recently formed the New York Solidarity Movement to educate communities of color about the Palestinian struggle. The nation's broadest antiwar coalition, United for Peace and Justice, at its first post-war national meeting, in June 2003, made fighting the Israeli occupation of the West Bank and Gaza as high a priority as fighting the U.S. occupation of Iraq. Hundreds, perhaps thousands, of individual activists have changed course, to put their energies into ending the Israeli occupation.

Vincent Lloyd, an African American religious studies student at Princeton, was a leader for many years of his campus's Living Wage Campaign, playing a key role in getting the university to convert temporary workers into full-time staff. Now he's the coordinator of Princeton Divest, which seeks to end university investments in corporations that do significant business in Israel. Charlotte Kates, a white first-year law student at Rutgers, used to agitate against racial profiling and for public housing; on campus, she advocated for the creation of a women's center. Now she's a leader of New Jersey Solidarity, which does community education in support of Palestinian liberation. Jordan Flaherty, a New York City union organizer, and Kamau Franklin, a member of the black nationalist Malcolm X Grassroots Movement, each joined the International Solidarity Movement in the spring of 2002. And on and on. The question of Palestinian oppression and Palestinian liberation has broken free from its tribal ways, gaining an entirely new prominence on the left.

At other times it was Vietnam, or Cuba, or El Salvador, or South Africa. But in 2003, as the second intifada nears the end of its third year, Palestine is the new cause célèbre, seen, in Kates's words, as "a central struggle in any fight for democracy and against imperialism." It's gotten to a point, says Faisal Chaudhry, a Harvard Law living wage organizer turned Palestine solidarity activist, where "not taking a position is seen as supporting what's going on there. Once the issue is raised, it becomes a measure of whether your group is critical and principled enough, anti-imperialist enough, consistent enough to take the right position—almost a litmus test." Flaherty, who had never done international solidarity work before taking off for Palestine, says, "I absolutely think that it's a defining issue on the left." So how did the issue gain such power—and what does it mean?

Mainstream Jewish organizations view this trend with alarm; the Anti-Defamation League (ADL) called criticism of Israel by antiwar protesters, for example, "an act of scapegoating both of the Jewish state and of Jews." Many liberal Jewish critics of the Israeli occupation are wary of the trend as well; as one rabbi wrote to an antiwar listserve, "this [debate] ignores many complexities about the Israeli-Palestinian-Arab conflict," and anyway, U.S. policy toward Israel and Palestine is "far, far less central" than its stance toward, say, Iran or Syria. But I see this explosion of interest in the Palestinian cause as a welcome development—not one born of bias, misinformation, or poor judgment, but rather a collective response to real world changes in the political landscape.

Radicals, particularly race radicals, have identified with the Palestinian struggle for decades, dating back at least to Stokely Carmichael's denunciation of "Zionist aggression" shortly after the 1967 war. In the 1960s and '70s, recalls Bob Wing, a longtime Bay Area activist and now the editor of the peace broadside *War Times,* "you had to be pro-PLO if you were a radical." But the attention was often shallow, and little actual organizing emerged on the American scene until after Israel invaded Lebanon in 1982—and then it was left largely to American Jews, Arab Americans, and the traditional peace-oriented church groups, such as Fellowship of Reconciliation. Only now have events converged to alter who is engaged in activist work on the issue of Palestine, how they are framing it, and how widely the issue is being taken up by the left as a whole. Many of these developments pose deep challenges to the old, tribal organizing models.

The most decisive turning point may have been the collapse of Oslo. After years of work to promote negotiations between the two sides, the failure of those talks to halt settlements, let alone create a viable Palestinian state, left the peace movement adrift. To many Palestinians, it marked the end of any hope that negotiations, on their own, could ever produce a just peace. The Jewish community, in denial about the tightening grip of occupation on the ground and the poverty of the Oslo deal, closed ranks around a single interpretation of the failed talks: Ehud Barak had made a generous offer and Yasser Arafat had rejected it.

By placing blame for Oslo's collapse squarely with the Palestinians, the Jewish community proved itself ready to embrace the leadership of Ariel Sharon, despite his sordid role in the massacre of refugees in Lebanon and his history as the architect of a settlement policy that had created such intractable obstacles to Palestinian statehood. Suicide bombings sealed the deal. "This shift to the right of the most elite part of the organized Jewish community quickly trickled down to local Jewish Community Councils, campus Hillels and liberal opinion," says Yifat Susskind, a former project director at the Alternative Information Center in Jerusalem and now associate director of the women's human rights group Madre. "It became untenable for Jews doing anti-occupation work to keep it 'in the family,' since the family wanted nothing to do with it." Jewish students who tried to get their footing through study groups on Palestine found themselves shut out of campus Hillel facilities; staffers at Jewish agencies faced discipline for circulating anti-occupation e-mails. Moderate groups such as Americans for Peace Now faded from view, while the new generation of radical Jewish outfits, such as Jews Against the Occupation, found themselves shut out of Jewish institutions. Other communities, meanwhile, were becoming far more receptive.

The launch of the second intifada in the fall of 2000—and the reoccupation of the West Bank in the spring of 2002—served as a global wake-up call about Palestinian suffering. Suddenly the Israel/Palestine conflict led the news almost daily. Richard Blint, a Caribbean American graduate student in American Studies at NYU, joined Students for Justice in Palestine around this time. He recalls that for him "it became a spectacle—the curfews, the roadblocks, the brutal nature of state power, the sense of frustrated diplomacy." And though much of the mainstream coverage focused on Palestinian suicide bombers and their Israeli victims, these stories were matched in volume by Indy Media postings and e-mail listserves whose missives focused almost exclusively on the attacks on Palestinians and the daily humiliations of occupation. Kates says the Palestinians' plight "went from something you heard about once a semester to your mailbox being full of news every day about what was going on in Jenin." The constancy of news from the region created the opening—Franklin and Chaudhry, who each had done work previously on East Timor, recall the organizing difficulties presented by the scant newsprint that Indonesia's violent occupation received—but the stark discrepancy between mainstream and alternative reports is what most sparked activist interest. "Perhaps the only thing more shocking than this power disparity [between Israel and the Palestinians]," Chaudhry said in a May 2002 speech promoting the Harvard/MIT divestment campaign, "is the ability to distort and misrepresent it to obscure its fundamental nature."

The events of September 11 deepened interest in the Palestinian experience, as many Americans struggled to learn about the region and discovered how reviled the Israeli occupation was throughout the Arab world. Racial justice activists, Franklin says, "began refocusing on international conflicts in a way we haven't seen in awhile, at least since the activism around Central America." This awakening to the rest of the world began earlier, but far more tentatively, after the massive antiglobalization demonstrations in Seattle in the fall of 1999. But September 11 accelerated the shift, stirring up discussion even among organizers whose work had been emphatically community-based throughout the 1980s and '90s. Dozens of racial justice groups around the country—who had traditionally focused on local urban agendas such as police brutality and the imprisonment boom—formed Racial Justice 911 to develop an international dimension to their work. As the Bush administration began its drive to war on Iraq, activist organizations across the spectrum, from left sectarian groups to environmentalists, women's organizations, and labor unions, enlisted in the fast-growing antiwar movement. The war itself forced activists to focus on the U.S. role in the region, and, just as during the first Gulf War in 1991, more and more people were suddenly talking about the Israel/Palestine conflict. More participants in the first significant antiwar march, in Washington, D.C., in April 2002, carried signs about Palestine than about Iraq. One speaker at the rally neatly expressed Palestine's new centrality in the left imagination with a call to "Globalize the intifada!"

The World Conference Against Racism in Durban in early September 2001 had already brought new energy to the Palestinian cause. American civil rights and racial justice advocates came to push slavery reparations but found their efforts stymied by the intransigence of the U.S. government delegation over proposed language on Palestine (only exacerbated by the circulation of some genuinely anti-Semitic literature). Eric Mann, a founder of the Bus Riders Union in Los Angeles, writes in his book *Dispatches from Durban* about the galvanizing impact the U.S. position had on the American NGO delegation, forcing a debate over whether delegates saw the Palestinian cause as a frontline struggle against racism. The answer, for many of them, was yes. The eventual walkout of the official U.S. delegation only further convinced activists to back the Palestinians' demands. Mann himself returned home to build support for Palestinian rights within the Bus Riders Union, whose organizers now distribute fact sheets on the occupation during their rounds on city buses. Directly on the heels of the conference came September 11 and its political sequel the Patriot Act, which made Arab Americans and Muslims the targets of roundups, registration, racial profiling, street violence and prolonged detention. "The demonization of Arabs reached extreme levels," says Wing, and the centrality of the Palestinian movement grew accordingly.

Debates began to rage throughout the antiwar movement about whether or not to take on the Israeli occupation, but, echoing the events at Durban, concerns that the issue might be divisive, and efforts by Jewish activists to achieve "balance" in the language, only gave the cause more prominence. In Boston area antiwar groupings, Chaudhry says, "some people were urging that global economic issues be taken up, but people were more or less friendly to working on the cost of war in our communities, so that debate was overcome pretty easily. But when the issue of Palestine came up, there was definitely a sense that this was a challenge—did we have the strength to deal with this." Kates says her education efforts gained little attention at Rutgers until a Jewish student group labeled them anti-Semitic; after that the occupation became a campuswide topic.

This expanded activist interest, springing from such diverse political circles, has opened the door to a complete political rethinking of the Israel/Palestine conflict. New, more expansive frameworks have arrived that leave behind the old tribal model of two peoples with competing claims and dispense with the assumption that Jews have a privileged voice on the issue. These activists have rewritten a story that was once about "Jews" and "Palestinians" as one, in Chaudhry's words, about "an oppressing entity and the people they're oppressing." They have replaced the language of "conflict" and "peace" with that of "occupation" and "justice."

Activists schooled in the movement against corporate globalization, and influenced by the growing international human rights movement, brought to the conversation the more abstract and objective standards of human rights and international law. "It's a people-versus-systems approach, rather than this identity versus that identity," says Susskind. "It takes the conflict out of the realm of the subjective and emotional connections to Israel and how great it was to visit the kibbutz when you were little or the sense that the conflict is so 'complicated,' and allows people to come to the same conclusions they would about other countries who engage in these practices." At the same time, the Bush administration's explicit plans for empire have allowed more Americans to see Israel's actions in relation to their geopolitical value to the United States, and this has in turn popularized anti-imperialist and anti-colonialist views of the Palestinian struggle. With U.S. plans to remake the region so clearly enunciated, Israel's role as the colonial administrators of U.S. regional interests has come into sharper relief—and the suspect theory that the tail is wagging the dog is losing its last shreds of credibility. "The idea that the United States backs Israel because of Jewish political power is ridiculous," says Hany Khalil, an organizer with United for Peace and Justice. "There is now a very clear coincidence of political vision between the neocons in the administration, Jewish and non-Jewish, and the right-wing government in Israel. And in that geopolitical vision, Israel functions as a watchdog against Arab nationalism."

All of the younger activists I spoke with are intensely preoccupied with U.S. complicity in the occupation, not just as failed mediators, but as active accomplices. They are aware that Israel receives more U.S. foreign aid than any other country, surpassing $3 billion a year; that the Israeli occupation, along with the Israeli economy, would collapse without that aid; that many of the weapons used to enforce and deepen the occupation are U.S.-made; that indeed the bulldozer that crushed ISM activist Rachel Corrie to death was an American-made Caterpillar. And so prison and sweatshop activists, trained in tracing financial holdings up the food chain, went to work uncovering their universities' investments in Israel and launched campaigns to divest. Local solidarity groups planned consumer boycotts of Caterpillar and sit-ins at Starbucks, which has plans to open dozens of stores in Israel. Experienced anti-occupation activists broke the mold with the U.S. Campaign to End the Occupation, which points its demands exclusively at the U.S. government, not at Israel. This focus on the United States is useful in two important ways: It gives Americans a sense that they are implicated in the occupation and therefore have the right to weigh in—relieving them of the expectation, enforced by American Jews for many years, that they had to become experts on the issue before getting involved. And it allows activists to defend themselves from spurious charges of anti-Semitism, since it is their own government, not Israel, at which they're directing their attentions. This local prism is also deeply motivating: Americans have a difficult time relating to distant suffering, but once it's their corner coffee shop, their university, their government helping to fund human rights abuses, the issue becomes visceral. "We say, 'This money is going to buy these bulldozers that you can see running over someone,'" Lloyd says.

Together, these changes offer a real challenge to most Jews, even longtime peaceniks. Those who identify even a little with Israel tend to view this broadening movement against the occupation with anxiety: They sense something suspicious about all of these non-Palestinians and non-Jews singling out Israeli nationalism as uniquely wrong. Some Jews have retreated into traditional formations, such as the creation of the Zionist anti-occupation group Brit Tzedek v'Shalom, which seeks to balance "car[ing] deeply about Israel" with "the achievement of a negotiated settlement" and promotes a constructive engagement strategy that would fund the relocation of settlers back behind the Green Line. Those American Jews who are diasporists by sensibility, who wish to lead political lives that do not focus on Israel, find that the growing centrality of Palestinian liberation on the left forces them, uncomfortably, to get engaged. The years-long efforts of many committed Jewish peace activists to lead subtle community education work that might allow Jews and Palestinians to understand each other's worldviews is threatened with becoming irrelevant and obsolete. And, perhaps most devastatingly to those who wish to redeem the Jewish community from its moral bankruptcy, these changes signal that moving the Jewish community on the issue of Palestine is a strategy that is becoming at best irrelevant and at worst a lost cause. "Our goal should not be to reach Jews. They'll come last, kicking and screaming," says Phyllis Bennis, a Jewish founder of the U.S. Campaign. "There's still a problem of perception that Jews have more of a right than non-Jews to criticize Israel. But my line is, 'Get rid of it.'"

Charlotte Kates, the young Rutgers activist, said to me at one point, "Israel is a racist state, an imperialist state—it is and it should be a pariah state." There's something a little bit shocking about these words, even for someone like me who has never had any special identification with Israel. But if that's what it takes to bring down the occupation, and finally end Israel's oppression of the Palestinians, Israel should absolutely become a pariah state. The way students during my college years in the mid-1980s danced at parties to "Sun City" and wore ANC colors; the way corporations were shamed into ending their investments in South Africa and pop musicians were shunned for performing there, the time has come when Israel must be totally isolated by world opinion and forced, simply forced, to concede.

The road to that victory will be littered with e-mail postings that are a bit strident and flyers that are insensitive to Jewish history. It will be populated by activists who are young, brash and unknowledgeable, a handful of whom will carry placards that read "Zionism = Nazism" in a crude attempt to open old Jewish wounds. Israel will become a punching bag for every good reason and maybe a couple of bad ones, too. And so what? This new wave of activism has healthy roots, ones that tap deep into despair at the worsening occupation and anger at U.S. complicity—not into ancient wells of Jew hating. "Where we are tied in various ways to injustice against others," Chaudhry said, straightforwardly, in that May 2002 speech, "decent people seek to end these ties." Zionists themselves once dreamed of "a state like any other." And that comes with accountability.

Those difficult, agonizing conversations within Jewish spaces, attenuated to the pressing weight of Jewish suffering and aspiration; those carefully planned Palestinian-Jewish dialogues; those passionate efforts to push the Jewish community to refuse to stand for the occupation any longer—this work may still serve a purpose. But it is far too slow, and faces too much resistance, to any longer truly serve the Palestinian cause. It has become a project, rather, of saving the Jewish soul.

Israel has proven its intransigence. And no effort tough enough to overpower that government's belligerence will ever emerge from the American Jewish community, given its current political direction, no matter how hard those of us on the radical fringe push and cajole. But new activists can and will throw down the gauntlet, framing the issue in ways that are not overly shaded by history, but which simply look at the current situation, name it for what it is, and demand that it end. This path does have the potential to help bring about Palestinian liberation, and so it's exactly what we need. We Jews can join in—many of us will—but we don't own this movement anymore.

If We Really Care About Israel: Breira and the Limits of Dissent

Michael E. Staub

"Are we, in the end, one people?"
Arnold Jacob Wolf, 1977

Not long ago, a friend phoned me in a fit over the PBS *NewsHour with Jim Lehrer.* Apparently David Brooks, influential conservative pundit and senior editor of *The Weekly Standard,* was on, and he'd just been asked to prognosticate which Democratic candidate for president in 2004 would likely get the most support from Jewish voters. "Why, Joe Lieberman, of course," Brooks had said. And so my friend, who, I should add, is a left-leaning, antiwar, opposed-to-the-occupation, and in-a-bitter-feud-with-her-likes-to-think-of-itself-as-liberal-shul-over-how-to-respond-to-the-ugly-militaristic-manifestations-of-contemporary-Zionism kind of Jew, had called in frustration to ask what she—or we—could do to protest such blatantly offensive spin-doctored offal. I hadn't a clue, I said. Let it go, I said. Yet here I am now, still reliving the moment, and feeling more than a little aggrieved myself.

Quite a long time ago, while I was still probably in high school, I heard the legendary stand-up comedian and political satirist Dick Gregory. I don't remember too much of his performance, though I imagine (since this would have been the early seventies) that the Watergate scandal, the illegal bombings of Cambodia, fasting (Gregory always seemed to be fasting), and the prospect that Nixon might get booted from the White House would all have been likely topics. However, what I do remember clearly is Gregory pausing several times during his monologue, taking a sip from a glass of water, looking out silently at the audience, and then quietly saying: "You young people here tonight. You've got a big job."

Which is to say only this: We American Jews who oppose the Israeli occupation of Palestine and oppose the growing preeminence of hawkish Jews like Joe Lieberman, who cringe at the news (in the *Jerusalem Post*) that "it's an open secret that presidential advisor Karl Rove sees the Jewish vote as critical to [George W. Bush's] reelection chances in 2004" and who mourn over reports (in the *Forward*) that "American Jews may be poised on the edge of a historic shift to the right," we've got a big job. For however much we might like to pride ourselves on our historic commitment to solid liberal principles, or a tradition of respecting dissent within our community, the actual track record of American Jews on both counts is rather spotty, I'm afraid. This is a distressing and painful thing to acknowledge.

Which brings me in a roundabout way to the historical subject of this essay: Once upon a time—a mere three decades ago—a left-center alliance of prominent American Jews formed a national organization that sought to challenge what they perceived already at that time to be the rightward drift of American Zionism. This organization provided public forums where contentious topics like Palestinian nationalism, the occupation, the settler movement, and the rise of religiously legitimated right-wing Zionism could be engaged in open debate. Its founders hoped to bring together liberal communal leaders of an older generation (many of whom had been active in sixties civil rights and antiwar protests) with members of the Jewish counterculture and Jewish radical movements around matters of shared urgency. And they wished to lessen sectarian divisions within the community by building a coalition with both secular and religious, as well as both Zionist and non-Zionist elements. And not least of all, they aimed to acknowledge and endorse feminism's powerful impact on nearly every dimension of American Jewish communal existence.

The coalition was named Breira, and it survived for four tumultuous years (1973–77). Its proposals on Israeli-Diaspora Jewish relations and Palestinian nationalism generated fierce international debate over the limits of public dissent and conflict in Jewish communal life. Virtually every major American Jewish organization and American Jewish newspaper took a public stand on the group, and positioned itself as either for or against the open discussions Breira advocated.

Yet comprehensive studies of recent American Jewish history do not mention Breira. To a remarkable degree Breira is simply forgotten; when I spoke about Breira in 2000 to an audience of American Jewish historians, I found no one under the age of 45 who had even heard of the group. Such loss of memory continues to have consequences for what is imaginable for young Jews in the present.

The story begins in late 1973 when, in the stunned aftermath of the costly Yom Kippur War, an alliance of diverse members of the American Jewish community joined together to establish Breira: A Project of Concern in Diaspora-Israel Relations. As for the name, member Bill Novak explained:

> Breira is Hebrew for "alternative," but in Hebrew the word has much richer connotations than in English. For years Israelis have used the phrase *ein breira*—there is no alternative—to explain their situation, their attitude, and, increasingly, the policies of their government. Over time, the phrase has acquired more and more of a kind of official usage, to the point where, like the American notion of "national security," *ein breira* is sometimes used indiscriminately and reflexively as a defense of the status quo. Calling a Jewish organization "Breira" was a challenge to that usage. (It was also a comment about the importance of Israel and the Hebrew language, a point which seems to have been discounted by most observers.)

Breira called for an end to the occupation of lands seized by Israel in 1967, and it proposed a two-state solution as "now more than ever the chief possibility for a peaceful, long-term resolution of the Middle East conflict." It emphasized not only the mutual responsibility of Israeli and Diaspora Jews to one another, but pinpointed specifically the domestic American Jewish atmosphere discouraging debate. As the group's founding statement emphasized, "this is the reason we join together now—we deplore those pressures in American Jewish life which make open discussion of these and other vital issues virtually synonymous with heresy."

In a relatively short time, Breira appeared well on its way to becoming precisely what its founders intended: a sort of dovish alternative both to the mainstream American Israel Public Affairs Committee and to the more militant right-wing religious Zionism of the Jewish Defense League or Gush Emunim (Bloc of the Faithful). Among its members and supporters were such respected American Jewish writers and intellectuals as Steven M. Cohen, Paul Cowan, Arthur Green, Irving Howe, Paula Hyman, Jack Nusan Porter, Henry Schwarzschild, and Milton Viorst. And given a surge in grassroots communal disillusionment with the deadlocked nature of Israeli-Palestinian relations after the Yom Kippur War, Breira also gained enthusiastic endorsements from at least six overlapping quarters. First, it found support from socialist Zionist groups, especially Hashomer Hatzair and its allied organization, Americans for a Progressive Israel—both of which had been active for decades. Second, Breira quickly attracted approximately one hundred Reform and Conservative rabbis; notable among these were Eugene Borowitz, Balfour Brickner, Everett Gendler, Robert Gordis, Richard Levy, and Joachim Prinz. Third, Breira drew considerable support from numerous Hillel Foundations across the United States. While they would later be mocked as "incubators of Breira," Hillels across the country proved remarkably receptive to this new peace initiative; at least eight Hillel directors (including those at UCLA, Dartmouth, Carnegie-Mellon, Adelphi, Temple, and Yale) served on Breira's advisory committee.

Fourth, Breira also concretized aims emerging out of the larger and more amorphous phenomenon known as the radical Jewish youth movement. Already early in 1973, at Rutgers University's Hillel, a conference of Jewish student activists initially raised the idea for a group which would provide an alternative to establishment Jewish communal views on Zionism, as well as Israeli military policies and attitudes towards Palestinians. Many (though not all) of these activists were themselves radical Zionists, such as those involved with the Jewish Liberation Project in New York. The fifth strand of support for Breira, and possibly the most influential, came from the Jewish counterculture and the *havurah* movement; prominent *havurot* like the New York Havurah and Fabrangen in Washington, D.C., proved particularly helpful. (The New York Havurah, for instance, contributed its small office space where Breira began publishing a newsletter, *interChange*, in September 1975.) Finally, and crucially in terms of how the intra-communal controversy over Breira's actual intentions would later explode, the group's staff and advisory committee also included individuals with prior affiliations with American Jewish peace organizations on the New Left. Notable among these were Don Peretz, Barry Rubin, John Ruskay, and Rabbi Arthur Waskow.

Yet what remains most striking about Breira, as one observer already wrote in 1978, is that despite the prominent participation of radical Jews within it, the organization's official platform "hardly constitutes a call to the barricades." Breira did *not* position itself as "out there" on the left wing. To the contrary, Breira also sought deliberately to gain moderate—and even neoconservative—support; as Breira executive director Bob Loeb said at the time: "We are a coalition which is not predicated at all on a left-right debate." And the group did successfully draw prominent Jewish academics and communal spokespersons like Nathan Glazer, Charles S. Liebman, Jacob Neusner, and Michael Wyschogrod into its circle of sympathizers. This is hardly surprising given that, as Bill Novak would point out, "the members of Breira had all the right credentials: they had been involved all their lives with Jewish schools, Jewish youth groups, seminaries, summer camps, programs in Israel, Jewish publications, and the like." Moreover, Breira consistently asserted its loyalty to Zionism. As a Breira statement from 1975 announced:

> Our immediate and overriding concern is peace in the Middle East. Our concern grows out of our love and respect for the people and the land of Israel as well as our understanding that the continuity of Jewish life in the Diaspora is inextricably linked to the existence of Israel.
>
> We are not innocent bystanders. If we share the anxieties about Israel's policies, we have the responsibility to say so. If we detect mistakes which might have catastrophic consequences, we must not ignore or swallow our concern. . . . For the sake of Zion, we shall not be silent.

Thus, Breira represented a dissenting Jewish voice, but it was a voice that saw itself coming, as one Breira publication put it, "from within the mainstream of the American Jewish community and from a more moderate perspective" than the "extreme" views one heard from groups like Rabbi Meir Kahane's Jewish Defense League. This distinction needs to be kept in mind in view of how rapidly the terms of debate surrounding the group would shift. Its members understood—and expected—that going public with American Jewish criticism of Israeli policies towards the Palestinians would generate debate and controversy. But it is safe to say that Breira members could in no way have anticipated the intense barrage of assaults the group would ultimately provoke.

Jewish communal and professional response to Breira went through three phases. The first phase was the longest; it lasted almost three years from late 1973 until mid-1976. During this time, there was a widespread sense that although Breira was raising unpleasant issues, these issues were important, and that indeed a sizable segment of the American Jewish community agreed with Breira's positions. The nationally distributed *Jewish Post and Opinion,* for instance, thoroughly covered Breira's policy statements. Its editorials on the group acknowledged that the group's views were causing conflict, but held that intra-communal debate only benefited the American Jewish community. "Actually, we seem to need to learn all over again that differences of opinion, even those strongly held, are healthy," stated a *Jewish Post and Opinion* editorial from 1974. Yet the *Jewish Post and Opinion* had long maintained a liberal editorial policy, and would be expected to embrace a new peace initiative like Breira.

On the other hand, a more indicative communal bellwether might be the Washington, D.C., area newspaper *Jewish Week.* Again, it too remained remarkably even-handed in its coverage of Breira. This was notable not least because a *Jewish Week* editorial from 1971 had seen fit to upbraid American Jews who publicly dissented from Israeli official policies, going so far as to argue that there was "no place for them in the American Jewish community" because their actions "can and do help to undermine Israel's cause before the American people." It was notable as well because *Jewish Week* editor Philip Hochstein had a notorious track record of red-baiting radical Jews; additionally, *Jewish Week* carried a regular column by right-wing commentator I. L. Kenen, executive director of AIPAC, on how the news media covered Middle East issues. In short, Hochstein would have been well-informed on Breira and what it stood for, and could easily have undermined it from the very outset.

Significantly, despite this history of Jewish anti-leftism, *Jewish Week*'s handling of Breira was often conciliatory. One editorial even conceded that Breira might have a point when it charged that "perhaps Israel erred during the long years since the war of 1967 in not having done more to promote" dialogue with the Palestinians (though it added quickly that "it is misleading to suggest that the option is now open"). More significant, though, in terms of getting the word out to the Washington Jewish community, is that (until early 1976) *Jewish Week* repeatedly reported statements by local Breira spokesperson, Rabbi David Saperstein, associate director of the Religious Action Center of the Union of American Hebrew Congregations. More than once, Saperstein was also provided a column where he could rebut the views of American Jewish hawks on the Middle East conflict. Against Herbert A. Fierst, chairman of the Washington chapter of the American Jewish Committee, whose concern for Israel (he said) obligated him to support increased U.S. defense spending, Saperstein wrote: "If we really care about Israel, let us not give into any kind of blackmail on the question of the Jewish community's support for the military budget." And against *Near East Report* editor Wolf I. Blitzer (who argued that "As American Jews, I am sure that we can find better things to do than tell Israelis what is—or what isn't—in their best national security interests"), Saperstein queried: "Are we going to stand up and say to the American people, you can be for national rights of the Palestinians and be strong supporters of Israel, or, by our silence, are we going to force Americans to choose between support of Israel and support of the Palestinians just because Israeli policy at this moment make the two seem incompatible?" Given a self-consciousness over how such open debates within Washington's Jewish communal leadership might likely also influence members of Congress, *Jewish Week*'s balanced handling of Breira and what it advocated becomes all the more striking.

Throughout this initial phase, Breira continued to publicize its positions, refine its arguments, and expand its national membership. It sponsored lectures by leading American Jewish commentators, like *Jewish Spectator* editor Trude Weiss-Rosmarin, as well as Israeli doves, like Matityahu Peled, a retired Israeli Defense Forces major general. It published a collection of essays by Israeli doves and regularly invited Israeli intellectuals in the peace movement to write for its monthly newsletter, *interChange;* these contributions called for direct negotiations with the Palestine Liberation Organization, advocated the formation of a self-determining Palestinian state, and criticized the settlement movement and Gush Emunim. Repeatedly, Breira sought (with no small degree of initial success) to lay claim to the center of American Jewish political discourse on the Middle East, and thereby reverse a rightward swing of the ideological pendulum under way at least since 1967.

During Passover week in 1976 Gush Emunim organized a march of more than thirty thousand supporters of the settlements through the West Bank. The march resulted in clashes in which one Arab was killed and several were injured by Israeli security forces. This fatal confrontation, taken together with the death of six Arab Israelis in the Galilee area, prompted the Breira Executive Board to draft an "Open Letter to Israel's Leaders." Dated April 7, 1976, it read in part:

> We are grieved by the tragic events of the past weeks in the occupied West Bank and within Israel proper. . . . Police action, even when justified, will not end growing Arab civil resistance to the Israeli government's plan for the expropriation of Arab and Jewish land in the Galilee, nor will it end growing frustration in the captured territories over Israel's nine-year occupation. Rigorous suppression of Arab dissent serves only to strengthen Arab nationalism and to weaken faith in Israeli and Jewish commitment to the human and national rights on which Israeli society was founded and is maintained.

With the distribution of this April 7 letter to leading Israeli government officials, the second phase in the Breira controversy commenced. On May 3, the *Washington Post* ran a headline that read: "U.S. Jews Beginning to Go Public in Criticism of Israel." Breira was named as a group calling on Israel to "turn its occupied territories on the West Bank into a separate Arab state and pull back to its 1967 boundaries." This, the *Post* added, "is a proposal argued widely in Israel, but rarely heard in this country, where criticism of what Israel does has come to be equated with an attack on Israel's existence." The article quoted Breira members Joachim Prinz and Balfour Brickner, as well as outspoken Orthodox rabbi Henry Siegman, executive director of the Synagogue Council of America, who was not a Breira member, but who also publicly advocated a withdrawal by Israel to its pre-1967 boundaries, "with the exception of Jerusalem and minor border rectifications." More sympathetic publicity of Breira followed. The following week, a *New York Times* editorial noted that Breira was "picking up wide support among influential Jewish intellectuals in its criticism of Gush Emunim, overcoming as well the misapprehension of many Jewish Americans that criticism of Israeli policies would be seen as a rejection of Israel." However, and although Rabbi Alexander M. Schindler, chairman of the Conference of Presidents of Major American Jewish Organizations, said at the time that there was "a new openness to divergent viewpoints and I am determined to keep that openness alive," and Rabbi Siegman agreed that American Jews were currently experiencing "a new openness and willingness to criticize certain specific issues" within Israel, there were powerful indicators that this optimism would prove premature, and that a tightening of the reins on dissent was already under way.

Several leading Jewish communal figures stepped forward to condemn the April 7 letter. These critics used diverse strategies to deflate Breira's impact. Rabbi Stanley Rabinowitz, president of the Rabbinical Assembly (Conservative), said of Breira members: "It is arrogant of them to sit in their ivory towers and pass judgement, with nothing to lose by making the wrong choice." Rabbi Israel Klavan, executive vice president of the Rabbinical Council (Orthodox), stated: "What they are doing is weakening Israel's bargaining position." And (although in 1972 he had warned that "American Jewry will not become a 'colony' of Israel. We insist on the right to criticize Israel when criticism is needed, even if that criticism is likely to be exploited by Israel's enemies"), Rabbi Arthur Hertzberg now observed that public criticism of Israeli policy inadvertently fed into anti-Israeli propaganda, citing as an example how a critical statement he had once made about Israel had been manipulated by an Arab UN delegate.

Almost all at once, Breira experienced its first real hostile backlash. Within weeks, several more Jewish communal leaders now publicly excoriated Breira. Hyman Bookbinder, Washington representative of the American Jewish Committee, noted how there was "a shrillness, a self-righteousness, [and] a certitude" about the group that disturbed him. And Bookbinder harshly added: "I don't believe Israel needs to be lectured about morality." A *Hadassah* newsletter slammed Breira members as "Cheerleaders for Defeatism," lumped Breira together with anti-Zionist groups, and warned that "every Hadassah member should be alerted to anticipate and reject the advances of these organizations with their dogmas that run counter to Israeli security and Jewish survival." Meanwhile, forty-seven rabbis published a signed statement that accused Breira of promoting a position "practically identical with the Arab point of view." And also that May, Harold M. Jacobs, president of the Union of Orthodox Jewish Congregations of America, and Fred Ehrman, chairman of the UOJCA Israel

Commission, issued a joint statement that demeaned Breira representatives Prinz and Brickner for their "diaspora mentalities" and for their "cheap shots at the Israeli government," which performed "a great disservice by highlighting to the American people the division that may exist within the Jewish community in regard to the administered territories." The UOJCA statement characterized Breira as "dangerous and divisive," charged that the group's public dissent was "undermining the morale of the American and Israeli Jewish communities," and recorded UOJCA's official support of Gush Emunim and the settlement movement.

In June 1976, when more than one hundred representatives of the Conference of Presidents of Major American Jewish Organizations met in New York, "the debate over debate" dominated the discussion, just as it also would that same month at annual meetings of the Synagogue Council of America and the American Zionist Federation. At the Presidents Conference, Eugene Borowitz spoke in favor of Breira, advocating an official policy endorsing the possibility of American Jewish dissent on Israeli policy, while Fabian Schonfeld defended Gush Emunim and challenged the right to dissent. By the end of the conference, Alexander Schindler sought middle ground when he suggested that criticism of Israel might be restricted to the Jewish press. However, this conciliatory move did little to reduce heightening animosity between supporters and detractors of the right to American Jewish dissent on Israel.

As controversy over its actions continued to heat up, Breira's newsletter *interChange* stayed on the offensive against its detractors. In May 1976, it had circulated a public letter, "The Time Has Come to Say NO to Gush Emunim," signed by over one hundred prominent Breira supporters. These supporters included Aviva Cantor, Phyllis Chesler, Leonard Fein, Betty Friedan, Vivian Gornick, Grace Paley, Muriel Rukeyser, Morris Schappes, Charles Silberman, Ted Solotaroff, I. F. Stone, and Alvin Toffler. The letter read in full:

> We American Jews who are ardent supporters of Israel's existence encourage all peace forces in Israel in their demonstration on the eighth of May against the proposed Jewish settlement in Kadum on the West Bank.
>
> Like our brothers and sisters in Israel, we feel that further Jewish settlement in the occupied territories is an obstacle to peace efforts.
>
> We will join with all people committed to a secure Israel in building a just and equitable peace.

In the same issue, and reversing precisely the rhetoric of Breira's opponents, Balfour Brickner bluntly asserted: "It is neither distortion nor exaggeration to accuse the Gush Emunim and their supporters of undermining the security and threatening the survival of the State of Israel." In June, *interChange* opened with an Irving Howe essay entitled "For Free Discussion in the Jewish Community"; it also reprinted the *Post* article and the *New York Times* editorial, and offered a concise summary of the anti-Breira UOJCA statement. In short, Breira appeared in little mood to be conciliatory toward its opponents.

In the later months of 1976, during a period that might have seemed like a lull, the storm over Breira was actually about to break. Right-wing American Jewish elements supportive of Gush Emunim and the settlement movement were moving ahead with an analysis that Breira provided aid and comfort to anti-Israeli forces, and was thus not to be trusted. On this front, the right-wing journal *American Zionist* took the lead, leveling accusations that—by going public with a private Jewish communal debate—it was Breira that directly threatened Israeli survival. Breira was an organization comprised not of doves, a first *American Zionist* essay sarcastically intoned, but really of pigeons, and it was well-known that flocks of pigeons "constitute a public health menace in many large cities, not to mention a public nuisance." A second *American Zionist* article asserted that Breira abused its right to free speech when it brought intra-Jewish disunity to the attention of the wider gentile world. "The Jews who cry 'Foul!' in public must realize the treacherous consequences of their efforts," the magazine concluded. "Ramifications are felt not by them, but by fellow Jews thousands of miles away."

Such crass and seemingly over-the-top attempts to cast Breira's members as illegitimate—indeed, inauthentic, traitorous, and anti-Jewish—Jews could not dampen the enthusiasm of the coalition, flush with what correctly must have seemed like the moment it stood on the threshold of both popular acceptance and widespread credibility. Yet the reversal of Breira's fortunes arrived swiftly. Few could have foreseen how close at hand the end turned out to be.

On November 1, 1976, in New York, and then again on November 15 in Washington, D.C., several American Jews met with Sabri Jiryis, an Arab Israeli author with close ties to the PLO, and Isam Sartawi, a leading Palestinian intellectual and (according to the State Department) a member of the Fatah Revolutionary Council. Among the Jews present at the meetings were: Herman Edelsberg, recently retired director of the B'nai B'rith International Council; David Gorin, the newly appointed Washington area regional director of the American Jewish Congress; Olya Margolin, Washington representative of the National Council of Jewish Women; Rabbi Max Ticktin, assistant national director of the B'nai B'rith Hillel Foundations; and Rabbi Arthur Waskow, resident fellow of the Institute for Policy Studies in Washington, D.C. Ticktin and Waskow were also members of Breira's executive committee, as well as members of Fabrangen. The meetings were arranged by the American Friends Service Committee, a Quaker organization. By mutual consent, the meetings were to be kept secret; additionally, the American Jews made it understood that they were present solely as private citizens, not as representatives of any agency or association.

On November 23, Wolf Blitzer reported in the *Jerusalem Post* that the meetings had taken place, and within days the meetings made headlines also in the American Jewish press. There followed a rapid flurry of condemnations. The Conference of Presidents of Major American Jewish Organizations stated that it "vigorously opposes and deplores any meetings—official or unofficial—with the PLO." (Interestingly, borrowing and reconfiguring the language of Breira, its reasoning was that such contacts "could tend to undermine the peace process.") B'nai B'rith, the American Jewish Congress, and the National Council of Jewish Women all issued policy statements that denounced the meetings; Gorin received a public reprimand from the AJCongress. Additionally, Stanley Rabinowitz charged that Breira now appeared to be "fronting for the PLO."

At the same time, *Jewish Week* rethought any prior reluctance to rip into Breira; an editorial in January 1977 now queried: "Why, of all the many millions of Arabs with whom one might seek dialogue, has the Breira inner dictatorship elected to approach the PLO?" Another editorial stated that "it is most obnoxious to find American Jews conferring with terrorist agents who state as their purpose the manipulation of American Jewish influence to shape Israel's policies." And yet a third *Jewish Week* editorial upstaged the first two by adding a reference to Nazism into the equation: "There is no doubt that American Jews have 'the right' to question Israel's policies, but it is a certainty that they have a prior duty to unmask the brutal intransigence of Israel's Arab enemies, and to fight the appeasement mentality of a world that seems to have forgotten the massive price civilization paid for appeasement at Munich."

Thus it was in this already overheated rhetorical tinderbox that the third and final phase of the Breira controversy was announced by a front-page headline in *Jewish Week* on January 27, 1977: "Scholar accuses Breira of pro-PLO 'obsession.'" The scholar in question was Rael Jean Isaac, described as "a scholar of Jewish affairs, whose earlier work was 'Israel Divided,' a study of the opposed forces in the Jewish state's political and social struggles." The text in question was a thirty-page pamphlet, *Breira: Counsel for Judaism*, which argued that Breira had no authority to speak on behalf of the American Jewish community. The neutral characterization of its author served only to make her analysis of Breira appear that much more credible.

A closer look at Isaac's background, however, revealed a less than neutral observer. In her book, *Israel Divided: Ideological Politics in the Jewish State*, Isaac had detailed how the settlement movement in Israel drew upon what was "normative" in Jewish religious tradition. According to Isaac, "the peace movement, on the other hand, derives from a deviant but traditional strain that saw the basic task of Zionism as reaching agreement with the Arabs." Isaac's thesis hinged on this distinction. It was to misread both Jewish history and religion, Isaac stated, if one failed to grasp that "while over a thousand years of Hebrew sovereignty in the Land of Israel boundaries expanded and contracted, the core area where Hebrew sovereignty was first asserted, maintained for the longest period, and reestablished after exile, was what is now Jerusalem and the Israeli-occupied West Bank." Moreover, one should not "look upon Zionism as yet another movement of national liberation—which can then be paralleled to the Arab nationalist movement which developed only slightly later," because such comparisons "ignore the foundation of modern Jewish nationalism in religious tradition." In short, Isaac's book offered scholarly legitimation to what was still a seldom

discussed aspect of contemporary Jewish political life: the ascendance of a religious right both in Israel and the Diaspora. In retrospect, this would all fit
neatly together with the news (belatedly disclosed) that Isaac belonged to Gush
Emunim and served on its advisory board in the United States.

At the time, however, the Isaac pamphlet carried no visible ideological baggage, and was interpreted rather as a balanced account of Breira and the key
individuals who helped bring it into being. In a chatty and affable style, and
with the stated goal of understanding better one "puzzling feature of Breira,"
namely the group's "overriding obsession . . . [that] the solution to the Arab-
Israeli conflict is a PLO-dominated state on the West Bank and in Gaza," Isaac
flashed back to the sixties:

> Breira is one of the many organizations which grew out of the social activ-
> ist thrust in the United States that can be traced to the Civil Rights move-
> ment of the early 1960's. For some Jews the decisive experience was being
> pushed out of that movement. Jews were disproportionately prominent
> among whites within it, and when they found themselves accused by re-
> sentful blacks of usurping power in a movement that rightfully belonged
> to blacks, some of them began to reexamine and reassert the Jewish iden-
> tity they had discarded in deference to universalist concerns for human
> justice and dignity. For others the decisive experience was not the civil
> rights movement but the anti-war movement and the student movement
> which it precipitated, and which led many to a whole new radical politics,
> that of the so-called New Left. In this political vision America, especially
> the government and the big corporations, became the fountainhead of
> all oppression, of her own people and of the third world with which those
> in these movements identified. And the task became creating a revolu-
> tion that would transform Amerika, which the activists customarily spelled
> with a "k" to indicate its surrealistic evil character, into America. Racist,
> oppressive, corrupt, imperialist, capitalist Amerika, through the revolu-
> tion, would be transformed into egalitarian, socialist, free America.

This paragraph represented "a detour," Isaac acknowledged, but it was "a detour that leads to the heart of our subject: we will be introducing leaders of
Breira, their ideologies, and the methods by which they work to achieve their
goals." Armed with a license to stray, Isaac then seized it—and launched ahead
for twenty more pages to name-drop virtually every organization that Rabbi Arthur
Waskow had ever joined or been remotely affiliated with. What did the mani-
fold left-liberal impulses of the sixties have to do with this one individual? According to Isaac, Waskow "was in fact an organizing genius for the whole network
of associations whose personnel was eventually to become important in Breira."

Indeed, Isaac's real target was Waskow, because Waskow had made the mistake during the sixties of making radical New Left claims about Judaism itself.
For instance, Waskow believed, as did all radical Jews (according to Isaac), that

the state of Israel "far from advancing the distinctively Jewish mission, impeded it." Having arrived at this view, Isaac concluded that for the Jewish radical "the way was clear to supporting the political tastes of the far left for Arab over Israeli on Jewish religious grounds." And it had been precisely such anti-Zionist sentiments among radical Jews that had led directly to a decision to establish Breira in the winter of 1973. Isaac even connected the B'nai B'rith Hillel Foundations to this unholy Jewish anti-Israeli radical alliance because Max Ticktin belonged to Fabrangen and because Breira member Albert S. Axelrad, Hillel director at Brandeis, had also participated in the Jewish Campaign for the People's Peace Treaty (which Waskow had also joined). At times, it appeared as if merely being in the same room with Waskow—or with anyone, really, who uttered something inflammatory about Israel or Zionism—was enough to win a permanent place in Isaac's anti-Zionist hall of shame. And this, of course, included just about every liberal or former radical Jew now associated with Breira.

Finally, Isaac dismissed in advance the countercharge that her opposition to Breira might be part of a "witch hunt" or due to "McCarthyism." As Isaac pithily noted: "The assumption in such a reaction is that there are no witches and the accusers are pursuing figments of their imagination." According to Isaac, however, Breira's record spoke for itself; what the group was actually accomplishing was a legitimization of American Jews' "growing sense of distance from Israel, the feeling in their bones that may never be allowed to consciousness that in the future Israel will be for them not a source of pride and a haven against possible storms but a burden, economically, politically, emotionally." If this was what Breira aimed to accomplish, Isaac concluded, then so be it. But members of such a group "should not be able to pass themselves off as 'prophetic' critics and dedicated guides" for Israeli policies: "If Jews want to organize on behalf of the Fatah, that is their privilege. But let them call it 'Jews for Fatah' and not 'Breira.'"

Such rhetorical tactics resisted counterattack because everyone Isaac tarred with the brush of anti-Zionism *had* said what she said they said, or been present at the meeting she said they attended. But there was very little doubt also that her guilt-by-association-with-Waskow strategy functioned above all as an attempt to destabilize the left-center, secular-religious, Zionist-non-Zionist coalition that Breira had sought to build. And the strategy worked.

Breira started to fall apart from within. Joachim Prinz and Jacob Neusner immediately made separate announcements that they had resigned from the group. Prinz had never agreed with the Breira position that Israel should return to pre-1967 borders, but shied away from direct criticism of the group; Neusner was more eager to publicize his current dislike for his former associates. At around the same time, Alan Mintz, a member of the Havurat Shalom in Somerville, Massachusetts, and the organizer of the Rutgers University Hillel conference that had led to the founding of Breira, published a widely discussed critique of Breira. Most damaging may have been Mintz's charge that "Breira often seems simply out of touch with the emotional rhythms of the Jewish People."

According to Mintz, Breira had become an organization insufficiently sensitized to "*ahavat yisrael,* unconditional love for the Jewish people." Given the other difficulties experienced by Breira at that moment, such charges were even more wounding than they might have been otherwise.

Matters got worse still when the Jewish Community Council of Washington, D.C., passed a resolution stating that it "deplores Breira's methodology and platform" because its members "seek to divide and politicize American Jewish support of Israel." However bitterly ironic such a resolution might have felt to die-hard Breiraniks (as they were sometimes called), the group was quickly losing its credibility as a voice of moderation within the Jewish community. Increasingly, Breira was simply getting painted as a PLO front working for Israel's ultimate destruction.

On February 20, 1977, in Chevy Chase, Maryland, Breira convened its first national membership conference, attended by three hundred people. Outside the hall, Jewish Defense League members distributed the Isaac pamphlet, shouted slogans like "Hell no, we won't go from Hebron or Jericho," "There is no Palestine," and "We remember Munich," and waved placards that read, "Not One Inch of Retreat," "Death to Breira," "No Deals with Baby-Killers," "Breira is the Choice of Death," and "Breira Means Suicide." Inside the convention hall, however, there was little sign that Breira was prepared to back down. It reconfirmed its call for "the immediate cessation of Jewish settlement of the occupied territories" and proposed that "while Jerusalem will continue to serve as the capital of Israel, the Arab part of the city could become, after the establishment of peace, the capital of a Palestinian Arab state." It explained as well that it adopted these views because "we love Israel. We cherish the cultural treasures and the many moral examples it has given us. And we similarly affirm the richness of the Jewish experience in North America and are eager to explore and extend its possibilities." Moreover, and significantly, Breira declared its commitment to advancing domestic change. Its platform argued not only that "our Jewish prophetic values demand that we fight oppression and work to bring about economic and social justice in the American society in which we live." The platform also insisted that there was a need to eliminate "stereotyped sex roles in Jewish communal life" and to support "non-sexist education; and the Jewish feminist movement," and contended that although "we endorse the forms of traditional Jewish family life . . . they are not the only legitimate social units for Jews in American society. We must pursue means of integrating Jews living in extended families, single people, and gays into the normative Jewish community." However, the context for grasping the import of these policy statements was now being set not by Breira, but rather by its ideological opponents. And in *that* context, what Breira stood for was increasingly beginning to look more like unflattering caricature, and less like real life.

For instance, *Reconstructionist* editor Ira Eisenstein, who made a point of noting that he'd quit Breira a year before, wrote in February 1977 that "there is a serious question whether safe and fairly prosperous American Jews, from their comfortable armchairs in the USA, have the moral right to urge policies upon Israelis which could well involve their very lives and the life of the State." While defenders of Breira, like historian Melvin I. Urofsky, stated that the attacks on Breira were "creating a McCarthyite atmosphere" and were serving only to "polarize the community between the young and the old, between liberals and conservatives," the innuendo that Breira represented an elite clique of radical chic intellectuals proved difficult to counter. Here was an anti-left technique as old as the Cold War itself; it had served successfully to mobilize popular class resentments against American leftists and their sympathizers already since the late 1940s. Those who denounced Breira therefore portrayed themselves also as crucially more in touch with an imagined Jewish public. Often their armchairs were just as comfortable as those of the Breira members they criticized. And yet it was the elitist image of Breira that stuck.

In short, Breira was losing the public relations battle over its own image. In April 1977, *Commentary* picked up the anti-Breira cause, citing at length what it characterized as "a well-documented pamphlet," and recycling once again (and repeatedly) the claim that Rabbi Arthur Waskow was a PLO supporter. Author Joseph Shattan saw Breira's perspectives in the years since the Yom Kippur War as particularly unfortunate since during this period "the political fortunes of the state of Israel have reached perhaps an all-time low," adding that since 1973 "Israel has become increasingly isolated in the world as a whole, shunned even by many of its former friends and treated as a pariah by the community of nations." Hewing closely to the analysis served up by Rael Jean Isaac, Shattan delivered yet another installment in *Commentary*'s ongoing project of assessing Jewish left-liberalism in psychopathologizing terms, explaining how so many otherwise seemingly well-intentioned Jewish leaders could allow themselves to get lured into Breira in the first place:

Liberal guilt, a desire to be on the side of "liberation" and "progress," a weariness at having to uphold Israel's cause when that cause has gone out of odor or has come to seem hopeless, even an unconscious and paradoxical wish to be, for once, on the side their government may be leaning toward . . . [But] what strikes the observer above all in such mental maneuvers is the unspoken desire, born, perhaps, of the feeling that Israel has become an intolerable burden, to distance oneself as a Jew from Israel's fate. Because this desire cannot be confronted honestly, reality is denied or redefined, one's intentions become cloaked in the language of moral rectitude, and a conviction takes hold that the "solution" to Israel's dilemma is both simple and at hand.

Despite continued and concerted efforts by the dwindling number of Breira members to counter these charges, largely by accusing their accusers of orchestrating a campaign to destroy them, these countercharges tended to get written off, and proved largely ineffective. By late 1977, Breira was dead.

Had it been the assaults from outside the group that led ultimately to the dissolution of Breira? And had it been the move of Breira's critique into the mainstream American press that prompted those assaults? With close to three decades of hindsight, several former Breira members each responded recently to these questions with a flat "no." These former members now recall the group's demise as mainly the result of internal wrangling—over the authority of the executive director, for instance. Not that vicious attacks from outside the group made matters any easier. While citing "implosion" as the key reason for Breira's untimely end, a leading member added that "maybe the bashing helped drive us to slit each other's throats, but maybe not." And another leading member saw the "friendly fire" of fellow liberals who opted vocally to abandon the movement as the main cause for the group's collapse.

Yet it would be hard not to conclude that the hawks had triumphed over the doves. Breira had been destroyed, and in subsequent years its collective memory would largely be lost. And in retrospect, given that the 1970s were a decade marked primarily by widespread Jewish communal retreat from issues of social justice, the Breira controversy and its outcome might appear almost inevitable. Yet it is important also to recall that there emerged numerous American Jewish forums to replace Breira, notably the progressive broad-based coalition, New Jewish Agenda (formed in 1980), *Tikkun* magazine (founded in 1986 as the liberal-left Jewish alternative to *Commentary*), as well as a variety of Jewish peace groups, like Americans for Peace Now, Jewish Peace Lobby, and Jewish Peace Network, established throughout the United States during the next quarter century.

Yet despite definite indications that revitalized left-liberal activity within the American Jewish community followed the death of Breira, it would also be an error to underestimate how that death did represent "a watershed in contemporary American Jewish life," as historian Jacques Kornberg predicted in 1978. The shutting down of dissent around Breira so disturbed Irving Howe that it led him to remark: "Now I remember why I had nothing to do with the Jewish community all these years." Although labeled a pro-PLO front, what Breira truly represented, according to Breira national chairperson Rabbi Arnold Jacob Wolf speaking at the annual convention of the Rabbinical Assembly in May 1977, was a national Jewish group that had "recovered more young Jews, more 'New Left' Jews, more angry Jews, more intellectual Jews than any organization in the recent history of the United States." And although several groups subsequently emerged to promote the causes of Breira, it is not at all certain that they could really claim the same. Instead, American Jews turned primarily inward, not only away from social justice, but also away from one another. This did not signal necessarily any loss in Jewish faith or Jewish conviction; on the contrary, the decades that ensued saw continued religious renewal within the community.

But those decades also witnessed a profound splintering; this occurred to such a extent that the community—if it ever had been a community—could scarcely again even pretend to speak in one voice, believe in one faith, or act as one people. Thus, the 1970s may well have been the decade when American Jews moved subtly but conclusively from being One People (*K'lal Yisrael* in Hebrew) to becoming many peoples.

In *Number Our Days* (1978), her brilliant observer-participation study of elderly Jews living our their lives at the Aliyah Senior Citizen's Center in Venice, California, anthropologist Barbara Myerhoff described at length how much anger and negative emotion these old people expressed toward one another. Bitter quarrels and outright conflicts were a fact of life that these old people deeply lamented, yet nonetheless engaged in with ritualized regularity. In her analysis of their angers, Myerhoff offered also possible insight into the role in-fighting may have played in postwar debates over activism and identity in American Jewish life:

> Anger is a powerful indication of engagement between people, the very opposite of indifference. It may be regarded as the most dramatic proof of responsiveness and caring. . . . It is a basic form of remaining attached. And among people who are not inevitably bound together, anger may become a refutation of the possibility of separating: Anger is a form of social cohesion, and a strong and reliable one. To fight with each other, people must share norms, rules, vocabulary, and knowledge. Fighting is a partnership, requiring cooperation. A boundary-maintaining mechanism—for strangers cannot participate fully—it is also above all a profoundly sociable activity.

By the end of the 1970s, American Jews still fought, and continued to fight, with one another. And we would fight, and continue to fight, with one another into the twenty-first century and right up to the present day. But there has been a noticeable change. The fighting remains fierce, but not quite so fierce as it has been in the past; American Jews seem just to have less to express to one another altogether. We simply share less than we once did. And with the loss of shared norms, the anger that once served—however paradoxically—as a distinctive and reliable form of social cohesion and as a boundary-maintaining mechanism, has also lessened, and that collectivity known as a Jewish people has also come closer to an end.

Sources

Blitzer, Wolf I., and David Saperstein. "Should U.S. Jews Urge Concessions? Pro and Con," *Jewish Week* 8–14 Apr. 1976: 18.
Eisenstein, Ira. "The Breira Controversy," *Reconstructionist* 43 (Feb. 1977): 3–4.

Fein, Leonard J. "The Assault on Breira," *Moment* 2 (May 1977): 11–13+.

Hyer, Marjorie. "U.S. Jews Beginning to Go Public in Criticism of Israel," *Washington Post* 3 May 1976: A2.

Isaac, Rael Jean. *Breira: Counsel for Israel.* New York: Americans for a Safe Israel, 1977.

———. *Israel Divided: Ideological Politics in the Jewish State.* Baltimore: Johns Hopkins UP, 1976.

Kornberg, Jacques. "Zionism and Ideology: The Breira Controversy," *Judaism* 27 (Winter 1978): 103–114.

Mintz, Alan. "The People's Choice? A Demurral on Breira," *Response* 10 (Winter 1976–77): 5–10.

Myerhoff, Barbara. *Number Our Days.* New York: Simon and Schuster, 1978.

Novak, William. "The Breira Story," *Genesis* 2 16 Mar. 1977.

Proceedings of Breira's First Annual Membership Conference. New York: Breira, 1977.

"Scholar Accuses Breira of Pro-PLO 'Obsession'," *Jewish Week* 27 Jan.–2 Feb. 1977: A1.

Schwartz, Jacques. "Why Our Doves Are Pigeons," *American Zionist* 67 (Sept. 1976): 23–26.

Shattan, Joseph. "Why Breira?" *Commentary* 63 (Apr. 1977): 60–66.

Urofsky, Melvin I. "Breira Battle Turning into a Witch-Hunt," *Jewish Observer and Middle East Review* 26 (31 Mar. 1977): 8+.

"Why We Fear Open Discussion," Editorial, *Jewish Post and Opinion* 29 Nov. 1974: 6.

Wolf, Arnold Jacob. "American Jewry and Israel: The Need for Dissent," *Conservative Judaism* 31 (Winter 1977): 29–34.

Five Short Essays

Henry Siegman

A Profile of Henry Siegman

by Chris Hedges

New York Times
June 13, 2002

As a young refugee, Henry Siegman found himself fleeing advancing German troops in Belgium early in World War II. He, his pregnant mother and younger brothers and sisters stumbled into one of the worst debacles of the war—the frantic retreat of Allied troops at the Battle of Dunkirk. They huddled in a pitch-black cellar as the fighting raged overhead. In the morning, to the horror of the young boy, the door was kicked open by victorious German troops.

This scene, the subsequent months of hiding in Vichy France, the constant efforts to elude the roundups of Jews and the eventual flight to Casablanca and passage to America, come back to him now regularly. He says that what he went through as a child makes it easier to understand what it is like to be a Palestinian living under the "fear and humiliation" of Israeli occupation.

Now a senior fellow at the Council on Foreign Relations, Mr. Siegman says that it is this empathy for the plight of the Palestinians that has made him a pariah among American Jewish groups.

"We have lost much in American Jewish organizational life," he said. "I was a student and admirer of Rabbi Abraham Heschel. I read his books. We were friends. We marched together in the South during the civil rights movement. He helped me understand the prophetic passion for truth and justice as the keystone to Judaism. This is not, however, an understanding that now animates the American Jewish community. Without that understanding there is little to distinguish the call of Jewish leaders for Jewish unity and solidarity from the demands made by narrow nationalist movements that too often degenerate in xenophobia."

No faith or denomination is immune from a swing to the right, he said, but American Jewish leaders face a special conundrum with the conflict between the Israelis and the Palestinians. And as the conflict intensifies, the voices of opposition to Israeli policy among American Jews have withered away.

"American Jewish organizations confuse support for the state of Israel and its people with an uncritical endorsement of the actions of Israeli governments," he said, "even when these governments do things that in an American context these Jewish organizations would never tolerate. It was inconceivable that a Jewish leader in America twenty or thirty years ago would be silent if a political party in the Israeli government called for the transfer of Palestinians—in other words, ethnic cleansing. Today, there are at least three such parties, but there has not been a word of criticism from American Jewish organizations."

In 1933, when the Nazis took power in Germany, Mr. Siegman's father, Mendel, fled with his family to Antwerp, Belgium, and eventually to the United States.

In New York, Mr. Siegman studied to be ordained a rabbi. He joined the United States Army and served with combat troops as a chaplain in Korea, where he earned a Bronze Star and a Purple Heart.

The Korean War, coupled with his own childhood experiences in Europe, inclined him to those in Jewish life who saw social justice as central to faith. He went on to become the head of the American Jewish Congress for sixteen years, before joining the council.

But for many Jews, he says, there came to be new definitions of faith, ones that he says turned the ideology of the Jewish state into "a surrogate religion."

"The support for Israel fills a spiritual vacuum," he said in his corner office on Park Avenue. "If you do not support the government of Israel then your Jewishness, not your political judgment, is in question."

Mr. Siegman does not speak with the rage of indignation but with quiet disappointment. Most of his brothers and sisters are so angered with his stance that he cannot discuss the issue with them.

"There is only one brother who I am able to enter into a political discussion with," he said.

He insists that along with the glaring moral failure of American Jewish leaders is a failure to understand that the kind of repression meted out to the Palestinians damages Israel's security. He says he believes that the Palestinians will eventually get a state, but one that will cost so much blood and create so much enmity that it will poison relations between Jews and Palestinians for generations. He calls the Palestinian struggle for a state "the mirror image of the Zionist movement" that led to the creation in 1948 of Israel.

"This does not excuse suicide bombings," he said, "but the way Israel deals with these outrages is suspect as long as they are exploited to extend the occupation and enlarge Israeli settlements."

"Future Jewish historians who will be writing about our times will not be kind to us because of such political and moral blindness," he said. "In a recent demonstration in Washington in support of Israel, the demonstrators drowned out a spokesman for the administration, Deputy Secretary of Defense Paul Wolfowitz, a hawkish supporter of Israel, because he dared to express sympathy for the suffering of the Palestinians. This is why I do not look to leaders of Jewish organizations, or to the political leaders of Israel, many of whom are Jewishly illiterate, to define for me the meaning of Jewish identity or solidarity. Classical Jewish sources are a far more reliable guide."

Jewish Ethics and Terrorism

Henry Siegman

from The Jerusalem Post International Edition, *August 5–11, 1984*

THE DISCOVERY of a Jewish terrorist organization in Israel has evoked remarkably little comment from American Jewry. Of course, they found the phenomenon of Jewish terror repugnant; that repugnance was taken for granted. The episode was seen essentially as a problem in law enforcement, which the Israeli authorities could fully be relied on to deal with—as indeed they are doing.

It became quickly apparent, however, from the agitation that this development occasioned in Israel, that the phenomenon raised far deeper issues. Members of this conspiracy were not criminals or "crazies," but solid citizens. Moreover, surveys revealed that a surprisingly large number of Israelis (over 30 percent) were sympathetic to the terrorists. Yet, the intense concern and consternation in Israel found no resonance in the American Jewish community.

The seeming lack of interest of American Jewry must surely say something important—and, I suspect, disquieting—about the nature of the relationship of American Jews to Israeli society. It seems to be a relationship that, despite fund-raising slogans that declare "we are one," does not go much beyond public relations considerations. American Jewry does not really feel implicated in the internal character and problems of Israeli society.

It goes without saying that American Jews care deeply about Israel's security and survival, and for its good name abroad. They take intense pride in its public image as a modern society that is in the forefront of scientific and technological advances. And they celebrate its democratic and egalitarian ethos.

For all of this, however, American Jews do not feel organically linked to Israeli society. Unlike Israelis, for whom the phenomenon of Jewish terror raised fundamental questions about their society and its values, American Jews have given no evidence that their own values were in any way implicated or challenged. The question in America was not what does this Jewish terror say about *us*. It was not seen by American Jews as a problem that demands a re-examination of ethical and religious assumptions.

Apparently, we are not nearly as "one" as the slogan would have it.

If it is true, as we American Jews have argued so consistently, that Zionism and Judaism are inseparable, then surely this violent expression of Zionism cannot be dismissed as a problem for Israeli nationalism that has no implications for American Jews. Does Jewish nationalism have within it the same dark proclivities that lurk in all nationalisms, and that can erupt in a destructive chauvinism? Are such tendencies incompatible with the fundamental ethos of Zionism? More important, are they "un-Jewish"?

These are questions that have agitated Israelis, but they have no echo in American Jewish life.

Even more distressing has been the ambivalent response to this phenomenon of Jewish terrorism from the Orthodox community in the U.S., no less than in Israel. Revulsion to Jewish terror was most pronounced among Israeli secularists. The Orthodox response, on the other hand, seems to suggest that for this segment of the community (i.e., those who are most observant of religious law and rituals), non-Jewish life is less valuable than Jewish life. Indeed, for some it seems to be virtually worthless, except for the concern of *ma yomru hagoyim* (what will non-Jews say?). What this says about the ethical standards of Orthodox Judaism is painful to contemplate.

The problem of the ethical insensitivity of the religiously observant community, and most particularly of its leaders, is hardly new. During the most brutal phases of the American war in Vietnam, I asked in the pages of an American Jewish publication how morally sensitive Orthodox Jews can come to terms with the indifference of Orthodox religious leaders to the slaughter that was taking place in Vietnam. At that point in the war, some of the most conservative sectors of American society, many of whom—in finance, industry and corporate life—had not been known for the delicacy of their social conscience, were deeply shaken by the devastation inflicted by American forces on Vietnamese civilians. But our *gedolim* (religious leaders) remained unruffled. It was as if the lives of Vietnamese women and children destroyed by American "carpet bombing" did not matter.

The record of Orthodox indifference to social concerns is sadly consistent. There was no Orthodox involvement to speak of in the American civil rights struggle in the 1950s and '60s. If there was a single head of a yeshiva who was deeply moved by the plight of blacks in America during that period, he managed to keep such feelings well under control. (Whatever the moral implications of current expressions of black anti-Semitism, and they are serious indeed, it was not an issue in the '50s and '60s.)

The situation is not much different in Israel. I do not believe anyone in Israel looks to the Orthodox establishment, whether it be the official Chief Rabbinate, the heads of yeshivas or the *gedolei hatora* (Torah sages), for instruction and leadership on issues of social concern. Pain and outrage over Sabra and Shatilla did not come from Orthodox religious leaders; vigilance for civil rights and civil liberties in Israel does not come from the Orthodox political parties; and pressures for social policies that address issues of poverty and social injustice do not come from the Orthodox either. It is sad but true that in all of these areas, the voice of conscience is far more likely to come from secular than from religious quarters.

The record of Orthodox leadership in matters of ethics and social concerns seems to give the lie to the claim that the *Halachic* discipline makes for ethical sensitivity. On the contrary, the closer Orthodox leaders stand to the religious right (which is to say, the closer they are to *Halachic* Judaism), the more indifferent they seem to be to anyone's hurt but their own.

Of course, there have been "modern" Orthodox rabbis and scholars, both in Israel and in the U.S., who have condemned Jewish terror and have raised the larger ethical issues. Paradoxically, they have made matters worse, for their critique of the religious right seems to be shaped more by their Western cultural sensibilities than by *Halachic* imperatives. The *Halachic* sensibility seems to be more authentically represented by those who are indifferent to Jewish terror.

For religious Jews, both in Israel and in America, the question is whether in real life—not just in sermons and in apologetic polemics—the *Halachic* discipline makes for ethical sensitivity. Those who believe that it should make for such sensitivity face a monumental task: to free the *Halachic* from the mean-spirited constraints imposed on it by its putative guardian and to release the enlightenment and compassion it contains to *all* created in the image of God. It is a monumental task because those who are engaged in it are relegated to the fringes of Orthodox Jewish life. Those who occupy the center view them with suspicion and disdain.

There are some who will argue that the problem is one of priorities. Given limited energies and resources, the Orthodox community chooses to apply them to internal Jewish concerns. They are wrong, for the issue of ethics is joined precisely at the point where self-interest impinges on the interest of others. A morality that so narrowly calculates self-interest as to leave no compassion for others does not deserve the name "morality." More important, it does not deserve the name "Jewish." That it seems to deserve the name "Orthodox" is the heavy burden Orthodox leadership must bear.

It Does Concern the Diaspora

Henry Siegman

from The Jerusalem Post, *July 8, 1986*

May an American Jew have opinions on the General Security Service affair, and may he voice them publicly?

There seems to be a view among some American Jewish organizations that the General Security Service affair is an "internal" Israeli matter, therefore not an appropriate subject for public comment by American Jews. That is how a former chairman of the Conference of Presidents of Major American Jewish Organizations characterized the affair, when he urged Jewish organizations not to issue any statements about it.

It should be noted, parenthetically, that the Conference of Presidents is mistakenly seen by Israelis as a kind of super organization that sets policy for the American Jewish community. It does not. Its role is far more limited; the Conference serves as a convenient address for visiting Israelis, and it speaks for the organized Jewish community to the American administration on matters affecting U.S.-Israeli relations (and on those matters only) when it is authorized to do so by its member organizations. Its standing derives from the voluntary participation of its member agencies.

In any event, the American Jewish Congress did issue a public statement on the GSS affair, expressing its concern over the granting of immunity to the head of the Shin Bet in an apparent effort by the Israeli government to head off an investigation into its secret services.

While recognizing Israel's vulnerability as a nation under constant siege, and its need to protect the secrecy and anonymity of its intelligence agencies which constitute Israel's first line of defense against the relentless terror to which it is subjected, the American Jewish Congress nevertheless questioned whether the granting of immunity would not do harm to Israel's standards of justice and the rule of law. The Congress statement suggested "there are better ways (than the granting of amnesties) of balancing urgent security considerations and the integrity of a lawful society."

It is interesting that this criticism of the government's action—certainly mild by comparison—was characterized by one Israeli newspaper as "harsh" and "severe." Apparently, Israelis agree that the GSS affair is an "internal" matter, and that non-Israelis should "butt out."

I arrived in Israel shortly after the American Jewish Congress issued its statement, and had occasion to participate in many discussions of the GSS controversy with various Israelis. I came to realize from these discussions that the Shin Bet affair raises questions far more important in their implications for the future of this country than many Israelis and most American Jews seem prepared to concede.

At the outset, the notion that this matter is "internal," and therefore off-limits to outsiders, should be disposed of. Of course, it is internal, but that is hardly a category that creates immunity from comment and criticism from concerned parties outside the country. The only relevant question involved here is whether the matter is significant or not, whether it raises questions that are ethically and politically substantial. Perhaps the only internal matter off-limits to outsiders are elections in a democratic society.

What struck me most about the discussions and debates over the affair among Israelis is that they focus almost exclusively on political and narrow legal questions. Did Deputy Prime Minister Shamir know about the GSS action, or is the head of the Shin Bet lying? Is it politically astute of the Alignment to press for an inquiry at the time, or is this the wrong issue over which to go to new elections? Is there an internal rivalry within the GSS? Was it right for the GSS to have falsely implicated an army officer? These are some of the questions one hears debated. But almost no one seems agitated over the alleged killing by the secret services of two Arab terrorists *after* the terrorist action had been terminated. To the contrary; I suspect that had Shamir gone before the public and stated, "I am the man who ordered the killing of the two Arabs and I take full responsibility for my action," his political stock would have skyrocketed.

One frequently hears in Israel (including in the Knesset) astonishment that such a furor should have been created over the killing of two Arab terrorists.

That astonishment says something not only about the obvious revulsion Israelis feel towards terrorists, but also about their sense of the value of Arab life.

Terrorists, Arab or otherwise, should be given the death sentence. Terrorism should be a capital offense. Its perpetrators should be hunted down wherever they are. They are a scourge to be wiped off the face of the earth.

But when terrorists have been taken into custody within Israeli territory wherein Israeli law applies, the law cannot be superseded by the secret services. Once terrorists have been taken into custody, no civilized society turns over the power of life and death to its security forces. More to the point, no Jewish society should do so.

If terrorists deserve the death sentence, let the Knesset pass the necessary legislation and let the sentence be imposed by the courts. The killing of persons as a form of punishment is not the prerogative of secret service agencies. That the far-ranging debate over the GSS affair focuses so little on this critical point should be a matter of the gravest concern.

The recurring theme in the discussions I have overheard is that the reason an inquiry into this matter is inconceivable is because it might bring to light similar actions by the GSS. I do not for a moment believe that such actions are in fact common practice.

But those who advance such alleged practices by the GSS as the reason not to have an inquiry obviously believe such practices to be the norm. Apparently, it does not seem to occur to them that this should make an inquiry into the GSS even more necessary, not less so.

All security services, even in the most democratic of societies, operate to a certain extent outside the normal legal framework. But the leeway too many Israelis are prepared to allow their secret services is unprecedented. They do so, apparently, because of their belief—elevated to the level of sacred myth—in the integrity and infallibility of the Shin Bet. They are all "good guys," patriotic to the point of complete selflessness. Most important, they are secure in the knowledge that these extraordinary practices are applied to Arabs only. I suspect that if the secret services were believed to apply these alleged arbitrary decisions of life and death to the Jewish citizens of Israel as well, the reaction of Israelis would be quite different.

This raises once again the painful question of the extent to which Arab life has become cheapened because of nearly 40 years of Arab hostility and violence against Israel. It is an issue, I believe, that should be taken far more seriously than it has been. There was a time when it was possible to avoid dealing with it because of the belief that it was a consequence of circumstances that would change. But the situation is clearly not a passing one.

For most Israelis, it is a permanent condition, unlikely to change in their lifetime. Of course, the Arabs have only themselves to blame, but that is hardly a consolation for what this situation is doing to the Jewish soul.

Leaving this question aside (which one ought not), is there really a correspondence between the myth about Israel's security services and the reality? Are the security forces in Israel, unlike security forces in other democratic countries, so perfect as to be entrusted with the kind of latitude that Israelis are prepared to give them? Is it really so unthinkable that what a secret service is permitted to do with Arabs, they will one day feel free to do with Jews as well?

The fact is that the current GSS affair was brought to light when several of the service's senior officials decided to bring the matter to the prime minister's attention. Ironically, it is the very same people who argue for the immunity and sacrosanct status of the secret service who accuse these officials of being motivated by professional and personal jealousies. It seems not to occur to them that a secret service susceptible to these common human frailties cannot, at the same time, be seen as comprised of infallible supermen. In any event, in a democratic society, no bureaucracy, no matter how legendary its reputation, should be allowed to operate without the strictest accountability to the society which it serves.

These are some of the wider implications of the GSS affair. One can disagree, of course, with particular answers to the questions raised but what one cannot do, however, is to attempt to silence the discussion of these critical issues, or to dismiss the concern of Jews outside of Israel by describing the matter as an internal affair. It is undoubtedly internal. In fact, it is so internal that it touches the innermost values of a society and, therefore, the concern and involvement of Jews everywhere should be welcomed and encouraged.

The Perils of Messianic Politics

Henry Siegman

from The Jewish Week, *April 28, 1988*

The criticism directed at me by several Orthodox organizations is indicative of a phenomenon in Jewish life that cannot be ignored.

The Orthodox groups accuse me of saying that "Jewish religious tradition" values non-Jewish life less than Jewish life, thus providing fodder for anti-Semites. In fact, I said no such thing. What I said was that some of those who *oppose* territorial compromise hold such a view; I did not ascribe that view to "Jewish religious tradition."

The issue would not be worth further comment were it not for the fact that there are political forces in Israel that do ascribe a level of sanctity and holiness to Jewish existence, individual and collective, which they do not ascribe to others. It should be clear that it is not the notion itself that is objectionable, but its peculiar application by these groups to the current political situation.

To be sure, the issue is not this or that classical Jewish text. Jewish tradition is sufficiently rich, complex and diversified to enable the proponents of virtually any ideology to read their prejudices back into specific texts of their choosing; such selective exercises prove absolutely nothing about normative Judaism.

Indeed, it is not even the choice of text that matters, but what one does with it. A text that has a noble purpose can be used for ignoble ends. Thus, for example, the concept of eternal war with Amalek, the ancient nation that ambushed the Israelites in the desert, has served for generations as a symbol of Jewish opposition to evil and immorality. However, by applying that text literally to the Palestinians, as some Gush Emunim ideologues have done, a noble text is used to dehumanize an entire people.

Similarly, the literal application of a text concerning the three choices that were offered the ancient Canaanite residents of the land of Israel—to flee, to accept Jewish rule, or to fight—to the current population in the territories provokes ugly sentiments never intended by the text. It leads to such bizarre phenomena as the call by Rabbi Chaim Druckman, a leader of the National Religious Party, for the total obliteration of the Arab village of Beita in retaliation for its alleged role in the death of an Israeli girl.

What is so distressing, therefore, about fundamentalist trends in Israel's political culture—and their resonances in American Jewish life, as evidenced by the Inquisition-like demands of these Orthodox organizations—is, among other things, their distortion of normative Judaism.

These trends are influenced profoundly by the ideology and political activism of Gush Emunim, the territorial settlers' movement, who seek to replace the democratic socialism of Israel's Zionist founders with an ultra-nationalist and eschatologically based fundamentalism. According to this ideology, the essence of the Israel-Arab conflict is metaphysical, not political; the allegedly raging anti-Semitism of the non-Jewish world is a necessary component of that metaphysics.

The resolution of the Arab-Israel conflict is seen, therefore, along lines preordained by the imperatives of Jewish eschatology—whose demands are absolute and not subject to compromise—rather than by the give-and-take of normal political processes.

These trends are not to be dismissed as an esoteric phenomenon, of interest only to scholars and theologians. To the contrary; no one can understand what is going on in Israel's political life without reference to this fundamentalism, for it is the single most coherent and vigorous political force in Israel today.

Recent polls in Israel project that Meir Kahane's Kach party will grow to four seats in the upcoming November elections, making it as large as the National Religious Party, and that Techiya, the ultra-nationalist party to the right of Likud, also will enlarge its mandate significantly.

If that weren't enough, at its recent national convention, the National Religious Party—since the founding of the state the model of moderate religious Zionism—ousted its leadership and replaced it with right-wing ideologues. The combination of these three parties alone—all to the right of Likud—could result in nearly fifteen seats in the next Knesset.

What this portends for the coming Israeli elections is a radical shift from a political culture based on rational and democratic principles of governance to one that is shaped by principles of messianism, extreme nationalism and religious fundamentalism. The potential this holds for the gradual alienation not only of American Jews and of most other diaspora Jewish communities, but also of a substantial segment of Israel's own population, many of whom are already entertaining the unthinkable notion of abandoning a society they and their parents shaped, is tragic beyond imagining. The implications of that emerging political culture is one that the leaders of Jewish federations here, of the United Jewish Appeal and, not least, of our cultural institutions would do well to ponder.

In any event, what distressed the Orthodox leaders who attacked my speech is not the statement they (falsely) attributed to me, but my call for a repudiation of a narrow nationalistic and religious fundamentalism that is threatening ascendancy in Israel's political life. It is a fundamentalism whose goal is nothing less than substituting what it considers to be authentic Jewish forms of governance for Western-style democracy. A redefinition of "who is a Jew" to read out of Judaism some Conservative and Reform Jews is the least of the changes such governance would bring about.

That was the burden of my speech, which was critical of a reactionary Zionism that is exclusionary, that distinguishes—even within Israel itself—between the so-called "national camp" and other political parties that are implicitly smeared as traitorous; that distinguishes between the Jewish people in Israel and Jews outside of Israel, who risk being accused of making common cause with anti-Semites if they express dissenting views; that sees the non-Jewish world as a monolith bent on the Jewish people's destruction—that is a Zionism of the diaspora, of an uncertain, unproud and unfree people.

Instead, I urged a Zionism "that is inclusionary; that unites and does not divide; that reflects the optimism, confidence and openness of a truly free people: in short, a Zionism that is faithful to its founders and to the sense of justice and universalism that is the legacy of our prophets, those first lovers of Zion."

Far from seeking to create divisions within the Jewish community, I called for a rededication to a Zionism that "will make far more explicit the underlying solidarity and unity of Jews all over the world—not with any particular Israeli party, or policy, or politician, but with the Zionist enterprise and the Jewish people as a whole."

When Oslo Finally Dies

Henry Siegman

from The Jerusalem Post, *July 17, 1998*

In recent weeks, Prime Minister Binyamin Netanyahu and his spokespeople have issued daily pronouncements about the "narrowing gap" between Israel's position and the U.S. administration's initiative calling for an Israeli redeployment of 13.1 percent in the West Bank.

Far from heralding an imminent agreement between Israel and the Palestinians, these pronouncements are intended as a cover for the inevitable formal collapse of the Oslo peace process that began with such high expectations nearly five years ago.

While the U.S. administration wasted two years deluding itself about Netanyahu's "real intentions," relying on his alleged pragmatism and commitment to the implementation of Israel's undertakings under the Oslo Accords, Netanyahu waged a relentless and effective war against those accords, aimed at killing the peace process.

He has been brilliantly successful in wearing down everyone—Israelis, Palestinians, Jordanians, Egyptians and, finally, Americans as well—making all of them weary and sick of the process. It is "a success" for which the U.S., but above all the Israelis themselves, will unfortunately pay dearly. Prospects for an Israeli-Palestinian agreement will not improve in the slightest even if Netanyahu were to agree at the last moment to accept the American proposal.

He is a past master at preventing implementation of agreements that hold any promise of accommodation to Palestinian demands, while shifting the blame to the Palestinians themselves. He has already fully laid the groundwork for such obstruction by announcing that everything is nearly in place for Israel's acceptance of the American idea, except for the Palestinian lack of reciprocity.

It is a tactic Netanyahu has resorted to repeatedly these past two years to camouflage his own government's violations of reciprocity, which include Israel's failure to allow the opening of an airport and seaport in Gaza and safe passage between Gaza and the West Bank, the failure to release Palestinian prisoners as promised, and—above all—unilateral actions by Israel in Jerusalem and in the West Bank, such as housing projects, the enlargement of settlements and the construction of major roadways, to preempt issues that were to be discussed in the final-status negotiations.

Even if the Netanyahu government were to redeploy the IDF in accordance with the American proposal, the prospect for the progress of the final-status issues (borders, Jerusalem, refugees and water) is nil. The deadline of May 1999, which under Oslo marks the end of the negotiations, would be impossible to meet even if there were an abundance of good will between the parties. (If such good will existed, however, the deadline for reaching an agreement could have been extended.)

Under the present circumstances, which are marked by profound mistrust, hostility and a continuing determination by this Israeli government to treat Palestinians not as partners in a peace process but as closet terrorists, May 1999 could well trigger a sudden downward spiral that will return the region to the conflict and violence that characterized it for nearly half a century.

The possibility, if not the likelihood, of such disastrous consequences is attested to by Israel's own army intelligence. While last summer the IDF intelligence service concluded that the likelihood of war in 1998 was low and that they did not expect serious clashes with the Syrians or the Palestinians, they now say that the probability of war in 1999 has risen dramatically.

They conclude that if the political impasse continues, there could be a large-scale flareup with the Palestinians and the Syrians in 1999. And in those circumstances, there is no reason to believe that Israel's peace agreements with Egypt and Jordan will hold.

Earlier this year, *Ha'aretz* warned that Israel's situation today is chillingly similar to the period preceding the Yom Kippur War, "a disaster brought on by a diplomatic freeze, boastful self-confidence, contempt for the Arab adversary and a nation which followed its leaders into destructive apathy. It takes no great imagination to see how today's march of folly is returning Israel to the bloodshed of previous blindness."

Given the imminent proliferation of missiles and weapons of mass destruction, the damage to Israel following a collapse of the peace process could be incalculable. If what lies ahead is the scenario described by the IDF's intelligence, Israelis will have no one to blame but themselves.

Arab countries are always lectured by Israelis that, unlike its neighbors, Israel is a democracy. And so it is. What distinguishes a democracy is that its citizens have the possibility of repudiating leaders whose policies they reject, especially in parliamentary systems such as the Israeli one, whose Knesset can oust the prime minister.

They have not done so, and will therefore have few claims on others in dealing with their failure's consequences. You cannot repudiate U.S. diplomatic efforts in the name of Israeli democracy, and then demand that the U.S. intervene in the conflict triggered by that repudiation in order to save the Middle East's "only democracy."

Deal with Fundamentals

Henry Siegman

from The Jerusalem Post, *February 7, 2002*

In the face of Palestinian Authority Chairman Yasser Arafat's inability or unwillingness to restrain Hamas and Islamic Jihad—and even some of his own Fatah-affiliated forces which are now sponsoring Hamas-style suicide bombings—the

Bush administration seems to have decided to "unleash" Prime Minister Ariel Sharon by removing restraints on Israeli retaliations against Palestinians it had previously insisted on.

To believe that this is a prescription for ending terrorism is folly. To the contrary, it is a prescription for the "Lebanonization" of the occupied territories and of Israel's own heartland. How much more blood needs to flow in the streets of Jerusalem and Tel Aviv, not to speak of Ramallah, Nablus and Gaza, before it finally registers with Israeli and U.S. policymakers that efforts to end the violence that are based solely on revenge killings only inflame and accelerate terrorism? There is a long line of shahids (suicides) waiting for the privilege of blowing themselves up for their cause. Each Israeli reprisal attack brings new cohorts of shahids into Hamas's ranks.

Large segments of the Israeli public continue to support Sharon's intention to continue on this self-destructive path only because they believe there is no alternative. But an alternative does exist, and always did. That alternative does not entail acquiescence to Palestinian terrorism.

But if revenge killings are the only Israeli response, then the country is on the road to eventual self-destruction. Palestinians, who have lived in misery and deprivation for more than half a century and have little to lose, will outlast Israelis who are accustomed to the comforts and per capita income of advanced Western societies.

If Israel's punishment of Palestinian terrorism is to serve as a deterrent rather than a provocation to greater terrorism, Israel must offer Palestinians a clear alternative to violence that leads not to vague "confidence-building," or a new "incrementalism," but to viable statehood.

For such an alternative to be credible, it must include an Israeli commitment to return to political negotiations as soon as terrorism abates, without imposing impossible conditions that Sharon has insisted on until now; an immediate halt to settlement construction; and an acceptance of the principle of Israel's withdrawal from the West Bank and Gaza to essentially the pre-1967 border.

To refuse to offer such an alternative to the Palestinians on the grounds that former prime minister Ehud Barak offered it two years ago and it was rejected by Arafat—which is the common objection one encounters in Israel—is entirely disingenuous. If the 1999 offer was based on Israel's recognition of Palestinian rights, these rights have not disappeared. If it was based on Israel's "generosity," it was not a serious or politically viable offer to begin with.

In the real world, Sharon's government will never offer an alternative to its policy of ever-escalating revenge killings. It is therefore the United States that should declare its vigorous support for such an alternative. To be sure, the U.S. cannot make Israeli policy. But if the U.S. is clear about what it believes is the right and necessary thing to do, Israel will eventually do it.

When U.S. president Dwight D. Eisenhower declared, without equivocation, that the 1956 invasion of Egypt by Israel, Great Britain and France was wrong and needed to be reversed, all three countries pulled out promptly. A great power, particularly one that has become the world's only great power, does not need to send planes and troops to make its point.

It is time for Washington to deal with the fundamentals of the conflict, and not to avoid them by focusing instead on so-called "confidence-building" strategies; that is a cop out. The only way to build confidence is to give Palestinians reason to believe they can achieve their goal without resorting to violence. This requires far more than the U.S. entertaining a "vision" of a "State of Palestine" in an indeterminate future. Without an explicit and credible non-violent alternative that would lead to statehood, the very term "confidence-building" is quite meaningless. What is it we expect Palestinians to have confidence in? Sharon's goodwill?

The U.S. commitment to the Palestinians must be balanced with an equally clear commitment to Israel that if terrorist incursions continue across the new Palestinian state's border, the U.S. will fully support the most severe Israeli countermeasures to eliminate that threat. As it is, Israel has a proven ability to stop cross-border aggressions from all of its neighbors—Egypt, Jordan, Syria and Lebanon—none of whom prevents such incursions because of its affection for the Jewish state. Israel has a proven record of failure in suppressing what is essentially a civil war with a people under its own occupation.

Israel's insistence on a continuation of measures that have bred only increased terrorism in the past, in the belief that more of the same will somehow yield different results, is madness. The last thing the U.S. should be doing is encouraging such madness.

Of Dogs and Tails: The Changing Nature of the Pro-Israeli Lobby, The Unchanging Nature of the U.S.-Israeli Alliance

Phyllis Bennis

A nalysis of the U.S. relationship with Israel has long been characterized by debates over who calls the shots. Who wags whom, which is the dog and which is the tail? Is the pro-Israeli lobby in charge of foreign policy or do Washington's strategic thinkers and official policy-makers determine its trajectory? In fact neither version alone answers the question. It is, rather, the intersection between the two main arenas of U.S.-Israeli relations, the domestic/political and the international/strategic, that serves as the main locus of U.S. decision-making. Analysts with long years of accountability to the lobby's institutions move through revolving doors into State Department or White House positions. Government officials recognize the lobby's power to build popular support for policies that would otherwise be hard to sell.

According to Frank Gaffney, a leading pro-Israeli hawk and former Reagan administration official, supporters of Israel find a warm reception at the White House. "It's the old issue of pushing on an open door," Gaffney said. "You are seeing American government policy being profoundly influenced by beliefs that are shared by the pushers outside and the people on the inside."[1] And the relationship between the strategic and the political goes back as far as the origins of U.S.-Israeli relations. Those ties began, with the creation of the state of Israel in 1948, in tandem with the emergence of the Cold War. From the beginning, the key element in the relationship was the expectation in official Washington policy circles that Israel—quickly deemed a more reliable U.S. ally than any of the pro-Western Arab governments—would be able and interested in serving important U.S. interests in and around the Middle East region. Domestic political returns, by taking advantage of Jewish community interest in providing for Holocaust survivors unwelcome in the U.S. and Europe, were anticipated by Washington from the beginning.

While the United States had supported Israel from the time of the founding of the state, Washington's large-scale economic and military aid did not emerge

1. Silverstein, Ken & Scherer, Michael, "Born-Again Zionists," *Third World Resurgence* magazine, Malaysia, Sept.-Oct. 2002.

until after the 1967 war, when Israel's military showed its prowess against the combined capacity of several Arab armies. Only then did U.S. strategists begin to recognize just how important Israel could be in carrying out the global reach of Washington's Cold War.

And simultaneously with that escalation in official aid and support came massive public support for Israel. The breadth of political support, and its bipartisan nature, was never simply because the pro-Israeli lobby was well-organized or well-connected or wealthy. Rather, broad U.S. support for Israel was always rooted in the fact that the goals of the lobbying networks supported, rather than challenged, the traditional definitions of U.S. national interest as defined by the Pentagon, the White House and the State Department. Israel would continue to play a key role as a strategic U.S. surrogate and junior partner in fighting the Cold War in the region and, for many years, far afield in Africa, Asia and Latin America.

In the Middle East, Israel's overwhelming military superiority kept nationalist Arab regimes in check, and was important in suppressing nationalist uprisings in other Arab countries. Tel Aviv's willingness and ability to carry out delicate military projects on behalf of Washington that might otherwise be constrained because of U.S. domestic concerns, also helped solidify the close relations between Israel and the CIA and the Pentagon, as well as the State Department and Congress. Throughout the Cold War, Israel provided arms, training, and other military and intelligence support to a host of unsavory dictatorships in Africa, Latin America and elsewhere, whose main claim on U.S. backing was based on their anti-Soviet stance. Israel armed UNITA rebels in Angola and RENAMO in Mozambique, backing their guerrilla campaigns aimed at destabilizing those newly independent African countries. Israel developed long-standing ties with the Somoza dictatorship through its last years in Nicaragua, and then continued with a major role in backing the Reagan administration's favorite terrorist organization, the Contras whose civil war devastated that impoverished country. Elsewhere in Central America, the Israeli Galil rifle replaced the U.S.-provided M-16 as the weapon of choice for repressive armies and powerful government-supported death squads. The Guatemalan arms purchases from Israel picked up steam after public pressure in the United States forced a downsizing of direct military aid from Washington to the Guatemalan junta. And Israel maintained long-standing strategic economic, industrial, military and eventually nuclear weapons ties with apartheid South Africa. Those were only some of these tasks.

With the end of the Cold War, Israel's role as a bastion against Soviet penetration of the strategic Middle East begins to wane in significance. It did not disappear altogether, of course. The $270 million transmitter ($30 million given to Israel in 1989 for site preparation costs alone) built in the Negev desert to broadcast Voice of America propaganda to formerly Soviet Central Asia and Africa was only one example of its continued usefulness.

Even after the Cold War, the three pillars of U.S. policy in the Middle East remained constant: maintaining a strong Israel, ensuring control of Middle Eastern oil, maintaining strategic reach. The end of the Cold War and the collapse of the Soviet Union, and the U.S. military victory in the 1991 Gulf War rewrote the political map of the Middle East. But the key U.S. regional interests—ensuring market-friendly stability for creation of a "New Middle East," the post–Cold War Middle East version of NAFTA—took on new primacy.

Israel's role came under new U.S. scrutiny, although not under serious challenge. With the end of Cold War-driven proxy wars in Africa, Asia and elsewhere, the primacy once placed on military force shifted in favor of economic and market realignments. During Operation Desert Storm, the U.S.-enforced Arab coalition against Iraq, a key component of Washington's new Middle East strategy, meant Israel had to be kept out of the fighting. Patriot anti-missile systems and other expensive military hardware were shipped to Tel Aviv, and protection of Israel became a key task for the U.S.-controlled "coalition" forces. The Israeli military's technological advances contributed to the Pentagon's capacity, but a public role for Israel in the anti-Iraq coalition would have shifted the politically vital role of Arab regimes from difficult to impossible to maintain in the face of massive popular opposition. A few in the media murmured that perhaps Israel was moving out of the asset column and into the liability side for the United States. But those voices were quickly squelched with the reminder that Israel was itself a target of Iraqi scuds during Desert Storm.

Serious recent challenges to Washington's partnership with Israel have been extraordinarily rare. In 1980, one of the first actions of the Carter Doctrine (responding to the Iranian revolution with a more aggressive Middle East–wide agenda) involved sending advanced AWACS communications planes and F-15 fighter jets to Saudi Arabia at the request of the king, who felt threatened by the overthrow of his former ally, the Shah of Iran. Israel and its U.S. supporters fought bitterly against Washington approving the sale of the F-15s to Saudi Arabia. It was the first major, public break between the pro-Israeli lobby and the foreign policy establishment, but in the end (by a very close vote in the Senate) regional stability and control of oil temporarily trumped Israel and the sale was approved—though with the condition that Israel's security not be eroded. Israel's Ambassador Ephraim Evron announced that his country would now expect increased U.S. military aid to compensate.[2] That was fine with the United States, and Israel was designated to play a key role as Washington's junior partner in implementing the Carter Doctrine.

The other challenge came with Bush Senior's announcement in 1992 that he would condition a $10 billion new loan guarantee on an Israeli agreement to freeze settlement activity in the occupied territories. The Bush plan was to deduct the amount of money Israel spent on settlements from the $10 billion. But before the loan was finalized congressional opposition and cries of outrage from the Clinton campaign emerged, and Bush signed off on the loan without

2. Raines, Howard, "President Praises Senate's Action as Statesmanlike and Courageous," *New York Times*, Oct. 29, 1981, cited in Tivnan, op. cit.

an Israeli agreement on a settlement freeze. Bush was defeated, as was the hard-line Likud government of Prime Minister Yitzhak Shamir. But Congress eventually imposed a rider to the appropriations bill requiring the deduction for settlement spending. Immediately Clinton's top Middle East official, Martin Indyk (who had earlier founded the Washington Institute on Near East Policy as a think tank for the main pro-Israeli lobby group AIPAC), announced that the administration would find a way to provide full funding. When the State Department estimated that Israel spent $437 million on settlements in 1993, that amount was deducted from that year's portion of the loan. Soon after, the U.S. authorized Israel to take $500 million worth of U.S. military supplies from NATO warehouses in Europe.[3]

U.S. support for Israel has taken numerous and varied forms. But the two most important aspects of that support come in the form of billions of dollars of unconditional economic and military aid, and in providing diplomatic protection to Israel, particularly in the United Nations, to prevent Tel Aviv from being held accountable for its violations of international law and UN resolutions.

In the years following the Gulf War the U.S.-Israeli alliance gained new strength. Despite major cuts in U.S. foreign aid programs all over the world, aid to Israel remained untouched. The privileges that only Israel receives from the United States continued. From the beginning, aid to Israel came with special perks. Unlike all other countries in the world who are required to spend their entire aid allotment on U.S. goods and services, Israel is allowed to siphon off about a quarter of the aid to invest in its own military research and production. Israel also receives its stipend in a lump sum at the beginning of the fiscal year, allowing a significant increase in interest payments.

And aid to Israel has remained the highest percentage of U.S. aid, totaling 25 percent of the entire foreign aid budget. In February 2003 the Congressional Research Service issued a new report on U.S. foreign aid to Israel from 1949 through fiscal year 2002. The total was a breathtaking $87.104 billion. But in fact that figure was significantly too low. It excluded such grants as the $1.2 billion provided to Israel after the Wye River agreement in 1998, later subsidies for "refugee resettlement," and more. Bringing the total up to date through early 2003, and adding in such recent items as the additional $1 billion in military grants and $9 billion in loan guarantees included in President Bush's war budget of March 25, 2003, the *Washington Report on Middle East Affairs* calculates the total from 1949 to reach $97.5 billion.[4] And that, of course, doesn't include whole other categories of aid—including the tax-exempt status of private donations to the Jewish National Fund and other quasi-official and offi-

3. Zunes, Steven, "The Strategic Functions of U.S. Aid to Israel," www.geocities.com/CapitolHill/Senate/7891/zunes.html.

4. McArthur, Shirl, "A Conservative Tally of Direct U.S. Aid to Israel: $97.5 Billion—and Counting," *Washington Report on Middle East Affairs*, May 2003.

cial arms of the State of Israel in the form of contributions to numerous Jewish charities. Only Israel maintains that tax-exempt status.

Beyond the question of economic and military aid, the United States serves as Israel's key diplomatic backer, especially in the UN. From the mid-1970s on, the UN saw overwhelming support for an international peace conference under the auspices of the UN to resolve the conflict, for all parties including Israel and the PLO taking part in those talks. It was the kind of approach that would, as the Cold War wound down, prove at least relatively successful in crisis zones across the world—bringing together opposing parties to talk under UN auspices.

But Israel absolutely rejected UN involvement, viewing the UN as implacably antagonistic to Israeli interests and the General Assembly as hostile territory. Assembly votes critical of Israel usually reflected a near-consensus in favor (sometimes with some rather abashed abstentions), while only two countries voted against—the United States and Israel itself. Tel Aviv on its own would have been unable to stand against those initiatives. Alone, its refusal would have brought it universal opprobrium and the likelihood of serious sanctions. But U.S. commitment to bolstering a reliably pro-U.S. ally in the sometimes volatile and always strategic Middle East meant that Washington agreed to back Tel Aviv's rejectionism as far as it wished to go.

In general the United States stood aside while the Assembly passed numerous resolutions condemning and demanding an end to Israel's occupation of the West Bank, the Gaza Strip and Arab East Jerusalem. There were serious exceptions, including Washington's refusal to grant Yasser Arafat a visa to address the Assembly in 1988, and the high-profile pressure campaign in post–Gulf War 1991 to force the Assembly to revoke its 1975 "Zionism is a form of racism" resolution. But while their language was often tough, the resolutions lacked any means of exacting compliance; Assembly resolutions do not carry enforcement power like those of the Security Council. The pressure was limited to publicity and public opinion, neither of which was taken very seriously by Israel. Without access to any implementation mechanism, Assembly resolutions were routinely passed, routinely excoriated by Tel Aviv and Washington as evidence of UN "bias," and routinely ignored.

After the Cold War, the use of vetoes in the Security Council dropped dramatically—until the Council tried to pass a resolution condemning new Israeli settlement construction that was tightening a ring of settlements surrounding Arab Jerusalem. Then Washington's veto came into play again. And throughout the 1990s the United States maintained its refusal to allow the UN to play a substantive role in Israel-Palestine diplomacy.

During the second intifada that began in September 2000, further efforts were made in the Security Council and in the General Assembly to intervene, to provide protection for Palestinians living under occupation from the assaults, assassinations, house demolitions and other depredations of the Israeli military, as well as for Israeli civilians threatened by the consequences of occupation, including suicide bombers. But the United States ensured that no such measures were taken.

The crisis escalated, matched by growing international outrage. Within the first two weeks of March 2002, 160 Palestinians and 60 Israelis were killed. Israel besieged Bethlehem's Church of the Nativity, where Palestinian militants had taken refuge, soon joined by international solidarity activists. UN Secretary General Kofi Annan harshly criticized Israel's use of advanced military equipment, including U.S.-provided attack helicopters and F-16 fighter jets as well as tanks against Palestinian neighborhoods and refugee camps. "You must end the illegal occupation," he said to Israel on March 12. "You must stop the bombing of civilian areas the assassinations, the unnecessary use of lethal force, the demolitions and the daily humiliation of ordinary Palestinians." The United States and Britain blocked the Security Council from endorsing Annan's statement on the grounds that Israel's invasion of Palestinian land during the 1967 war was not necessarily illegal.

Not surprisingly the increased repression led to a new round of Palestinian attacks, including two suicide bombings in late March which killed numerous civilians inside Israel. Israel ratcheted up the violence with a massive offensive that roared across the West Bank on March 29, reoccupying Palestinian cities and towns. The Israeli offensive came to a head in the Jenin refugee camp, where in April 2002 occupying troops launched a full-scale raid, leaving scores of Palestinians dead, many buried under the debris of bulldozed houses destroyed in the attack. According to international human rights organizers, more than fifty Palestinians were known to have been killed; twenty-eight of them were non-combatant civilians, including children. After the fighting, a strict curfew prevented aid agencies and ambulances from reaching the injured, the homeless, and the bodies of those buried in the rubble. The UN Special Coordinator in the occupied territories, Terje Roed-Larsen, called the destruction by the Israeli army "morally repugnant," and said that "combating terrorism does not give a blank check to kill civilians." On April 13 Kofi Annan called on the Security Council to send a "robust" international peacekeeping force to the region, based on Chapter VII of the UN Charter, meaning enforceable through military force.

Security Council discussions quickly rejected such a plan, but settled on sending a UN fact-finding mission to investigate. On April 19 Israeli Foreign Minister Shimon Peres agreed to accept such a team. But within days Israel reneged on Peres's commitment, first arguing over the composition of the team (which included the former president of Finland and a retired U.S. Army general) and other technicalities, and finally completely rejecting the UN team. U.S. officials accepted the Israeli position, claiming that the Jenin investigation issue had become a "distraction" from the peace process. Washington refused to press Israel to abide by the UN decision, and refused to allow the Security Council to enforce its resolution. On May 1 Kofi Annan, unable to move without U.S. support, called off the investigation altogether. The following day, a report by

Human Rights Watch indicated that the IDF's abuses in the Jenin refugee camp constituted "grave breaches of the Geneva Conventions, or war crimes."

Support at Home

Buoyed by the world-class photo-op of September 1993, when he presided over the signing of the Israel-PLO accord on the White House lawn, Bill Clinton emerged as the most pro-Israeli president—until Bush Junior would have his chance. Clinton's pro-Israel stance was not the political commitment of a centrist Democrat. Unlike his vice president, Al Gore, who had maintained a long-standing loyalty to Israel and to the pro-Israeli lobby while still a senator, Clinton took up the pro-Israel posture seriously only after reaching the White House. Throughout the Clinton years, the most important component of the lobby was rooted in the Jewish community—largely liberal, mainly supportive of the center-left Labor Party in Israel, and overwhelmingly Democrats. But even in that period, another sector of pro-Israel sentiment—along with organizing, money and increasing influence—was on the rise in American political life. It was centered in the conservative Republican, theologically Zionist, pro–Likud Party, Christian right.

Fundamentalist Christians and Right-Wing Israelis: The Unholy Alliance

In January 1998, hours before he was scheduled to meet President Clinton in the Oval Office, Israeli Prime Minister Benjamin Netanyahu, staying at the Mayflower Hotel just three blocks away from the White House, was shaking hands with one of Clinton's most vociferous fundamentalist Christian right-wing critics. Rev. Jerry Falwell, among other things, had been using his highly rated TV program to sell a widely discredited videotape accusing the president of peddling drugs and being involved in the death of former White House deputy counsel Vincent Foster, who committed suicide. He was also deeply involved in mobilizing support for Israel.

Netanyahu was rallying all the backing he could muster in Washington to dissuade the Clinton administration from "pressuring" him to force Tel Aviv back to the stalled peace talks. (The "pressure" Netanyahu was worried about was merely the threat of a public statement of U.S. goals for the Middle East "peace process"—no one believed Clinton was even considering actual pressure.) After his meeting with the Israeli leader, Falwell said, "there are about 200,000 evangelical pastors in America, and we are asking them all through e-mail, faxes, letters, telephone, to go into their pulpits and use their influence in support of the State of Israel and the prime minister."[5]

5. Published in *The New York Times,* January 21, 1998.

The Falwell-Netanyahu meeting was only one episode in a twenty-five-year-old unholy alliance between Netanyahu's right-wing Likud Party and the American right-wing fundamentalist Christians. What began to change during Clinton's second term was the emergence of the highly organized Christian Zionist movement as a dominant force within both the professional pro-Israel lobby and the community of popular support for Israel, once overwhelmingly Jewish.

It was Israeli Prime Minister Menachem Begin, years before, who first recognized the increasing influence of fundamentalist Christians. In the early 1980s, he decorated Falwell with the Jabotinsky medal—named for the founder of the Zionist terrorist organization Irgun—a few years after Falwell imposed himself on the political scene with the establishment of his influential Moral Majority organization.[6] Begin, who came to power in 1977 after a long social-democratic period in Israel, sought natural allies in right-wing American circles. An aide was instructed to meet with American fundamentalist Christians and "explore the depth of their pro-Israel sentiment." The outcome was astounding. In 1977 full-page advertisements started to appear in major U.S. papers, all declaring the support of Christian organizations for Israel and its policies, such as the immigration of Soviet Jews. In 1981, after Israel bombed the French-built Iraqi nuclear power reactor at Osirak, Begin telephoned Falwell and asked him to do some publicity for Israel. Falwell, in his many TV appearances, defended Israel's air raid on Osirak[7] at a time when the Reagan administration itself condemned the raid as a violation of international law. Begin paid Falwell back with the medal.

This alliance between the Israeli right and the U.S. Christian right has been cemented in a very long process shaped by ideological/theological, international, and U.S. domestic considerations. The global significance of the strategic basis for strong U.S.-Israel relations came under question for a time, as did the operational importance of Israel as a cat's paw for U.S. power in the oil-rich Middle East after the fall of the Soviet Union. Domestically the influence of organized right-wing Christian groups skyrocketed within U.S. politics. The 1994 Republican sweep in the House of Representatives brought to power a number of right-wing Christians, and helped consolidate Congress as the most significant institution backing Israel's "most favored friend" position in U.S. foreign policy.

Ideologically, these evangelical Protestants believe the second coming of Christ must be pre-conditioned by the "return" of all the Jews to the land of Israel, and the creation of a Jewish entity ready for the Messiah. As a result, they support not only Israel as an existing state, but the Zionist project of "returning" Jews from around the world to Israel. Of course what is never mentioned is the

6. Tivnan, Edward, *The Lobby: Jewish Political Power and American Foreign Policy* (New York: Simon and Schuster), 1987, p. 181.

7. Melman, Yossi and Raviv, Dan, *Friends in Deed: Inside the U.S.-Israel Alliance* (New York: Hyperion), p. 354.

anti-Semitic belief in what happens next. After the return of the Jews to Israel other developments are anticipated to hasten the realization of this biblical promise—including, by the time of the second coming, the conversion or death of the all the Jews. This part of the Christian Zionist agenda is, not surprisingly, played down by both the evangelicals and their allies in the Likud. (Although in 1999 when Jerry Falwell declared that the Antichrist is alive and Jewish, the Anti-Defamation League did say that the remarks bordered on "anti-Semitism at best and [are] anti-Semitic at worst."[8])

Christ Will Come Back

The fundamentalist connection to Israel dates back to the nineteenth century during a revivalist movement in American Protestantism. For the last one hundred years, American evangelicals had their sight set on Palestine not only as missionaries and pilgrims, but also, in the second half of the twentieth century, as supporters of Israeli policies. Throughout this time they waited and anticipated, in line with their biblical beliefs, the second coming of Christ. Many of today's U.S. fundamentalists still adhere to this millenarian theology, according to which the return of the Jews to Palestine is a pre-condition for the appearance of the Messiah. Jews and Israel are merely a stepping-stone in this mythological scheme of things.

Lobbying Congress from this religious biblical ground dates back to this era. William Blackstone, a Chicago Methodist and a prominent figure in the early pro-Zionist Christian movement, was able in 1891 to gather the signatures of forty-three leading congressmen, governors, mayors and industrialists on a petition submitted to then-President Benjamin Harrison asking him to lead an international effort in support of a Jewish state in Palestine. By the 1980s some estimates put the figure of membership in right-wing Christian organizations, listeners to Christian radio stations, and part- or full-time activists as high as 61 million Americans.[9] And by the second Bush administration, right-wing Republican senators and congressmembers represented the most vociferous support for Israel—particularly those from states with infinitesimal Jewish populations. In March 2002, for instance, Oklahoma Senator James Inhofe announced on the floor of the Senate that he supports Israel as a strategic ally, as a roadblock to terrorism, and "because God said so."[10]

The Formation of the Unholy Alliance

It was in the mid-1980s that the American Israel Public Affairs Committee (AIPAC), Israel's major lobbying group on Capitol Hill, started re-aligning itself with the rising right wing in the United States.

8. Silverstein & Scherer, "Born-Again Zionists."
9. Tivnan, p. 182.
10. Silverstein & Scherer, "Born-Again Zionists."

AIPAC correctly understood that the American far right's commitment to Israel was qualitatively different from the conventional support lent by the various U.S. administrations to the Zionist state, support historically based within the U.S. global anti-Soviet strategy. Moreover, the far right paid little attention to Israel's dismal human rights record. An AIPAC insider said :

[W]e are becoming more "neo-conservative." We want to broaden Israel's support to the right—with the people who do not care about what is happening on the West Bank but care a lot about the Soviet Union.[11]

A majority of those people were right-wing Protestant fundamentalists who viewed support to Israel as a key to the political and spiritual survival of the United States. Those Christians were ready to lend support to Israel even after the breakup of the "Evil Empire" because their position was rooted more in theology than in the strategic and defense considerations, even those most ideologically based, of Washington foreign policy elites in the State Department, the Department of Defense or the CIA.

According to Robert Kuttner of *The New Republic,* the benefit was mutual. AIPAC and its controversial links to scores of local pro-Israel PACs started "delivering Jewish financial backing to candidates far to the right of positions that most Jews hold on most issues. Incumbent conservative Republicans have discovered a cynical formula. They have only to demonstrate sufficient loyalty to Israel and they can all but lock out their Democratic challengers from a substantial fraction of Jewish support."[12]

Seeing that Christian right-wing groups have successfully targeted one pro-Israel liberal candidate after another for defeat "because of their positive votes on abortion, civil rights and social spending and war and peace . . . the pro-Israel money has moved well to the right of most Jewish voters."[13] This was combined later with attacks by the traditionally Jewish parts of the lobby— AIPAC, the Council of Presidents of Major Jewish Organizations, and so on —in the explicit targeting of progressive African-American members of Congress who took balanced, rather than one-sidedly pro-Israeli, positions on the Middle East. In 2002 congressmembers Cynthia McKinney of Georgia and Earl Hilliard of South Carolina were defeated against challengers backed by the pro-Israeli lobby.

Many liberal American Jews were disturbed by this alliance between American and Israeli rightists. Liberal Jews, who tend to favor abortion rights, oppose prayers in public schools, and defend the separation of church and state, were

11. Tivnan, p. 181.

12. Quoted in Curtiss, Richard, *Stealth PACs: Lobbying Congress for Control of U.S. Middle East Policy* (Washington, DC: The American Educational Trust), 1996, pp. 81–82.

13. Ibid., p. 82.

alarmed by the right-wing Likud governments in Israel, and by Tel Aviv's Washington lobbyists allied with extreme conservative fundamentalists on these issues. The problem was compounded by the structure of the organized Jewish community, in which a plethora of right-wing organizations committed to a hardline pro-Israeli agenda, largely succeeded in controlling the most influential coalition organizations, AIPAC and the Council of Presidents, using those groups to speak in the name of all Jews.

The fundamentalist agenda, says Robert Zimmerman, president of the American Jewish Congress, threatens "the freedoms that make Jews safe in America."[14] But the AJC's view is not supported by other major Jewish American organizations. The rift goes deep in organizations such as the Anti-Defamation League. Nathan Perlmutter, Director of the Anti-Defamation League of B'nai B'rith, dismissed concerns of liberal Jews about fundamentalist support for Israel saying "Praise God and pass the ammunition."[15]

The dangerous cynicism underlying such an unholy alliance was perhaps best captured by Lenny Davis, former chief of research for AIPAC and later second in command of the Israeli embassy in Washington, who said, "until I see Jesus coming over the hill, I am in favor of all the friends Israel can get."[16]

"All the Friends Israel Can Get"

After Clinton's failure, at the Taba talks in early 2001, to cement his place in history with a follow-up Israel-Palestine photo-op, the Bush presidency initially looked like it might bring some changes in U.S. support for Israel. This was, after all, an oil industry administration, without close ties to Israel, without dependency on the pro-Israeli lobby or on Jewish voters. Even in the first responses to the attacks of September 11, it seemed that the Bush White House might break with long-standing tradition and put some real pressure on Israel. After all, moving against terrorist targets in the Islamic and Arab worlds required maintaining good relations with Arab governments; Sharon's aggressive anti-Palestinian policies could undermine that.

Then the domestic came back into play with the international/strategic. Shortly after the attacks, when Israel launched its brilliantly orchestrated campaign of parallelism, the Bush administration reversed course and embraced Sharon as a long-lost partner. The Israeli line was essentially based on a "now you know how it feels" perspective, linking the terrorist attacks, American victims, and the aggressive U.S. military response to Palestinian attacks, Israeli victims, and the—therefore—legitimacy of Israel's military response. Israel's military occu-

14. Ibid.
15. Tivnan, p. 182.
16. Ibid.

pation, and its continuing violence, had no role in the new U.S.-Israeli "anti-terrorism" partnership.

All of this was made easier by the preeminent characters in the Bush administration—the neo-conservative ideologues for whom defense of Israel was a cornerstone of their worldview. Until September 11, the neo-cons, including Dick Cheney, Paul Wolfowitz, Richard Perle, Lewis Libbey, and more, had to battle the pragmatists grouped around Secretary of State Colin Powell. Both sides appeared to have Bush's ear. But after September 11, backed by Secretary of Defense Donald Rumsfeld, the ideologues and the militarists took over.

These officials were not new to Washington power. While many of them had been out of office throughout the Clinton years (often after serving in the Reagan and first Bush administrations), they had maintained economic power and political influence through several organizations. The Project for the New American Century (PNAC), created at the beginning of the 1990s, gave voice to an aggressive new global strategy crafted for the post–Cold War era, a new U.S. foreign policy based on an unbridled militarism, increased Pentagon budgets and unchallenged unilateralism, starting with the overthrow of several Middle Eastern governments. Their founding document was deemed so extreme that the Republican Party leadership shelved it, distancing themselves from these reckless elements.

Another organization was the Jewish Institute for National Security Affairs (JINSA), where support for an empowered, militarized Israel joined the broader conception of increasing U.S. power and strategic reach. During the Clinton years officials supporting Israel's Labor Party rotated into key positions in the White House, the Pentagon, the State Department, and the National Security Council. They came from pro-Israeli think tanks such as the Washington Institute for Near East Policy, the American Enterprise Institute and elsewhere. In turn, the Bush administration pulled into its centers of power the pro-Likud neo-con hawks of JINSA, PNAC and related institutions.

And after September 11, what had once looked too extreme even for the Republican Party's right-wing leadership suddenly became acceptable: embrace of the notion that there is a military solution to every political problem; the legitimation of preemptive war and first strikes; calls for a new generation of "usable" nuclear weapons; an early obsession with the overthrow of the Iraqi government; and a new and different definition of a "new Middle East." This vision was rooted in a plan for pro-American regimes being imposed on countries after the forcible overthrow of governments in Iraq, Syria, the Palestinian territories (referring to the Palestinian Authority, of course, not to Israel as the occupying power), Iran, even Saudi Arabia itself. And if the consequences included the collapse of the Jordanian monarchy, well, military solutions could be easily imposed there too.

One of the most significant aspects of JINSA is that (despite the name) it is not made up only of Jews. But the JINSA affiliates do hold something in common: power. Their unshakable defense of Israeli strength and militarism reflects a worldview consistent with that of the ideologues within the Bush administration. According to Jason Vest, writing in *The Nation*, "Until the beginning of the current Bush Administration, JINSA's board of advisers included such heavy hitters as Dick Cheney, John Bolton (now Under Secretary of State for Arms Control) and Douglas Feith, the third-highest-ranking executive in the Pentagon. Both Perle and former Director of Central Intelligence James Woolsey, two of the loudest voices in the attack-Iraq chorus, are still on the board, as are such Reagan-era relics as Jeane Kirkpatrick, Eugene Rostow and [Michael] Ledeen—Oliver North's Iran/contra liaison with the Israelis."[17]

It is through JINSA's board that the links between U.S. officials (current and former) and Israel, specifically the Likud Party, become very clear. In a parallel development, some of the same authors of the PNAC paper of 1992 drafted a 1996 version for Israel. Designed as a campaign strategy for then-candidate Bibi Netanyahu, the document was entitled "Making a Clean Sweep," and proposed a new set of Israeli policies including abandoning the [then-viable] Oslo process, telling the Palestinians they would never achieve an independent sovereign state, issuing military threats against Syria and Iran, and moving to make Israel an even greater military power. Beyond the military aspect, "Clean Sweep" also reflected a broader right-wing social and economic agenda, encompassing privatization, tax cuts, and shifting spending even more toward the military. Much of it reflected an Israeli version of the New American Century plan for the United States, centered on increasing military spending and military reach.

And it is also clear that ties to both U.S. and Israeli military contractors link these advisers with currently powerful policymakers. According to Vest, "the behemoths of military contracting are also well represented in JINSA's ranks. For example, JINSA advisory board members Adm. Leon Edney, Adm. David Jeremiah and Lieut. Gen. Charles May, all retired, have served Northrop Grumman or its subsidiaries as either consultants or board members. Northrop Grumman has built ships for the Israeli Navy and sold F-16 avionics and E-2C Hawkeye planes to the Israeli Air Force (as well as the Longbow radar system to the Israeli army for use in its attack helicopters). It also works with Tamam, a subsidiary of Israeli Aircraft Industries, to produce an unmanned aerial vehicle. Lockheed Martin has sold more than $2 billion worth of F-16s to Israel since 1999, as well as flight simulators, multiple-launch rocket systems and Seahawk heavyweight torpedoes. At one time or another, General May, retired Lieut. Gen. Paul Cerjan and retired Adm. Carlisle Trost have labored in LockMart's vineyards. Trost has also sat on the board of General Dynamics, whose Gulfstream subsidiary has a $206 million contract to supply planes to Israel to be used for 'special electronics missions.'"[18]

On the other hand, old-style Israel lobby funds also help bolster JINSA and its allies in and out of government. American real estate mogul Irving Moskowitz,

---

17. Vest, Jason, "The Men from JINSA and CIP," *The Nation*, 15 August 2002.
18. Ibid.

for instance, has been well known for years as the key financier of Ateret Cohanim and other extremist Israeli settler organizations, including the group that engineered the opening of a long-closed tunnel under the Haram al-Sharif in 1996, leading to days of violence and seventy deaths. Not coincidentally, he happens to be a JINSA board member and major donor to both JINSA and its allied Center for Strategic Policy.[19]

The intersection of these pro-Israeli right-wing ideologues, the arms industry, influential institutions and powerful people in government make the question of who are the dogs and who wags the tails essentially moot. When Defense Secretary Donald Rumsfeld speaks dismissively of the "so-called occupied territories" while Ariel Sharon acknowledges the "occupation," the real difficulty of challenging the inextricably tangled U.S.-Israeli alliance becomes frighteningly clear, as does the need to create an entirely new Middle East policy for the United States.

19. Ibid.

Wings

Aurora Levins Morales

Cuba y Puerto Rico son	*Cuba and Puerto Rico*
de un pájaro las dos alas.	*are the two wings of one bird,*
Reciben flores y balas	*receiving flowers and bullets*
en el mismo corazón.	*into the same heart.*

Lola Rodriguez de Tió

Two wings of one bird said the exiled poet
whose words burned too many holes of truth
through the colonial air of a different iron-toothed occupation.
Nothing divides the suffering of the conquered.
Two wings, she said, of a single bird, with one heart between them,
taking bullets and roses, soldiers and prison bars and poetry,
into one pulse of protest. One bird she insisted
as the ship pulled away from San Juan headed for Havana, 1879.

A century later we are still the wounded wing,
fluttering, dragged through the waves, another empire
plucking feathers from living flesh. *White egret among the foam,*
cried another poet, returning after long years in the dry solitude of Spain:
garza, garza blanca. Those ruffled reefs are infested now
with unexploded bombs. Pastures where white birds
still grace the backs of cattle, are dusted with the toxic waste
of rehearsal for invasion, that seeps into the blood of children,
so that cancer is a required course in the high schools of Vieques,
giving a whole new meaning to the term "drop out."
I was born into an occupied country. I am that wing.

What kind of Jew are you, receiving bullets and roses
as if in a Palestinian heart?
I am the Jewish great-great-granddaughter of Puerto Rican slaveholders.
I am the Puerto Rican great-great-granddaughter of Ukrainian socialists.
I am the surviving branch of a family tree split at the turn of the last century
holding the photograph of nameless cousins

who missed the last train to Siberia
and fell into the trenches of summer
as Nazi armies rolled across the farmlands of Kherson.
I am the educated granddaughter of a Puerto Rican seamstress
who never went past the eighth grade,
whose fingers bled into the spandex of sweatshop assembly line girdles,
a long subway ride from the barrios where she lived, the granddaughter
of an electrician wiring battleships in the Brooklyn Navy Yard, of a
 communist studying law at night and serving deli by day, and of a
 social worker
trying to plug the holes in immigrant lifeboats.
I am a daughter of occupation and conquest, of deportation and escape.
I am a daughter of people who were outgunned and refused to die.
I am a colonial subject with a stone in my hand when I listen to the news.
I am a fierce Latina Jew holding out a rose to Palestine.

I am the Jewish grand-niece of a Puerto Rican WWII soldier
cracking up in the bloody Pacific, in the service of an army
that always sent the brown men in first. I am the Puerto Rican cousin
of Jewish evacuees trying to flee eastward, shot in the back
by Ukrainian collaborators who lived just down the road.
I am the daughter of red pacifists married in the year of Korea,
a two-winged child conceived as the Rosenbergs died, born as Lolita
 was shackled into her quarter century of punishment for shooting
 into the air.
I was born Jewish in an occupied Caribbean land, speaking Spanish
with the accent of escaped slaves and hungry coffee laborers,
because my great-grandfather would not fight Japan for the Tsar,
because he evaded yet another imperial draft, and washed up in New
 York City
where barrio meets shtetl, girl meets boy and solidarity was my lullaby.

What kind of independentista are you, to weep for Israeli soldiers
drafted into accepting atrocity as a fact of life,
beating out the ritmo of kaddish for colonialists killed in rightful revolution
on the conga of your caribe heart?
I am the proud cousin of a banned Boricua writer climbing out of his
 deathbed
to raise the flag of Puerto Rico on the third anniversary of the U.S.
 invasion, just two weeks before he died of tb contracted in the bitter
 prison cells of Valladolid.
I am a distant relative of the first woman of Puerto Rico
burned by the Inquisition in the name of Christ, for being a secret Jew.

I am the descendant of hacendados
who worked their own slave children to the bone in tobacco fields
    ripening
over the traces of uprooted plantings of casabe,
and of the pale brown daughters of dark women,
taken into the marriage beds of landholding men,
criada servants deemed good enough for younger sons,
setting their wide cheeks and mouths into their children's bones.
I am the descendant of invaders and invaded,
now riding high on history's wheel, now crushed below,
of those evicted and their village burned,
of those who rode the horses and set the flames.

What kind of song is this? Whose side are you on?
Two wings, I say with the exiled poets of my country
to my dispossessed and dispossessing cousins
in the land it seems that everyone was promised.
Two wings with a single heart between them:
intifada and partisaner, refusnik and cimarron.
Nothing divides the suffering. One bird full of bullets and roses,
one bird with its wounded pinions,
one heart that if it breaks is broken.
I *know* there are two bloody wings,
but it is one bird trying to lift itself into the air,
one bird turning in circles on the ground, because
two wings rising and falling together,
is the forgotten principle of flight. Two wings
torn by tempestuous weather.
One bird struggling into the light.

Jews in America, in Israel, in History: Visions and Re-Visions

Jew vs. Jew:
On the Jewish Civil War
and the New Prophetic

Marc H. Ellis

A t the beginning of October 2000, days after the historic visit of Ariel Sharon
to the Temple Mount in Jerusalem, a visit that initiated the latest round of
Palestinian resistance to the continuing Israeli occupation of Jerusalem, Gaza,
and the West Bank, a rabbi where I live sent the following e-mail message to
her rabbinic colleagues in the United States: "In Waco we have a similar situation to Michael Lerner, though on a local, not national level. Baylor University, a Baptist University which professes to want close ties to the Jewish community,
has a professor, Dr. Marc Ellis, who is unabashedly pro-Palestinian. . . . Things
came to a head for us last week, when he was the only Jew interviewed by any of
the television stations about the Middle East. We are contacting the media to
let them know that he does NOT speak for the Jewish community, and that we
consider this biased coverage. Slanted news coverage is trouble enough, but to
have so much of this driven by Jews, who are either in the media or get media
attention . . . is tragic."

This message is interesting in a variety of ways, not the least of which is its
attempt to define dissenting Jews as outside the Jewish community. The rabbi's
e-mail is clear: she, along with the Jewish community, is *for* Israel; Jews who speak
against Israeli policies are pro-Palestinian and, hence, anti-Israel and the Jewish community itself. The tragedy is clear for all who read the rabbi's message:
good Jews support Israel no matter what its policies are; Jews who dissent from
these policies are hardly Jews at all.

Though this e-mail message can be seen as a personal attack in a local situation where Jews identify their distinction from the surrounding evangelical
culture in negative terms—we are not Christians; we are connected to the larger
Jewish world, we demonstrate our connection to the Jewish world by identification with Israel and by policing Jewish dissidents and Christians who speak out
on the issue—the mention of Michael Lerner signifies a larger issue at hand.

Lerner is known nationally and internationally as a progressive Jewish spokesperson and activist, founder and editor of *Tikkun*, which was begun in 1986 as
an attempt to counter the Jewish community's movement toward neo-liberal
and neo-conservative positions on a variety of political and cultural issues. A
central part of that rightward drift was the increasing centrality of Israel and
Israeli policies to American Jews after the 1967 war. This was confronted by dis-

senting Jews who saw the post-1967 occupation of Palestinian land, an occupation that featured expanding settlements around Jerusalem and in the West Bank, as unjust and destructive of Jewish ethics and tradition.

The first Palestinian intifada, beginning in December 1987, and the ensuing debate within the Jewish world about the Israeli policies of occupation and violent repression of the uprising, catapulted Lerner and *Tikkun* into the national spotlight. With strength of words and vision, Lerner, in a series of strong editorials, castigated Israel and American Jewish leadership for their violence and silence. And more. Lerner characterized the occupation policies of Israel and the brutal suppression of the Palestinian uprising as a betrayal of an inheritance of Jewish values and ethics, as well as a history of suffering, most recently in the Holocaust.

An Evolving Tradition of Dissent

The pages of *Tikkun* were filled with Jewish voices that said no to occupation and betrayal of Jewish values and history. What Lerner exposed—and no doubt by making it public, heightened—was a civil war between Jews, one that would now be played out on the national and international scene. Jewish leadership that wholeheartedly supported Israeli policies or, when questions were raised, counseled silence, would now be met by an articulate and growing number of Jewish dissidents not previously heard by the Jewish establishment or who had been actively discouraged from speaking, even forced, through intimidation, to be silent. What was at stake was the history and future of the Jewish people.

Jewish dissent vis-à-vis Israel had, of course, begun much earlier than the first intifada. At the turn of the twentieth century, Zionism was a decidedly minority movement among Jews, opposed by most religious and secular Jewish organizations in Europe and America. Even during the Nazi period and after, significant portions of Jewish life remained either indifferent toward or actively opposed to the creation of a Jewish state in Palestine. Opposition to a Jewish state was carried even by Zionists who opted for a cultural or spiritual understanding of a Jewish homeland. Hannah Arendt, Martin Buber, and Judah Magnes were among those who opposed a Jewish state even as they understood the importance of a Jewish homeland within Palestine to a Jewish future.

Since the creation of Israel, there have been a variety of dissenting actions and speech that address the hopes and aspirations of the Jewish people—a people that has certainly struggled and suffered in the throes of violence legitimated by religion and nationalism—to end the cycle of violence and atrocity. One thinks here of the soldiers under Yitzhak Rabin's command in the 1948 war who, educated in "cosmopolitan" ways, refused to cleanse Arab villagers from areas that would become part of the new Israeli state. These same soldiers, seeing Palestinians being displaced and forced across the borders, remembered the Jewish exile from Spain as an image which they glimpsed within the Palestinian catastrophe. The record of dissent continued during the Israeli bombing of Beirut in the 1980s, when some Israeli soldiers refused to serve in Lebanon. It accelerated during the Palestinian uprising when other Israeli soldiers saw, in the policy of might and beatings, images of Nazi brutality once carried out against Jews. For many Jews a transposition had taken place in Jewish life: Were Jews, in denying the rights of Palestinians, acting like those who had denied Jewish rights across the millennia?

After the Holocaust and Israel

As the tradition of dissent has grown over the years, Jewish leadership has become increasingly accepting of Israeli policies which, at different times in the last decades, shocked the Jewish world. Two different sensibilities have evolved in Jewish life: one speaks for or at least is silent about Israeli policies; the other increasingly speaks its mind in opposition to Israeli policy.

The al-Aksa intifada has raised the stakes significantly. The initial reports of Israeli tanks and helicopter gunships surrounding and menacing a defenseless civilian population brought a new realization of the ongoing campaign to demean and destroy the Palestinian struggle for dignity and statehood. This comes after almost a decade of peace talks, with the implementation of the Oslo accords constantly delayed and violated, the Rabin assassination, the Netanyahu era, the election of Ehud Barak, with settlements that grow ever bigger and more provocative and bypass roads and tunnels that cut through and around West Bank cities and villages. This second intifada has raised both the consciousness of Jewish dissenters and the rhetoric of Jewish leaders. Even those Jewish dissenters, who accepted Oslo and rebuffed those critical of that agreement who termed it too limited and unjust, have emerged in the shattering of Oslo with a new voice. Rather than policy implementation, they now speak of witnessing to values in the Jewish tradition, values that are being systematically violated. On the other hand, full-page paid advertisements from major Jewish organizations have appeared often in the *New York Times*. They call for Jewish unity in the face of Palestinian aggression and their refusal to accept the "offers" of the Israeli government for a final settlement of the Israeli-Palestinian conflict. Arafat is depicted as a warmonger who places children in harm's way. The bullets they receive from Israeli soldiers are blamed on the Palestinians themselves. In these calls for Jewish unity, the helicopter gunships used by Israel are not mentioned, nor is the closure of towns and cities. Israeli control of electricity and communication, of water and movement of people, as weapons of war, are not mentioned.

For many years dissent tied itself to Jewish innocence. Jews were innocent in suffering *and* empowerment, the argument goes: Zionism is something good, the national liberation struggle of the Jewish people. Israeli policies are sometimes wrong; these specific policies are aberrations and must be opposed. The opposition to certain policies is to bring Zionism and the Jewish state back into line, in a sense to recover their innocence.

Thus the Jewish establishment and Jewish dissenters have been arguing over the same turf—Jewish suffering and Jewish empowerment as innocent. Jewish leadership proclaimed this innocence as self-evident, Jewish dissenters as in need of recovery. Forgotten by both sides is an initial dissent that did not discuss Jewish innocence per se or even claim a right to a homeland uncontested by another people. In the emergency years of the post-Holocaust world, Magnes, Buber and Arendt desired fraternal bonds between Jews and Arabs in a changing Palestine and, whatever the claims of either people, they envisioned a mutual interdependent empowerment. Still, it is important to note that these initial dissenters were Western in their orientation and colonial in their mentality.

The anti-statist views of the early dissenters are important for this evolving tradition of Jewish dissent. Magnes, Buber and Arendt lived before and through the Holocaust and the creation of Israel. Their views of both events were informed by the *before* and *after*—between the before and after of the Holocaust, before and after the establishment of Israel. Thus they could anticipate and react to the formative events of contemporary Jewish history, and though the magnitude of the horror of the Holocaust had not been foreseen by them, their views of the choices before Zionism and the consequences of those choices were prophetic. For them the state itself, Israel as a Jewish state, was a recipe for disaster because of what ensues from the formation of any state. Certainly an insurgent European Jewish state in the Middle East would have extreme and negative ramifications on the Jewish religious and intellectual tradition. If the *raison d'etre* of Jewish life in Palestine became the creation, maintenance and survival of a nation-state, then the very reasons for a Jewish homeland—renewal of Jewish culture and language, social, political and cultural experiments in the postwar world, hope for the survivors of the Holocaust to find a place of peace and harmony, the revival of a an ancient religious community in its particularity but with a universal message—would be destroyed.

Jewish dissenters today come *after* the Holocaust and the formation of Israel. Though they have experienced the consequences of statehood, Jewish dissenters have been unable to articulate this clearly and boldly. Earlier dissenters understood that the state would skew Jewish values until the argument for the recovery of those values would be carried on in their very disappearance from Jewish life. Though contemporary dissenters have experienced this intimately, their inability to directly confront this fact is important. The reason seems to be a fear of being seen as outside the Jewish world or even against it and therefore against one's own Jewishness. Israel as a nation-state thus becomes the litmus test for Jewish loyalty and Jewish empowerment.

Once accepted, these parameters are impossible to push to their ethical conclusion. For if Israel, like any other nation-state, is not innocent, if its own trajectories have less to do with an ancient tradition and the pursuit of an individual and corporate ethical life, if it can, again like any nation-state, only use religion and religiosity for its own purposes, then calling Israel to its Jewishness is a lost battle; its Jewishness can only be dimly perceived as traditional and worthy of discussion in a spiritual way. The Jewishness that can be affirmed, the Judaism that is presently practiced in Israel and among Jewish leadership, is reminiscent of the ties that Christianity has had in nation-states after it was elevated from a persecuted sect to a state religion, that is a Constantinian Christianity that links church and state not only in the religious arena but in the intellectual world as well.

Constantinian Christianity was a new form of Christianity that transformed its witness to legitimation of the state and its policies in return for its elevation to respectability. Though the texts of the tradition and the symbolism of its deepest impulses remained, in fact a new religion evolved that used the subversive message of its early years as a cover for policies and the development of an orthodoxy that would have scandalized the early followers of Jesus. Certain arguments for Christian life, including its suspicion of the state and military, dropped away and were even turned around to an embrace of these arenas. Dissent was remembered only to be taken in by the tradition and transformed into views and visions that often contradicted the initial impulse celebrated by the community.

Many Christians have woken up to this Constantinianism and flee it like a person flees a burning building. Religion in service to the state serves only the state. In the end so much is justified by the state in religious language that the ethical center of any religion is gutted, spoken in words but its essence left behind, enacted ritually and contradicted in practice, until the practitioners themselves recognize that there is little, if anything, left. By that time the hierarchy is firmly ensconced and the dissenters are on the margins.

Isn't this what has happened to Judaism in our time, the embarkation on a Constantinian Judaism in service to the state and to power? And aren't Jewish dissidents in the same position that Christians find themselves in? Of course, the time is shorter as Judaism has developed this sensibility only in the last decades. The scope of Jewish Constantinianism is much smaller as the Jewish population is minuscule and concentrated compared to global Christianity. To be sure, there is also less on the line for Christians than Jews, for the Constantinianism of Christianity has become so widespread and diffused that no one Christian community seems immediately concerned about the other. Nor has the Christian community, at least in the West, come through an experience of suffering like the Holocaust. And Christianity at least pretends to a universality that the particularity of survival and flourishing has long since dissipated from Christian consciousness.

Yet with all of these caveats, the comparison of Constantinian Christianity to Constantinian Judaism is instructive: its arrival brings to an end the ethical precepts of any tradition and embroils the religion in legitimation of state policies that should be opposed. The elevation of that religion produces a leadership that persecutes its own contemporary prophets even as it holds ancient prophets up as part of its contribution to the world. In the end, Constantinianism defines a religion and the particular symbol structure means little. Constantinian Judaism and Christianity are, in essence and certainly in practice, the same religion.

Beyond Dissent

What are Jewish dissenters to do with this conundrum? On the one hand, they seek to argue as Jews, within the Jewish tradition and for a Jewish future. On the other hand, competing for the same terrain as Jewish leadership, dissenters enter into compromise, arguing ethics within a Constantinian Judaism that is beholden to the state and to power. Jewish leadership is fully assimilated to this Constantinianism in Israel and America, and most Jews follow this path to achieve security and affluence. Any ethical challenge, any headway that Jewish dissenters make, will be within a framework acceptable to the leaders of Constantinian Judaism.

Jewish dissidents are permanently within a cycle they did not begin and cannot control. They react rather than chart new directions. This reactive position limits thought and movement. It is always haunted by the powers that be and the accusations that can at any moment be hurled in their direction.

Trying to prove one's Jewishness in this arrangement is to be on the defensive, permanently it seems, and destined to fail the test. For how much more can ethics be challenged than by the wholesale dislocation of a people, aerial bombardments of defenseless cities, closures of towns and villages for weeks and months at a time, assassination squads and torture legitimated by the courts? How long before an ethical tradition is simply declared dead rather than argued for in compromise?

Here, too, it is important to understand that Jewish leadership is not in the main conservative in values or rhetoric. Just the opposite. The Jewish narrative in America, and for that matter in Israel as well, has been liberal in tone and content, even if betrayed in action and policy toward the Palestinians. It is not as if Jewish dissenters have argued with an avowedly conservative elite so a distinction in orientation is clear and unequivocal; liberalism, like Judaism, has been a shared framework. Morality, Jewish tradition, Jewish ethics, Jewish history and liberalism have been a shared universe of discourse.

Sharing this universe and appealing to it, both sides in the Jewish civil war have avoided the hard choices. Jewish leadership does not admit its Constantinianism; Jewish dissenters are not honest about the need to disassociate completely with this new Judaism, what Michael Lerner terms "settler Judaism." In fact both sides shy away from "settler Judaism" even as they embrace such a Judaism in the formation of Israel. Jewish leadership simply closes its eyes to settlers from 1948 on, while Jewish dissenters see settlers only in their post-1967 appearance. Even this is selective because most Jewish dissenters close their eyes to the post-1967 settlers in Jerusalem, preferring to speak about and chastise only the settlements outside of Jerusalem.

A further caveat about Jewish leadership and the complexity of Jewish dissent is crucial. Jewish leadership is most often thought of as found within Jewish organizations like the Anti-Defamation League and rabbinic associations. As important is the network of university-affiliated academics in administration, in Jewish Studies programs, and Holocaust Studies chairs. More than any other group, university-affiliated Jewish administrators and scholars, again mostly liberal in orientation, have stifled debate on university campuses around the country. Competing for their own legitimacy as Jewish scholars, they have often silenced their own voice and voices to the left of their positions. They, too, have been caught in the bind that forces compromise and arguments that twist logic so as to criticize without effectively challenging the dominant establishment. In fact, dissenting Jews, whether identified with the university or identified with *Tikkun,* have not only helped stifle dissent to the left of them, but in doing so have helped shield the Jewish world from a deeper understanding of the dilemmas Jews face as a people and a possible movement beyond the present impasse.

Could it be that Jewish dissent must free itself of the acceptable parameters of Jewish dissent? If this is the case, a hoped-for return to Jewish innocence must be left behind. Competing on the same turf, the competition to define what Judaism and Jewish life is all about must be downplayed. The very hope that Jewish dissent will become defining of Jewish life, the possibility that Jewish dissent will displace the present and become the next Jewish establishment, must be jettisoned.

In short, it may be that the agreed-upon parameters of the civil war, Jew vs. Jew, are obsolete, and can only result in a continuation of a cycle of legitimation and critique that leaves the Palestinian people suffering and the Jewish ethical tradition gutted. Like all renewal movements, Jewish dissenters seek to renew Judaism through calling it back to its best intentions and possibilities. Like all renewal movements, Jewish dissenters function in the shadow of and, to some extent, live off the power of Constantinian Judaism. Constantinian religiosity typically fights this renewal, absorbs part of it, and then claims it as its own even as the critique is transformed and vitiated. This was the fate of Christian reformers, often and later, at least in the Catholic tradition, named saints. Will Jewish dissenters escape this fate, losing the battle they rage while becoming fuel for the continuation and expansion of the very establishment they fight?

Clearly the entire concept of religion and religiosity, the very thrust of rabbinic Judaism, is part of the problem. So much of Jewish dissent, at least the dissent articulated in religious terms, seeks to rework the rabbinic tradition to recover the beauty and ethical sensibility within it. Of course, many Jewish dissenters have left Jewish religiosity all together, speaking their dissent in strictly secular terms. At times another battleground is found, between religious and secular Jewish dissenters.

Wars over Jewish identity multiply further, with secular Jews of different political and ideological persuasions accusing each other of abandoning secular Jewish identity. At the end of the day, one wonders if the very notion of Jewish identity, so hotly contested, is worth fighting over. Much of the fight is retrospective, arguing about what has happened to Judaism and Jewish life, rather than the possibilities of a future. Is this because there is an underlying anxiety that so little of depth of Jewish life is left that a future is not worth arguing over because there is little likelihood of a future?

The New Prophetic

Identity is always problematic, for all peoples, and religious identity is even more problematic, at least in the modern period. Identity is multi-layered and contested and, for Jews, the twentieth century bequeathed a pattern of events that has left Jews in a struggle over Jewish identity. How does a community, scattered and diverse, deal with the suffering of the Holocaust, the creation of Israel, and the ongoing policies of a settler state as it consolidates and expands its power and terrain? Within these events is the compression of the Jewish world from an extended diaspora to the centers of America and Israel and the empowerment of a people that just decades earlier were so weak as to suffer the annihilation of more than a third of its population. And now within the various civil wars of secular and religious Jews, for and against the Jewish establishment, a further displacement of Jews has taken place: Jews of conscience, who refuse the hypocrisy of the Jewish establishment and the compromises of Jewish dissenters, abandon the rearguard arguments about Jewish identity. They flee the Jewish world, even as they act and organize against Israeli policies of displacement and occupation.

Jews of conscience are in an exile that has no expectation of return and, perhaps because of their situation, no possibility of return. Could it be that the Jewish covenant, often invoked and so hotly contested, has fled the precincts of the articulate establishments, whether Constantinian or dissenter? Are these Jews of conscience, without claim or articulation, carrying the covenant into exile with them? Is this the last exile in Jewish history?

Jewish biblical scholars alert us to a continuing tension in Jewish history between prophecy and the canon. It seems, and perhaps this is true today, that each time the canon is nearly closed, and the claims of the prophetic are defined and sealed, there arise those who refuse that closure. Of course, the canon is always contested and constantly evolves, so, rather than being consigned to the biblical era, this drama is played out in every generation. The drama is heightened when a generation lives within and in the shadow of formative events of such magnitude as the Holocaust and Israel. In light of this contemporary history, is it any wonder that the prophetic is so difficult to embrace and articulate?

Despite the difficulty, it is hardly surprising that Jews of conscience are not welcome in the Jewish world. Nor is it surprising that the exile continues to grow as the debate over the canon, the acceptable way of Jewish identification, and the prophetic, the way Jewish life should be lived, is hashed out over and over again *as the displacement, torture and murder of Palestinians continues, even escalates.* It is almost as if Jews in exile realize that the central question of the relation of a nation-state and religious identity is a false question that will be argued for the sake of the Jewish community and Jewish history rather than the burning question of justice for Palestinians for its own sake.

Jews in exile refuse the internal debate because it goes nowhere. It does not lead to Palestinian freedom or a significant dealing with Jewish identity. Rejecting the Jewish civil war as a sophisticated game that will never respond to the fundamental questions, even and especially with a peace agreement that may come into being, Jews of conscience simply leave.

What Jews of conscience seem to be saying to the Jewish establishment and Jewish dissenters is that Jewish history as we have known and inherited it is over. The fight is no longer for Jewish survival or Jewish innocence; the very category of Jewishness is now mired in a quagmire that admits of no resolution or forward movement. The Jewish world as it has been known and inherited is no longer able to provide a future worth bequeathing to the next generation. The argument about identity is really about the spoils of a now-fragmented tradition. That argument takes one so far afield from anything approximating the inheritance of the Jewish ethical tradition that the spoils are not worth inheriting or, over time, reconfiguring. For Jews of conscience a level of hypocrisy has entered Jewish life from which there is no recovery, only a semblance of respectability that Jews reject when a similar reconfiguration is presented to Jews by Christians.

Christianity has long been infected by atrocity but the Jewish struggle, at least over the last two thousand years, has avoided this infection. Now with power, Jewish leadership pursues this infection almost as a badge of honor, a way toward respectability within the halls of empire. Perhaps Jews avoided perpetrating atrocity only because of Jewish powerlessness rather than because of a highly developed ethical tradition. Regardless, Jews of conscience refuse this atrocity as part of a long tradition of Jewish agnosticism toward religious claims that hide injustice. Is this not one of the most ancient of the traditions within Judaism, a refusal of idolatry to the state and to power?

Here the guide can only be the prophetic directed by a conscience honed in history. After Jewish suffering can we cause the suffering of others? Can a Jewish sense of the ethical be twisted with assertion and compromise then trotted out as a distinguishing aspect of the Jewish journey?

Contextualizing the Prophetic

In 1963, Emmanuel Levinas, the French Jewish philosopher, wrote an essay, "Judaism and the Present," in which he discerns the central trajectory of the Judaic sensibility and the role of the Jewish prophet. Judaism, he writes, is a "non-coincidence with its time, within coincidence: in the radical sense of the

term it is an anachronism, the simultaneous presence of a youth that is atten-
tive to reality and impatient to change it, and old age that has seen it all and is
returning to the origins of things." Of the prophetic within Judaism, Levinas
writes that the "most deeply committed man, one who can never be silent, the
prophet, is also the most separate being, and the person least capable of becoming an institution. Only the false prophet has an official function." Levinas
concludes his discussion of Judaism and the prophetic with this haunting and
perceptive challenge: "But this essential content [of Judaism and the prophetic]
cannot be learned like a catechism or summarized like a credo. . . . It is acquired
through a way of living that is a ritual and heartfelt generosity, wherein a human fraternity and an attention to the present are reconciled with an eternal
distance in relation to the contemporary world. It is an asceticism, like the training
of a fighter."

This summation of Judaism and the prophetic, this connection of the two
that cannot be severed without maiming, is for Levinas the essence of the Judaic and its contribution to the world. On the threshold of the twenty-first century, it is at one and the same time in danger of disappearing *and* reappearing
with incredible force. Constantinian Judaism is its disappearance in an announced
Jewish form; Jewish dissenters raise the Judaic in a fascinating and compromised
form; Jews of conscience testify to its survival without being able to articulate
this sensibility in symbol or meaning.

The procession of Judaism and the prophetic—this Judaic sensibility that,
according to Levinas, refuses idols, mystery and magic—accompanies these Jews
of conscience into exile. Determinedly agnostic toward eschatological claims
made by religion and the state, and refusing a pre-destined and confined pattern of worship and loyalty, Jews of conscience proceed into an uncertain future. The question of symbolic representation to self and others, of fulfilling
and passing the tradition down to their children, of proclaiming a special status or even deriving an ascendant status from the popularity of Judaism and
Jewish life in our time, remain unaddressed by Jews in exile.

Unlike Jewish dissenters, who always leave the door open for a return and
an inheritance of Jewish establishment life, Jews of conscience are far afield,
without signposts or destination. Holocaust is rarely discussed and Israel is seen
as a lost land, foreign territory, as other nation-states, including those within
which these Jewish exiles live. Of course, there are Jewish exiles within Israel
as well, and their voices are crucial to this exile, often arguing for the creation
of an Israel/Palestine that privileges neither religious affiliation nor ethnic identity.

It is as if the two central events of contemporary Jewish life can no longer be
remembered or raised because both have been betrayed. A silence is counseled
and practiced, lest a further betrayal occur. In some ways, Jews of conscience
embody what lies behind the civil war of the Jewish establishment and Jewish
dissenters, thus the exile. In other ways, Jews of conscience have left behind
this civil war because they see the war itself as avoiding the deeper challenges.
A Judaism and the prophetic, interpreted and guided by conscience, cannot

be so compromised in action and embroidered in militant and flowery language. Infected by atrocity, the Judaic limps along, is wounded and consorts with a Constantinianism of the establishment or even the dissenters. And yet what religion, culture or political tradition is without this wounding? Is it not a utopian projection, a wishful thinking and romanticized rhetoric that abandons the civil wars that abound in every tradition and culture? Do those in exile simply wash their hands of responsibility and complexity? Release from suffering and the ethical management of power are the engines of all traditions and systems that survive in the world. Here Jews of conscience are faulted by those who remain, hands dirty, in the fray. Is the exile a refusal of the challenge, a pretense to innocence where none is possible, an abandonment of the political world while others remain?

The suspicion of the prophetic in the world is highlighted here. The possibility of the Judaic sensibility, holding in tension the contemporary and the ancient, being present and absent, birthing and maintaining those "who can never be silent" and who are the "least capable of becoming an institution," is now derided. Even in the academy where the prophets are studied endlessly and held up as models of fidelity and religiosity, the possibility of contemporary prophets is downplayed. Those who embody these ancient understandings today, whose lives are fueled by them, are often ridiculed when the prophetic claim is made on their behalf. It seems a title too lofty, raising them above others, especially those who struggle in the "real" world. And after all, what would happen to the situation of Jews and Judaism, to the memory of the Holocaust and the security of Israel, if these situations were unattended by *realpolitik*? This high designation is often seen as egotistical. Is not the claim of one of truth over against the false, and can that claim be made in any arena, especially one fraught with so much complexity and anxiety as the Jewish path in the world?

Surely the prophetic has always been maligned in the present, the words of the prophet marginalized when they are spoken. Movements that carry the prophetic word have, in the main, been seen as forms of abandonment and betrayal. Religious establishments and dissenters within its framework have a vested interest in marginalizing the prophetic.

The biblical canon, as it is written and adopted by the community over time, also contributes to this marginalization. For the canon itself, preserving (and rewriting) the Pentateuch and the Prophets, reading them back and forth as a tension and corrective, the very reading of the texts on a regular basis in an established liturgical setting already decontextualizes and vitiates the hard demands of the raw experience found in both sections of the Torah. The biblical canon as it comes to be seals the prophetic in a way that the prophets, even those parts of the community who chastised and persecuted the prophets, would find difficult to recognize. Does that mean that the prophetic is permanently sealed?

Over the last two thousand years rabbinic Judaism has held sway and the canon it adheres to has been in force. In a situation of diaspora, at least in a European context, of an adversarial Christianity and relative powerlessness, it made sense to maintain the tension of the canon, a tension characterized by chosenness, wandering, suffering, study and prayer. Rabbinic Judaism is a Judaism of textuality and hope framed by a larger society that at best tolerates the presence of Jews, at worst seeks their removal.

Though it is often thought that the Holocaust and the questions it raised about God and powerlessness are the prime reasons for the breakdown of rabbinic Judaism, as important is the emergence of Jewish power in America and Israel and the end of the adversarial character of Western Christianity. The emergence of the Jewish world into a history of power and expansion, and now without the ongoing experience of ghettoization, rabbinic Judaism lost its contextual grounding, and, correspondingly, the canonical texts of Judaism, formed, affirmed, and studied only within rabbinic Judaism, lost their hold on Jews and Judaism.

The arrival of Holocaust theology after the Holocaust and the creation of Israel testifies to this process whereby rabbinic Judaism becomes a memory to be reflected upon. Here, rabbinic Judaism becomes a lost world of beauty and limitations; the Torah becomes a place of challenge where the very claims and tensions of the text are used as springboards for a radical questioning of God and God's fidelity found there. It is only a small step, then, to move outside of the new tension that Holocaust theology creates with rabbinic Judaism. Holocaust theology becomes dominant even, and perhaps because, it preserves aspects of the rabbinic, but since this is a retrospective preservation, new meanings arrive in Jewish consciousness that play off the old. In rabbinic Judaism, God chooses the Jews; in Holocaust theology, Jews choose Jews because Hitler played God. In rabbinic Judaism, God provided a promise to Israel that would come and go according to Jewish behavior and loyalty to God and God's ways; in Holocaust theology, the promise, especially of Jewish survival, flourishing and empowerment, has to be seized by Jews regardless of divine acknowledgment and sometimes in spite of God's absence.

Yet even here the innocence of Jews and Jewish life is preserved, indeed heightened by God's inability to protect Jews and the Nazi attempt to annihilate the Jewish people. In Holocaust theology the prophetic remains unannounced in specific terms or figures, at least as traditionally recognized by the rabbis. Rather, the prophets become the Holocaust theologians themselves—Elie Wiesel, a survivor of Auschwitz, for example, or those who further Jewish survival and empowerment, such as David Ben-Gurion, the first prime minister of Israel. As a bulwark of the state of Israel, America itself becomes part of the prophetic impulse in the post-Holocaust world, as does the Jewish community in America, especially after the 1967 war, because it unifies and mobilizes behind Israel without question or hesitation. Here Israel is the engine of the prophetic, the new center of the canon that is invoked with a regularity that is reminiscent of the cycle of Torah readings. A new Torah comes into being, with the tension in the traditional canon replaced by an alternating rhythm of suffering and empowerment in the contemporary world. Of the ancient Torah and the rabbinic framework, only that which speaks to the Holocaust and Israel is relevant. The ancient bends to the contemporary or is rejected.

Neither the rabbinic nor Holocaust eras, both responding to their own contexts, allows room for the prophetic without restraint. Both begin as subversive and insurgent theologies, only to become orthodoxies that diminish and refuse the context that evolves within their own ascendancy. The rabbinic initially refuses the Holocaust as a category that is religiously charged with depth and consequence; Holocaust theology refuses the critique of Jewish empowerment as worthwhile of consideration. The rabbinic refuses contemporary history of suffering and empowerment as defining; Holocaust theology refuses to acknowledge the arrival of Constantinian Judaism.

Sealing the Prophetic

The question remains: What is the prophetic critique of empowerment? If the rabbinic is subordinate to the events of Holocaust and Israel, and Holocaust theology masks the arrival of Constantinian Judaism, what resources are there for the prophetic? Theology is contextual; it arises in history to meet the needs of the present. Once subversive, these theologies give rise to orthodoxies that seek to fend off the meaning of contemporary events that challenge their hegemony. Each orthodoxy uses elements of the tradition that were once radical. Now they are used to buttress power.

Challenges to authority are always fraught with danger and accusation; with a small people concentrated in few areas and surrounded by powerful religions, cultures and militias, the stakes are high. For the Jewish community, a community that has certainly known danger, the Holocaust and the situation of Israel in its formative years only increase this sense of fragility. The creation of a nation-state, by its very nature an entity that aspires to permanence, represents a sea change in the tenuous relationship of religion, ethnicity and nationality that has characterized so much of Jewish history.

Though the emphasis on nationality in a structured and bounded way is not foreign to Jewish life, it is foreign to the Judaism and Jewishness known and practiced for the last two thousand years. In fact, it would be better understood to see Jewish nationality as a phenomenon of ancient Israelite life, rarely embodied, fiercely contested, and ultimately forsaken for reasons of political and religious intrigue and breakdown.

Though the biblical narrative is complex and its historical accuracy suspect, as a constitutional document that is foundational to rabbinic and Holocaust theology, its power is evident. The rabbis use the Talmud to interpret and determine the Bible's applicability to Jewish life. Holocaust theologians use both the Bible and Talmud to reinterpret Judaism and Jewish life after the Holocaust and the creation of the state of Israel. Yet the thrust of both the rabbis and the Holocaust theologians remain with the Jewish world as unempowered and suffering even after empowerment is achieved and suffering is diminished. Thus the canon is seen as internal Jewish discussion about leadership, God's will, historical events that affirm and/or contradict the covenant and the destiny of the Jewish people. Though the state of Israel emerges as a force within the era of Holocaust theology's argument with and ascendancy over rabbinic Judaism, its presence as a real political force with its domestic and foreign policy is almost never addressed.

Only in the last phase of Holocaust theology are the ethics of Jewish power discussed, and this as a rearguard defense of an Israel undergoing a relentless critique by Jewish dissenters over the invasion of Lebanon in the early 1980s and the policy of might and beatings instituted to crush the Palestinian uprising in the late 1980s and early 1990s.

In an era when the commanding voice of Jewish life issues not from Sinai but from Auschwitz, and when the central religious commandment of our time is empowerment rather than the critique of power, the prophetic must be disciplined and relegated to a secondary status. For, the argument goes, the unintended consequences of the prophetic demand, applied to the state of Israel, can only lead to the destruction of Israel and thus, a second Holocaust. Jewish life takes precedence over the prophetic and the ethics of Jewish power. After the Holocaust, no one, not even God, can override the Jewish nation-state in understanding and maintaining this mission.

In fighting this ban on the prophetic, Jewish dissenters are in a difficult, perhaps impossible bind. Like the Holocaust theologians, they affirm the end of the rabbinic era, at least rabbinic Judaism as it was practiced in Jewish history. Jewish dissenters affirm the Holocaust and Israel as central and the Holocaust functions as providing the need for Israel as well as its calling to embody justice for Palestinians. After all, if the suffering of the Holocaust justifies Israel as a nation-state for the survivors, it also mandates the refusal to cause others to suffer. The danger of Israel causing others to suffer is the danger of losing a mandate for Israel itself. For how to justify the empowerment of a people because of their suffering if in that empowerment another people is denigrated and displaced?

Clearly, the critique by Jewish dissenters of Israel is limited to the post-1967 occupation of the West Bank and Gaza and the "aberrational" policies that followed. In their view, despite the suffering caused the Palestinians in the creation of Israel, Jews had no choice but to found a nation-state after the Holocaust. Like Holocaust theologians, Jewish dissenters limit the prophetic in time and tone. They agree with each other that the undermining of Israel's *raison d'etre* and the power to maintain its existence is an unpardonable sin to be punished with excommunication from the Jewish world.

Though Holocaust theologians and Jewish dissenters agree on the arena and limits of disagreement, Jewish dissenters have over time retreated to the rabbinic framework in order to critique Holocaust theology. Here Talmudic interpretation is found again, mixed with a new-age sensibility, and the hard judgments and theological intervention of the prophets and God are eclipsed. Jewish dissent is a renewal Judaism that seeks to recover aspects of the Jewish tradition that have been left to languish by Holocaust theologians. The deep questions about God raised by the Holocaust are mixed and the developers of the textual reasoning movement, a later branch of Jewish dissent, are moving beyond the events of Holocaust and Israel completely.

When the question of God is left behind, at least in Judaism and Jewish life, events cannot be far behind. The original impetus of Jewish dissent in confronting the abuse of Israeli power, to argue from the Holocaust remains, but the need for resources to argue the depth of Jewish life, thus the recovery of the rabbinic in an age of Jewish empowerment, increasingly leave behind history. Thus Jews have reentered history with a power and vengeance unknown since the rabbinic has been in place.

In other words, Jewish dissent has argued from contemporary events and from the rabbinic tradition and within the limits agreed upon within the Jewish civil war. To do this the prophetic has had to be sealed even as it seemed on the precipice of being revived in the Jewish and non-Jewish world alike.

A New Voice

Has this sealing of the prophetic in an age of Jewish empowerment actually taken place? Has the suspicion surrounding the claims of the prophet taken hold? How is the prophetic to be discerned today? Do contemporary Jewish prophets need to meet a litmus test, hearkening back to the ancient Hebrew prophets or meeting the stringent, if not impossible, requirements of Holocaust theologians and Jewish dissenters? Do prophets have to claim inspiration by God today as they did in ancient times? Do they need to promise safety and flourishing in the land of promise if the people return to God's commandments? In short, do the prophets of contemporary life have to speak within a context that is not their own or within a civil war that seeks to tie the prophetic voice to an empowerment that dislocates another people?

The context of the prophetic today is empowerment and an assimilation to the state and power hitherto unknown in Jewish history. At the same time, religious language, including the language of the Bible, is alluded to by those in power. That same language is used by Jewish dissenters. Their struggle to become the next Jewish establishment also demonstrates an assimilation to modernity, albeit with certain divergent understandings of the pace and terms of that assimilation. It is not as if Jewish dissenters are in exile, passing a prophetic judgment that, if accepted, will pave the way for their return. Return itself is suspect and comes within a nation-state setting, which Holocaust theologians and the Jewish establishment uphold, while Jewish dissenters critique on its margins. The return in the form of a nation-state limits its ability to fulfill even the compromise that the dissenters argue for, as the forces for justice in domestic and foreign policy of any state are typically on the margins.

Insofar as the dissenters still hold out the possibility that the Jewishness of Israel is determining rather than the imperatives and tensions of the nation-state itself, then they are permanently in denial. Within the return has come a disenchantment with the nation-state itself, among Jews in Israel and beyond, and an exile within Israel is forming. Contrary to the Jewish establishment, Holocaust theologians and Jewish dissenters, the diaspora aspect of Jewish life is reasserting itself at the very moment when many Jews call for the end of the diaspora in light of the Holocaust and Israel.

What does this reassertion of the diaspora mean for Jewish life and for the prophetic? Does it mean that Judaism is fundamentally diasporic in its sensibility and that the tensions found in its canonical text make it almost impossible to maintain a faithful religiosity in a nation-state claiming Jewish affiliation? In terms of the prophetic, the promise of land, the threat of exile and the hoped-for return, while within the canon, have been so throughly disciplined by the rabbis and compromised by the actualities of power that the cycle seems to have runs its course. The prophetic has been found within the canon and has now been lifted from it, shorn of certain aspects and deepened in others. Even the claim of God's instrumentality and voice are muted. Does this mean that the very source of the prophetic and the very claims of the prophets can no longer be made?

A new voice has appeared. And most often the reassertion of the diaspora is not found in the rabbis or the dissenters who seek to reclaim Jewish innocence by averting their eyes or washing their hands of the Holocaust and Israel. Religious language itself has become so compromised that the very notion of religiosity, no matter how beautifully rendered and appealingly presented, is anathema.

The new voice of the prophet is therefore doubly hidden, unable to skirt the loss of innocence by abandoning history and Jewish complicity in the dislocation of Palestinians and the destruction of Palestine, and unable to travel with a community that hides its power in religious words and song. Since God has been used and abused in this process, the new voice has difficulty with the very concept of God. What could one expect from the prophetic who has barely survived the use of religion by Constantinian Christianity, only to be pursued by the God of Constantinian Judaism?

The arrival of helicopter gunships as the witness of the Jewish people, as central to Jewish life as the Torah once was, and the gathering of millions of Jews in a nation-state that in its creation caused a catastrophe for the Palestinian people, do not demonize Jewish history or relegate it only to a colonial and imperial power. The militarization of Jewish life and thought can be recognized and opposed without condemning the struggles and limitations of Jewish history as foretold through the biblical canon or a history of rejection and ghettoization. The idea that a people's history is uni-directional, without evolution of thought and practice, and without choices that have been made and can be made again, is a form of determinism and racism that others have used against Jews and Jews have used against others. So, too, the idea of separation of peoples as desirable and permanent for the protection and projection of identity. That Jewish history has come to an end as we have known and inherited it does not mean that Judaism, the very touchstone of the Judaic, has lost its force in the world. It only means that the contemporary expression in Jewish life masks a deeper sensibility that in its renewed expression cannot be expressed in language identifiably Jewish.

Militarization of religious discourse, like the militarization of social and political discourse, does not vitiate core values or witness. On the contrary, it heightens the need for such expression even as it severs the language and conceptual framework that has been the vehicle for its expression. Thus the Jewish exile without religious language is absolutely to be expected. It is inevitable that after the experience of Constantinian Christianity, the refusal of Constantinian Judaism in its starkest and most consistent form should be found among secular Jews of conscience who have come into solidarity with the Palestinian people.

For some these exiles are an example of abandoning the difficult path of empowerment and the language that path could embrace beyond oppression. But the experience, borne out again during the al-Aksa intifada, is that operating within is simply attempting to hold the line on the amount of oppression, the percentage of loss of Palestinian land and freedom, the degree to which militarization of Jewish life will be tolerated.

The cycle of violence will remain, between Jews and Palestinians and within the Jewish world. The moral force will always be usurped by power, held in abeyance when unneeded and called in the voice of loyalty when required. The prophetic will never be free. Rather, helicopter gunships at the ready, the construction of the "security" wall around the Palestinian population of the West Bank—unmentioned by diplomats and the Jewish establishment, intended to seal off and permanently ghettoize Palestinians—continues unabated. This concrete wall stands over twenty feet high, ringed by barbed wire and sniper towers. It should remind Jews of other times and places in Jewish history, and it stands now at the center of Jewish life, defining us as a people who have chosen violence, complicity and silence.

Some time ago I suggested that we replace the Torah in the Ark of the Covenant with helicopter gunships. Since military power defines Jewish life, we should be honest about what we worship—power and might. At the most meaningful moment of worship, we bow before that which secures us. Once it was the covenant and Torah; now it is helicopter gunships and the wall. And what of the soldiers in the sniper towers? Do they protect the Jewish people like the Torah was to protect us? Do they guard the covenant? The Jewish people? Do they guard God?

At this point in our history, only the free prophets can point the way forward. Their power is limited, to be sure, and the cycle of violence will, at least for the foreseeable future, continue. In this cycle more Palestinians, and some Jews, will die. Those deaths will be accompanied by the delay of freedom for Palestinians, and the long and eventful history of Jewish suffering and struggle will be stripped of meaning. The free prophets have no power to grant this freedom or to salvage this history, only to witness the possibility of another way that joins Palestinians and Jews in a bond that brings forth life rather than death.

Jewish Days and Nights

Adrienne Rich

Every day in my life is a Jewish day. Muted in my house of origin, Jewishness had a way of pressing up through the fissures. But only in my college dormitory years did it become a continuous conversation, as Israel was declared a nation-state, Brandeis University was founded, the first private university committed to diversity. (The Holocaust went almost unmentioned in those late 1940s–early 1950s of postwar optimism and amnesia.) On a first date I was taken for a walk by an intense young man who talked about Kafka, and whose first name was the same as my father's. Too intense, it felt; I had been deciding that at college I would be "normal," not "special."

Jewishness was muted in my house of origin but the sense of specialness was not: that house was—intensely—different from the homes of my middle-class, non-Jewish friends. For one thing it was full of books. I started off intellectually in my father's eclectic library, which included Maimonides and Dostoevski, Spinoza and Carlyle, Dante and Darwin, Edwin Arnold's *The Light of Asia* and Oscar Wilde's poems, Ibsen and William Blake, Heine and Cervantes and Sigrid Undset, a set of Chekhov's stories and a big blue volume of the *Trial of Jeanne d'Arc*. Medical books (he was a pathologist) were on the lowest shelves; books deemed unfit for young eyes stored high up under the ceiling—an unexpurgated edition of the *Thousand and One Nights*, a manual for *Ideal Marriage*, both revelatory (once I was able to get at them) about heterosexual erotics. No Freud, no Marx; Veblen's *Theory of the Leisure Class*, a title that caught my eye but did not hold me. Also Bernard Shaw's *The Intelligent Woman's Guide to Socialism and Capitalism*, but since in my teens I had not yet heard of either system I passed on that interesting title.

I'm remembering a library I was foraging in between 1938 and 1947, accumulated since my father's youth. So every day in my life even then was, in fact, a Jewish day, little as I thought about it.

Because the freedom of that library—whatever its limitations—let me know that it's possible and necessary to be interested in everything: Hindu mythology, the mud-blotted villages of Chekhov's peasants in Tsarist Russia, the sound of an eighteenth-century English poem (*I wander through each charter'd street / Near where the charter'd Thames doth flow*) or Bible cadences: *Would to God I had died for thee, O Absalom, my son, my son;* and the French Revolution. To assume that philosophy, history, foreign literatures in translation, novels, plays, poetry of many kinds, belonged together in one room of the mind. That there are many worlds with many texts worth reading—this included my father's admiration for Arab culture, partly "orientalist" but with deep respect for its learning, especially its medicine, its architecture, its dignity.

Elsewhere I have described my father as an "assimilated Jew." He was also a Southerner, born in Birmingham, Alabama, to parents (Ashkenazic and Sephardic) who had reason to be careful about their Southern Christian neighbors. But I believe that in his mind, for various reasons, every day of his life was a Jewish day. It was also a day of thinking about science, the description of objective phenomena, the relation of disease to its environment—micro and macro. During most of my childhood, for ten years, besides teaching medical students and running a department, he was writing a comprehensive text on tuberculosis. His promotion to full professor was held up by anti-Semitism (the Johns Hopkins School of Medicine, modeled on the German academic system, had never had a Jewish department chair).

These memoiristic paragraphs are my way of suggesting that a Jewish day can have many dimensions. When I think—daily—about American Jews and Israel, about Zionism and the Middle East, about intellectual and political life in this country and elsewhere, I start from there. A library. An attitude.

The Israeli novelist Shulamith Hareven, born in Europe, has described herself as more Levantine—by disposition and sympathies—than Ashkenazic Israeli:

> Authentic Levantism means the third eye and the sixth sense. It is the keen sensitivity to "how," the knowledge that "how" is always more important than "what"; therefore every true artist is a kind of Levantine. It means a perpetual reading between the lines, both in human relations and in political pronouncements—an art no Israeli political leader has yet succeeded in acquiring. . . . Levantism . . . is the tacit knowledge that different nations live at different ages, and that age is culture, and that some nations are still adolescent, among them, quite often, Israel. And it is the bitter experience that knows that everything—every revolution, every ideology—has its human price, and there is always someone to pay it. It is the discerning eye, the precise diagnosis, that sees the latent narcissist in every ideologue. It is the joke at his expense, and the forgiveness.

What Hareven is describing is the dynamic life of what in the United States we woodenly term "multiculturalism," giving it an ideological salute with little sense of how it might be, has been, lived, over centuries, not in the Middle East only, along rivers and trade routes, in villages and cities and in the exchange of letters and manuscripts, medicinal herbs and culinary spices, surgical and musical instruments, poetry and dance, food and seeds and attitude.

But this *is* what Jews have lived, sometimes turning outwardly toward it (perforce if in covert resistance—the Marranos), sometimes assuming that an intellectually vibrant dominant culture (Enlightenment Germany) could absorb us harmlessly,[1] sometimes living theocratic, hemmed-in, separatist, reductions of Eastern European Judaism (Mea She'arim, Williamsburg). Yet diaspora—a multifaceted condition—means never always, or anywhere, being just like other Jews. It means class and cultural difference, dissension, contradiction, different languages and foods, living in different ages and relationships to tradition, world politics and the "always/already" of anti-Semitism.

Edmond Jabès:

"Where do you come from, brother with the white face?"
"I come from that white part of the world where I was not."

"Where do you come from, brother with the dark skin?"
"I come from that black part of the world where I was not."

"Where do you come from, brother with the pale face and bent back?"
"I come from the boundless ghetto where I was born."[2]

Hareven ends her essay,

I am a Levantine because I see war as the total failure of common sense, an execrable last resort. And because I am a Levantine, all fundamentalists on all sides, from Khomeini to Kahane, will always want to destroy me and all Levantines like me, here and in the neighboring countries.[3]

Beyond the loss of millions of minds in the death camps, I wonder if there has been anything more impoverishing to Jewish ethical and intellectual culture in the second half of the twentieth century than the idea of Jewish sameness, Jewish unanimity, marching under one tribal banner. (Dissidence and argument are part of all human existence, in no way exclusively Jewish. But they have been acutely characteristic of Jewish life, political or religious, socialist or Talmudist: the question that begets a question.) This orthodoxy, relating to Jewishness

1. "Our enemies have never all at the same time persecuted us. So we have, now and then, found protection with a generous nation. But what a cruel game over the millennia, to save us a few relays on our inevitable march around the earth. –Reb Bosh." Rosmarie Waldrop, tr., Edmond Jabès, *The Book of Questions*, vol. I. Middletown, CT: Wesleyan University Press 1976, p. 138.

2. Jabès, p. 139.

3. Shulamith Hareven, *The Vocabulary of Peace: Life, Culture and Politics in the Middle East*. San Francisco: Mercury House, 1995, pp. 82–83, 86. For a deeper critical and historical exploration, see Ammiel Alcalay, *After Jews and Arabs: Remaking Levantine Culture*. Minneapolis: University of Minnesota Press, 1993.

and Israel, has long prevailed in self-declared mainstream American Jewish circles (centering around synagogues and Jewish philanthropies), and has been received—indeed, welcomed in many quarters—as the official Jewish voice.[4] It has framed such concepts as Zionism; the absolute historical uniqueness of the Final Solution (hideously unique in some ways, in other ways a successor and predecessor of other genocides); on the representative character of European Jewish experience, whether in western or eastern Europe (a historical ignorance or marginalizing of Jewish histories and cultures in those parts of the world colonized by Christian Europe). This Eurocentrism has been absurdly parochial (Hareven notes American-born Golda Meir's horror at the Middle Eastern—Levantine—food she found Israelis eating), racist even toward other Jews, and disastrously blind and deaf to those non-Jews whose fates in suffering were and are linked to Jewish fates (as in "a land without a people for a people without a land"). The history of Zionism itself, within Europe, as a much-debated and debatable strategy, has been conveniently submerged. Israel itself, and U.S. military aid to Israel, have until recently been untouchable by controversy or criticism.

Clare Kinberg, a longtime activist for justice within several Jewish communities, and a founding editor of the Jewish feminist journal *Bridges,* has told this story:

> Recently I was speaking with some younger activists about the deep divisions within the Jewish community, and the difficulty of expressing a "peace with justice" agenda within Jewish settings in the U.S. The experience of younger activists is that the last two years of explosive violence in Israel have so terrorized the [U.S.] Jewish community that any sympathy for Palestinian suffering is equated with betrayal. The Jewish community has never been so divided, the young activists told me. My perspective is a bit different.
>
> In the early 1980s, at a public meeting with the Israeli consulate at the St. Louis Jewish Community Center, I asked a question based on my reading of former Jerusalem Deputy Mayor Meron Benevisti's "five minutes

---

4. "There is no elected body that is authorized to speak on behalf of American Jews. The Conference of Presidents of Major Jewish Organizations, with a right-of-center orientation, has presumed to fill that vacuum, and they have consistently supported the policies of right-wing Israeli governments in the name of American Jews. The American Israeli Public Affairs Committee (AIPAC) exists for the purpose of lobbying Congress to support Israeli governmental policies and actions. These oligarchies have persistently reduced Israel to their ideological preferences by ignoring its critical opposition...One might have hoped that religious Jews who pray several times a day for peace and who affirm the traditional teachings about the supreme worth of human life would rise up against the subjugation and humiliation of the Palestinians. Most regrettably the opposite has been the case." (Rabbi Ben-Zion Gold, "The Diaspora and the Initifada" in *Boston Review,* Vol. 27 #5, October/November 2002.)

to midnight" thesis: Do you think Jewish settlement on the West Bank might make it harder for Jews and Palestinians to eventually reach a negotiated agreement? For this question, I was spit on and physically chased from the room.

Kinberg goes on:

Now, twenty years later, my question is mundane. A November 2002 survey of American Jews revealed that 51.7 percent supported a solution to the conflict on the basis of the Clinton Proposals—two states, evacuation of most settlements, withdrawal to the 1967 border with adjustments, and a shared capital in Jerusalem . . . Twenty years ago mere mention of ideas such as this landed and branded you outside the community.

Ignorance—or suppression—of the Jewish tradition of secular heretics and radicals who have repeatedly emerged at the crossroads of culture and thought. An idolatry of certain select aspects of Jewish experience at the expense of others. An American Jewish default toward the Holocaust when politically challenged, a tendency to privilege Jewish suffering over all the sufferings of human history. A pulling away from centuries of Jewish conversation about justice, ethics, human rights, property, our obligations to others, toward Israel-centric chauvinism, fundamentalist ideas of blood and soil. These have been part of the price paid for middle-class Jewish American identity—and for the problematic and controversial "whiteness" of American Jews, the idolatry of class success that has disidentified itself from American class and racial struggles.

That intellectual price reveals itself where neoconservative Jews accept Christian Identity fundamentalists as their "pro-Israel" allies[5] or where Jewish students on university campuses are prompted to treat critiques of Israel and the occupation or protests against the unholy alliance between the Bush and Sharon governments as anti-Semitism, pure and simple. Anti-Semitism, crude and subtle, certainly exists on campuses. Universities are not charmed moral spaces. But to reduce every question to anti-Semitism is to become infected with anti-Semitism's toxic spirit. (Not to do so is surely difficult for young Jews raised in the pro-Israel monologue, facing controversy and politics perhaps for the first time. I well remember arguing politics out of my father's mouth, at college, not really wanting to know that there were other arguable positions of which I hadn't a clue.) It is of course scalding to be called a "self-hating Jew" if you won't name yourself a Zionist. It's also a psychologizing pseudo-diagnostic label for a real, historical political position.

---

5. "The Zionist Organization of America recently presented its State of Israel Friendship Award to Pat Robertson, who has declared America to be a 'Christian nation' and believes in the conversion of the Jews after the Second Coming." (*The Nation*, January 6, 2003, p. 8.)

The ideas of Jews like Marx and Rosa Luxemburg fired a Jewish generation who were mostly non-Zionist, believing that if social revolution could ignite
throughout the world there would be less and less room for anti-Semitism in a
socialist international community. Many of that Eastern European generation
emigrated to America to vitalize labor, antiracist and socialist movements in
the United States. But even Zionist pioneers, as the Marxist historian Isaac
Deutscher points out, were imprinted with revolutionary socialist ideals which
they carried to Palestine: ideas of egalitarian community, of mending the division between mental and manual labor.

Writing in the '50s and early '60s of a very new Israel, Deutscher remarks
that as a young Marxist he had been anti-Zionist; after the Final Solution he
described himself as a "non-Zionist"—a position he would argue with leading
Israelis including Ben-Gurion and Moshe Sharett. Critical of nationalism, recognizing Zionism's inevitable realization at the end of World War II, he was
certainly taken with Israel's energies and contradictions; he felt the utopian,
collective, secular attractions of the kibbutz and also saw its role as military outpost:
"The bastions of Israel's Utopian socialism bristle with Sten-guns." He did not
minimize Israeli danger; his sense of the meaning of Palestinian dispossession
and displacement now seems tone-deaf for an internationalist. (As was common in the 1960s, he recognized no Palestinians, only Arabs in general.) He
also noted that Israel's economy, only partly because of Arab boycotts, had virtually no base apart from American Jewish donations and U.S. aid.

I first read Isaac Deutscher's *The Non-Jewish Jew* in 1982, a time of newly re-
minted left Jewish identity in the United States, of a Jewish feminism trying to
locate itself in multiracial feminist identity politics. Into this burst the massacres
in Sabra and Shatila, the first intifada and a sharpened consciousness of Palestinian presence, history and politics. I found colleagues and comrades among
Jewish activists—feminist, lesbian, gay, communist, socialist, offspring of communists—reckoning with the wasteland bequeathed by Stalinism and McCarthyism,
and with the acute tension between the antiracist, anticolonial politics we believed in and the question of Israel. Let's say those were not easy years. Deutscher's
book went past me, as it were; even its title sounded too much like escapism.

Rereading it in the past months I found it mostly acute, generous, accessible—the essays of a former *cheder*-prodigy from Poland who, intended for a
rabbi, turned from religion; got expelled from the Polish Communist Party
over the question of international social revolution vs. "socialism in one country;"
lived in exile, became an anti-Stalinist historian who eloquently made English
his fourth or fifth language, wrote respected and lasting biographies of both
Stalin and Trotsky, and to the end kept his eye on Jewish complexity and its
relationship to the hope of international socialism. In 1954 he wrote of Middle
Eastern politics:

> As long as a solution . . . is sought in nationalistic terms both Arab and
> Jew are condemned to move within a vicious circle of hatred and revenge.

... In the long run a way out may be found beyond the nation-state, perhaps within the broader framework of a Middle East federation.[6]

—Shulamith Hareven's sense of Levantism in political terms.

I've said that "American Jews" have paid an intellectual and spiritual price for the narrowing of sight demanded by conformity and reliance on Israel as surrogate identity. Part of this price has been estrangement of many Jews from any Jewish affiliation. But of course, in reality, American Jews disagree like all other Jews, past and future. I share the hopes of those working to create a specific counter-voice to AIPAC and the Council of Presidents of Major Jewish Organizations, as the organizers of Brit Tzedek v'Shalom (Jewish Alliance for Justice and Peace) seek to do—an intervention in the monologue. I'm grateful for the multiracial coalition work of Jews for Racial and Economic Justice in New York, and the Los Angeles–based Progressive Jewish Alliance, activists who recognize that American Jews have every reason to oppose, as Jews, the accelerating dismemberment of democracy in and by the United States. And for international groups like Women in Black, Rabbis for Human Rights, and especially Israeli-Palestininan groups like Bat Shalom and Ta'ayush. My days usually begin with reading emailed bulletins from the Jewish Peace News, whose critical and balanced editorial comments accompany articles from international sources including *Ha'aretz* and *Al-Ahram,* the *Jerusalem Post* and the Electronic Intifada, as well as periodicals in the United States, Britain and Europe.

The white-out of American Jewish dissent is starting to crack like old plaster, even under Bush administration moves to paralyze and penalize all dissent. The cynicism of official United States support for an expansionist Israel grows more obvious as American troops (and a preemptive nuclear policy) are being massed against Iraq, and as Israeli democracy quivers like a reed. But the mobilization of public antiwar sentiment, from a remarkable spectrum of Americans, including thousands of Jewish activists, is also mounting as I write this. And the words and actions of Israeli dissidents, including feminists, "refuseniks" and high school students, groups like Gush Shalom, New Profile and the Israeli Committee Against House Demolitions, have borne courageous, often physically endangered witness to "another Israel."

Israeli Jews are a fractured population, between European, Levantine, Ethiopian, U.S.-born, Russian, Israeli-born and newer immigrants, secular and observant, left-wing and right-wing, with in-group differences as well. Neither Israeli nor Palestinian society is a seamless, monochrome garment: hope as well as difficulty lie in this recognition. Yet mainstream sources of information in the United States convey only one-dimensional representations of all this internal complexity, and organized American Jewish opinion has yet to become as expressive of po-

6. Deutscher, *The Non-Jewish Jew and Other Essays.* Oxford University Press, 1968; Boston: Alyson Publications reprint, 1982, pp. 116–117.

litical differences and contradictions as the Israeli press has been, even under a military government in a climate of increasing insecurity.

Emeritus Harvard Hillel Rabbi Ben-Zion Gold, describing himself as as a lifelong Zionist, a survivor of the camps, "devoted to Israel," calls on American Jews to

> discover their own focus, independent from Israel . . . to link up with [the] proud history of the Diaspora. They have to rediscover their cultural, religious and political gravity. . . . At present, the task of Jews who are committed to the welfare of Israel is to hold up the critical mirror for Americans and Israelis . . . a thankless but important task.
>
> . . . It is not American Jewish criticism that has created sympathy for the Palestinians. It is the suppression of millions of Palestinians over thirty-five years that has done it. It is a pity that the Israeli government has never expressed regret for the harm it has done the Palestinians during the occupation. An ounce of compassion would go a long way.

And perhaps the nineteenth-century word "Zionism"—so incendiary, so drenched in idealism, dissension, ideas of blood and soil, in memories of victimization and pursuant claims of the right to victimize—perhaps the use of this word, by Zionists, post- Zionists and anti-Zionists alike, needs to dissolve before twenty-first-century realities. Israel's "right to exist" is still questioned and challenged in some quarters. Yet it does exist—buttressed by an unprecedentedly reckless U.S. military-industrial complex—as an expansionist nuclear state, with a thirty-five-year history of military occupation, in a world where the right to exist is endangered for all, some more immediately than others. Israel is no longer, if it ever truly was, a "place where Jews can be safe," in a world where national borders have become so discrepant with actual human migrations and displacements, where religious zealotry and imperial will outpace ethical understanding and where the urgency of possible extinction is everywhere heavy on the air; a world where Jewish survival is inextricable from the survival of everyman and everywoman. Like the United States, Israeli civil society is permeated with contradictions and social inequities, promises and betrayals, chauvinism and self-interrogation. The citizens of neither nation can, in good faith, afford the illusion of exceptionalism.

Would a new focus for American Jews transcend voting for a (Democratic or other) party hack who happens to be Jewish? Moving beyond myth and monologue, would it become a critique of false loyalties, an argument with power and privilege? A new relation to the "proud history of the Diaspora?"

Somewhere in the close distance someone is asking: *But—do you love the Jewish people?*

—What do you think I'm doing here?

Isaac Deutscher ended his 1954 essay on "Israel's Spiritual Climate":

. . . . sometimes it is only the music of the future to which it is worth listening.[7]

Every day was a Jewish day for the socialist intellectual who provocatively called us to acknowledge the possibility of a "non-Jewish Jew." Not a Jew trying to pass, deny or escape from the wounds and fears of the community, but a Jew resistant to dogma, separatism, to "remembering instead of thinking" in Nadine Gordimer's words—anything that shuts down the music of the future.[8] A Jew whose solidarity with the exiled and persecuted is unrestricted. A Jew without borders.

The most thoughtful of my brothers turned to me and said:
  "If you make no difference between a Jew and a non-Jew, are you, in fact, still a Jew?"[9]

I began with a Jewish library. As I write these sentences there's a disc playing—Solomon Burke singing "None of us are free/ while one of us is chained."[10]

He's not a Jew. But it's a Jewish night. One of my Jewish days and nights.

7. Deutscher, *The Non-Jewish Jew,* p. 117.
8. Nadine Gordimer, *A Sport of Nature.* Penguin Books, U.S.A., 1988, p. 234.
9. Jabès, *The Book of Questions,* p. 61.
10. Solomon Burke, "None of Us Are Free" on *Don't Give Up on Me.* Epitaph/ANTI Fat Possum Records (1999).

Why Israel Must Choose Justice

Arthur Miller

*The following speech was delivered on June 25, 2003. The Jerusalem Prize honors liter-
ary achievement in the field of freedom of the individual in society.*

I wish to thank you for this honor and for allowing me to join the distinguished
list of authors who were past recipients of the Jerusalem Prize. The awarding
of this prize in recognition of my work as a writer also cites my activities in defense
of civil rights. As a past president of International PEN, the association of writers from around the world committed to the defense of the freedom to write,
I have visited many countries with various political systems, at times to try to
get writers out of jail, at other times simply to reinforce local PEN centers in
their struggle, quite often, to continue to exist. To tell the truth, I never wanted
to spend time away from my desk, but it may be that as a Jew of a certain generation I was unable to forget the silence of the 1930s and '40s, when Fascism
began its destruction of our people, which for so long met with the indifference of the world. Perhaps it is because I have tried to do something useful to
protect human rights that I know how hard it is to make good things happen.
At the same time, my experience tells me that most people by far continue to
believe in justice and wish it to prevail.

Because I have at least a sense of the many terrible contradictions in Israel's
situation vis-à-vis the Palestinians, I am also conscious of my distance from the
day-to-day realities. So I am not going to lecture or try to persuade. The fundamentals of my views are simply that Israel has the right to exist, and the Palestinians likewise, in a state of their own. With the expansion of settlements I have
witnessed, initially with surprise and then with incredulity, what seemed a self-
defeating policy. I am not going to pursue conflicting arguments with second-
hand knowledge, but merely to say the obvious—that the settlement policy appears
to have changed the very nature of the Israeli state and that a new birth of a
humanistic vision is necessary if the Jewish presence is to be seen as worth preserving. To put it perhaps too succinctly—without justice at its center, no state
can endure as a representation of the Jewish nature.

I might fill in some of the background of these views, because this background
is what provides the stark contrast for me with the present tragic situation. I
have not been without some small experience with political Israel. I was invited
to attend the Waldorf dinner in 1948 to celebrate the Soviet Union's recognition of the State of Israel, which was the first and for a time her only international acknowledgment. The very idea of a nation of Jews existing in modern
times was hard to imagine then. It was almost as though a scene out of the Bible

were being reenacted, but this time with real people smoking cigarettes. Imagine! Jewish bus drivers, Jewish cops, Jewish street sweepers, Jewish judges and the criminals they judged, Jewish prostitutes and movie stars, Jewish plumbers and carpenters and bankers, a Jewish president and parliament and a Jewish secretary of state. All this was something so new on the earth that it never dawned on me or, I think, on most people, that the new Israel, as a state governed by human beings, would behave more or less the same as any state had acted down through history—defending its existence by all means thought necessary and even expanding its borders when possible. In 1948, from the prospect of New York at any rate, the very idea of a Jewish state was defensive, since it was under almost perpetual attack. It existed at all as a refuge for a people that had barely escaped a total genocidal wipeout in Europe only a few years earlier. And so it was, I think, that the predominant sense of things at that Waldorf celebration was that, having passed out of the control and domination of others, the time had come for Jews to act normal.

Naturally, it never occurred to most people, certainly not to me, what normal really meant. In that ebullient Waldorf moment and afterward one heard little or nothing of the dark side of the history of new states, especially their sharp collisions with other peoples in the same or contiguous areas. For some years, especially in the United States, a certain idyllic Israel existed in the public imagination, and for some it probably still does. The Israel of the kibbutz, of the rescued land, of the pioneers and the pioneering cooperative spirit reminiscent of summer camp. There was inevitably a lot of psychological denial in this picture, just as there always is in the nationalist picture of any nation. I was not a Zionist, but I certainly participated, however unwittingly, in this kind of denial—although it did seem rather odd to hear Golda Meir responding to a question about the Palestinians by saying, "We are the Palestinians." But this seemed about as harmless as the American president's habit of resolving the harsh inequalities in American society by pridefully declaring, "We are all Americans."

The Jewish obsession with justice goes back to the beginnings, of course. Job, after all, is not complaining merely that he has lost everything; he is not some bourgeois caught in an economic depression. His bewilderment derives from a horrendous vision of a world without justice, which means a world collapsed into chaos and brute force. And if he is called upon to have faith in god anyway, it is a god who in some mysterious manner does indeed still stand for justice, however inscrutable his design may be. Israel in that Waldorf moment meant the triumph of sheer survival, the determination to live a dignified life. Israel also signaled the survival of a temperament, the continuing Jewish entanglement in the mesh of life, and somehow the Jewish engagement with eternal things.

In short, Israel was far more than a political entity, let alone a geographic place, probably at least in part because it was so far away and the distance turned it into something approaching an artistic expression, a sort of bright vision of productive peace. However it may have evolved, it appears at this distance that from the assassination of Rabin onward the settlement policy and the present leadership's apparent abandonment of Enlightenment values before the relentless suicide bombings and the inevitable fear they have engendered have backed the country away from its visionary character and with it the Waldorf prospect of a peaceful, progressive, normal society like any other. What is left, so it appears, is its very opposite—an armed and rather desperate society at odds with its neighbors but also the world. That it remains the only democracy in the area is easily glossed over as though this were not of great consequence, such is the hostility surrounding the country in many minds. Maybe the hypocrisy in this conflict is no greater than usual, but it is certainly no less.

Is it because the country is the country of the Jews that this hostility has found so little resistance? I think so, but not for the obvious reason of congenital anti-Semitism, at least not entirely. It is also because the Jews have from their beginnings declared that God above all means justice before any other value. We are the people of the book and the book, after all, is the Bible, and the Bible means justice or it means nothing, at least nothing that matters. The shield of Israel, it seems to me, was that here in this place a kind of righting of the scales of justice had at last taken place, this people had in fact survived the mechanized genocide and had come back to once again work the land and raise up new cities. This Israel, in my experience, soon earned the admiration and respect of people, many of whom, to my knowledge, had had no special regard for Jews or were even hostile to them. This refusal of death and embrace of life resonated out into the world, and it seems to me now as it did half a century ago, this was Israel's shield, quite as much as her valor in arms.

It may be futile to argue with a repeated story that every modern nation has gone through in its development—a democratic system for its own citizens, and something quite different for others outside its physical and psychological boundaries. Israel's misfortune, as the current leadership and its partisans no doubt see matters, is the lateness of its arrival on the scene, long after a colonial mentality was thought not only normal but praiseworthy. Whole long blocks of very solid buildings still stand in London, Vienna, Paris, which were once filled with offices whose function was the administering of the lives and fates of peoples thousands of miles away in climates that no European would ever see. Post-Rabin Israel, no doubt as an act of defense, is nevertheless asking not only that the clock stop but that it turn backward to allow Israel's expansion into lands beyond its borders.

Finally, I believe it would be a mistake to attribute so much of the world's resentment of this policy to anti-Semitism. The United States, incredibly to most Americans, is experiencing a very similar aversion in the world, and very possibly for similar reasons. The American administration has turned an extraordinarily hard and uncompromising face to the world, and along with a certain arrogant self-righteousness in its tone has alienated a lot of people who only a short while back were genuinely commiserating with us over the bloody attacks of 9/11. It was not long ago, after all, that the French—yes, the French—were declaring in some banner headlines, "We Are All Americans Now."

It may have struck some of you that what I have been talking about is basically public relations—the impact of Israel as an image before the world—rather than the hard questions of security and new arrangements with the Palestinians. But my inspiration in this goes a long way further back into history than the public relations industry. Thomas Jefferson, writing the American Declaration of Independence, inserted into it a phrase no doubt to help justify the new democracy's decision to break away from the British Empire. Thus he hoped to appeal to the forbearance of a hostile world of monarchy and imperialism. The Declaration, he said, was written "In decent respect for the opinions of mankind." In short, the weak, newly born society needed the world's friendship or at least its toleration even as it was prepared to go to war for its independence.

There too something unique was being ushered into a largely hostile world; the British were the enemy and French support was purely strategic, the monarchy having no use for this new democracy whose influence it suspected might endanger the regime. But Jefferson and his friends understood and accepted that no nation can for long endure, whatever the urgency of its defenses, with less than respect, let alone contempt, for the rest of mankind in its longings for justice and equity for all. But my own belief is somewhat less than pessimistic. A nation's history does count a great deal in determining its future. Jewish history is extremely long and is filled, as I have said, with an obsession with justice. It is a terrible irony that, in a sense, the State of Israel today is being attacked by those wielding visionary ideals that were born in the Jewish heart. It is time for Jewish leadership to reclaim its own history and to restore its immortal light to the world.

Living with the Holocaust: The Journey of a Child of Holocaust Survivors

Sara Roy

This essay was originally given as the Second Annual Holocaust Remembrance Lecture at the Center for American and Jewish Studies and the George W. Truett Seminary, Baylor University, on April 8, 2002.

Some months ago I was invited to reflect on my journey as a child of Holocaust survivors. This journey continues and shall continue until the day I die. Though I cannot possibly say everything, it seems especially poignant that I should be addressing this topic at a time when the conflict between Israelis and Palestinians is descending so tragically into a moral abyss and when, for me at least, the very essence of Judaism, of what it means to be a Jew, seems to be descending with it.

The Holocaust has been the defining feature of my life. It could not have been otherwise. I lost over 100 members of my family and extended family in the Nazi ghettos and death camps in Poland—grandparents, aunts, uncles, cousins, a sibling not yet born—people about whom I have heard so much throughout my life, people I never knew. They lived in Poland in Jewish communities called shtetls. In thinking about what I wanted to say about this journey, I tried to remember my very first conscious encounter with the Holocaust. Although I cannot be certain, I think it was the first time I noticed the number the Nazis imprinted on my father's arm. To his oppressors, my father, Abraham, had no name, no history, and no identity other than that blue-inked number, which I never wrote down. As a young child of four or five, I remember asking my father why he had that number on his arm. He answered that he had once painted it on but then found it would not wash off, so was left with it.

My father was one of six children, and he was the only one in his family to survive the Holocaust. I know very little about his family because he could not speak about them without breaking down. I know little about my paternal grandmother, after whom I am named, and even less about my father's sisters and brother. I know only their names. It caused me such pain to see him suffer with his memories that I stopped asking him to share them.

My father's name was recognized in Holocaust circles because he was one of two known survivors of the death camp at Chelmno, in Poland, where 350,000 Jews were murdered, among them the majority of my family on my father's and mother's sides. They were taken there and gassed to death in January 1942. Through my father's cousin I learned that there is now a plaque at the entrance to what is left of the Chelmno death camp with my father's name on it—something I hope one day to see. My father also survived the concentration camps at Auschwitz and Buchenwald and because of it was called to testify at the Eichmann trial in Jerusalem in 1961.

My mother, Taube, was one of nine children—seven girls and two boys. Her father, Herschel, was a rabbi and *shohet*—a ritual slaughterer—and deeply loved and respected by all who knew him. Herschel was a learned man who had studied with some of the great rabbis of Poland. The stories both my mother and aunt have told me also indicate that he was a feminist of sorts, getting down on his hands and knees to help his wife or daughters scrub the floor, treating the women in his life with the same respect and reverence he gave the men. My grandmother, Miriam, whose name I also have, was a kind and gentle soul but the disciplinarian of the family since Herschel could never raise his voice to his children. My mother came from a deeply religious and loving family. My aunts and uncles were as devoted to their parents and they were to them. As a family they lived very modestly, but every Sabbath my grandfather would bring home a poor or homeless person who was seated at the head of the table to share the Sabbath meal.

My mother and her sister Frania were the only two in their family to survive the war. Everyone else perished, except for one other sister, Shoshana, who had emigrated to Palestine in 1936. My mother and Frania had managed to stay together throughout the war—seven years in the Pabanice and Lodz ghettos, followed by the Auschwitz and Halbstadt concentration camps. The only time in seven years they were separated was at Auschwitz. They were in a selection line, where Jews were lined up and their fate sealed by the Nazi doctor Joseph Mengele, who alone would determine who would live and who would die. When my aunt had approached him, Mengele sent her to the right, to labor (a temporary reprieve). When my mother approached him, he sent her to the left, to death, which meant she would be gassed. Miraculously, my mother managed to sneak back into the selection line, and when she approached Mengele again, he sent her to labor.

A defining moment in my life and journey as a child of Holocaust survivors occurred even before I was born. It involved decisions taken by my mother and her sister, two very remarkable women, that would change their lives and mine.

After the war ended, my aunt Frania desperately wanted to go to Palestine to join their sister, who had been there for ten years. The creation of a Jewish state was imminent, and Frania felt it was the only safe place for Jews after the Holocaust. My mother disagreed and adamantly refused to go. She told me many times during my life that her decision not to live in Israel was based on a belief, learned and reinforced by her experiences during the war, that tolerance, compassion, and justice cannot be practiced or extended when one lives only among one's own. "I could not live as a Jew among Jews alone," she said. "For me, it wasn't possible and it wasn't what I wanted. I wanted to live as a Jew in a pluralist society, where my group remained important to me but where others were important to me, too."

Frania emigrated to Israel and my parents went to America. It was extremely painful for my mother to leave her sister, but she felt she had no alternative. (They have remained very close and have seen each other often, both in this country and in Israel.) I have always found my mother's choice and the context from which it emanated remarkable.

I grew up in a home where Judaism was defined and practiced not as a religion but as a system of ethics and culture. God was present but not central. My first language was Yiddish, which I still speak with my family. My home was filled with joy and optimism although punctuated at times by grief and loss. Israel and the notion of a Jewish homeland were very important to my parents. After all, the remnants of our family were there. But unlike many of their friends, my parents were not uncritical of Israel, insofar as they felt they could be. Obedience to a state was not an ultimate Jewish value, not for them, not after the Holocaust. Judaism provided the context for our life and for values and beliefs that were not dependent upon national boundaries, but transcended them. For my mother and father, Judaism meant bearing witness, railing against injustice and foregoing silence. It meant compassion, tolerance, and rescue. It meant, as Ammiel Alcalay has written, ensuring to the extent possible that the memories of the past do not become the memories of the future. These were the ultimate Jewish values. My parents were not saints; they had their faults and they made mistakes. But they cared profoundly about issues of justice and fairness, and they cared profoundly about people—all people, not just their own.

The lessons of the Holocaust were always presented to me as both particular (i.e., Jewish) and universal. Perhaps most importantly, they were presented as indivisible. To divide them would diminish the meaning of both.

Looking back over my life, I realize that through their actions and words, my mother and father never tried to shield me from self-knowledge; instead, they insisted that I confront what I did not know or understand. Noam Chomsky speaks of the "parameters of thinkable thought." My mother and father constantly pushed those parameters as far as they could, which was not far enough for me, but they taught me how to push them and the importance of doing so.

It was perhaps inevitable that I would follow a path that would lead me to the Arab-Israeli issue. I visited Israel many times while growing up. As a child, I found it a beautiful, romantic, and peaceful place. As a teenager and young adult I began to feel certain contradictions that I could not fully explain but which centered on what seemed to be the almost complete absence in Israeli life and discourse of Jewish life in Eastern Europe before the Holocaust, and even of the Holocaust itself. I would ask my aunt why these subjects were not discussed, and why Israelis didn't learn to speak Yiddish. My questions were often met with grim silence.

Most painful to me was the denigration of the Holocaust and pre-state Jewish life by many of my Israeli friends. For them, those were times of shame, when

Jews were weak and passive, inferior and unworthy, deserving not of our respect but of our disdain. "We will never allow ourselves to be slaughtered again or go so willingly to our slaughter," they would say. There was little need to understand those millions who perished or the lives they lived. There was even less need to honor them. Yet at the same time, the Holocaust was used by the state as a defense against others, as a justification for political and military acts.

I could not comprehend nor make sense of what I was hearing. I remember fearing for my aunt. In my confusion, I also remember profound anger. It was at that moment, perhaps, that I began thinking about the Palestinians and their conflict with the Jews. If so many among us could negate our own and so pervert the truth, why not with the Palestinians? Was there a link of some sort between the murdered Jews of Europe and the Palestinians? I did not know, but so my search began.

The journey has been a painful one but among the most meaningful of my life. At my side, always, was my mother, constant in her support, although ambivalent and conflicted at times. My father had died a young man; I do not know what he would have thought, but I have always felt his presence. My Israeli family opposed what I was doing and has always remained steadfast in their opposition. In fact, I have not spoken with them about my work in over fifteen years.

Despite many visits to Israel during my youth, I first went to the West Bank and Gaza in the summer of 1985, two and a half years before the first Palestinian uprising, to conduct fieldwork for my doctoral dissertation, which examined American economic assistance to the West Bank and Gaza Strip. My research focused on whether it was possible to promote economic development under conditions of military occupation. That summer changed my life because it was then that I came to understand and experience what occupation was and what it meant. I learned how occupation works, its impact on the economy, on daily life, and its grinding impact on people. I learned what it meant to have little control over one's life and, more importantly, over the lives of one's children.

As with the Holocaust, I tried to remember my very first encounter with the occupation. One of my earliest encounters involved a group of Israeli soldiers, an old Palestinian man, and his donkey. Standing on a street with some Palestinian friends, I noticed an elderly Palestinian walking down the street, leading his donkey. A small child no more than three or four years old, clearly his grandson, was with him. Some Israeli soldiers standing nearby went up to the old man and stopped him. One soldier ambled over to the donkey and pried open its mouth. "Old man," he asked, "why are your donkey's teeth so yellow? Why aren't they white? Don't you brush your donkey's teeth?" The old Palestinian was mortified, the little boy visibly upset. The soldier repeated his question, yelling this time, while the other soldiers laughed. The child began to cry and the old man just stood there silently, humiliated. This scene repeated itself while a crowd gathered. The soldier then ordered the old man to stand behind the donkey and demanded that he kiss the animal's behind. At first, the old man refused but as the soldier screamed at him and his grandson became hysterical, he bent down and did it. The soldiers laughed and walked away. They had achieved their goal: to humiliate him and those around him. We all stood there in silence, ashamed to look at each other, hearing nothing but the uncontrollable sobs of the little boy. The old man did not move for what seemed a very long time. He just stood there, demeaned and destroyed.

I stood there too, in stunned disbelief. I immediately thought of the stories my parents had told me of how Jews had been treated by the Nazis in the 1930s, before the ghettos and death camps, of how Jews would be forced to clean sidewalks with toothbrushes and have their beards cut off in public. What happened to the old man was absolutely equivalent in principle, intent, and impact: to humiliate and dehumanize. In this instance, there was no difference between the German soldier and the Israeli one. Throughout that summer of 1985, I saw similar incidents: young Palestinian men being forced by Israeli soldiers to bark like dogs on their hands and knees or dance in the streets.

In this critical respect, my first encounter with the occupation was the same as my first encounter with the Holocaust, with the number on my father's arm. It spoke the same message: the denial of one's humanity. It is important to understand the very real differences in volume, scale, and horror between the Holocaust and the occupation and to be careful about comparing the two, but it is also important to recognize parallels where they do exist.

As a child of Holocaust survivors I always wanted to be able in some way to experience and feel some aspect of what my parents endured, which, of course, was impossible. I listened to their stories, always wanting more, and shared their tears. I often would ask myself, what does sheer terror feel like? What does it look like? What does it mean to lose one's whole family so horrifically and so immediately, or to have an entire way of life extinguished so irrevocably? I would try to imagine myself in their place, but it was impossible. It was beyond my reach, too unfathomable.

It was not until I lived with Palestinians under occupation that I found at least part of the answers to some of these questions. I was not searching for the answers; they were thrust upon me. I learned, for example, what sheer terror looked like from my friend Rabia, eighteen years old, who, frozen by fear and uncontrollable shaking, stood glued in the middle of a room we shared in a refugee camp, unable to move, while Israeli soldiers were trying to break down the front door to our shelter. I experienced terror while watching Israeli soldiers beat a pregnant women in her belly because she flashed a V-sign at them, and I was too paralyzed by fear to help her. I could more concretely understand the meaning of loss and displacement when I watched grown men sob and women scream as Israeli army bulldozers destroyed their home and everything in it because they built their house without a permit, which the Israeli authorities had refused to give them.

It is perhaps in the concept of home and shelter that I find the most profound link between the Jews and the Palestinians, and perhaps, the most painful illustration of the meaning of occupation. I cannot begin to describe how horrible and obscene it is to watch the deliberate destruction of a family's home while that family watches, powerless to stop it. For Jews as for Palestinians, a house represents far more than a roof over one's head; it represents life itself. Speaking about the demolition of Palestinian homes, Meron Benvenisti, an Israeli historian and scholar, writes:

> It would be hard to overstate the symbolic value of a house to an individual for whom the culture of wandering and of becoming rooted to the land is so deeply engrained in tradition, for an individual whose national mythos is based on the tragedy of being uprooted from a stolen homeland. The arrival of a firstborn son and the building of a home are the central events in such an individual's life because they symbolize continuity in time and physical space. And with the demolition of the individual's home comes the destruction of the world.

Israel's occupation of the Palestinians is the crux of the problem between the two peoples, and it will remain so until it ends. For the last thirty-five years, occupation has meant dislocation and dispersion; the separation of families; the denial of human, civil, legal, political, and economic rights imposed by a system of military rule; the torture of thousands; the confiscation of tens of thousands of acres of land and the uprooting of tens of thousands of trees; the destruction of more than 7,000 Palestinian homes; the building of illegal Israeli settlements on Palestinian lands and the doubling of the settler population over the last ten years; first the undermining of the Palestinian economy and now its destruction; closure; curfew; geographic fragmentation; demographic isolation; and collective punishment.

Israel's occupation of the Palestinians is not the moral equivalent of the Nazi genocide of the Jews. But it does not have to be. No, this is not genocide, but it is repression, and it is brutal. And it has become frighteningly natural. Occupation is about the domination and dispossession of one people by another. It is about the destruction of their property and the destruction of their soul. Occupation aims, at its core, to deny Palestinians their humanity by denying them the right to determine their existence, to live normal lives in their own homes. Occupation is humiliation. It is despair and desperation. And just as there is no moral equivalence or symmetry between the Holocaust and the occupation, so there is no moral equivalence or symmetry between the occupier and the occupied, no matter how much we as Jews regard ourselves as victims.

And it is from this context of deprivation and suffocation, now largely forgotten, that the horrific and despicable suicide bombings have emerged and taken the lives of more innocents. Why should innocent Israelis, among them my aunt and her grandchildren, pay the price of occupation? Like the settlements, razed homes, and barricades that preceded them, the suicide bombers have not always been there.

Memory in Judaism—like all memory—is dynamic, not static, embracing a multiplicity of voices and shunning the hegemony of one. But in the post-Holocaust world, Jewish memory has faltered—even failed—in one critical respect: it has excluded the reality of Palestinian suffering and Jewish culpability therein. As a people, we have been unable to link the creation of Israel with the displacement of the Palestinians. We have been unwilling to see, let alone remember, that finding our place meant the loss of theirs. Perhaps one reason for the ferocity of the conflict today is that Palestinians are insisting on their voice despite our continued and desperate efforts to subdue it.

Within the Jewish community it has always been considered a form of heresy to compare Israeli actions or policies with those of the Nazis, and certainly one must be very careful in doing so. But what does it mean when Israeli soldiers paint identification numbers on Palestinian arms; when young Palestinian men and boys of a certain age are told through Israeli loudspeakers to gather in the town square; when Israeli soldiers openly admit to shooting Palestinian children for sport; when some of the Palestinian dead must be buried in mass graves while the bodies of others are left in city streets and camp alleyways because the army will not allow proper burial; when certain Israeli officials and Jewish intellectuals publicly call for the destruction of Palestinian villages in retaliation for suicide bombings or for the transfer of the Palestinian population out of the West Bank and Gaza; when 46 percent of the Israeli public favors such transfers and when transfer or expulsion becomes a legitimate part of popular discourse; when government officials speak of the "cleansing of the refugee camps"; and when a leading Israeli intellectual calls for hermetic separation between Israelis and Palestinians in the form of a Berlin Wall, caring not whether the Palestinians on the other side of the wall may starve to death as a result.

What are we supposed to think when we hear this? What is my mother supposed to think?

In the context of Jewish existence today, what does it mean to preserve the Jewish character of the State of Israel? Does it mean preserving a Jewish demographic majority through any means and continued Jewish domination of the Palestinian people and their land? What is the narrative that we as a people are creating, and what kind of voice are we seeking? What sort of meaning do we as Jews derive from the debasement and humiliation of Palestinians? What is at the center of our moral and ethical discourse? What is the source of our moral and spiritual legacy? What is the source of our redemption? Has the process of creating and rebuilding ended for us?

I want to end this essay with a quote from Irena Klepfisz, a writer and child survivor of the Warsaw ghetto, whose father spirited her and her mother out of the ghetto and then himself died in the ghetto uprising:

> I have concluded that one way to pay tribute to those we loved who struggled, resisted and died is to hold on to their vision and their fierce outrage at the destruction of the ordinary life of their people. It is this outrage we

need to keep alive in our daily life and apply it to all situations, whether they involve Jews or non-Jews. It is this outrage we must use to fuel our actions and vision whenever we see any signs of the disruptions of common life: the hysteria of a mother grieving for the teenager who has been shot; a family stunned in front of a vandalized or demolished home; a family separated, displaced; arbitrary and unjust laws that demand the closing or opening of shops and schools; humiliation of a people whose culture is alien and deemed inferior; a people left homeless without citizenship; a people living under military rule. Because of our experience, we recognize these evils as obstacles to peace. At those moments of recognition, we remember the past, feel the outrage that inspired the Jews of the Warsaw Ghetto and allow it to guide us in present struggles.

For me, these words define the true meaning of Judaism and the lessons my parents sought to impart.

Rally 'Round the Flag

Douglas Rushkoff

When I was a kid attending services at Larchmont Temple, a classical Reform synagogue that boasted Joan Rivers as a regular member, my mind would wander from the monotoned responsive readings to pretty much anything else available. I played simple games in which I mentally listed the many logical inconsistencies in the service—from the professional organ player and chorus to the way the Torah was paraded around like one of those idols toward which we're supposed to be so wary.

But, growing up as I did during the most well fought and well publicized of the Israeli wars, what I always ended up pondering the longest and most intently were those two flags on either side of the stage. (Yeah, I know now it's called the *bima,* but I still have a hard time understanding what use it has other than distancing the costumed rabbi and cantor from the congregation that they should be a part of, and putting some big donors on display. So the word "stage" stands.)

The flag on the left was American, and the one on the right was Israeli. Which one was I supposed to be looking at when I worshiped? Which one deserved our allegiance? Why were they even in the temple, to begin with? Does God care about our nationalities? Do we have both of them up there just to cover our bets?

I figured the one we Jews really believed in was the Israeli flag. The one with the Jewish star. That was *our* country, after all. But then why did we have an American flag up there, too? This, I concluded, was a precaution in case a gentile walked in during the middle of services and wanted to know why we were all worshipping a Jewish flag. Weren't we Americans?

So the Jewish flag was our real flag—our secret flag—and the American flag was our conspicuous nod to the nation that we called home. Just so no one thought we were unpatriotic, or, worse, communists (like grandma).

But when we went to the wedding of my brother's fourth grade teacher, there was no flag. It was held in a Catholic church. Hmph. I supposed that because they didn't have a nation to defend, they didn't have to put up their own flag. They were just a religion, not a country. And since they didn't have to prove anything about their allegiance, they didn't bother to put up an American flag, either.

The dual flags in temple became a metaphor for me of the role of Jews in America. We were guests in America, pretending to be Americans, but when we got together behind closed doors we were actually some sort of Israelis. Why did we always say "next year in Jerusalem" if we didn't mean it, somehow? My brother and I used to ask our parents if we were really supposed to be wishing to go to Israel, where they have all those wars. "Just for Passover," my dad told us.

This notion of Jew as closet Zionist was confirmed by the Jewish youth groups I joined as a teenager. We went on weekend retreats where we'd walk around in the woods, smoke pot, make out, and then participate in "programming" meant to show us just how much we loved Israel. It's the same woods-sex-and-song formula used to attract youth to an entirely more nefarious ideology in an earlier era, and it worked just as well. I left those weekends believing I would gladly die in a war for Israel—but not for the United States.

I can't help but wonder now, however, which of those two flags in synagogue truly reflected Jewish values—the one representing the Jewish state, or the one representing a state that, at least in intention, favors no religion at all? Is a Jewish state Jewish, or a breach of the most fundamental principles of Judaism?

As a fan of the Torah, I've spent most of my Jewish-related reading time learning about ancient Israelites who had no country of their own. Is it just coincidence that the cut-off point for these holiest of our holy books occurs immediately before the Israelites invade Canaan (at their God's behest) and begin their first experiment in running a nation?

The Exodus is a myth about gaining freedom from idols. It's a story celebrating a people who see through the false icons of the Egyptian civilization, and come to understand the way that attention to such idols leads to inhumanity towards people. This is why Egypt—the first-born civilization—had to be put down. By sacrificing a lamb, the mythic Israelites were not saving their children from a plague-happy God, but blaspheming the highest god of the state religion— precisely during the Egyptian New Year festival during which they were supposed to worship him.

In revolutionary zeal, they put the blood of this god on their doors, at once betraying the nation of which they were a part, and liberating themselves of allegiance to a god they very likely would have prayed to, themselves. These were the workers of Goshen, after all, and most likely had nothing to do with any Hebrew immigration four mythic centuries earlier. (I like to think of the plagues not as attacks on our Egyptian captors, but as desecrations of Egyptian gods—blood desecrating the Nile, locusts desecrating the corn, darkness desecrating the sun. To me, those drops of spilled wine at the Seder seem much more like mourning our own smashed idols than the pain and suffering of our captors.) But such analysis is shunned in most corners, today, lest it threaten those who maintain a literal or historical interpretation of Torah mythology.

The Torah, like the vast majority of Jewish lore, is better appreciated as allegory than as any sort of historical chronicle. From what we can tell, the audience for whom its stories were intended understood this quite well. They knew that Jacob's sons were not real people, but symbolic of the many tribes who rallied together around a new conception of God that was not dependent on a locality or common race.

Once the Israelites enjoyed a nation of their own, prophets from Samuel to Isaiah tried desperately to keep them from turning their God into yet another nation-saver, like those of their contemporaries. Some prophets even saw the loss of Israel as a valuable lesson in transcending the illusory security of a divinely protected nation.

Exile forced the Jews to pack up their religion for the road. The ancient rituals of the centralized Temple, themselves a replacement of barbaric rites of child sacrifice, were replaced by prayer and scriptural analysis. The Torah and Talmud became the new, virtual Temple. And ethical behavior—which can be practiced anywhere—replaced citizenship.

Ironically, perhaps, this focus on text and discussion over blood rites made Jewish houses of study—the Beit Midrash—the most popular religious institutions on the block. Non-Jews and Jews alike crowded into them to enjoy free-spirited conversations unfettered by the top-down doctrine of the official empire's religion.

Guests of the nations in which they lived, Jews couldn't own land. So they became merchants, bankers, and translators, specializing in mediating the transactions of others. As such, they depended on free and open commerce between nations that were ordinarily suspicious of one another, and developed radically pluralistic philosophies in the long search for a "unified field theory" of civilization. For if the world were really one connected place, it would include the Jews, too.

But as many nations' most visible advocates of such cosmopolitan strides, the Jews were also persecuted as dangerous agents of change, particularly among nations who were having a hard enough time maintaining a national and racial identity in the face of the challenges of a more fluid civilization.

Everywhere the Jews went, there was a local god and local government with whom to contend. As nation-states developed, they institutionalized their local religions and myths of racial origin. For centuries, Jews stood as evidence of those who denied the reality of those religions while attempting to cohabitate with their believers. Whenever a fledgling monarch felt the foundations of his faulty reign failing, the Jews were singled out as the non-believing foreigners who threatened the sanctity of the state.

Jews always seemed to have two opposite reactions to this situation. There were the thinkers, like the prophets, Hillel, Maimonides, and Spinoza, who saw in nationhood and the persecution it brings not a goal, but an idol to be smashed. It was Spinoza who conceived the notion of a separation of church and state, and the right of any person to believe in the god he or she chooses. It was an Enlightenment philosophy that led almost directly to the American Revolution. Right about the same time, Isaac Luria's myths of return from exile were reaching widespread acceptance as factual prophecy. Riding on this wave, a Jewish "messiah," Shabbatai Zevi, had convinced at least 80 percent of the world's Jewish population that judgment day was upon us, and that they should pack up their things and head for Israel. So while some seem to understand that the only Jewish answer to national religion is to separate these two irreconcilable priorities, the other side—usually in the majority, at least economically—believes that the better strategy is for Jews to create a nation of their own. Rather than teaching the world how ultimately immoral it is to institutionalize a religion into a government, they prefer to join them in their theocratic shortsightedness.

It's hard to blame them. After a good millennium of persecution and exile by one nation after another, the status of "welcome guest" had become an impossible aspiration. Between 1421 and 1494 alone, the Jews were exiled from thirteen nations by official decree. The pogroms, the Dreyfus Affair, and the Nazis, to name just a few highlights on the persecution hit parade, were enough to convince even progressive Jews that, until the world became more civilized, a compromise was in order. The Jews would need a state of their own.

But the Jewish state is just that: a compromise of Jewish ideals, and not their realization. It has, no doubt, saved Jewish lives. At the same time, however, its unchecked descent into religious self-justification threatens Judaism itself.

For in order to protect this nationalized refugee camp—especially by those of us here in America who do so through financial proxy—we have had to inculcate ourselves with some very un-Jewish ideas. The most glaring of these is the notion that Jews need to control all of biblical Israel in order for the messianic age to begin. It's not a commonly held belief within secular Israel—but it sure is in the disputed territories, and especially here in the post–1967 generation United States. That's why Brooklynites radicalized in this fashion leave their safe homes and fine jobs in favor of settling the West Bank. It's also why Israel's greatest allies are the most radically fundamentalist Christians of the United States—the same ones who blame 9/11 on the sins of New Yorkers—but who share the belief that land is a prerequisite for grace. Messianism leads to strange bedfellows.

Torah itself is sacrificed to the cause. It is interpreted in the most literal way possible in order to justify each new land grab. *See? This parcel was deeded to Abraham. It says so right here in Genesis!* And this new need to interpret Torah in a literal fashion reduces covenant to a real estate contract. It conflates the sacred space created by divinely inspired allegory into the flat, mundane time line of political history. We get a claim on some land, but we lose our religion in the process.

Nation-states were not invented by God, but by people. Look up the Treaty of Versailles for how that happened. Nation-states are social constructions—agreements that all those people living in the region from, say, Tuscany to Sicily are now Italians, with a shared heritage and religion. This religious and ethnic identity is invented and retrofitted, not an original part of the human condition.

And just as all the other nation-states developed false myths of ethnic identity in order to generate ethnocentric patriotism, now the Jews are doing it, too—in spite of the fact that our religion, such as it is, was designed to avert just such a scenario. We are wrong. Judaism is not a race, but an idea. Jews come from an assortment of tribes who allied in the desert around a single notion: that human beings are not simply born into their reality, but can make the world a better place.

It is our enemies who attempted to define us promoters of universalism as a race, and we who have allowed ourselves to adopt their view. Pharaoh is the first character in the Bible to call the Israelis "a people." The Inquisitors of Spain first called the Jews a "race," in order to justify persecution against people who had successfully converted to Catholicism with a new crime: our blood. And Hitler, exploiting some of Carl Jung's musings, was the first to publicize the myth of a Jewish "genetic memory." Now, in the face of science and basic genetics, famous New York intellectuals publish rebuttals of my efforts to break these misconceptions, citing the existence of Tay-Sachs disease as proof of a Jewish race.

I am not against Israel, and I'm most certainly not against the Israelis, who tend to have a much more progressive and secular understanding of the role of nationhood in sustaining the Jewish people and an experimental system of government founded on Jewish ethical principles. They should be applauded for their efforts.

It is American Jews, insisting that the biblical character God literally gave a specific piece of land to all people who accept the covenant (or the race of people descended from the mythic figure Abraham), who have mired Israel and Judaism in the worst stripes of fundamentalism. There are better ways to support the existence of Israel—ethical, social, political, financial and even military—than to claim that it is the Lord and one true God's will. The fact that American Jews today now have a nation to defend, a race to keep pure, and flag to wave just like everybody else is not a step toward true Jewish emancipation. It's the ultimate form of assimilation.

At the very least, we must consider the possibility that Israel is not the ultimate realization of Jewish ideals, but a temporary surrender of those ideals to the greater necessities of survival in a world plagued by angry religious states with cruel and murderous ethnocentric policies.

In a sense, the real Jewish nation—at least in principle if not its most recent deeds—is the United States, which was founded on more consistently Jewish ideals than Israel, herself. Unintentionally, the Arabs are right when they paint America as a great Zionist conspiracy. It is the true, if troubled, experiment in religious freedom and secular self-rule initiated by Moses so many ages ago.

If I had to pick a flag that best represented the spirit and law of my Torah, it'd be the one on the left.

On a Zion in the Wilderness

Blanche Wiesen Cook

Who is a Jew, and where is Zion? What do we know, and how do we know it? As a studious daughter of the secular diaspora, educated to consider myself an American Jew, not a Jewish American, these questions haunt my life, as they haunt our history. I was brought up to believe that Jews pursued learning, tithed themselves for community betterment, protected and helped people in want or need or trouble. These things my family affirmed, and ignored all debates about whether Jews represented a religion, an ethic, a culture, or a nation. Always a tiny minority everywhere, Jews understand discrimination, abuse, slavery. When we moved from the Bronx to Queens my mother and I walked around the neighborhood uprooting signs that read: "No dogs or Jews allowed." It never stops, this bigotry and hate; and in times of change and trouble it grows and grows.

In the context of hatred and Holocaust we rejoiced for Israel, a center of hope and Homeland, where Jews could sing and dance and be safe, and where labor Zionists imagined a socialist democracy that would heal the wounds of war and create a new era of work, health, and dignity for all people in a new time of peaceful coexistence. But Israel was attacked and in desperation militarized and hardened. As Israel transformed, corrupted by violence/occupation/aggression, Palestinians, long denied and neglected in refugee camps and diaspora, retaliated. Decades of terrorism and state terrorism ensued. Golda Meir, a hero to so many, declared in 1969 that Palestinians simply did not exist.

Positions hardened and peace groups organized and grew. There was a time when I struggled to ignore Israel/Palestine issues even as I wrote of empire and militarism. But that is no longer possible.

In 1991 the Cold War ended, and the wars of the twentieth century were immediately transformed into a new war without borders or boundaries, in a world without borders or boundaries. In this time of madness, with all rules and laws dismissed by the unipower, the world has been plunged into the most dangerous era in human history, a quagmire of death and dying. The epicenter of this new war, declared by a Christian fundamentalist president, who gloats, this is all war, all the time, nukes included, is Israel/Palestine. This bitter historical moment illumines, sharpens, and calls into question the very meaning of Jewishness and homeland, humiliation and suffering, war and massacre. How can Jews not relate to Palestinians and what they are going through?

Forged out of the fire of never-ending battles and promises of land and redemption, we have joined a 4,000-year-long war for place and primacy, resources and control. We have embarked on oil wars and water wars. But we have gone backward into the future and we are also in the vortex of religious wars. History begins at Sumer. Sumer, that place of antiquity and learning, the first cities, the first code of law, the first known writing, Ur on the Euphrates, the home of Abraham, the father of Judaism, Christianity, Islam. Ur, forevermore the word for first, just above and west of Basra, the biblical Garden of Eden, east of Sumer.

Archaeology, the unearthing of humanity's creations and written records, tells us much about the Book, illuminates the confusions, contradictions, battles of the Book. It all began in that first place: Mesopotamia, the ancient fertile land between the Tigris and Euphrates rivers, plentiful and frequently flooded, the cradle of western civilization, from the Sumerians to the Babylonians. Rich and substantial, the site of great cities, powerful towers, crossroads of civilizations. There were so many workers and slaves from so many places speaking so many languages, they created a monumental tower of Babel; and also famed gardens, recently a target of death in Nasariya, the site of the hanging gardens of Babylon in the time of Nebuchadnezzar, but that was later—during the Babylonian captivity when the scribes took their stories for their Book.

First, we have been told, Abraham and his family left Ur in circa the twenty-first century B.C.E. for Canaan, the land promised by God to Abraham. But Canaan was a rich and already settled land, an area of commerce and plenty, and Abraham's tribe were deemed invaders by the Canaanites (Phoenicians) to the north, and the Egyptians to the south. They were repelled and the battles went on, and on. For hundreds of years and thousands of deaths Abraham and his sons and their sons warred and warred—with each other and their neighbors. It all began with Abraham of Ur, Sarah the Priestess, and Hagar the Egyptian: Isaac, Ishmael, and Jacob—renamed Israel, the father of twelve tribes who never could abide each other, and divided and warred, and there were eventually two kingdoms, Israel to the north, and Judah to the south. They were destroyed, and the wars went on. Invasion, plunder, war—always trumpeted by God's promise, God's wrath, God's jealousy, God's goodness. Always bracketed by exhaustion, suffering, the need to repair; promises of peace, amity, justice, love, dignity, redemption, respect, and the rule of law.

From an historical point of view the Bible is a swamp of blood and patriarchal insanity. (The Book of Amos, for example, leaps to mind.) It documents bloodlust, betrayal, and hope. I write this as a small U.S. junta with no memory of international law, no concern for human progress or the needs of humanity, has plunged its citizens and the world back into the pages of the Book. They have the gall to name their new and mightiest (presumably non-nuclear) bomb MOAB: that place where every resident was condemned to weep and howl, mourn and wail; its people forever deprived of joy and singing. As the bombs fell on Baghdad, one of earth's oldest cities and sacred sites, uprooting families, creating uncounted casualties, words of raw jubilance exposed contempt for history.

Triumphant, the United States failed to ask the question of conquest: Watchman, what of the night? Troops stood idly by as the Museum of Antiquity was invaded and plundered. The National Museum of Iraq, storehouse of the cen-

turies, repository for 7,000 years of humanity's treasures, was the site of warning by historians and archaeologists worldwide. Nobody can ever say we did not
know to protect this place.

We may never know what was lost. Many artifacts and documents have long
been at the Lourvre, and in British, German, and U.S. universities whose archaeologists went out to dig and study. Hammurabi's Code has long been in
books, and gives us a sense of the loss. Four thousand years ago Hammurabi
called himself "King of Babylon, Sumer, and Akkad, and the Four Quarters of
the World." He ruled over "civility and commerce," and ruled well: "Lasting water
I provided for the land of Sumer and Akkad. Its separated peoples I united.
With blessings and abundance I endowed them. In peaceful dwellings I made
them live."

The day after the Museum of Antiquities was rendered rubble, the National
Archives and Koranic Library were burned. This cultural calamity is a crime against
all humanity. It compares with other global horrors: the burning of Alexandria
and Constantinople; Spain's destruction of Mayan, Incan, and Aztec cultures.
But this happened on America's watch, during an illegal "preemptive" war in
opposition to the protests of millions of people worldwide. And so one must
pause to ask: Who are we now? How do we fight for peace in a time of war?
Why does this have so much to do with Jews and Zion, with American Jews of
the secular diaspora? How do those of us schooled to think spirituality is about
responsibility and love consider paths toward a peaceful future? In this bitter
moment, when silence is mandated by American Zionists who scorn discussion
and reject criticism of Israeli deeds—actions once deemed despicable and called
pogroms—we must disagree, organize, protest. We must fight to break the cycle
of terrorism and violence which feeds on fear, encourages passivity, and breeds
hatred that ensures continual escalating unbearable violence.

There is no time for silence, no space for error. Who are we now: a divided
people confronting a planet of confusion. Fundamentalists are the scourge of
this moment. They believe they are chosen people destined to rule. So many
chosen peoples, so few places to rule. In 1947 Jews of Europe, the remnant of
the Shoah, were told they were to settle a Zion in a Wilderness, a waste space
for a wasted people. The prophetic said: Divide the Land and Let the Peoples
Grow. But war followed war, and after 1967 Israelis became occupiers, aggressors. They dared build homes for their children on the myth of the original
myth: here is a land without people for a people without land. Every people,
Zionists emphasized, needs a state, a nation, their own Homeland. Palestine is
today the core of Arab politics, even though fundamentalists despise secular
Palestinians. There will be no peace until this issue is resolved. The settlements
of conquered territories should simply be turned over to Palestinians. But there
is nothing simple about that: Water rights, giant fences, uprooted fruit trees,
fertile fields and occupied houses bulldozed. Bitterness rules. Nobody is safe.
Who will take a road map to peace seriously while settlements are still under
construction? How can we stop the slaughter and the terror? What has happened

to the people of the Book who wrote of law, justice, freedom and forgiveness? There is now only the rule of vengeance, an eye for an eye, many eyes for an eye. A state with planes, tanks, and bulldozers facing broken shattered neighborhoods armed with stones and suicide bombers. What is a viable state? Where is respect for life? Why has Mordechai Vanunu been isolated in solitary confinement for almost twenty years because he revealed the facts of Israel's nuclear arsenal?

There are Jewish physicians in Israel fighting for human rights, led by Ruchama Marton, a woman who every day fights for justice and healing. There are Women in Black, International Solidarity Movement, and Dirty Laundry, thousands and thousands of Israelis, Palestinians, and internationals worldwide who struggle to stop the indignities and create conditions for a peaceful alternative to carnage, brutality, death. There is no alternative to activism. While contempt and hatred for Jews and fanatical violence intensifies, Palestinians are treated as Jews were treated during the 1930s: Their lives devalued and diminished, they are deprived of dignity, work, safety. Without a homeland, Palestinians are refugees, and in greater Israel limited to ghettos within barrier walls—locked in, and locked out.

What does it mean to be a secular Jew demanding peace now? We are Jews of the modern age, beyond Pale and patriarchy, Jews who survived medieval crusades, the expulsion from Spain. My mother, Sadonia Ecker Wiesen, was very interested in the expulsion from Spain, and called herself Sephardic. An American Jew from an "old" family that mostly converted to Christianity, the Eckers were German assimilationists, perhaps Sephardic. One vivid memory: our mothers watching in horror when we played at Nazi murderers kidnapping and killing little Jewish children on the porch of a friend's house. The mothers watched us speechless from behind a curtain; we noticed them when we stopped rolling and screaming, and stopped playing, feeling that we had somehow hurt our mothers. By then my mother was a Zionist. Not that she wanted to go to Israel, but she wanted Israel to be a homeland of safety and respect for Jews who were hated and abandoned by all Europe.

By then I was a Zionist too. As the only girl in my Hebrew school in the Bronx, I was earnest, competitive, tough. World War II had just ended, and I was a member of Young Judea. We sold trees for Eretz Yisrael, and sang Zionist songs. On my twelfth birthday, I received Doris Katz's memoir, *The Lady was a Terrorist During Israel's War of Liberation*, with an introduction by Konrad Bercovici. I never doubted that if I could I would be a member of the Stern Gang. The British policy involved cruelty, bigotry, humiliation. They sank ships, bulldozed houses. Ruth Gruber reports that a refugee boy was shot in the face when he threw an apple at a British soldier. In the Bronx, I never went anywhere without my gang. We bested the bullies, our schoolbags stuffed with jars of paste and dangerous sharp-edged things. I never doubted the rightness of our toughness. Never Again meant Israel would live, and girls could walk free through the streets of the Bronx, even to Hebrew school. But even then, or soon after, as a high school debater and college politician, Never Again meant the end of suffering, abuse, humiliation for all. It meant, at war's end, repair, a new beginning, justice and dignity for all.

My journey toward this ethic intensified at Hunter College. I studied anthropology with Dorothy Cooke Jensen, colleague of Samuel Noah Kramer (*History Begins at Sumer*). With Z. Drescher and the Dean of Students, Katharine Louise Hopwood, I attended both the Jewish Theological Seminary and Union Theological Seminary. After Dean Hopwood suggested that I convert to Christianity because it would be so much better for my career, and I refused, the three of us decided to study theology and religious history at night. And so we did, and new questions emerged. Abraham Joshua Heschel gave us a philosophy of religion, *Man Is Not Alone*. And we learned more about redemption, forgiveness, the endless quest for the meaning of life, the journey for justice:

> It is true that our reason is responsive to reasonable arguments. Yet, reason is a lonely stranger in the soul, while the irrational forces feel at home and are always in the majority . . .
>
> With a capacity to hurt boundless and unchecked, with the immense expansion of power and rapid decay of compassion, life has become a synonym for peril. . . . How shall we replenish the tiny stream of integrity in our souls?

I wrote *Eleanor Roosevelt: Volume II* (1933–39), curled in agony. There was evidence that could not be denied that ER and FDR knew fully about events in Hitler's Europe as they disrupted and dislocated Europe's Jews. They knew and they said nothing. More than that, FDR ordered ER to say nothing, to write nothing about what they knew. This was the bitter time, before the burning time. It was the time that might have been used to prevent war and the Shoah. Nothing was done to stop Hitler between 1933 and 1939. The United States traded with Germany, blockaded democratic Spain, and in every way maintained a Silence Beyond Repair concerning Europe's communists and Jews, Hitler's specific targets. Of the great history books, David Wyman, much embattled and criticized by Roosevelt defenders, documented in *Paper Walls* the effort to keep refugees out of America, 1938–1941; and *The Abandonment of the Jews, 1941–1945*. To factor in what ER knew and the deals made, all at the expense of Jews, including oil deals with Ibn Saud regarding U.S. access to Saudi Arabia's oil, leaves me horrified and still curled in agony throughout the ongoing process of writing volume III. In the end, there is no way to understand this bitter moment, without appreciating the enormity of the horrors that defined the twentieth century.

War brutalizes, and in war there are no final victories. The agony and humiliations of one war bleed into the next. Nothing is ever settled until it is settled right. As we look at Israel, unwilling to delineate its borders, an occupying army humiliating a hopeless impoverished people, the old questions arise. Are Israelis treating Palestinians the way the British treated them? Will the killing and vicious acts of revenge on both sides ever end? Is Israel a democratic secular state, or a theocracy? Is it, in the words of Peter Bergson (Hillel Kook), that great Jewish freedom fighter who went to the United States to build a Jewish army to fight for a free Palestine, a Jewish homeland that was to be a multicultural democratic secular state with a Constitution, now reduced to "a ghetto with an army"?

From 1948 to 1956, Israel was almost continuously threatened by war. Harry Truman had reluctantly recognized Israel because of Eleanor Roosevelt's lobbying and President Dwight David Eisenhower was not convinced that had been a good idea. His international staff was dominated by Arabists and oil interests, particularly in the CIA. In 1953, his Operations Control Board (OCB), composed of senior State and CIA analysts, issued a report, "Israel's Fundamental Problems." It concluded that border disputes reflected Israel's "economic and financial plight." Basically there were too many new settlers admitted "too rapidly into a country which possesses almost no natural resources." Whether Israel might develop a "viable economy" was "very uncertain." There were no minerals, no coal, no iron, no oil. Israel's budget depended on foreign loans, contributions, and "funds advanced by the U.S. Government." (There were also German reparations advanced after 1952.) The Arab blockade was effective; Israel had few markets. Israel's response was to expand its territory and enhance its population.

On 25 October 1953, Prime Minister David Ben-Gurion called for an end to these problems within ten years, and preparations were under way to admit two million immigrants from the Middle East, North Africa, and Soviet states. The OCB projected: "This unrealistic approach can only lead to further economic and financial difficulties, and will probably result in additional pressure to expand Israel's frontiers into the rich lands of the Tigris and Euphrates valleys, and northward into the settled lands of Syria." Such expansionism, the OCB opined, was promoted by "a considerable element in the Army, the Government, and among the people." But the OCB concluded that so long as "realists" like Ben-Gurion remained in power and were able to "control the expansionists," Arab hostility might be ameliorated, if not eliminated.

According to Ruth Gruber, after 1967, David Ben-Gurion advised Israel to give up the territories. Their occupation would, he said, destroy Israel—and the soul of the people. In the 1970s, Israel's great General Matti Peled arrived in the United States to protest the new settlements and warn of the bitterness emerging in the occupied territories, where water pipes were being rerouted. Palestinian communities were being parched, wrecked. Disaster was imminent. The people were caused to suffer, olive groves were being uprooted, fruit trees destroyed. It was wicked and wrong. Today, his granddaughter killed by a suicide bomber, his daughter tours the world with Palestinian mothers, with Families of the Bereaved, for hope, forgiveness, peace.

But some American Zionists deny Jews the right to protest Israel's policies. When I publicly quoted Marc Ellis's *Toward a Jewish Theology of Liberation,* a gift to me from Marshall Meyer (who always called Zionism a Jewish Liberation Movement), I was attacked by the head of Zionists of America, who snarled that Rabbi Meyer and Marc Ellis were anti-Semites. The paragraph that caused him such distress was a simple question: Was Martin Buber's vision of a shared land, co-operatively and peacefully developed by Arab and Jew, now irrelevant, "a memory better left alone," or was the possibility of reconciliation, a "turning away from domination to relation, which is at the same time peace with the Palestinian people and a recovery of Jewish witness," still possible? [106–7]

Now, with urgency and dread, we must work to end the 4,000-year-long war of the Book. There must be a negotiated peace, with justice. The deserts might be allowed to bloom, the water shared, fair market prices for oil assured, dignity and freedom for all. And after the illegal occupation of the West Bank and Gaza ends, and Palestine becomes a viable state, the world's crises might be returned for adjudication to the United Nations. In the north of Iraq, in the ancient cities of Mosul and Kirkuk, Kurdestan may come into being. Then there is Chechnya, Russia's Moslem breakaway republic. Factor in Sinkiang, known as East Turkestan, the land of the Moslem Uighers, China's breakaway republic. Factor in Tibet, and the pipeline from the Caspian Sea. Factor in oil and pipeline-istan. Factor in ancient hatreds, Hindu and Moslem, India (never a unity except during the hundred years of the Raj), and Pakistan (composed of Pashtun, Afghanistan, Kashmir, Iranstan). Factor in U.S. promises to go to war against Syria, Iran, North Korea. What would it take to achieve peace? What would it take to return to the promise of the United Nations, forged out of 40 or 60 million dead after World War II? What would it take to return to the promise of the Universal Declaration of Human Rights, and really breathe meaning into the hope of a just future? Only the UN, all 200 member nations, meeting and negotiating in concert can prevent a global conflagration.

We are now in the grip of war and calamity. To avoid chaos people must fight for a humane and peaceful future. It is still true: without vision the people perish. In a world flooded by armaments of unlimited danger, we must end the agony— the crazed cycle of bulldozed homes and bombed buses, humiliation and misery. If we are to survive, we must work for a miracle. Young people must have more to live for than to die for. There is nothing simple about building peace, creating security, acknowledging respect. But we have a tradition to build upon. In Abraham Heschel's words: "Judaism is not another word for legalism. The rules of observance are law in form and love in substance. The Torah contains both law and love. Law is what holds the world together; love is what brings the world forward."

How can we replenish the streams of love and humanity to honor the truths of our incredibly connected planet?

Sources

W. F. Albright, *The Archeology of Palestine* (Pelican Books, 1949, 1960)
Roane Carey & Jonathan Shainin, *The Other Israel: Voices of Refusal & Dissent* (The New Press, 2002)

Jimmy Carter, *The Blood of Abraham* (University of Arkansas Press, 1985, 1993)

Blanche Wiesen Cook, *The Declassified Eisenhower* (Penguin, 1981, 1984)

————, *Eleanor Roosevelt*, vols. I & II (Viking-Penguin, 1992, 1999)

Marc Ellis, *Toward a Jewish Theology of Liberation* (Orbis, 1990)

Bruce Feiler, *Abraham* (William Morrow, 2002)

Henri Frankfort, *The Birth of Civilizaton in the Near East* (Anchor, 1951)

Ruth Gruber, *Inside of Time.* (Carroll & Graf, 2003)

Abraham Joshua Heschel, *Man Is Not Alone* (Jewish Publication Society, 1951)

————, *God in Search of Man* (Jewish Publication Society, 1956)

Samuel Noah Kramer, *History Begins at Sumer* (Anchor, 1959)

————, *Sumerian Mythology* (Harper Torchbooks, 1961)

Savina Teubal, *Hagar the Egyptian: The Lost Tradition of the Matriarchs* (Harper, 1990)

————, *Sarah the Priestess: The First Matriarch of Genesis* (Swallow Press, 1984)

Barbara Tuchman. *Bible and Sword: England and Palestine from the Bronze Age to Balfour* (Knopf, 1956)

David Wyman & Rafael Modoff, *A Race Against Death: Peter Bergson & the Holocaust* (The New Press, 2002)

————, *The Abandonment of the Jews, 1941–45* (Pantheon, 1984)

New Outlook, The Washington Symposium, November/December 1979

David Wyman, *Paper Walls, 1938–1941* (Pantheon, 1968, 1985)

A Blessing to the Families of the Earth

Rabbi Arthur Waskow

Once upon a dream, I imagined the two peoples that share the narrow land between the Jordan and the Sea becoming a model for peacemaking to the peoples of the earth.

Was peace between them easy? No. For there are no obvious boundaries between the two peoples, and they both feel deep yearning for the whole land each calls its own. Precisely because their journey from hostility to peace has been hard, I felt that if they could walk the journey, their path would matter to all the peoples, whose path is also hard.

For we all live on the great unboundaried earth, and most peoples love a scrap of land some other people loves as well. In our generation of H-bombs and global scorching, the journey to Peace has seemed hard—but necessary.

It even seemed both canny and uncanny that the need for all the peoples to make peace came due in history at precisely the same time that the two families of Abraham met up once more in that tiny land where he had herded sheep.

Uncanny: The workings of the God of Abraham—Whose Torah taught that the seed of Abraham would become a blessing to all the families of the earth.

Canny: The churnings of history had through Modernity brought the Jewish people to nationhood in the ancient land, had through Modernity brought the Palestinian community to nationalism and a nascent nation there, and had through Modernity brought all the peoples to the brink where transformation meets disaster.

The upshot? It has all come about precisely as I dreamed—but with all the colors reversed into their opposites. The green of life turned to the red of blood and fire, silver hope turned into black despair.

The two peoples do indeed teach many others. Arik Sharon responds to brutal terror with still more brutality, creating an infinite spiral of rage and death, keeping himself in power by creating hopeless dependency upon his mini-imperial vision; and look!—he becomes the model and the most dependable ally for a would-be real Emperor, a big enough American to bestride the narrow world on tanks of oil and make perpetual war on boasts of Christian triumph. It is not that the Emperor fought his war against Iraq for the sake of his older, smaller brother Arik, for the sake of Israel, for the sake of the Jews. The conspiracists of right and left who blame the war upon the Jews, for good or ill, ignore that the Cowboy of the Apocalypse has much bigger fish to fry, much bigger cities to burn, a much bigger world to control.

The stakes were power at home and power overseas. At home, the unelected President could consolidate power by becoming Commander-in-Chief. He could transfer hundreds of billion of dollars to the ultra-rich, make destitute the poor, impoverish the workers, and rob the middle class of its pensions and its stock holdings by turning attention to a real live video game called Shock and Awe.

Overseas, stationing the U.S. military in the heart of the oil region meant control of the planet. The world remade in the image of Texas—not democracy but corporate oligarchy.

And on the reverse side of the historical phonograph record, the dark obbligato shadows Bush and Sharon. Just as Sharon teaches Bush, so Hamas teaches Al Qaeda. The terrorists of Hamas pour blood on the streets of Tel Aviv and Jerusalem, and look!—a global band of Muslim terrorists learns to pour yet more blood on the streets of New York and Washington.

Can we find anywhere in this a blessing from the two families of Abraham to the other families of earth? Is there any alternative to the war between Israel and Palestine, or the U.S. war against Iraq today, Iran tomorrow, Allah knows who next week?

It is not enough to say: Put a team of UN inspectors in Iraq. Or, set a peacekeeping team of U.S./UN soldiers separating the two peoples in Twice-Promised Land.

These might be useful, but nowhere near enough. What has gone sour is an entire vision of planetary connection and relationship. Treaties to make peace between Israel and Palestine, to heal the earth from CO_2, to ban land mines, to create an International Criminal Court—all spinning down the sour drain. They had too few supporters to make the Imperial Corporations and the one remaining Super-state accept their authority.

Wintertime for decency. But what dies in winter leaves deep-buried the seeds of new and unexpected life. The one blessing of these terrible two years has been the firm though frightened grass-roots solidarity between some Israelis and some Palestinians and some *menshlikh* human beings from abroad . Women who held hands around Jerusalem. Men who together rebuilt Palestinian houses that had been bulldozed down. Rabbis who helped harvest olives when Israeli settlers were shooting at the Palestinian farmers. Israeli and Palestinian families whose very own children have been killed by "the other side"—joining to mourn both sets of children, all of them the seed of Abraham. Joining to mourn their children together as Isaac and Ishmael came together to mourn their father Abraham—and by their grieving were released to live face to face at peace with one another. Israeli soldiers who refused to serve in the Occupation, and Palestinians who demanded that the suicide bombings cease. Italians, Brits, Frenchfolk, Americans who fed and healed and cried. And died. Yes, one of them—an American—died, crushed under an American-built, American-sold bulldozer.

No, I take that back. Not "American" built or sold, but Global Corp built, Global Corp sold, Global corpse killed.

These networks of resistance are not "international," not between the nation-states, but transnational. Crossing all the official Boundaries. Just as the Global Corporations cross all Boundaries, but with one difference: These are seeded at the grass-roots. These are the real seed of Abraham, and they could become a blessing to all the families of the earth. For the treaties that look beyond the old-time boundaries also need constituencies that exemplify nonviolence: Germans and Americans who together will boycott the U.S. car companies that make SUVs. Who will put opaque "indictment" notices, crazy-glued and stet-faced, upon their windshields—for the crime of poisoning the earth. And whisk away on bikes.

Brits and Colombians and Canadians and New Yorkers who will "die" from simulated land mines in front of the offices of the generals and senators who have refused to ban them. And then arise to dance the music of the peoples who are dying as leftover wars continue to explode. Lawyers who will serve on unofficial alternative war crimes "courts" to cry out justice on those accused of terrorism or of war crimes, to hear whatever evidence can be gathered, serve subpoenas on those who refuse to testify.

People who will not only march against the Iraq War but buy some food to be delivered to Iraqi children—and give the Attorney General an affidavit that they have committed this illegal deed of love.

Americans who learn from the Israeli-Palestinian Circles of Bereaved Families to mourn all the dead—not only U.S. soldiers but Iraqis too, and others. Who create Funeral Processions for the Dying and the Not-Yet-Dead of this war. Group after group after group of mourners, with many, many coffins, each and all in silence, except for a muffled drumbeat, and everyone wearing black. Mourning those who have already died and the Not-Yet-Dead: U.S. troops and civilians, Iraqi troops and civilians, UK troops and civilians, Israelis and Palestinians, Kuwaitis and Kurds, Egyptians and Jordanians, who might be killed as the TV War gives cover to terrorists and vigilantes and armies of all stripes; Saudi and Gulf States citizens who might be killed as a result of burning oil wells, depleted uranium bombs, and other long-term environmental effects of the war; Americans, Africans, Indians, Burmese, Venezuelans, etc., who will die of hunger, homelessness, polluted water and air, etc., as a result of money spent on this war instead of healing the sick, feeding the hungry, housing the homeless, protecting the earth.

The front and rear of the funeral march to be made up of a great banner in rainbow colors: THEY ARE NOT YET DEAD: SAVE THEIR LIVES. STOP THIS WAR AND THE NEXT THREE, NOW.

Something, someone, died this winter past: The American Republic, Uncle Sam. And yet—What dies in winter leaves deep-buried the seeds of new and unexpected life.

On February 15, 2003, the great round earth, convulsing, gave birth to something new: A planetary community. Grassroots globalization. Millions gathering on every continent to assert that planetary community, not imperial war, should be the way to deal with dangers like terrorism and weapons of mass destruction.

The real seed of Abraham, who mourn their forebear's death and then join hands across the walls that are supposed to separate them, are the seed that offers blessing to the world.

Dislocated Identities:
Reflections of an Arab-Jew

Ella Habiba Shohat

I am an Arab Jew. Or, more specifically, an Iraqi Israeli woman living, writing and teaching in the United States. Most members of my family were born and raised in Baghdad, and now live in Iraq, Israel, the United States, England, and Holland. When my grandmother first encountered Israeli society in the '50s, she was convinced that the people who looked, spoke and ate so differently—the European Jews—were actually European Christians. Jewishness for her generation was inextricably associated with Middle Easternness. My grandmother, who still lives in Israel and still communicates largely in Arabic, had to be taught to speak of "us" as Jews and "them" as Arabs. For Middle Easterners, the operating distinction had always been "Muslim," "Jew," and "Christian," not Arab versus Jew. The assumption was that "Arabness" referred to a common shared culture and language, albeit with religious differences.

Americans are often amazed to discover the existentially nauseating or charmingly exotic possibilities of such a syncretic identity. I recall a well-established colleague who, despite my elaborate lessons on the history of Arab Jews, still had trouble understanding that I was not a tragic anomaly—for instance, the daughter of an Arab (Palestinian) and an Israeli (European Jew). Living in North America makes it even more difficult to communicate that we are Jews and yet entitled to our Middle Eastern difference. And that we are Arabs and yet entitled to our religious difference, like Arab Christians and Arab Muslims.

It was precisely the policing of cultural borders in Israel that led some of us to escape into the metropolises of syncretic identities. Yet, in an American context, we face again a hegemony that allows us to narrate a single Jewish memory, i.e., a European one. For those of us who don't hide our Middle Easternness under one Jewish "we," it becomes tougher and tougher to exist in an American context hostile to the very notion of Easternness.

As an Arab Jew, I am often obliged to explain the "mysteries" of this oxymoronic entity. That we have spoken Arabic, not Yiddish; that for millennia our cultural creativity, secular and religious, had been largely articulated in Arabic (Maimonides being one of the few intellectuals to "make it" into the consciousness of the West); and that even the most religious of our communities in the Middle East and North Africa never expressed themselves in Yiddish-accented Hebrew prayers, nor did they practice liturgical-gestural norms and sartorial codes favoring the dark colors of centuries-ago Poland. Middle Eastern women similarly never wore wigs; their hair covers, if worn, consisted of different variations on regional clothing (and in the wake of British and French imperialism, many wore Western-style clothes). If you go to our synagogues, even in New York, Montreal, Paris or London, you'll be amazed to hear the winding quarter tones of our music which the uninitiated might imagine to be coming from a mosque.

Now that the three cultural topographies that compose my ruptured and dislocated history—Iraq, Israel and the United States—have been involved in a war, it is crucial to say that we exist. Some of us refuse to dissolve so as to facilitate "neat" national and ethnic divisions. My anxiety and pain during the Scud attacks on Israel, where some of my family lives, did not cancel out my fear and anguish for the victims of the bombardment of Iraq, where I also have relatives.

War, however, is the friend of binarisms, leaving little place for complex identities. The Gulf War, for example, intensified a pressure already familiar to the Arab Jewish diaspora in the wake of the Israeli-Arab conflict: a pressure to choose between being a Jew and being an Arab. For our families, who have lived in Mesopotamia since at least the Babylonian exile, who have been Arabized for millennia, and who were abruptly dislodged to Israel forty-five years ago, to be suddenly forced to assume a homogenous European Jewish identity based on experiences in Russia, Poland and Germany, was an exercise in self-devastation. To be a European or American Jew has hardly been perceived as a contradiction, but to be an Arab Jew has been seen as a kind of logical paradox, even an ontological subversion. This binarism has led many Oriental Jews (our name in Israel, referring to our common Asian and African countries of origin, is Mizrahi or Mizrachi) to a profound and visceral schizophrenia, since for the first time in our history Arabness and Jewishness have been imposed as antonyms.

Intellectual discourse in the West highlights a Judeo-Christian tradition, yet rarely acknowledges the Judeo-Muslim culture of the Middle East, of North Africa, or of pre-Expulsion Spain (1492) and of the European parts of the Ottoman Empire. The Jewish experience in the Muslim world has often been portrayed an an unending nightmare of oppression and humiliation.

Although I in no way want to idealize that experience—there were occasional tensions, discriminations, even violence—on the whole, we lived quite comfortably within Muslim societies.

Our history simply cannot be discussed in European Jewish terminology. As Iraqi Jews, while retaining a communal identity, we were generally well integrated and indigenous to the country, forming an inseparable part of its social and cultural life. Thoroughly Arabized, we used Arabic even in hymns and religious ceremonies. The liberal and secular trends of the twentieth century engendered an even stronger association of Iraqi Jews and Arab culture, which brought Jews into an extremely active arena in public and cultural life. Prominent Jewish writers, poets and scholars played a vital role in Arab culture, distinguishing themselves in Arabic-speaking theater, in music, as singers, composers, and players of traditional instruments.

In Egypt, Morocco, Syria, Lebanon, Iraq and Tunisia, Jews became members of legislatures, of municipal councils, of the judiciary, and even occupied high economic positions. (The finance minister of Iraq in the '40s was Ishak Sasson, and in Egypt, Jamas Sanua—higher positions, ironically, than those our community had generally achieved within the Jewish state until the 1990s.)

The same historical process that dispossessed Palestinians of their property, lands and national-political rights was linked to the dispossession of Middle Eastern and North African Jews of their property, lands, and rootedness in Muslim countries. As refugees, or mass immigrants (depending on one's political perspective), we were forced to leave everything behind and give up our Iraqi passports. The same process also affected our uprootedness or ambiguous positioning within Israel itself, where we have been systematically discriminated against by institutions that deployed their energies and material to the consistent advantage of European Jews and to the consistent disadvantage of Oriental Jews. Even our physiognomies betray us, leading to internalized colonialism or physical misperception. Sephardic Oriental women often dye their dark hair blond, while the men have more than once been arrested or beaten when mistaken for Palestinians. What for Ashkenazi immigrants from Russian and Poland was a social *aliya* (literally "ascent") was for Oriental Sephardic Jews a *yerida* ("descent").

Stripped of our history, we have been forced by our no-exit situation to repress our collective nostalgia, at least within the public sphere. The pervasive notion of "one people" reunited in their ancient homeland actively disauthorizes any affectionate memory of life before Israel. We have never been allowed to mourn a trauma that the images of Iraq's destruction only intensified and crystallized for some of us. Our cultural creativity in Arabic, Hebrew and Aramaic is hardly studied in Israeli schools, and it is becoming difficult to convince our children that we actually did exist there, and that some of us are still there in Iraq, Morocco, Yemen and Iran. Western media much prefer the spectacle of the triumphant progress of Western technology to the survival of the peoples and cultures of the Middle East. The case of Arab Jews is just one of many elisions. From the outside, there is little sense of our community, and even less sense of the diversity of our political perspectives. Oriental-Sephardic peace movements, from the Black Panthers of the '70s to the new Keshet (a "Rainbow" coalition of Mizrahi groups in Israel) not only call for a just peace for Israelis and Palestinians, but also for the cultural, political, and economic integration of Israel/Palestine into the Middle East. And thus an end to the binarisms of war, an end to a simplistic charting of Middle Eastern identities.

Interrogate My Love

Daniel Boyarin

As long as I can remember I have been in love with some manifestations of Christianity (not always ones that my Christian friends would themselves love, or even approve). Tennessee Ernie Ford singing on television the hymn "The Garden" moved me to tears when I was a child (I won't pretend to remember how old). For an oddly gendered teenager, St. Francis, the Sissy, proved an incredibly tantalizing figure of a man. Later on it was medieval Christian art and architecture, the cathedrals of Europe, the spirituality of Meister Eckehart and Jakob Böhme. Still later, and most significantly, it has been the writings of the Fathers of the Church (and their excluded others, the Christian heretics) that have been most riveting to me, pulling me into a world so close to that of my own beloved rabbis of late antiquity and yet so foreign as well, a world in which oceans of ink (and rivers of blood) could be spilt on questions of detail in the description of the precise relationships between the posited persons of a complex godhead, a world, as well, in which massive numbers of men and women could choose freely and enthusiastically to live lives without the pleasures of sex and the joys of family. I find this world endlessly moving, alluring, even at its most bizarre to me. For the last decade or so I have devoted much, much of my time and spirit to learning the languages of and understanding something of the inner and outer worlds of those early Christian men and women who wrote such texts and lived such lives.

Some Jews, it seems, are destined by fate, psychology, personal history, or whatever, to be drawn to Christianity.[1] I have to come clean and confess that I am one of those Jews. I cannot, of course, deny the problematic aspects of that desire; desire is frequently unruly and problematic. Christians, of course, have been bloody rotten to Jews through much of our histories, and Jews, when occasionally given the chance, have taken their turn at being rotten to Christians, as well. This desire seems sometimes to be not entirely unlike the "love" that binds an abusive couple to each other. Nevertheless, it is there. The question is, then, what creative use can be made of problematic desire, not only what pleasures can it engender but also what utile can it be in the world?

1. If I am at all plausible in my reading, this category of "some Jews" may go historically very far back indeed. Boyarin, Daniel, *Dying for God: Martyrdom and the Making of Christianity and Judaism*. The Lancaster/Yarnton Lectures in Judaism and Other Religions for 1998, 26–41. Stanford: Stanford University Press, 1999. My own, perhaps dangerous, identification with Rabbi Eliezer is presumably clear by now to anyone who is paying attention.

Some Jews who are so absorbed by Christianity have been induced by that affection to convert and become Christians. I have not, held back by an even more powerful libidinal commitment to the religion, the memories, the thick history, the literature and liturgy of diasporic rabbinic Judaism as practiced for nearly the last two millennia. Perhaps, better than "greater" or "lesser" in characterizing these investments, I should distinguish between a love of who I am, diasporic rabbinic Jew, and a desire for a different other, the subject of Christianity.

As I have been doing my research over the last decade into the intimacy between patristic Christianity and talmudic Judaism, portions of the work have been presented in many venues. On one occasion, when I had delivered a lecture on the Gospel of John as a Jewish sermon, a very upset undergraduate arose from the audience to inquire: Who are you and why are you trying to take our Gospel away from us? On another occasion, a group of Christian ministers asked me why I was not a Jew for Jesus (not in an effort to convert me to that movement but rather to understand what it is that makes me not one). At still another time, in Jerusalem on one memorable occasion, I was asked explicitly by the organizer of a conference, Dr. Alon Goshen-Gottstein, to reflect on the implications of this work for the present and future. On all of those occasions, I disengaged from the question that was being asked, falling on the last resort of the scholarly scoundrel: "I'm just trying to figure out what really happened!" In a more ongoing sense, I had experienced this research as a pleasing and restful withdrawal from cultural wars in which I have been engaged for so long, for once not seeking (so I thought) to defend or attack, to apologize or polemicize, but simply to describe and analyze. But something was disturbing me; something was sapping my strength from even continuing the work. I came to a total standstill. Overnight it became clear to me that I cannot evade the good and hard questions that the undergraduate at Grinnell asked, that the ministers asked, that Alon had asked of me. It turns out, of course, that this scholarship was no less political and no less fraught for me personally than anything else I have ever done. Something seems to frighten me here, either some boundary that I am afraid, for myself, that I am threatening to breach, or perhaps, a fear that I will be perceived to have breached such a boundary and be marginalized or excluded from a community to which I still fervently desire to belong. But there's no way out of this now other than to go right through the middle of it.

Why does my psyche drive me to "come out" in order to continue my work? Why need I tell about the love that (almost) would not dare to say its name, the love of this Orthodox Jew for Christianity? Even more grandiosely, I could pose the question (but very hesitantly, almost taking it back as I ask it), what purpose might this strange attraction play? Perhaps it has led me to be able to listen to the ways that the affiliation between what we call Judaism and what we call Christianity is a much more complex one than most scholars, let alone most layfolk, imagine and that that complexity has work to do in the world, that we can learn something from it about identities and affiliations. The world that I have found in my research is one in which identities were much less sure than they have appeared to us until now, in which the very terms of identity were being worked on and worked out. Not only had there not been the vaunted "parting of the ways," but Christianity was deeply engaged in finding its identity, its boundaries and even busily and noisily sorting out what kind of an entity it would be, what kind of an identity would it form. There was no telling yet (or even now) what the telos of the story would be. Non-Christian Jews, and especially an important group of Jewish religious elites, were busy, as well, working hard to discover how to define their own borders in a discursive world being dramatically changed by the noise that Christians were making, soundings of "New Israels," "true Jews," and "heretics." "Judaism"—an anachronism—was up for grabs as well, as it were, by which I don't mean only the by now well-accepted notion that there was no normative Judaism, only Judaisms, but something more. Even rabbinic Judaism was struggling to figure out for itself what a "Judaism" is and who, then, could be defined as in and out of it. Those definitions were carried out by inscribing people as heretics, as Jewish-Christian hybrids, or as the rabbis would name them, *minim*, creatures who don't fit into any categories, monsters.

The extraordinary practice of anatomizing, pinning down, making taxonomies of Christians who are not somehow "in" seems an integral part of the answer to the question: What kind of a thing will Christianity be? Integral to that heresiological answer as well was a response to Jews who would not be Christians, or, better put, a response to the question of how the mapping of a border with something that Christianity will call Judaism will make the new Christian self-definition as a "religion" work. As an important, even vital, part of the answer to these questions, Christian discourse from the second through the fifth centuries, at any rate, kept producing a species of heretics called "Jews" and "Judaizers," hybrids, "monsters," to use the terminology of one of the earliest of Christian writers, Ignatius of Antioch: "It is monstrous to talk of Jesus Christ and to practice Judaism" [Magnesians 10:3]. These very monsters were to appear as a heresiological topos of the orthodox Christian writers who almost constantly figured heresy as a hydra. The rabbis, in those same centuries, produced an analogous response, a discourse as well of the pure and the authentic opposed to the impure, the contaminated, the hybrid, the *min*.

I speak here, then, for the monsters. But why? What right do I have to do so? I am not, after all, a heretic from either the orthodox Christian or orthodox Jewish point of view, neither a Judaizing Christian nor a Christian Jew [a *min*], for all my attraction to Christianity and Christians. I do not choose, in any way, to be a Messianic Jew, a Jew for Jesus, or anything of that sort, but actually, to be just a Jew, according to the flesh and according to the spirit. Let me state here the obvious, the simple, the straightforward, and definitive: I do not believe that Jesus the son of Joseph of Nazareth was (or is) the Messiah, let alone do I subscribe to even higher christological glories ascribed to him as "Son of God." I am not, I think, a Jew against Jesus but there is no credible sense in which I could be construed as a Jew for Jesus either. I do not seek, of course, covertly (as sometimes Jews for Jesus do), or overtly, to convert myself or any other Jew to Christianity, nor claim that Christianity is the true Judaism, nor preach that somehow Jews must accept John as Gospel truth.

There is, therefore, a conundrum here. On the one hand I occupy an "orthodox"—or at least quite conventional—form of Jewish identification, belief, and practice, but on the other hand, find myself driven to write a history that calls the very terms of that orthodox identity into question. I need to figure out in what way the position of monster, of heretic, calls me in order to discover the meaning of my work to me. I think I read the record, in some sense, from the point of view of the hybrids, the heretics, not because I wish, then, to revive their particular religious modality, whether we call it Jewish Christian or find some other name for it, but because there is some other sense in which the position of those "monsters" is close enough to my own to call me to it, to identify with it, as my place. My first apparent apologia must, it seems, give way to another, deeper one.

For all the conventionality of my self-identification as an Orthodox Jew, I am seriously out of step with my community at this moment, in a position of marginality that is frequently very painful to me. The present is a time in which Jewish orthodoxy has been redefined as including the unquestioning support for a political entity, the State of Israel, and all of its martial adventures. My own vaunted "love" for Christianity has become suspect to me at this moment, for I am writing in a time (2003) in which many Jews and many powerful Christians (millennial enemies) are suddenly strange bedfellows, collectively engaged in a war/wars against Muslims. Ariel Sharon's war of ethnic cleansing against the Palestinians is applauded by fundamentalist Christians, and American President George W. Bush's crusade against Iraq is cheered by most Jews in the name of a battle against Muslim terrorists. (Ironically—but not accidentally—just as in the first Crusades, Arab Christians are assimilated to Muslims by the discourse of both the Jewish and American Christian anti-Muslim campaigns.)[2] Already I have heard rumblings, ominous warnings, that the import of my critical work is precisely that, of aiding and abetting in the forging of a new identity of Jews and Christians against the Muslims. Perhaps my transgressive love is not transgressive enough, maybe even, in the current social-political context, not transgressive at all but the enactment, or potential enactment, of a dangerous liaison.

2. My colleague, Prof. Ibrahim Muhawi, writes to me in a personal communication: "Eastern Christianity has always had a bad time with the Western variety, beginning perhaps with the Crusades. But there is also something which is more than merely Eastern Christianity; there is also a Semitic Christianity (the same Semitic Christianity with which you deal in your book)—Arab (Eastern Orthodox, Greek Catholic, Coptic, Maronite), Chaldean, and a number of other offshoots. The alliance of certain brands of American Christianity with Zionism is at the same time an alliance against Arab Christians like me." I wish to thank him for this very important intervention. I was in danger of a very significant occlusion.

I have been repeatedly asked in the last year or so why my inquiry does not engage the history of Islam as part of the history of Judaism in the same way that it engages Christianity. Once again, I have until now taken the easy way out: It is not in my period of research. I cannot continue to evade the hard question at this time of crisis, but I am hoping that there is at least the embryo of an answer in the very research itself. Indeed, in some sense this kind of historical scholarship can only be justified to me now, via an allegorical—or perhaps I mean anagogical—reading of it. I think that while the historical sense of the historical research concerns Christians and Jews in late antiquity, its moral sense lies elsewhere, paradoxically in an interrogation of the easy and terrible alliances between most Jews and many Christians against Muslims in the present.

I and all of us (especially Jews) who dissent from a version of a Jewish-Christian alliance that brands the Palestinians, Saddam Hussein, and Osama bin Laden as equally and demonically Islamic terrorists are labeled by both Jews and Christians as Jewish anti-Semites. This is powerfully reminiscent to me of Jerome many centuries before stigmatizing Jews who were Christians, Christians who were Jews, as heretics and declaring them confidently "neither Jews nor Christians." The mind boggles and the imagination is beggared at the spectacle of right-wing Protestant presidents, Southern Baptist fundamentalist preachers (historically no friends of the Jews), and the Jewish president of Harvard University, speaking from the (Christian) pulpit at Harvard Memorial Church (historically no site for the championing of Jews), making common cause in demonizing those, Jews and others, who dissent radically from Israeli policy and practice toward the Palestinians. How bitterly ironic to find the latter pulpit being used to label Jewish and other signers of a petition calling on universities to divest from apartheid Israel as "anti-Semites!" I and other Jews who dissent from Jewish support of Israel are being labeled heretics.

On the stairs of my synagogue, in Berkeley, on Rosh Hashana this year, I was told that I should be praying in a mosque and versions of this, less crude perhaps, are being hurled at Jews daily by other Jews. I don't wish to romanticize my situation. It is not I who is suffering; my only personal pain is the pain of living on the margins, and that, too, has its privileges. More piercing to me is the pain of watching a tradition, my Judaism, to which I have dedicated my life, morally disintegrating before my eyes. It has been said by many Christians that Christianity died at Auschwitz, Treblinka, and Sobibor. I fear—G-d forbid—that my Judaism may be dying at Nablus, Daheishe, Beteen (Beth El), and al-Khalil (Hebron).[3] The violent actions taken in the name of defense may help some

3. By writing "my Judaism," I hope to be evading the very essentialist trap that my book sets out to counter. I do not wish to be understood, however, as claiming that even "my" Judaism is a wholly politically correct thing; it is rabbinic Judaism warts and all, but no version of that ever incorporated the total disdain for any but Jewish lives and bodies that seems—I hope I am wrong—to characterize the lion's share of self-identifying Jews in the world today.

Jewish bodies survive (and even that only dubiously, temporarily, momentarily), but they threaten to empty Jewish existence of all meaning, to make hollow the resistance for two thousand years to being dissolved into the majority. If we are not for ourselves, other Jews say to me, who will be for us? And I answer, but if we are for our selves alone, what are we?

Crusades have historically been very bad for Jews. The attempts of historical Christendom—which is not coeval, of course, with the Church as mystical body of Christ—to dominate the world, to make the whole world Christendom, left in their wake the second most ghastly trail of Jewish blood in all of history. But now, when fundamentalist Protestant forces in the United States mobilized as well by money and power of other sorts, are seeking such a domination again, heedless of the horrors of violence and war, my people are making common cause with this new crusade, imagining somehow that those horrors will strengthen, protect, and defend us. Let us make no mistake, the motivations of the invasion of Iraq are as classically colonialist as any invasion in history. On the secular front, there is clearly the economic motivation; the oil must be secured for American economic interests, to make George Bush and his friends even wealthier. However, on the religious front, the same old contempt for Islam that has motivated Christians for centuries is being played out. Powerful religious forces in the United States hope to be there alongside of Bechtel, "rebuilding" Iraq, turning mosques into churches, and these forces, as well, are arrayed in an unholy alliance with the real and justified fear of Jews, as well as the Jews' own paranoia and religious/national megalomania against Islam and against Muslims, who are everywhere demonized. I call on Jews of good sense and good will to recognize that down this path leads only moral and ultimately physical annihilation for Jews, and I call upon Christians of good sense and good will to struggle against those forces within the larger world of Christian religious community that seek, once more, to turn the whole world Christian. These ways are not the ways of the Torah all of whose ways are peace and they are not the ways of the Prince of Peace who came, as he says, to fulfill the Torah. It boggles the mind that Jews who a decade ago were protesting the desire of the Southern Baptist convention to convert all Jews to Christianity now see in those same religious figures, groups, and leaders their allies against Islam, that Israeli and Jewish leaders routinely sup with the ilk of Jerry Falwell and no one considers this bizarre and dangerous. This is not the *Versöhnung* that we have sought, nor the intended consequence of our historical reimagining of the relations of Judaism and Christianity in antiquity.

In my scholarship, I suggest that the borders between Judaism and Christianity have been historically constructed out of acts of discursive (and too often actual) violence, especially acts of violence against the heretics who embody the instability of our constructed essences, of our terrifying bleedings into each other. I ask whether we can transform transgressive desires for the proscribed other, for proscribed otherness, from a phobic moment within ourselves that produces ever more violent attempts to repress them and insist on purity into something like what the best love should be, a psychic (in the allegorical instance, social) situation in which one seeks the good of another out of the autonomy and security of a self. Can observing the processes through which a self (two selves) was formed enable a rewriting of the story of self, of Jewish self and Christian self, not only with respect to each other but also, or perhaps especially, as each separately and both together encounter new others? Paradoxically, it is my transgression of that unholy alliance of Jews and so many Christians (but not, indeed, all Christian groups, let alone all Christians)—a transgression born paradoxically at least in part of my attraction to Christianity and with it my interest in the time of blurred identity—that constitutes my monstrosity, my heresy.

Seeing the complexities of identification and desire, the roads crissing and crossing through which identities, entities, ultimately Christianity and Judaism, were forged in late antiquity might help, a bit, in the greatest, most acutely emergent task with which Jews (in the end it comes to this for me) are faced right now, once again to maintain our existence, our cultural, religious memory without sacrificing the very meanings of that existence, continuity, and memory on their own altar, without fetishizing borders and boundaries in the enactment of an ethnic cleansing that finally, in my view, negates the very meaning of Jewish survival until now. If we have only been for ourselves, what are we? As I write, in occupied Palestine, literal physical boundaries of barbed wire and electrified fencing are being raised to separate violently one "People" from another. In the process of maintaining our own identities (and now I address Christians—and, indeed, Muslims as well), can we learn the lessons of the past and prevent ourselves at the eleventh hour from the path of new and even more violent heresiologies? Jews and Christians are called upon at this moment to learn from our own difficult histories, without in any way rendering those histories equivalent phenomenologically or morally—and do something different now.

No Return

Ammiel Alcalay

Dear Lord Rothschild,

[London] 2 November 1917

I have much pleasure in conveying to you, on behalf of His Majesty's Government, the following declaration of sympathy with Jewish Zionist aspirations which has been submitted to, and approved by, the Cabinet:

"His Majesty's Government view with favor the establishment in Palestine of a national home for the Jewish people, and will use their best endeavors to facilitate the achievement of this object, it being clearly understood that nothing shall be done which may prejudice the civil and religious rights of existing non-Jewish communities in Palestine, or the rights and political status enjoyed by Jews in any other country." I should be grateful if you would bring this declaration to the knowledge of the Zionist Federation.

Yours sincerely,
Arthur James Balfour[1]

One has to stop for a second, looking at this Balfour Declaration, a text notable for its esoteric racism in which the whole Palestinian drama has been inscribed. . . . Suffice it to reiterate here that, through this text, a government, that of Great Britain, delegated a land, Palestine, over which it exercised no sovereignty in either law or fact, for the benefit of a religious community, the Jews, then almost wholly living outside of that land.

In turn-of-the-century Palestine, despite the efforts of the Zionist movement, the Jewish population represented scarcely 9 percent of the inhabitants, and the Jews of pure Palestinian stock, around 60,000 souls, made up a minute proportion of the world Jewish population. But nevertheless, oh marvel of marvels, the Declaration wished to "respect" the rights and equity of the Arabs, 91 percent of the population, by qualifying them as the "non-Jewish communities in Palestine," to make sure nothing would prejudice their "civil and religious rights." But there is not one word in

1. This brief but crucial text can be found in a very useful new collection, *The Middle East and Islamic World Reader*, edited by Marvin E. Gettleman and Stuart Schaar (New York: Grove Press, 2003), p. 170.

the text about the political rights of these bizarre "non-Jewish communities," the Palestinian people, whom they refuse to name, just as any possibility of their collective existence is eliminated by depriving them of any and all political rights.

In the same vein, the text stipulates, with astonishing asymmetry, that nothing should prejudice "the rights and political status enjoyed by Jews in any other country." A futurist text, if you will, the declaration is inscribed in the Arab memory as a monument to perversion, marked annually by mourning.

Georges Corm
[*Le Proche-Orient éclaté 1956–2003*
(*The Near East Fragmented 1956–2003*)][2]

Arcane from the inside,
explode and

dead reckoning
RKN,

think in roots,
and of a people suicided,

who bring their chains
to funerals that are blasts

of a resistance
everyone understands
and everyone resists understanding
Jack Hirschman[3]

1.

This futurist text, like a virus gone mad, has incinerated any idea of the book, and now only inscribes the earth by bulldozer, crushing bodies, houses, or-

2. The clarity and erudition found in Georges Corm's work is very hard to come by in an American context, regardless of which part of the political spectrum one looks at; author of more than a dozen important books, none of them, as one has come to expect, have been translated into English; this quote is from *Le Proche-Orient éclaté 1956–2003* (Paris: Gallimard, 2003), pp. 469–70 [my translation].

3. From an unpublished poem, "The Apocryphon Arcane" (2002), by Jack Hirschman, prolific poet, translator, and important Jewish radical whose work is more widely recognized outside of the United States.

chards and olive groves, marking time in what we have come to call "history:" 1948, 1967, 1982, 1987, 2002—the disaster, the defeat, the invasion, the uprising, the incursion. Tales of land, water and people: tales of oranges, olives, almonds and figs.

2.

I'm not quite sure how we ended up going together, but I remember driving out to a prison from Jerusalem with some friends. It must have been sometime around 1979. I don't know exactly why we went, but the windows were open in the small car and there were waves of dry heat beating against us that just became more and more oppressive the closer we got to the prison, located somewhere in the desert. There had been some disturbances in the neighborhood my friend lived in—people had blocked the streets off with burning tires and set the dumpsters on fire to keep the police out as protests mounted over the lack of housing and cuts in the subsidies on bread, milk, oil, flour and sugar. One of the guys in the car was a junkie who had been active in the Black Panthers.[4] I guess we must have been going out so he could visit someone, but I think there were a bunch of people that we spoke to standing outside the prison who were protesting something. Here everyone grew up together and knew each other—the guards, the prisoners, and those who'd come to see friends and family. Conditions were notoriously bad and the addict, Upright Son (which is how his name translated), told me in detail what he'd gone through when he'd been forced into solitary and had to kick cold turkey. Most of the prisoners had names like mine: Alfandari, Almosnino, Alhadef, Algazi, Altaras, Abulafia.

3.

I remember him as if I'd just seen him: black leather jacket, a party button on each lapel, beret perfectly pitched at an angle resting on his hair, a stack of papers at his feet, a dozen or so copies tucked under his left arm, and one held out in his right hand. I'd go every week when the paper came out—I was only 13 or 14, and he couldn't have been much more than 16. He'd ask me what I thought of the last issue, and we'd stand there and talk in between him hawking the paper, greeting people, and keeping an eye out for trouble. We talked about *The Battle of Algiers,* which played pretty regularly in those days. 1969, maybe

4. There is very little information available on the Israeli Black Panthers, the most important Israeli social movement of the 1970s, in English; recently, however, filmmaker Eli Hamo and poet, journalist and scholar Sami Shalom Chetrit released a video called *The (Israeli) Black Panthers Speak;* information can be accessed through: *http://www.kedma.co.il/Panterim/PanterimTheMovie/PanterimMovieEng.html.*

1970. Going back to that time, I feel like an archaeologist of sorts as I dig through
the traces to see what made me, what made *us* tick.

As I wade through piles of cheap paperbacks (priced between 75¢ and $2.45),
I see a deep rift we haven't yet begun to account for. From 1969 to 1972 Avon,
Bantam, Ballantine, Harper Perennial, Dell, Anchor, Vintage, Grove, Ace, New
American Library, Pocket Books and many other publishers brought out books
like: *Getting Busted: Personal Experiences of Arrest, Trial and Prison; Soledad Brother:
The Prison Letters of George Jackson,* introduction by Jean Genet; *Look for Me in the
Whirlwind: The Collective Autobiography of the New York 21; If They Come in the Morning*
by Angela Davis, Rachel Magee, the Soledad Brothers and Other Political Pris-
oners; *Prison Journals of a Priest Revolutionary* by Philip Berrigan; *Seize the Time* by
Bobby Seale; *For Us the Living* by Myrlie B. Evers, widow of Medgar Evers; *One
Day, When I Was Shot,* James Baldwin's screenplay based on *The Autobiography of
Malcolm X;* Dick Gregory's *Political Primer; Famous Long Ago* by Raymond Mungo;
I Ain't Marchin' Anymore by Dotson Rader; Lenny Bruce's *How to Talk Dirty and
Influence People;* *"R.F.K. Must Die!": A History of the Robert Kennedy Assassination
and its Aftermath; In Red & Black: Marxian Explorations in Southern & Afro-American
History* by Eugene D. Genovese; *The Middle of the Country: The Events of May 4th
As Seen By Students & Faculty at Kent State University; The Long Walk at San Fran-
cisco State* by poet and novelist Kay Boyle; Paul Goodman's *Speaking and Lan-
guage: Defense of Poetry;* Dudley Randall's *The Black Poets; In a Time of Revolution:
Poems From Our Third World,* edited by poet Walter Lowenfels; *The San Francisco Poets,* edited by poet David Meltzer, founder of *Tree* magazine; *The East
Side Scene: American Poetry 1960–1965; A Caterpillar Anthology,* edited by poet
and translator Clayton Eshleman.

How many of my students recognize these names? How many professors?
Critics? People in general? Now everything fits into a category (niche markets
by color, gender, class and profession, baubles for the academic, the esoteric,
believers and nonbelievers, gun-toters and vegetarians), and it's become almost
impossible to find anything you're not already looking for:

so many romes to go

o rome of scots
and rome of brits
of slavs and spics
jewrome arabrome
romeafrique
no can go home
no mo rome

o rome

4.

In July 1969, a delegation of the Black Panther Party is introduced and hosted at the First Pan-African Cultural Festival in Algeria by Abraham Serfaty. In the first issue of *The Black Scholar*, Nathan Hare, a man born on a sharecropper's farm near Slick, Oklahoma, who went on to get his doctorate at the University of Chicago and become the head of the first Afro-American Studies Program at San Francisco State University, wrote an account of the Festival:

"There was a battle in Algiers in late July, with lighter skirmishes both old and new, and emerging signs of struggle which now lurk ready to boomerang around the world in the years (and months) to come. The troops came together, African generals and footsoldiers in the war of words and politics that splashed against the calm waters of the Mediterranean Sea—in the First Pan-African Cultural Festival—from everywhere in greater numbers than ever before; from San Francisco to Senegal, from Dakar to the District of Columbia . . .

"Hundreds of delegates came from thirty-one independent African countries and representatives from six movements for African liberation, from Palestine to Angola-Mozambique and the Congo-Brazzaville. And there were Black Panthers and 'black cubs' and old lions from the American contingent. Secretly exiled Eldridge Cleaver chose this occasion to reveal his whereabouts, and expatriated Stokely Carmichael came with his South African-exiled wife, Miriam Makeba. Kathleen had her baby during the festival, and there was Panther Minister of Culture, Emory Douglass, international jazz artists, such as Nina Simone and Archie Shepp, and Julia Hevre (the late Richard Wright's daughter now living in Paris).

"LeRoi Jones (whose passport had been held up) could not get over, but there were: the serious and quietly charismatic young poet, Don L. Lee; Carmichael lieutenants, Courtland Cox and Charlie Cobb; Panther Chief of Staff, David Hilliard, who had to return to the United States before the festival was over to take care of a crisis with Chicago Police; and the compassionate black Parisian poet, Ted Joans. There were many young black Americans who had not been invited, but who had cared enough to piece together their own fare."[5]

Back in the USA, the FBI aggressively exploited an issue that had begun to present itself in the summer of 1967 when, at the National Convention for a New Politics in New York, two members of the Student Nonviolent Coordinating Committee (SNCC), James Forman and Rap Brown, "led a floor fight for a resolution

---

5. This text appeared in one of those great cheap paperbacks, not mentioned previously: *New Black Voices*, edited by Abraham Chapman (New York: New American Library, 1972); Hare's text is called "Algiers 1969: A Report on the Pan-African Cultural Festival," p. 426.

condemning Zionist expansion."[6] Just a few months after the Festival in Algiers, the Counterintelligence program, otherwise known as COINTELPRO, embraced a fundamental axiom of Israeli propaganda: to be against Zionism is to be an anti-Semite. Rabbi Meir Kahane was chosen as an efficient vessel to convey this message since, as a memo put it: "Rabbi KAHANE's background as a writer for the NY newspaper "Jewish Press" would enable him to give widespread coverage of anti-Semetic [sic] statements made by the BPP [Black Panther Party] and other Black nationalist hate groups not only to members of JEDEL [Jewish Defense League] but to other individuals who would take cognizance of such statements."[7] Fabricated letters, like the one below, went out:

Dear Rabbi Kahane:

I am a Negro man who is 48 years old and served his country in the U.S. Army in WW2 and worked as a truck driver with "the famous red-ball express" in Gen. Eisenhour's [sic] Army in France and Natzi [sic] Germany. One day I had a crash with the truck I was driving, a 2½ ton truck, and was injured real bad. I was treated and helped by a Jewish Army Dr. named "Rothstein" who helped me get better again.

Also I was encouraged to remain in high school for two years by my favorite teacher, Mr. Katz. I have always thought Jewish people are good and they have helped me all my life. That is why I become so upset about my oldest son who is a Black Panther and very much against Jewish people. My oldest son just returned from Algers [sic] in Africa where he met a bunch of other Black Panthers from all over the world. He said to me they all agree that the Jewish people are against all the colored people and that the only friends the colored people have are the Arabs.

I told my child that the Jewish people are the friends of the colored people but he calls me a Tom and says I'll never be anything better than a Jew boy's slave.

Last night my boy had a meeting at my house with six of his Black Panther friends. From the way they talked it sounded like they had a plan to force Jewish store owners to give them money or they would drop a bomb on the Jewish store. Some of the money they get will be sent to the Arabs in Africa.

They left books and pictures around with Arab writing on them and pictures of Jewish soldiers killing Arab babys [sic]. I think they are going to give these away at Negro Christian Churchs [sic].

6. Ward Churchill and Jim Vander Waal, *The Cointelpro Papers: Documents from the FBI's Secret Wars Against Dissent in the United States* (Boston: South End Press, 2002), p. 135; this essential book sheds much light on understanding the extent to which limitations on dissent have become internalized and normalized since the 1970s.

7. Ibid., p. 136.

I thought you might be able to stop this. I think I can get some of the pictures and books without getting myself in trouble. I will send them to you if you are interested.

I would like not to use my real name at this time.

A friend

"It is further suggested that a second communication be sent to Rabbi KAHANE approximately one week after the above described letter which will follow the same foremat [*sic*], but will contain as enclosures some BPP artifacts such as pictures of BOBBY SEALE, ELDRIDGE CLEAVER, a copy of a BPP newspaper, etc. It is felt that such a progression of letters should then follow which would further establish rapport with the JEDEL and eventually culminate in the anonymous letter writer requesting some response from the JEDEL recipient of these letters."[8]

Other memos, from 1970, describe further operations and their results:

"2.   Operations Being Submitted

On 2/27/70, a correspondence was directed to individuals known to have attended a BPP [Black Panther Party] fund-raising function at the home of the well known musician, LEONARD BERNSTEIN. This correspondence outlined the BPP's anti-semetic [*sic*] posture and pro-Arab position."

3.   Tangible Results

On 5/7/70 [NAMES BLACKED OUT] both of whom have furnished reliable information in the past, advised that on that date approximately 35 members of the Jewish Defense League (JDL) picketed the Harlem Branch of the BPP in NYC. The purpose of this demonstration was to show that the JDL feels the BPP is anti-Semetic [sic] in its acts and words.

Also on the above date, approximately 50 members of the JDL demonstrated outside of the Bronx, New York BPP Headquarters for the aforementioned reasons.

In view of the above actions by the JDL it is felt that some of the counterintelligence measures of the NYO [New York Office (of the FBI)] have produced tangible results."[9]

8. Ibid., p. 137.
9. Ibid., pp. 162–63.

5.

At an event to raise money for medical relief at the beginning of the al-Aqsa intifada, I quoted a story recounted by Abraham Serfaty, the same man who had hosted the Black Panthers in Algiers, in a "salute to the African-Americans":

> I remember my father, when I was about ten, telling me once in the synagogue: "Zionism is against our religion." And I recall the pilgrimage with my parents, when I was 14, to the tomb of Rabbi Amran Ben Diwan, in an olive grove in Asjen, right near Ouezzane. What did it matter that belief in God was a thing of the past, I couldn't root this scene from my being any more than the olive trees could uproot themselves from their terrain, that ancient olive grove that so many of my ancestors had prayed in. My roots were there, in the depths of that soil. Could I accept that my Moroccan Jewish brethren had gone to the Holy land, that land of Palestine from which Rabbi Amran had come, in order to uproot olive trees?[10]

As if that wasn't clear enough, I read what Serfaty had written in 1982, following Sabra and Shatilla: "That religion of peace, justice, and mutual respect, has been transformed by them into a religion of hatred, war and injustice. What a disgrace to the sacred memory of our ancestors! That assassins like Begin and Sharon used their mercenaries to massacre women, children and elderly people in the name of Judaism. What a disgrace and what a sacrilege."[11]

When I was through speaking, an entourage of ultra-Orthodox men waited off stage to greet me and one, stepping out from the group and extending both arms to take my hand, exclaimed: "Who was that sage you spoke of?"

6.

In 1991 I got a letter postmarked "Central Prison; Kuneitra, Morocco," dated June 24. I had met Christine Daure-Serfaty some months before, when she had come to New York to accept a human rights award in her still imprisoned husband's name. Happy for the recognition but appalled at the institutional merchandising of pain and suffering she sensed in the proceedings, we immediately hit it off. She told me that the only visitors her husband might eventually receive had

10. One of the most important political prisoners in the Arab world for many years, Abraham Serfaty is virtually unknown in the United States; none of his books have been translated into English and his position as a major anti-Zionist Jew certainly has played a part in this; the quote is from *Écrits de prison sur la Palestine* (Paris: Arcantere, 1992), p. 16 [my translation].

11. Ibid., p. 30.

to be related. Because of our common background, she suggested I pose as a long-lost cousin, an American searching for "roots." I proceeded to write to Abraham, not quite knowing what to expect. By now an internationally known figure, Serfaty had been captured in 1972, brutally tortured and held at the infamous desert prison of Tazmamart; in 1977 he was given a life sentence for "openly plotting to overthrow the monarchy," and "offences against state security." A mining engineer by profession, he had been active in the communist party and belonged to a clandestine Marxist group. By the time he wrote to me, his conditions had improved and the long letter (beginning "Dear Friend, Your letter of May 2 gave me great pleasure. I am already familiar with your texts in *Middle East Report* and, moreover, I have long hoped to enter into contact with a younger, militant anti-zionist Jew whose sensibility is representative of Oriental Jews maintaining some rapport with this ethnicity in relation to the State of Israel"), was typed out on thin paper and neatly pasted into an aerogramme. The Gulf War had only been officially over for a few months and Bosnia was on the verge of a siege that would last over three years.

7.

After the assassination of Martin Luther King in 1968, rebellions and riots broke out in 125 cities across the United States; after Robert Kennedy's assassination, tanks sealed Miami Beach off from demonstrators and rioters too close to the Republican Convention; in Chicago, police battled demonstrators outside the Democratic National Convention; on Moratorium day in November 1969, millions across the country staged antiwar demonstrations; in December, police assassinated Black Panthers Fred Hampton and Mark Clark. In 1970, U.S. troops invaded Cambodia: students were shot and killed at Kent State and Jackson State universities. In 1971, Colonel Robert D. Heinl, Jr., in "The Collapse of the Armed Forces," wrote: "By every conceivable indicator, our army that now remains in Vietnam is in a state approaching collapse, with individual units avoiding or having refused combat, murdering their officers and non-commissioned officers—drug-ridden, and dispirited where not near-mutinous."[12] In 1971, the Vietnam Veterans Against the War, along with mothers whose sons were killed and their supporters, carried out Dewey Canyon III, "a limited incursion into the country of Congress." On the final of several days of protest, some 800 decorated veterans stepped up to a microphone in front of the barricades blocking access to the White House, made a statement, and

12. Colonel Robert D. Heinl, Jr., "The Collapse of the Armed Forces," in *Vietnam and America,* edited by Marvin H. Gettleman, Jane Franklin, Marilyn B. Young, and H. Bruce Franklin (New York: Grove Press, 1995), p. 327.

threw their Bronze Stars, Silver Stars, Purple Hearts, and campaign ribbons over the fences.[13]

In high school—1969, 1970, 1971—if you wore an army jacket, it meant you were against the war. But that would soon change, with imagery and stories of POWs and returning vets facing a purportedly hostile homecoming. It took ten years to reverse the famous image of General Loan, head of South Vietnam's police and intelligence, firing a pistol into the head of a prisoner; it took ten years to hand that gun over to a North Vietnamese officer and replace the NLF prisoner with an American POW forced to play Russian roulette. It took ten years, but it happened, in *The Deer Hunter*, in 1978.[14] In the meantime, the Middle East had taken center stage and "Israel, or a certain image of Israel, came to function as a stage upon which the war in Vietnam was refought—and this time, won."[15] In 1979, U.S. Ambassador to the United Nations Andrew Young was forced to resign because of contacts with the PLO. The revolution was almost complete: sights could be set on Beirut, barely limping but still alive.

8.

In *Memory for Forgetfulness*, Mahmoud Darwish describes the effects of a vacuum bomb, used by the Israeli air force on an eight-story apartment building near Sanaya Gardens in West Beirut:

> A vacuum bomb. It creates an immense emptiness that annihilates the base under the target, the resulting vacuum sucking the building down and turning it into a buried graveyard. No more, no less. And there, below, in the new realm, the form keeps its shape. The residents of the building keep their previous shapes and the varied forms of their final, choking, gestures. There, below, under what a moment ago was under them, they turn into statues made of flesh with not enough life for a farewell. Thus he who was asleep is still sleeping. He who was carrying a coffee tray is still carrying it. He who was opening a window is still opening it. He who

13. Certainly one of the most moving acts in American history, this action is very well documented in a book that, of course, remains out of print; the current positions of its primary author, John Kerry, one of the Democratic candidates for the presidency in 2004, are indicative of the political distances that have been traveled since that period; *The New Soldier* by John Kerry and Vietnam Veterans Against the War; edited by David Thorne and George Butler (New York: Collier Books, 1971).

14. For a brilliant analysis of this reversal of imagery, see H. Bruce Franklin, *Vietnam and Other American Fantasies* (Amherst: University of Massachusetts Press, 2000), pp. 14–17.

15. From Melani McAlister's groundbreaking and important book, *Epic Encounters: Culture, Media and U.S. Interests in the Middle East, 1945–2000* (Berkeley: University of California Press, 2001), p. 159.

was sucking at his mother's breast is still suckling. And he who was on top of his wife is still on top of her. But he who happened to be standing on the roof of the building can now shake the dust off his clothes and walk into the street without using the elevator, for the building is now level with the ground. For that reason the birds have remained alive, perched in their cages on the roof.[16]

In "Beirut Guernica," Fawwaz Traboulsi writes:

Guernica 1937: testing ground for the latest models of the Nazi death machines on the eve of World War II. A new generation of incendiary bombs. The study of the effects of air raids on a civilian population.

Beirut 1982: testing ground in the atomic age for the latest models in the arsenal of the U.S. war machine:

Semi-nuclear bombs,
smart bombs,
laser-guided bombs,
implosion,
cluster,
fragmentation,
concussion,
and phosphorous bombs . . .[17]

9.

In 1945, Moise Ventura, the chief rabbi of Alexandria, delivered a sermon called "An Echo of the Atomic Bomb," which began: "The state of the discovery of the atomic bomb marks the historic moment of the most spectacular explosion of materialism, that world system founded on the principle of the eternity and indestructibility of matter."[18]

16. From Mahmoud Darwish's masterpiece, *Memory for Forgetfulness: August, Beirut, 1982;* translated by Ibrahim Muhawi (University of California Press, 1995), pp. 76–7.

17. From Lebanese writer, journalist and translator Fawwaz Traboulsi's powerful work *Guernica-Beirut,* originally published in Beirut in 1987. This excerpt appears as "Beirut Guernica: A City and a Painting," in *For Palestine,* edited by Jay Murphy (New York: Writers and Readers, 1993). Traboulsi is the translator into Arabic of Marx, Engels, Gramsci, Isaac Deutscher, John Reed, John Berger, and many others.

18. A major scholar who wrote seminal texts on Saadia Gaon and Moses Maimonides, Moise Ventura is a completely forgotten figure and only one of hundreds of prominent Arab Jewish intellectuals whose biographies and thought have been completely excised from the narrative of contemporary Jewish life; Ventura expressed bitter

10.

The scheduled release date for Mordechai Vanunu (the former nuclear techni-
cian drugged, beaten and kidnapped in Rome under the orders of then-
Defense Minister Shimon Peres and taken to Israel where he disappeared for six
weeks before being tried in secret and given an eighteen-year sentence, more
than eleven years of which were served in solitary confinement), is April 22, 2004.[19]

11.

Meir Vanunu, harassed and threatened with imprisonment for campaigning on
his brother's behalf, wrote: "The Lebanon war of 1982 had a great effect on the
development of his views in the following years, in fact, already, before the war,
he refused to train or to be trained in his army reserve service, and chose to work
in the kitchen instead. In his geography degree he took a special interest in acid
rain and its effects on the environment. He went on to study for a Masters degree in Philosophy, became an assistant lecturer and lectured in philosophy. When
I try to explain myself and to others how he came to do what he did, I draw the

---

disillusionment with Europe while still harboring hopes for a revitalized Middle East
where Jews would continue to have a central role in an integrated society. In a New
Year's Sermon given in 1942, Ventura said: "After the lamentable failure of Western
civilization, the Orient is again called upon to play an important part in the cultural
life of Nations. The Orient means Egypt, Palestine, Syria, Iraq; more specifically, the
Semites—Jews and Arabs—are again called upon together to play a vital role within
the scene of history. Everyone whose mental capacities are in free working order must
recognize that today the enemies of the Jews are as well the enemies of the Arabs—
that is, the enemies of civilization." This text, and the one referenced by this footnote,
both appear in *Soupirs et espoirs: Échos de la guerre, 1939–1945* (Paris: Libraire Durlacher,
1948), pp. 76, 88, and 99 [my translation].

19. The importance of public awareness in the United States about the Vanunu case
cannot be overemphasized, particularly now, after the patently false reasons given for
the U.S.-led invasion and occupation of Iraq. The double standards regarding Israel's
possession of weapons of mass destruction, nuclear, chemical, and biological, and various
demands by Egypt, Iraq, Syria, Iran and other countries in the region to have Israel
comply with the Nuclear Non-Proliferation Treaty (to which they are NOT a signatory),
can only be described as outrageous and potentially cataclysmic. Information on
Mordechai himself, as well as his potential release, is available through: The U.S. Campaign
to Free Morechai Vanunu / Felice Cohen-Joppa, coordinator / P.O. Box 43384 / Tuc-
son, AZ 85733 / Phone/Fax: (520) 323–8697 / e-mail *freevanunu@mindspring.com*.
In addition, it is very important that people write to Vanunu in prison, both to bolster his own spirits and to make the Israeli government aware of the fact that people are
concerned about his fate. Letters should be addressed to: Dr. Mordechai Vanunu / Ashkelon
Prison / Ashkelon, ISRAEL.

following picture. On one hand, a man who in his daily reality was deeply involved in the philosophy of those such as Nietzsche, Sartre, Spinoza, and Kierkegaard, and on the other hand faced the reality of his work as a full time night-shift worker at the nuclear complex half an hour from the university." Later, from prison, when he could finally write, Mordechai let his brother know that: "I did not want to be a hero. I did not want to be famous. I did not want to perform this act but I knew if I had not done it, no one would."[20]

12.

In a proposal tabled during the first ever Israeli parliamentary discussion touching on such issues ("On nuclear weapons and Mordechai Vanunu," held February 2, 2000), member of parliament Issam Makhoul asked the following questions:

Last year a story appeared in the media, according to which Israel exports part of its nuclear waste to be buried in Mauritania, in Africa. I ask the Prime Minister: Is this true? Has Israel adopted the criminal colonialist practice of polluting the Third World, which European countries abandoned some years ago following the struggle of the green organizations?

I ask the Prime Minister: What is the condition of Israel's nuclear missile sites near Kfar Zechariah on the outskirts of Jerusalem, and near Yodfat in the Galilee? Are there additional sites?

I ask the Prime Minister: How is it that plants in which the missiles are manufactured and atom bombs are made are located in the most densely

20. This quote is from "My Brother's Motives" by Meir Vanunu, and appears in *Voices for Vanunu: Papers from the International Conference, Tel Aviv, October 1997; An International Symposium of Experts and Whistleblowers,* chaired by Professor Joseph Rotblat (London: The Campaign to Free Vanunu, 1997), pp. 11–12; in addition to Nobel Prize–winner Rotblat (a member of the secret team developing the atomic bomb at Los Alamos during the Second World War, and founder of the Pugwash Conference on Science and World Affairs), participants included Daniel Ellsberg (former consultant for the Rand Corporation and whistleblower on the Pentagon Papers); nuclear physicist Dr. Frank Barnaby; Judge Amadeo Postiglione, director of the Scientific Secretariat for the Promotion of the International Court of the Environment; Dr. Hugh Dewitt, senior scientist at the Livermore National Laboratory in California; Dr. Vil Mirzayanov, former director of the State Research Institute for Organic Chemistry and Technology in Moscow, arrested and charged with revealing secrets on chemical warfare research in 1992 but cleared through international protests; Dr. Alla Yaroshinskaya, former deputy in Gorbachev's Supreme Soviet, and recipient of the Right Livelihood Award, often referred to as the Alternative Nobel Peace prize; leading Israeli lawyer and activist Avigdor Feldman; psychiatrist Dr. Ruhama Marton, founder and director of the Association of Israeli and Palestinian Physicians for Human Rights; actress Susannah York, and many others.

populated areas in Israel, in the center and in Haifa? I ask the Prime Minister: Do you understand that the Biological Institute in Nes Tsiona, which is where Israel manufactures its biological warfare, is set in a residential area, which is a crime against the residents of Israel and the neighboring countries?

And what about the risk of an earthquake? The reactor in Dimona is located over the Syrian-African rift. An earthquake similar to the one that occurred in Turkey last year would crack the reactor, and Israel would be covered with radioactive dust. If that happens, there would be nothing left but say goodbye, and die a terrible death.[21]

13.

Mordechai's palm, facing out of the tiny window of the paddy wagon, with the name and date of the flight on which he was abducted, tied to a stretcher: "They brought me here like Kunta Kinte, chained up like a slave."[22] Bound and gagged in court, a motorcycle helmet strapped over his head: the *Jerusalem Post* byline: "Yes, the law does allow for people to 'disappear.'" Locked up in a cell no bigger than himself, the lights on twenty-four hours a day, a video camera constantly pointed directly at him: "What kind of justice is there in this state and where are all the defenders of human rights? How did the authorities manage to gag them all without putting them in prison or holding them in solitary confinement?"[23]

21. This document can be found at: *http://www.pnnd.org/debate_in_the_knesset_on_nuclear_weapons_and_mordechai_vanunu.html*.

22. From "Vanunu's Abduction," *Sunday Times* (London), August 9, 1987.

23. Communication by Mordechai Vanunu to his brother Meir from prison; printed in *News From Within* (vol. III, nos. 5–6; March 31, 1987). *News From Within*, published by the Alternative Information Center, then directed by Michel Warschawski, remains a vital source of information. In 1987, the offices of the Alternative Information Center were raided under the British Emergency laws, primarily used to detain Palestinians without charges or warrants. Warschawski faced a twenty-month prison term for providing printing services (a handbook on how to resist arrest) to a "hostile organization." Allen Ginsberg visited Jerusalem to collect information on this case (as well as cases of Palestinian journalists who had been imprisoned) for the PEN Freedom to Write Committee; attempts to make strong statements on these matters were either significantly qualified or fully suppressed by a faction in PEN led by Cynthia Ozick. Characteristically, Ginsberg paid attention and was well aware of the Vanunu case. In a sold-out performance at the Jerusalem Cinemateque on a Friday night, in the heart of white, liberal Ashkenazi cultural life, the faithful had come to hear the great American poet. At the end of his performance, accompanied by Steven Taylor on guitar, Ginsberg sang a song by Tuli Kupferberg, one of the founders of the Fugs, dedicated to Mordechai Vanunu. Along with two companions, I jumped up and burst into wild applause before we looked around to realize no one had budged. You could hear a pin drop. I thought we were going to get lynched.

14.

Like the invisible scars neurologically imprinted on a prisoner deprived of any human contact, there is no return from consciousness: "The individual can compel the establishment, can say to it, You are accountable to me. The individual can expose the dark machinations of any regime in the world, in any sphere, by means of civil disobedience. . . . An action like mine teaches citizens that their own reasoning, the reasoning of every individual, is no less important than that of the leaders. . . . They use force and sacrifice thousands of people on the altar of their megalomania. Don't follow them blindly."[24]

15.

In 1998, there were just a few references to Mordechai Vanunu in the American press: a few scattered news articles, some AP dispatches, one item each on CNN and NPR. *The New York Times* did not mention him once. In Britain, on the other hand, according to the Nexis database, mainstream outlets did at least forty-five major stories on Vanunu, with sixteen appearing in the *Sunday Times*. Many Nobel Prize winners, prominent intellectuals and public figures have campaigned on his behalf. When he was temporarily taken out of solitary in 1999, he spoke of the methods he used to survive: "I developed a way to deal with this nightmare. I waged a totally conscious war against the messages the prison was trying to get through to me. I brainwashed myself to create a system of checks and balances to counteract them. I checked myself continuously to make sure I wasn't going off track. It was like an obsessive trance. I knew that if I stopped that would be the end of me. I could never allow myself to become apathetic. I looked at things only with my own rationale. I couldn't afford to allow any room for pain or emotions. It would have broken me like a twig. If I would have thought about all the things that I missed I would have collapsed."[25]

24. Communication to Meir Vanunu; see note 21, above.

25. These quotes are from a story by Andy Goldberg, appearing in the electronic version of the London *Sunday Times* (April 19, 1998); it can be accessed at: *http:// webhome.idirect.com/~occpehr/ campaign/vanunu/times.html.* The information on references to Vanunu in the press is from an article by Mark Gaffney, "Mordechai Vanunu: Pre-eminent Hero of the Nuclear Age," accessible at: *http://www.counterpunch.org/ gaffney01312003.html.* Gaffney is the author of one of only two books in English on Vanunu, that I am aware of: *Dimona: The Third Temple? The Story Behind the Vanunu Revelation* (Brattleboro, VT: Amana Books, 1989); and *The Woman from Mossad: The Story of Mordecai Vanunu and the Israeli Nuclear Program* (Berkeley: Frog Ltd., 1999) by Peter Hounam, the British journalist who broke the Vanunu story for the *Sunday Times*.

16.

plutonium for memory uranium for forgetfulness
the chosen people is 200 bombs that don't exist
in Dimona acid raining on Bengazi and Tripoli
Algiers Oran Casablanca Rabat and Marrakesh
the Nile the Tigris and the Euphrates glow
the Orontes lights up Gilgamesh chips and
cinders float over this imploding planet

My Patriarch Problem—and Ours

Richard Goldstein

If I forget thee, O Jerusalem, will I lose my right arm? (I'm a leftie.) Will the finger of God impale me? (It might be interesting.) Will the Mossad demand a pound of flesh? (I can spare it.) Not likely any of the above—so, *eppes*? Why can't I forget thee? This question has a special meaning to me as a gay Jew, but I want to answer it through the prism of gay Palestinians. A number of them have been living illegally in Israel and working as male prostitutes. In August 2002, Yossi Klein filed a credible report in *The New Republic* about these sexual refugees. They had been grotesquely abused at home, by their families or by the Palestinian Authority; forced to sit on Coke bottles, dropped into pits of sewage, and such. In the eyes of their tormentors, these young gay men were, ipso facto, collaborators with Israel. My gaydar told me otherwise.

Klein's piece was a brief on behalf of the outcasts, but also an implicit *kvell* about the moral superiority of the Jewish state. This is how Palestine treats its homos, while we let ours run free. Israel is by far the gay-friendliest nation in the Middle East (notwithstanding the recent call by the leader of a religious party for the execution of homosexuals). Tel Aviv has a visible queer scene, and there are homo-themed films of the sort that would shock Christians who think of Zion as a warm-up for the Rapture. Yes, a trannie represented Israel at a European song festival, and yes, a gay war hero served (briefly) in the Knesset. Yes, this is an attempt to project a humanistic image of the Jewish state, but, also yes, it's an expression of the communitarian impulse that makes Israelis think of gays as just another group of exotic citizens, a homo tribe in a polyglot society.

Of course, the embrace extends only to gay Jews. Those Palestinians Klein wrote about? A more recent piece in *The Gay and Lesbian Review* describes their fate at the hands of the Israeli secret police. Threatened with exposure, some of the refugees were pressured into collaborating and, when they were no longer useful, deported to the territories, where they were picked up by the Palestinian police. In this cycle of persecution, Israel, the region's defender of gay rights, compounds the abuse.

Is an ethic genuine if it applies exclusively to members of your group? That question can be asked of most Israeli values. But what about the Palestinian ethic that permits the persecution of gays? As anti-occupation activists point out, the embrace of Sharia, the Islamic law that severely punishes homosexuality, is a recent phenomenon in Palestine, the product of a siege mentality. But not every society in crisis turns anti-gay. I suspect that homophobia in Palestinian culture is a marker of the boundary between that nation-in-exile and Israel. If the occupier is gay-friendly, the occupied will be anything but.

The same is true of the Arab world in general, where fundamentalism arose as a rooting out of the West (and of course, the West had no objection, until recently, to a nationalism that oppressed women and gays). Among Palestinians, this belief system was nurtured by the Jewish occupation, just as Israel's abandonment of its liberal tradition was accelerated by terrorism. The very different fate of gay people in both societies is a consequence of the conflict between them. Virtue and villainy have less to do with it than chronic pain.

Like most progs, I'm drawn to cultures of resistance. But I won't accept the fashionable double standard applied to sexual oppression committed by the oppressed. I don't forgive bitch-slapping rappers and I can't look the other way when Palestinians torture gays. So, shortly after Klein's piece appeared, I made a number of calls about this situation to human rights groups, gay and otherwise. Further investigation was needed before a judgment could be made, I was told. A year later, little had changed. "We've done research about violence against gay American teens, but, to my knowledge, not about this," a spokesperson for Human Rights Watch told me.

The director of the International Gay and Lesbian Human Rights Commission said she would discuss the gay Palestinian issue with her staff and then get back to me. She never did. I did come across dispatches from gay conservatives demanding that the persecution be addressed. Their tone was polemical and predictably directed at the silence of the left. Here was an issue that allowed them to condemn the enemies of Israel and assert the rights of fellow gays. Of course, the homocons never noticed that the humane Jewish state had refused to take these threatened goyim in, just as most gay leftists dedicated to the Palestinian cause hadn't spoken out about its homophobic tendency. I noticed both, but failed to act. I told myself I didn't have enough information. But in fact, the words of my editor were ringing in my ears. "Anything that makes Israel look good!" he had said when I pitched the story. I didn't want to provide that kind of aid, yet I was tempted to do precisely that. So I never ventured into this terrain. The reason for my bad faith is clear to me now: It was my Jerusalem complex.

I have never been a Zionist. As a teenager, I would tell anyone who raised the subject of *aliyah*, "If I wanted to live in a desert, I would move to Arizona." I saw the whole Zionist project as a sexless sing-along with ring dances that had nothing to do with the bluesy grinds I loved. The oppression of the Palestinians wasn't yet on my horizon; the American media had made their suffering easy to overlook. This was mostly about my desire to flee from Jewish power—and also from the power of Judaism.

I hated the stolid synagogue where my parents dragged me on the High Holies. I had to sit there for three hours watching men sway and chant incomprehensibly. Their transfixion, their unrinsed breath, the *tsitses* that bobbed below their talises, brushing their crotches: All of it repelled me. It must also have fascinated me, since I can still call up the memory. That male rapture was so different from the comic Judaism I knew at home: the ten-minute Seders, the *yahrtzeit* glasses recycled for juice, the exemption from the kosher laws granted to bacon. This was nothing like the resonant sight of men touching the Torah with their *tsitses* and then touching their lips. Those men seemed charged with a primordial bolt. It frightened me, because it was my first inkling of a homoerotic bond with God and the sages.

Let it be said that I married a Jewish woman. But when I set out on my own to have a gay life, I dated only *shaygetzes*. I told myself it was the familiarity of Jewish men that drove me to pluck the fruit of Christendom (especially WASPs, the most exotic citrus to a child of the swarthy Bronx). Yet I also lusted after Italians, who were nearly as familiar to me as Jews. There was something else behind the recoil reflex. It had to do with terror and guilt about turning the bond of the patriarchs into a sexual passion. My feelings about this were so conflicted that they couldn't be processed, even as erotic fantasy. The result was a block against sex with Jewish men.

All of this dovetailed with my feelings about Israel, which were formed by countless images of tan and shirtless men. Paul Newman's conquering brow, on display in the film *Exodus* always showing somewhere in the Bronx, was as distasteful to me as the mastery of Hollywood moguls or Garment Center *machers*. They reeked of cigars, an utter absence of faith in the world, and a grasp of human folly that consolidated their will to power. For me, this will always be the essence of Jewish machismo. I've kept my distance.

Yet there are things about being Jewish I adore. Anything Yiddish: Those curling, shoulder-shrugging cadences; the fatalism in every phrase; the delicious sensation of turning German into something perverse. Yiddish-inflected English automatically carried a conditional tone—as in "How should I be?" This send-up of certainty invited me to imagine a different kind of Jewish man, untethered by the guide wires of patriarchy, flying off into the clouds like some luftmensch out of Chagall, hands outstretched in a gesture at once welcoming and pleading: Come, boychick, I will take you home. This, of course, was my father.

From him I learned a patchwork version of the *mamaloshen*, along with the most unpronounceable Yiddish explicative—that cross between "oy" and "feh" that so perfectly expresses the experience of a European Jew in the *gildene/treyfene medina*, the golden and polluting land of America. My father's Judaism was intensely personal. He had visions of rabbis and tales of the miracles they had performed, saving his life as a child in the tenements on more than one occasion. It was real rock-of-ages stuff, but it had no social dimension. In shul he steered clear of other men, praying in a solitary mumble. He wasn't given to patriarchal bonding, and he rarely had anything to say about Israel. My mother was the Zionist of the family—but also an assimilationist who believed that if she sent me to school with a white shirt and a hankie I would be welcomed into the legions of Disney. She sold raffles for Hadassah and issued casual pronouncements like, "Why can't they leave that poor little country alone?" I would point out that Israel was a nuclear power with an expansive view of its manifest destiny, and she would smile. "My little Communist," she called me, expressing her satisfaction at my upward mobility. In a sense her ambition for me inspired my anti-Zionism. I was above such sectarian leanings, and I looked with contempt at my Jewish neighbors crowing over *Exodus* while complaining about blacks no longer willing to be *schvartzes*. It seemed to me that this same obliviousness had been present in the Zionist project from the start.

Yet I couldn't quite repress the pride I felt every time a Jewish army beat back the Arabs. I, too, had been marked by the psychic wound left gaping by the Holocaust. In addition to the mortal toll, it dealt a fatal blow to the bond with the patriarchs that had always preserved us. Where were the ancients when the gas seared Jewish lungs? Where they had always been: in the Promised Land. Not that my neighbors were willing to give up even an episode of *I Love Lucy* for nirvana in the Negev. But for them no less than for the early Jewish settlers, I suspect, *eretz Yisroel* meant reconnecting with the sages.

The bosom of Abraham seemed suffocating to me. That beard, those robes, the willingness to sacrifice his son (until the Big Man told him not to) were enough to make me flee for the nearest uncircumcised buddy. Yet, to my horror, I had begun to fantasize about a young sabra named Ari, lion of the desert. We made love in the shifting sand, his gun by my side. I was too horny to consider the meaning of this fantasy, but I can see now that it was tied to a new and stirring image of Jewish masculinity. It never occurred to me that this mystique required a victim, and there was little to remind me of that terrible fact. Who saw Paul Newman kick a fellah off the land? We were the underdog, the pariah. What Palestinians?

When Israeli tanks invaded the West Bank, some Jewish American writers reacted to the world's opprobrium by *geshreying* about a "second Holocaust." They took that phrase from Philip Roth's masterfully ironic novel *Operation Shylock* and transformed it into something deadly earnest. They saw the real possibility of a nuclear exchange that would obliterate Tel Aviv and maybe the entire state. Who exactly had these bombs—and would use them given the probability that millions of Arabs would also die—was never made clear. All that mattered was that Israel was in danger of annihilation.

When I thought about the writers prone to this panic, I noticed a pattern. Zionists who had always been conservative weren't given to hysteria, but liberal Jews who had lately become disillusioned were. This was a very complicated closing of the wagons, part paranoia, part solidarity, part spiritual need. Adrift from their progressive moorings, and middle aged, they wanted to feel that patriarchal bond. If they couldn't achieve it by kissing the Torah, they could return to Abraham's bosom through Zionism. Their beards, a symbol of hip resistance in their youth, now gave them the grave and stolid look of Jewish sages in velvet paintings. We wear our quests. American Jews, as Leon Wieseltier has written, are the most fortunate Jews in history. For precisely that reason, there's a subtle sense of loss in the Jewish generation that entered the American mainstream, and it seems especially acute in men. With *zeyde* long gone, father dead or fading, and the prophets retired to Miami, where is the tie that binds these boychicks to the phallus of ages? Asking Jewish men to live without the patriarchs is asking a lot, especially now that Marx and Freud, the secular sages, are all but dethroned (and Seinfeld, let's face it, is no Abraham). In this vacuum, Israel has a primal significance quite distinct from what it represented at the time of its founding. Then, it seemed crucial to Jewish survival and renewal; now, the loyalty of American Jews stems from their security. It's a nostalgic solidarity that has no need to think of itself as progressive. And because this allegiance is metaphysical, it is blind to the complexities of cause and effect that actually define the situation of the Jewish state.

I don't mean to deny the recrudescence of anti-Semitism around the world— a sign that history isn't through with the Jews. But if the defensive posture of American Zionists were grounded in a sense of crisis, there would be a real debate about whether Israel makes us safer. Instead, there's an almost tyrannical consensus. The last time I dared to bash Ariel Sharon for his treatment of the Palestinians, on one of those cable-TV wrestling matches that pass for political discourse, I received three death threats. It wasn't the substance of my remarks but the fact that I'm Jewish and therefore a traitor to the covenant with Israel. I wouldn't call this outrage an expression of solidarity; it's more like phallus worship.

I'd like to think I covet cock, not the phallus. But that's too easy an assumption. Let's just say that my position as a gay man puts me in a highly ambivalent relationship to this primal instrument of male bonding. I hate it, I want it; I have it, I don't. I attack it, yet I'm afraid to live without it. This is pretty much the way I feel about Israel. No wonder it's so hard to criticize that piece of Jewish turf without feeling like I've smacked my father. If I forget thee, O Jerusalem, will He cut off my dick—or should I do it first? I wonder whether gay Palestinians have a similar conflict about their homeland. Presumably the refugees do, but there must be thousands of queers in the territories who haven't been heard from. Like the gay Hasidim I've interviewed, who lead double lives, they may be driven by a sense of loyalty to keep their sexuality under wraps. But what about their fantasies? Here is where we may connect, since we were shaped by two profoundly patriarchal religions. Gay Palestinians are caught in the clash of phallocentric cultures, but, in a sense, so am I. Though I don't live in fear of being seized by the brotherhood and thrown into a pit of shit, images of mortification at the hands of men and exile from their order are imbedded in my nightmares. This stigma, inscribed in dreams, could be the basis of a bond between gay Jews and Muslims. It just might contain the seeds of a new politics, one that challenges all sages and promised lands.

Imagine how the world would change if men asked the primal political questions: Why isn't it enough to love our fathers? Why do we need patriarchs?

Is There Still a Jewish Question?
Why I'm an Anti-Anti-Zionist

Ellen Willis

E arly '90s, post-Bosnia conversation with a longtime political friend I've met by chance on the street: "I've come to see nationalism as regressive, period. I can't use phrases like 'national liberation' and 'national self-determination' with a straight face anymore."

"You know, Ellen, there's one inconsistency in your politics."

"What's that?"

"Israel."

I'm not a Zionist—rather I'm a quintessential Diaspora Jew, a child of Freud, Marx and Spinoza. I hold with rootless cosmopolitanism: from my perspective the nation-state is a profoundly problematic institution, a nation-state defined by ethnic or other particularist criteria all the more so. And yet I count myself an anti-anti-Zionist. This is partly because the logic of anti-Zionism in the present political context entails an unprecedented demand for an existing state—one, moreover, with popular legitimacy and a democratically elected government—not simply to change its policies but to disappear. It's partly because I can't figure out what large numbers of displaced Jews could have or should have done after 1945, other than parlay their relationship with Palestine and the (ambivalent) support of the West for a Jewish homeland into a place to be. (Go "home" to Germany or Poland? Knock, en masse, on the doors of unreceptive European countries and a reluctant United States?) And finally it's because I believe that anti-Jewish genocide cannot be laid to rest as a discrete historical episode, but remains a possibility implicit in the deep structure of Christian and Islamic cultures, East and West.

This last point is particularly difficult to argue on the left, where the conventional wisdom is that raising the issue of anti-Semitism in relation to Israel and Palestine is nothing but a way of stifling criticism of Israel and demonizing the critics. In the context of left politics, the dynamic is actually reversed: accusations of blind loyalty to Israel, intolerance of debate, and exaggeration of Jewish vulnerability at the expense of the real, Palestinian victims are routinely used to stifle discussion of how anti-Semitism influences the Israeli-Palestinian conflict or the world's reaction to it or the public conversation about it. Yet that discussion is crucial, for there is no way to disentangle the politics surrounding Israel from the politics of the Jewish condition. Anti-Semitism remains the wild card of world politics and the lightning rod of political crisis, however constantly it is downplayed or denied.

My anti-anti-Zionism does not imply support for Ariel Sharon's efforts to destroy the Palestinians' physical, political, and social infrastructure while expanding Jewish settlements in occupied territory; or the disastrous policy of permitting such settlements in the first place; or the right-wing nationalism cum religious irredentism that has come to dominate Israeli politics; or, indeed, any and all acts of successive Israeli governments that have in one way or another impeded negotiations for an end to the occupation and an equitable peace. Nor do I condone the American government's neutrality on the side of Sharon. But I reject the idea that Israel is a colonial state that should not exist. I reject the villainization of Israel as the sole or main source of the mess in the Middle East. And I contend that Israel needs to maintain its "right of return" for Jews around the world.

My inconsistency, if that's what it is, comes from struggling to make sense of a situation that has multiple and at times contradictory dimensions. Israel is the product of a nationalist movement, but it owes its existence to a world-historical catastrophe. The bloody standoff between Israelis and Palestinians is on its face a clash of two nationalisms run amok, yet it can't be understood apart from the larger political forces of the post-1945 world—anti-colonialism, oilpolitik, the Cold War, the American and neoliberal triumph, democracy versus authoritarianism, secularism versus fundamentalism.

Indeed, the mainstream of contemporary political anti-Zionism does not oppose nationalism as such, but rather defines the conflict as bad imperialist national-ism versus the good liberationist kind. Or to put it another way, anti-Zionism is a conspicuous feature of that brand of left politics that reduces all global con-flict to Western imperialism versus Third World anti-imperialism, ignoring a considerably more complicated reality. But even those who are anti-Zionist out of a principled opposition to nationalism (including Jews who see the original Jewish embrace of nationalism as a tragic wrong turn) must surely recognize that at present, an end to nationalism in Israel/Palestine is not on either side's agenda. The question is what course of action, all things considered, will help in some way to further the possibilities for democracy and human rights as opposed to making things worse. I support a two-state solution that in effect ratifies the concept of the original 1948 partition—bracketing fundamental questions about Jewish *and* Palestinian nationalism—out of the non-utopian yet no less urgent hope that it would end the lunacy of mutual destruction and allow some space for a new Middle Eastern order to develop.

It looked for a while as if this might actually happen, and during that pe-riod, not coincidentally, there was a surge of discussion among Jews inside and outside Israel on the limits of nationalism and its possible "post-Zionist" tran-scendence. Now it's almost as if those years were a hallucination. Until recently, when a few fragile tendrils of sanity have surfaced in the form of the "road map" talks, the irredentists on both sides have been firmly in control, engaged in a deadly Kabuki dance whose fundamental purpose is to make a peace agreement impossible. Whatever the shortcomings of Ehud Barak's ill-fated Camp David proposal, it did move Israel onto previously non-negotiable territory, especially in its offer to share Jerusalem. In my view, the negotiations collapsed not because they had reached an impasse but, on the contrary, because they had finally become serious in a way that threatened Yasir Arafat's ability to walk the line between peacemaking and appeasing his rejectionist flank. Sharon set out to provoke violence by visiting the Temple Mount; the Palestinians gave him exactly what he wanted. The intifada, the suicide bombings and Arafat's complicity in them basically destroyed the Israeli left, while aside from a few intellectuals there seemed to be no serious Palestinian peace party. Meanwhile Sharon has used the need to defend against terror as an excuse to brutalize the Palestinian population. Any peace initiative must withstand this formidable collusion of enemies.

Nonetheless, leftists tend to single out Israel as The Problem that must be solved. That tropism is most pronounced among those for whom the project of a Jewish state is inherently imperialist, or an offense to universalist humanism, or both. (A young professor of brilliant intellect and anarchist inclinations, whose development I've followed since graduate school: "Why don't the Israelis just leave? Walk away from the state?" and in the same conversation, "Israel is the biggest problem I have as a Jew.") But it is also widespread, if often unconscious, among people who have no ideological objection to the Jewish state as such, including Jews who care deeply about the fate of Israel and are appalled by government policies they deem not only inhumane but suicidal. I've received countless impassioned e-mails emphasizing how imperative it is to show there are Jews who disagree with the Jewish establishment, who oppose Sharon. There is no comparable urgency to show that Jews on the left as well as the right condemn suicide bombing as a war crime, a horrifying product of totalitarian religious brainwashing, and a way to ensure there is no peace. At most I hear, "Suicide bombing is a terrible thing, but..." But: if Israel would just shape up and do the right thing, there would be peace. Would that it were so.

Along with this one-sided view of the conflict, the left has focused on Israeli acts of domination and human rights violations with an intense and consistent outrage that it fails to direct toward comparable or worse abuses elsewhere, certainly toward the unvarnished tyrannies in the Middle East (where, for instance, is the divestment campaign against Saudi Arabia?). No, I'm not saying it's reasonable to demand that critics of Israel simultaneously oppose all the violence, misery, and despotism in the world, or that complaints against Israel are invalid because Arab regimes are worse. Inevitably, at any given time some countries, some conflicts will capture people's imagination and indignation more than others—not because they are worse but because they somehow hit a nerve, become larger than themselves, take on a symbolic dimension. But that is exactly my point: left animus toward Israel is not a simple, self-evident product of the facts. What is the nerve that Israel hits?

Underlining this question are the hyperbolic comparisons that animate the anti-Israel brief, beginning with the now standard South Africa comparison—

the accusation that Israel is a "settler state" and an "apartheid state"—which has inspired the calls for divestment and for a boycott against Israeli academics. The South African regime, of course, was one whose essence was a proudly white racist ideology, a draconian system of legal segregation, and the denial of all political rights to the huge majority of people. To see Israel through this grid is to ignore a great many things: that Israel was settled primarily by refugees from genocide in Europe and oppression in Arab countries; that while Palestinian Israelis suffer from discrimination they are nevertheless citizens who vote, organize political parties, and participate in the government; that the occupation, while egregious, came about as a result not of aggressive settlement but of defensive war; that it continues because of rejectionism on both sides; that there is a difference between the nationalist and ultra-Orthodox militants who dream of a greater Israel and the majority of Israelis who once supported peace but turned to Sharon out of fear and cynicism. As for Israeli academics, they are independent and disproportionately active in opposing government policy, which leaves the boycott movement with no plausible rationale.

Even more fantastic is the Nazi comparison, often expressed in metaphors (Israeli soldiers as SS men, and so on). I imagine that most perpetrators of this equation, if pressed, would concede that Israel is not a totalitarian dictatorship with a program of world domination, nor has it engaged in the systematic murder of millions of people on the grounds that they are a subhuman race. But why do these tropes have such appeal? Where does it come from, the impulse to go beyond taking Israel to task for its concrete misdeeds, to lump it with the worst, most criminal states in history? That Israel is seen as a Western graft in the Arab Middle East (a view Israelis themselves would contest, given that most of the population comes from the Middle East and North Africa) and a surrogate for American power contributes to its symbolic importance as a target, as does an unconscious condescension toward Arabs that leads to a double standard of moral expectations for Israel and its neighbors. But it's impossible not to notice how the runaway inflation of Israel's villainy aligns with ingrained cultural fantasies about the iniquity and power of Jews; or how the traditional pariah status of Jews has been replicated by a Jewish pariah state. And the special fury and vitriol that greet any attempt to bring up this subject in left circles further suggests that more is at stake here than an ordinary political dispute—just as more is at stake in the Israel-Palestine clash than an ordinary border dispute.

At present, the Middle East is the flashpoint of a world ironically destabilized by the end of the Cold War, a world in a more volatile and dangerous state than at any time since the 1930s. And Jews are once again in the middle of the equation—in a vastly different position, to be sure, from the Jews of 1930s Europe; in a vastly different position *because* of what happened to those Jews; and yet the discourse about this set of Jews echoes certain familiar themes. The anti-Jewish temperature is rising, and has been for some time, in Arab and Islamic countries and in the Islamist European diaspora. I am speaking now not of the intemperate tone of left anti-Zionist rhetoric but of overt Jew-hatred as expressed in continual public denunciation of Jews and Zionists (who are assumed to be one and the same), ubiquitous propaganda tracts inspired by or imported directly from Nazi and medieval Christian sources, mob violence and vandalism directed against Jews, the execution of *Wall Street Journal* reporter Daniel Pearl, conspiracy theories like the widely believed tale that Jewish workers at the World Trade Center stayed home on September 11 because they had been warned.

Many on the left view this wave of anti-Semitism as just another expression, however unfortunately couched, of justified rage at Israel—whether at the occupation and the escalating destruction of the West Bank or at the state's existence per se. In either case, the conflation of "Zionists" and "Jews" is regarded as a misunderstanding of the politically uneducated. Which is to say, again, that Israel is The Problem—not only for Palestinians but for Jews as well. This is a serious failure of imagination, for in fact Israel's conflict with the Arab world owes more to the peculiar role played by the Jews in history, culture, and the Judeo-Christian-Islamic psyche than vice versa.

Half a century ago, Israel was supposed to have put a period to the long sordid history of Christian, European anti-Semitism, with its genocidal climax. Instead it turned out that the Europeans had in effect displaced their "Jewish problem," which Hitler had failed to "solve," onto new territory. This was true literally, in that Jewish refugees were now the problem of the Arabs, who didn't want them any more than the Europeans had, and worse, would be pressed, as Europe had never been, to deal with Jews not as a minority but as a sovereign nation in their midst. It was true geopolitically, in that Israel was slated to be a Western ally in a region struggling to overcome the legacy of colonialism—an alliance that would put Israel in the classic position of the Jew with a ruling-class patron, who functions as surrogate and scapegoat for the anger of the ruled. And it was true ideologically, in that the new state would become, for its neighbors, what the Jews had been to Europe—an unassimilable foreign body; a powerful, evil, subversive force; a carrier of contaminating modernity.

These developments exposed the core Zionist belief, that an end to the Jews' stateless condition would "normalize" Jewish life, as tragically naïve. For those on the Zionist left who believed that Jewish nationalism was a necessary but temporary expedient on the way to an international proletarian revolution, the post–World War II landscape offered little support: in Western Europe, the revolution did not happen; the Third World revolutions were nationalist ones; and the Soviet Union proved to be, among other things, virulently anti-Semitic. For right-wing Zionists of the Jabotinsky stripe, the embattlement of the Jews in Palestine justified a ruthless terrorism that in turn validated Arab violence, in adumbration of the present vicious cycle. Of course, the Israeli right has had no monopoly on regressive anti-Palestinian policies, but it has expressed most clearly and consistently that strain of bitter pessimism about the intractability of Jew-hatred to which few Jews, I suspect, are entirely immune. All right-wing nationalism (perhaps all nationalism) is rooted in paranoia, but in the case of the Jews, the paranoids indeed have real enemies; and the Zionist right's glorification of the Jewish warrior must be seen at least in part as a reaction to the stereotype of the soft, bookish Jew who went passively to the Nazi slaughter.

If Israel's conflict with the Palestinians and the Arabs generally cannot be understood without reference to the larger question of relations between Jews and the rest of the world, what of its audience—that is, the international community, including the American left? I'd argue that no one, Jewish or not, brought up in a Christian or Islamic-dominated culture can come to this issue without baggage, since the patriarchal monotheism that governs our sexually repressive structure of morality, and all the ambivalence that goes with it, was invented by Jews. The concept of one transcendent God has a double meaning: it proclaims the subordination of all human authority to a higher reality at the same time that, codified as "God the Father," it affirms the patriarchal hierarchy. The Jews, in their mythic role as the "chosen people" destined to achieve the redemption of the world through their adherence to God's law, embody a similar duality: they are avatars of spiritual freedom on the one hand, patriarchal authority and the control of desire on the other. In relation to Christianity and Islam, the Jews are the authors of morality but also the stubborn nay-sayers, setting themselves apart, refusing to embrace Jesus or Mohammed as the fulfillment of their quest.

In the patriarchal unconscious Jews represent the vindictive castrating father and the wicked, subversive tempter, the moral ideal we cannot attain and the revolution we dare not join. As such, Jews are an object of our unconscious rage at repressive authority as well as at those who tease us with visions of (evil) freedom; a subterranean rage that is readily tapped by demagogues in times of crisis. The ambiguous role of Jews also has a social shape: for complex reasons having to do with their outsider status and efforts to overcome or embrace it, Jews have been overrepresented in the ranks of the privileged as well as among political and social rebels. As a result, Jews are a free-floating political target, equally available to the right or the left, sometimes to both at once. This is why Jews are likely to surface as an issue in some way whenever the political climate heats up (American examples range from the anti-Communist crusades of the '50s, to the energy crisis and consequent debates over Middle East policy in the '70s, to the racial conflicts of the past several decades). Typically, attacks on Jews invest them with far more power than they possess—a tribute to their power as emotional symbols, but a distortion of social reality. In the end, the anger that collects around Jews is anger deflected from its real sources.

My point here is not that Israel should be exempt from anger. Israel is a nation-state. As such it has military, political, and social power. In the exercise of its power, it must be held accountable for its actions. Its misuses of power must be censured and opposed. The victims of its power can hardly be expected to be other than enraged. Yet as a Jewish state, Israel is also subject to layers of irrational anger, whether from antagonists who will not settle for a negotiated peace but demand that the foreign body be expelled, or from political critics who conjure up a monster that rivals Hitler. Israel's power, too, has been exaggerated, contingent as it is on the support of the United States: in the period of economic troubles, foreign adventurism, and revived protest we have entered, who knows what America will look like a few years from now, what our aims in the Middle East will be, what trade-offs we will make?

In the debates over Zionism and anti-Zionism, the situation of Jews is by no means the only question. But it is a question. Is it possible that Jews could once again be massacred? Given the rise of Islamic fundamentalism, the ubiquity of anti-Semitism in the Arab world, the anti-Jewish subtext in much anti-Zionist polemic along with the denial that any such sentiment exists—and given that in an increasingly murderous world the unthinkable takes place on a daily basis—I have to argue that the possibility cannot be dismissed. If there should be a mass outbreak of anti-Jewish violence it will no doubt focus on Israel, but it will not, in the end, be caused by Israel, and the hatred will not disappear if Israel does. Nor will it disappear with an Israeli-Palestinian settlement. Still, from this point of view as from so many others, an internationally brokered peace agreement is the first line of defense. And that agreement must allow Israel to retain its character as a haven for Jews, not as a validation of nationalism but as a gesture of international recognition that the need for such a haven has not yet been surpassed. It's not inconsistent to hope that this will not always be true.

Afraid

Grace Paley

1.

Jews are afraid these days. I'm Jewish so I'm afraid too. I'm afraid for my mother and father in their Russian Jewish youth 90 years ago, their high spirits and dangerous bravery. I'm afraid for my grandmother because she will have to find a wagon to bring her murdered son home. I am afraid for him. He falls down. He's been shot. It's pogrom time. My grandmother finds him among other dead boys. With all her strength, she lifts him, tips him into the wagon. He's seventeen. His name is Rusya. A photograph about two by three feet stands on the windowsill of my front room. When I walk into the room I see his intelligent Russian Jewish face and I am afraid for him. It will not be able to save him. I am afraid for my grandmother's sadness. It will never end. It is almost one hundred years old.

I am afraid for my grandchildren. Two of them are the great-great-great-grand-children of imported African immigrants (slaves). My grandchildren are called African American. I am afraid for those two little children. I am afraid of America.

2.

Ten or twelve years before World War II, my aunt, my mother's sister, visits us. She has come from a place called Palestine where she has lived as long as my parents have lived in this America. She came floating over the sea in a big ship. It was called the Grace Line. She gave me a wonderful button to pin on my dress. It said Grace. Then at the supper table she told my parents that she was ashamed of them. They had become members of the terrible American bourgeoisie. She herself had kept her socialist idealism alive, active in a place that would eventually be called Israel. My father ignored her rudeness politely, but thought it over. He said, What about the Arabs? You think they'll sit still? They'll eat you alive. My aunt said, You ignorant fool, we will live with them together. You'll see. My mother said, Maybe she's right. You don't know everything. Then the years passed as they do for nations as well as people, not always at the same rate.

3.

I am afraid for the Jews of Israel. A great people may not have had to become a small nation, despite promises made 2,500 years ago. Even He, its presumed

Author, did not imagine that His Book, made in Yavneh, so full of myth history prophecy law poetry, would carry us without the baggage of real estate (which must be defended) into the twenty-first century. A Book, a Testament of such beauty that you didn't have to believe in God in order to praise Him on the high holidays. With this Book, we have lived in the United States, France, Brazil, South Africa, Algeria. China! We spoke the languages of those countries; our voices live in their literature. Sometimes we speak with a Yiddish accent, or Ladino. This seems to be useful to those other languages, though they would deny it. They are so busy being nations.

4.

I was talking to my Indian friend from India the other day. She said her family had become obnoxious conservatives. What had America done to them? I talked to an Italian friend who said it was all impossible. With one set of anarchist grandparents and one set socialists, all the old uncles had voted Republican. My Irish friend thought his generation was sensibly progressive, but something had happened to his elders when they settled in a bad mood in South Boston.

This did not happen to the Jewish people for a long time. Their experience of enraged anti-Semitism kept their politics clear for some years. Also they had to state frequently, at home and in shul, "for we were strangers in Egypt." I thought a lot about that sentence when I was a kid. It meant, I thought, that we had to be nice to the two or three Christians who had inexplicably chosen to live in our noisy Jewish neighborhood.

5.

Now at one time, the Jews wanted a king. They'd had a couple of perfectly good prophets, but they said they really wanted a king. The prophet Samuel, with biblical experience and wisdom, pointed out that a king would require all sorts of taxes, olive orchards, concubines, etc.—a terrible expense. No, they said, they wanted to be like all the other nations and have a king—also, they'd probably need, like all the other nations, an army, airplanes, nuclear weapons, borders, checkpoints, and maybe a big wall and a lot more land.

6.

My father said, I told you they'd run into trouble. It's true my parents died years ago, but they still speak to me whenever I'm willing to listen.

My father continued. Anyway, what is this business of settlements? Probably mostly from Brooklyn? What do you mean they're tearing up trees and knocking down people's houses? Then the Arabs (he always says Arabs) for revenge they go after the Jews by killing themselves along with our people? Young boys and girls? They just give away their lives? I bet you one thing, there's some big shot fifty, sixty years old handling the whole business. Fifty-year-old people don't want to die. By the time they're sixty, even less. Then our people take revenge? Then back and forth? You heard the expression—Vengeance is mine, saith the Lord? They can't wait? My God, I'm glad I'm six feet under. And the Jews of America say all this is OK? They don't yell stop? I think they lost their Jewish minds. Us. Poor people hounded all over the earth for a couple thousand years and now they want to be the hounds?

I want to correct him, No, no, Pa, there are people on both sides. A lot who want to live like human beings. You would recognize them. He said sadly, I know, of course. Usually they're better, the people. But always in the end I have noticed how it grows, the state and its terrible power.

My mother who died thirty years before my talking father is shy. She wants to take my hand. Of course she can't. She's thinking about her sister and the grandchildren. All the children. She says, only have pity.

Enough, my father says. And they are gone.

Immature Song

Robert Pinsky

I have heard that adolescence is a recent invention,
A by-product of progress, one of Capitalism's

Suspended transitions between one state and another,
Like refugee camps, internment camps, like the Fields

Of Concentration in a campus catalogue. Summer
Camps for teenagers. When I was quite young

My miscomprehension was that "Concentration Camp"
Meant where the scorned were admonished to concentrate,

Humiliated: forbidden to let the mind wander away.
"Concentration" seemed just the kind of punitive euphemism

The adult world used to coerce, like the word "Citizenship"
On the report cards, graded along with disciplines like History,

English, Mathematics. Citizenship was a field or
Discipline in which for certain years I was awarded every

Marking period a "D" meaning Poor. Possibly my first political
Emotion was wishing they would call it Conduct, or Deportment.

The indefinitely suspended transition of the refugee camps
Must be a poor kind of refuge—subjected to capricious

Kindness and requirements and brutality, the unchampioned
Refugees kept between childhood and adulthood, having neither.

In the Holy Land for example, or in Mother Africa.
At that same time of my life when I heard the abbreviation

"DP" for Displaced Person I somehow mixed it up with
"DT's" for Delirium Tremens, both a kind of stumbling called

By a childish nickname. And you my poem, you are like
An adolescent: confused, awkward, self-preoccupied, vaguely

Rebellious in a way that lacks practical focus, moving without
Discipline from thing to thing. Do you disrespect Authority merely

Because it speaks so badly, because it deploys the lethal bromides
With a clumsy conviction that offends your delicate senses?—but if

Called on to argue such matters as the refugees you mumble and
Stammer, poor citizen, you get sullen, you sigh and you look away.

Inman Square Incantation

Robert Pinsky

Forgive us, we don't exactly believe or disbelieve
What the President tells us regarding the great issues
Of peace, justice and war—skeptical, but distracted

By the swarm of things. The young Romanian poet in L.A.
She said: "In Romania, bums are just bums, but here
In America the bum pushes a cart loaded with his *things*."

With a mean elfin look one of the homeless carters
In Alfred Vellucci Park will sometimes beg using
A stuffed dog, bear or bunny as a prop: the paper cup

Panhandled toward us passing marks puppetwise—
Can you spare a little for Teddy? Or *The Doggie's hungry*—
Crooning maternal parody, a wheedling mock-innocence.

The noseringed leather kids who haunt the T station seem
The reverse—feigned menace. But one bashed some black girls
On the train, using the kind of metal rod called an "asp."

Some money to feed the bunny? His little poetry reading.
And the plush animal a street sign among signs, his ad
For something more personal and abounding than just need.

His smirk knows a thing sharper than pity to block my way by
The brazen ten-foot tenor saxophone that marks Ryles,
To *Top Cleaners*, the bank machine and *Patel Quick Food Mart*.

The dictionary says that a thing is first of all an assembly.
Forgive the word "bums." Forgive "homeless," our sheepish
Euphemism. A Derelict is better for these forsaken.

Across the street from *Cerveija e Vinhos* and *Boston Improv*,
The Romanesque fire house's arches frame bas-reliefs
Of horse-drawn ladder & hose. Amid these signs of civic

Rescue and cleansing, diversion and provender, let's
Remember, you rat-faced beggar: I dislike you. Forgive me.
And if as I pass again from where I've been I choose to take

A dead president from my breast pocket where I stowed the thing
And put it in your cup, it isn't Charity, but superstition—a provisional
Wishful conspiring with the artist in you, son of a bitch, bastard.

The Jewish Question: The Israeli-Palestinian Conflict and Anti-Semitism

"Anti-Semitism," Israel, and the Left

Philip Green

The war on Iraq has unleashed some familiar conspiracy theories in recent months, on both the right and the left. Lyndon LaRouche laid blame for the coming war at the feet of "a nest of Israeli agents inside the U.S. government"; then Pat Buchanan blamed the U.S. invasion of Iraq on a "cabal" of Jewish intellectuals willing to "conscript American blood to make the world safe for Israel." On the other side of the tally, Democratic Representative James Moran declared, "If it were not for the strong support of the Jewish community for this war in Iraq, we would not be doing this," while a Democratic New York City Council member, Robert Jackson, attributed opposition to a local antiwar resolution to Jewish colleagues who saw New York only as their "home away from home" and believed the resolution would "not be in the best interests of the State of Israel."

The idea that Jews loyal to Israel over America were driving the United States to war gained enough force to garner mention in the editorial pages of the *New York Times* and the *Washington Post,* and finally ended up at the feet of Colin Powell, who, in what was surely a historical first for a secretary of state on the eve of armed conflict, was asked by a member of Congress to publicly disavow that a "cabal" was behind this war. Somehow, though, despite the broad circulation—and broad denunciation—of this poisonous idea, only the left seems doomed to bear the taint of anti-Semitism. Why should this be so? The furor over events in San Francisco leading up to the massive February antiwar marches is telling.

Rabbi Michael Lerner, the founder of *Tikkun,* claimed that he was excluded from a list of potential speakers at the Bay Area event because he had publicly criticized ANSWER, one of the sponsors, for being anti-Israel. What might have been a minor back-room squabble went public when a group of left writers (many affiliated with *The Nation*) circulated a petition on his behalf and Lerner himself detailed his charges in the pro-war *Wall Street Journal.* His story, headlined "The Antiwar Anti-Semites," condemned "anti-Semitism and Israel-bashing on the left." Letter writers to the *Journal* responded with barely concealed glee at Lerner's outing of the left, one opining venomously that "the American far left would no more tolerate criticism of its anti-Semitism than the Communists and Nazis tolerated criticism of theirs." Since that writer has certainly not been threatened with removal to the camps or the gulag, we can take his letter for what it really is: an attempt to blackmail "the far left" into silence on a crucial issue.

This fraught accusation of "left-wing anti-Semitism" surfaces so regularly that before considering it, we need to remind ourselves what anti-Semitism—the real thing—has actually looked like over the centuries. It had (and has) nothing to do with Israel or Zionism, but was rather a prototypical racist stereotyping, by means of which the alleged traits of certain individuals—"money-grubbing," "pushiness," moral degeneracy—are transformed via the alchemy of paranoid fantasy into the collective persona of "Jews" or "the Jew." For the anti-Semite, as for all racists, these racial distinctions are always invidious, never just descriptive.

This aspect of anti-Semitism has at times been disguised, since whereas for most other racisms the stigmatized group is alleged to be both morally and culturally inferior, anti-Semitism often combines an allegation of moral degeneracy or social inferiority with a paranoid fear of a dangerous superiority, or envy of supposed intellectual or economic attainment. Envy, though, is as unpleasant as disdain, especially in the form of litanies of what "your people" have so wonderfully accomplished. For the anti-Semite, then, the Jew is not just Jewish; he stands for something, and it's always something bad. At the same time, a collective personality having been established—the desire for world domination and control of international finance at its center—it is also read backward onto individuals, so that for the anti-Semite every Jew is potentially both a bearer of the group character and a part of the conspiracy. But precisely because that is the nature of classical anti-Semitism, we also have to insist that not every reference to a Jew or to Jews is by that token anti-Semitic; to be unable to distinguish ordinary political discourse from hate-mongering is to be willfully obtuse.

Congressman Moran's assertion about "the Jewish community" helps to make the distinction clear. Even devoid of hate-mongering (and followed by a sincere apology), this is a recognizable case of garden-variety anti-Semitism. Some Jews become all Jews, and their allegedly collective desire alchemically transmutes into domination of an entire nation's policies—even though public opinion polls show support for the war to be the same or weaker among Jews than among the population as a whole (as Moran himself acknowledged in his apology).

At the same time, it is not anti-Semitic to say, as Moran perhaps intended to say and as is often said on the left, that "the Jewish lobby is one of the biggest obstacles to a rational American Middle East policy." That statement is arguable, and hyperbolic, but at the same time perfectly reasonable in its broad outline—reasonable judgments are often arguable or hyperbolic. The main point is that there undeniably is a pro-Israel lobby in Washington composed in great part of the representatives of several major Jewish organizations, and if those organizations had their way American policy would always tilt unequivocally toward Israel: just as if the Irish political elite in Massachusetts had had their way policy would for many years have tilted toward Irish Republicanism; or would have tilted toward Mussolini in the 1930s if the major Italian-American organizations had had their way.

As Michael Kinsley pointed out in *Slate*, one of the strongest claims ever made for the power of this lobby can be found on the website of the American Israel Public Affairs Committee (AIPAC). But even this bit of self-inflation does not convict AIPAC's members of "dual loyalty," a charge that is still more likely to be raised by nationalists of the right, such as Buchanan, than by internationalists (or antinationalists) of the left. Ethnic identification with the homeland has always been central to American life, and has often had significant political consequences; any American history textbook that didn't mention it would have to be scrapped. When someone is Jewish, and acts upon the assumption that being Jewish carries with it certain interests and an obligation to defend those interests (as in the defense of Israel), the identification is not only relevant but even called for. This is especially true for those many Jews who feel that organizations like AIPAC do not speak for them, and thus choose to raise the specter of "the Jewish lobby" in order to critique it. One might avoid any implication of stereotyping to say, euphemistically, "the pro-Israel lobby in Washington," but it would also be pointless and obfuscatory.

In American politics, "Jewish" has a concrete, identifiable meaning, as any Democratic or Republican activist could tell us. It is only in extensions of this commonplace observation, such as Buchanan's hint of the ancient blood libel, or his and LaRouche's traditional and inflammatory anti-Semitic language of "cabal" or "nest"; or Congressman Moran's initial failure to acknowledge that Jews are as diverse a group as any other; or Councilman Jackson's implication ("a home away from home") that dual loyalty has become disloyalty, that a line that ought to be drawn is clearly crossed over. A fair-minded person, in short, looks for explanations of phenomena; the racist "explains" them by attaching them to his favorite race. So to "explain" American policy solely as the result of machinations of "the Jewish lobby," without mentioning oil, water, or expansionism; or the interests of the military-industrial sector; or the electoral and ideological utility of substituting guns for butter; or the way in which permanent crisis serves the interests of the Republican Party, is indeed to engage in anti-Semitism.

Conversely, it is misleading to mention all those factors and then, for fear of appearing anti-Semitic, omit all mention of "the Jewish lobby" or of the right-wing ideologues, who are also strong supporters of Israel, in key policy-making positions in the Bush administration. On the face of it, however, none of this has anything to do with the specifically anti-Israel sentiments that are indeed shared by many people on "the left," or in the antiwar movement. Therefore, when Michael Lerner alleges that the left engages in both "anti-Semitism" and "Israel-bashing," one looks for some examples of the former, let alone for any notable exemplars of it on "the left," considering that many of its most prominent voices signed an open letter opposing Lerner's exclusion from the rally. But one looks in vain. It may indeed be true—though how will we ever know?—that the San Francisco coalition would, as Lerner also suggested, have bent over backward not to exclude a black or gay person who wanted to speak, and yet was willing to exclude a Jew. But then the strength of this argument, if it has any, rests on the fact that in the United States people of color and gays can still quite reasonably claim the status of victimhood, with all that entails in our victim-conscious society; and Jews no longer can, to nearly the same extent. It should make Jews very happy, after all, that a "gentleman's agreement" among real estate agents or a redlined mortgage application will hardly ever be applied to them today, and that Jews as such are unlikely to be discriminated against in the courts, or to be beaten up as "Christ killers."

There is still more than enough anti-Semitic attitude around; and it may still, all in all, be historically insensitive for non-Jews, having welcomed Jews into the club, to assume that they can now be insulted as freely as anyone else; but it is not anti-Semitic. In any event, Lerner's case fell apart when subsequent reports satisfactorily established that he was excluded not because he's Jewish or a Zionist—there were, it turns out, already two rabbis with similar politics on the program—but because the rule about not having speakers who had publicly criticized sponsoring organizations had been put in place well before his name even came up.

Having been offered no evidence for the charge of anti-Semitism, then, we return to the original question of the relationship, if any, between anti-Semitism and "Israel-bashing," the only genuine point of departure for the right's (and Lerner's) imputation of "left-wing anti-Semitism." Certain things are obvious. Israel is a Jewish state. This is not a matter of controversy or denigration, but of proud self-assertion. It is a state to which Jews anywhere in the world have an unalloyed "right of return"; it is a state in which, at least in practice, Jews and only Jews are first-class citizens; it is a state governed almost entirely by Jews, in which every government in recent memory has included at least one explicitly Jewish party. The point is not that Israel should be criticized because of these facts but rather that one can't criticize anything about Israel without criticizing Jews.

But then the crucial question becomes: Is a state or its policies above criticism merely because it or they are composed of or made by Jews? The clear answer that the left's ideological enemies want to give to this question is yes: If you criticize Israel, you're criticizing Jews, and therefore you're an anti-Semite. That thousands of those critics, including many of the most distinguished (Noam Chomsky, for example), are Jews themselves doesn't bother the right-wing polemicists, who know they can always count on some conservative Jewish ally to talk about "Jewish self-hatred," a self-serving ideological concept without any clinical content at all, akin to the infuriating psychiatric notion that if you disagree with the analyst's interpretation of your motives you're merely displaying "resistance."

We can just as properly assert the contrary position, as the historian Eric Hobsbawm has done. He argues that the achievement of political rationality begins at home, so the first duty of a Scots intellectual is to oppose Scottish nationalism and the first duty of a Jewish intellectual is to oppose Jewish nationalism; just as, some of us might add, the first duty of a Jewish-American intellectual is to oppose American nationalism—or both nationalisms, for those who identify equally strongly as American and Jewish. If we consider the practical effect of these two positions, the simple nationalistic equation of "Israel" and "Jewish" has a lot to answer for. To the extent that self-anointed Jewish spokespersons, with the opportunistic assistance of the right, have worked to make Israel and Jewishness synonymous, it is they—and not the left—who have sown the dangerous seed of new waves of anti-Semitism. This is all too clear in Europe today, where the nationalist, ideological equation has helped to inflame the Arab youth who commit most of the anti-Semitic outrages attributed by American propagandists to "the French"—among whom, contrarily, it is chiefly the student left who participate in marches against anti-Semitism.

On the other hand, the anti-Semite Jean-Marie Le Pen actually sympathizes with Israel against its Arab enemies, not only because the latter are the more aggressive intruder into his version of a purified "nation" but also because in institutionalized Zionism he recognizes and appreciates a good, traditional European-style nationalism when he sees it. The sad truth, in other words, is that since the foundation of the State of Israel, Jews can no longer claim to be the "Jewish nation," wandering helplessly across the diaspora in search of a home. We—that is, those among us who want it—have a home now; but that home turned out to be a nation-state, and a state is just a state, founded (as most are) in violence, monopolizing (as all do) the means of repression. It is not a moral entity, but just an institutional means of organizing some people in a geographical area and excluding others, by force if necessary.

Nationalism, be it that of Irish Republicans or Anglo-Protestants, Israelis or Palestinians, is no better or worse than the actions committed in its name; no nation-state is better or worse than what it does to its own inhabitants, or in the world at large. In the case of Israel, as long as there are Palestinians clamoring to be allowed to return as full-class citizens to their (or their ancestors') homeland, and being denied that possibility, and killed in large numbers because they refuse to accept that denial, then their dispossession will be a constant and embittering source of enmity for Israel among those who sympathize with them.

That Zionists insist that the land of Israel is actually their historical homeland changes nothing; in the eyes of a disinterested observer, dispossession remains dispossession, no matter what the excuse for it. Is there not, though, a double standard operating here? Palestinians kill innocent people in the name of their nationhood, and seem to retain worldwide sympathy; when Israelis kill innocent people, they incur moral condemnation. In large part, this is because of the logic of the moral equation I've just described. Palestinians lost a home; Jews gained a state. By and large, people give more sympathy to the homeless than they do to states, especially when representatives of the state that expelled them from their homes now talk recklessly of achieving ethnic cleansing by making the expulsion total and permanent. But there is an even more critical factor operating against Israel as well, at least on the left—and here we come to the crux of the matter.

It is often said, angrily and truly, that Israel seems to occupy an exceptional place on the left's political hit list: Where is the critique of the Russians in Chechnya, of Turkey in Kurdistan, of China in Tibet? Actually, there has at times been quite a bit of such critique on the left, not to mention of Saddam Hussein himself. However, it does not seem of major relevance at a moment when the issue for Americans is the brutally one-sided assault we are witnessing in Iraq; and when even some of that assault's strongest supporters admit that it cannot achieve its purported aim—to bring "peace" and "democracy" to the Middle East—unless a mutually acceptable settlement on Palestinian rights is achieved first. Thus if there is a double standard here, Israel is not its primary object.

The truth is that the primary element in almost all left foreign-policy positions today is, and long has been, opposition to American imperialism. No doubt, this opposition has sometimes led elements of the left to romanticize the Third World and to exculpate its grossest tyrants, including those in Arab states. Such bending over backward to support any and all opponents or victims of the United States is a political and moral error, but again, it has nothing to do with anti-Semitism or "Israel-bashing." Whatever critique we ought to make of tyrants such as Saddam Hussein or opportunists such as Yasser Arafat, it remains the case that Israel is both the chief benefactor of American imperialism and its most visible outpost— our "most-favored nation." Israel's treatment of the Palestinians takes place under the umbrella of American protection, with arms paid for or supplied by the United States, with the unquestioning support of both major political parties. And more than any other nation today—unless one counts Tony Blair as a nation—it has hitched itself to the bandwagon of American belligerency. These two conditions—the asymmetrical moral equation and the relationship of Israel to the United States—are what left-wing "Israel-bashing" is all about; they explain its occurrence satisfactorily.

That is not to say that they excuse it; an explanation is not necessarily an excuse. For despite my earlier reference to the acceptance of Jews in the contemporary United States, there is still a terrible subtext here. Though Zionism originated as a response to nineteenth-century European anti-Semitism, it was finally given its material basis by the Holocaust. The State of Israel was thus born out of a terror at least as great as any people has ever had to undergo, and so the hideously destructive conflict between Palestinians and Jews over one of the smaller pieces of politically bounded land on the planet is one of the great historical tragedies of all time. Critics of Israel (I include myself among them) too often fail to see this tragic dimension; too often are capable of coldly forgetting, or seeming to disdain, this history when uttering our criticisms, or treating all of Israel as though it consisted of nothing but followers of Ariel Sharon. This constitutes a failure of human sympathy, though the failure is in no way idiosyncratic. Left, center—and nowadays especially right—people who are in the grip of ideological rigidity regularly forget the humanity of their opponents and view innocent people as only "collateral damage" arising from some policy or other.

In the case of American policy makers today, this is not an exception but the absolute core of their doctrine. As a member in good standing of the left, however, I like to think that we could do better than that. But as for the political content of the criticism of Israel, finally, no invocation of anti-Semitism is necessary to explain the intellectual and emotional outcome of the obvious facts I have stated. Left spokespersons, including Jews, say what they mean, and they hardly ever say "Jews" when they mean "Israel" or "the Israeli government." We do not think political attacks on France imply hatred of French people, or that attacks on the "axis of evil" imply hatred of Iranians, Iraqis and Koreans. Only with "Israel" and "Jews" is this crude equation being made, and it is not being made by Israel's critics, or even Israel's haters; it is being made by its apologists, and by the blowhards and bullies of the right.

The Charge of Anti-Semitism: Jews, Israel, and the Risks of Public Critique

Judith Butler

" . . . *profoundly anti-Israeli views are increasingly finding support in progressive intellectual communities. Serious and thoughtful people are advocating and taking actions that are anti-Semitic in their effect if not their intent.*"

Lawrence Summers, President of
Harvard University, September 17, 2002

When the president of Harvard University, Lawrence Summers, made his remarks that to criticize Israel at this time and to call upon universities to divest from Israel are "actions that are anti-Semitic in their effect, if not their intent,"[1] he introduced a distinction between an effective and intentional anti-Semitism that is controversial at best. Of course, the counter-charge has been that in making his statement, the president of Harvard has struck a blow against academic freedom, in effect, if not in intent. Although he himself made clear that he meant nothing censorious by his action, and that he is in favor of these ideas being "debated freely and civilly,"[2] his words nevertheless exercise a chilling effect on political discourse, stoking the fear that to criticize Israel during this time is to expose oneself to the charge of anti-Semitism. He made his claim in relation to several actions which he called "effectively anti-Semitic" which included European boycotts of Israel, anti-globalization rallies in which criticisms of Israel were voiced, and fund-raising efforts for organizations with "questionable political provenance."

Of local concern to him, however, was a divestment petition drafted by MIT and Harvard professors who oppose the current Israeli occupation and the treatment of Palestinians. Engaging this initiative critically, Summers asked why Israel was being "singled out . . . among all nations" for a divestment campaign, suggesting that the singling out was evidence of anti-Semitic aim. And

---

1. "Summers Says Anti-Semitism Lurks Locally," David Gelles, *Harvard Crimson*, September 19, 2002. The full transcript can be found at *www.yucommentator.com/v67i4/israelcorner/address.html.*

2. Remarks reported in *The Boston Globe*, October 16, 2002.

though Summers claimed that aspects of Israeli policy "can be and should be vigorously challenged," it was unclear how such challenges could or would take place without being construed in some sense as anti-Israel, and why those foreign policy issues, which include "occupation" and are, therefore, given the dispute over legitimate state boundaries, domestic policies as well, ought not to be vigorously challenged through a divestment campaign. It would seem that calling for divestment is something other than a legitimately "vigorous challenge," but we are not given any criteria by which to adjudicate the difference between those vigorous challenges that should be articulated, and those which carry the "effective" force of anti-Semitism.

Of course, Summers is right to voice concern about rising anti-Semitism, and every progressive person ought to be vigorously challenging anti-Semitism wherever it occurs, especially if it occurs in the context of movements mobilized in part or in whole against the Israeli occupation of Palestinian lands. It seems, though, that historically we are now in the position in which Jews cannot be understood always and only as presumptive victims. Sometimes we surely are, but sometimes we surely are not. No political ethics can start with the assumption that Jews monopolize the position of victim.[3] The "victim" is a quickly transposable term, and it can shift from minute to minute from the Jew atrociously killed by suicide bombers on a bus to the Palestinian child atrociously killed by Israeli gunfire. The public sphere needs to be one in which *both* kinds of violence are challenged insistently and in the name of justice.

If we think, though, that to criticize Israeli violence, or to call for specific tactics that will put economic pressure on the Israeli state to change its policies, is to engage in "effective anti-Semitism," we will fail to voice our opposition out of fear of being named as part of an anti-Semitic enterprise. No label could be worse for a Jew. The very idea of it puts fear in the heart of any Jew who knows that, ethically and politically, the position with which it would be utterly unbearable to identify is that of the anti-Semite. It recalls images of the Jewish collaborators with the Nazis. And it is probably fair to say that for most progressive Jews who carry the legacy of the Shoah in their psychic and political formations, the ethical framework within which we operate takes the form of the following question: will we be silent (and be a collaborator with illegitimately violent power), or will we make our voices heard (and be counted among those who did what they could to stop illegitimate violence), even if speaking poses a risk to ourselves? The Jewish effort to criticize Israel during these times emerges, I would argue, precisely from this ethos. And though the critique is often portrayed as insensitive to Jewish suffering, in the past and in the present,

---

3. For an extended discussion of how Zionism itself has come to rely upon and perpetuate the notion that Jews, and only Jews, can be victims, see Adi Ophir, "The Identity of the Victims and the Victims of Identity: A Critique of Zionist Ideology for a Post-Zionist Age," in *Mapping Jewish Identities*, ed. Laurence Silberstein (New York: New York University Press), 2000.

its ethic is wrought precisely from that experience of suffering, so that suffering itself might stop, so that something we might reasonably call *the sanctity of life* might be honored equitably and truly. The fact of enormous suffering does not warrant revenge or legitimate violence, but must be mobilized in the service of a politics that seeks to diminish suffering universally, that seeks to recognize the sanctity of life, of all lives.

Summers mobilizes the use of the "anti-Semitic" charge to quell public criticism, even as he explicitly distances himself from the overt operations of censorship. He writes, for instance, "The only antidote to dangerous ideas is strong alternatives vigorously defended." But with what difficulty does one vigorously defend the idea that the Israeli occupation is brutal and wrong, and that Palestinian self-determination is a necessary good, if the voicing of those views calls down upon itself the horrible charge of anti-Semitism?

Let us consider his statement in detail, then, in order to understand both what he means and what follows logically from what he has said. In order to understand Summers' claim, we have to be able to conceive of an "effective anti-Semitism," one that pertains to certain kinds of speech acts, which either follows upon certain utterances, or is said to structure those utterances, even if it is not part of the conscious intention of those who make the utterance itself. His view assumes that such utterances will be taken up by others as anti-Semitic, or will be received within a given context as anti-Semitic. If his claim is true, then there will be one way or, perhaps, a predominant way of receiving them, and that will be to receive them as anti-Semitic arguments or utterances. So it seems we have to ask what context Summers has in mind when he makes his claim; in what world, in other words, is it the case that any criticism of Israel will be taken to be anti-Semitic.

Now, it may be that what Summers was effectively saying is that, as a community, largely understood as the public sphere of the United States, or indeed, of a broader international community which might include parts of Europe and parts of Israel, the only way that a criticism of Israel can be heard is through a certain kind of acoustic frame, such that the criticism, whether it is of West Bank settlements, the closing of Birzeit and Bethlehem Universities, the demolition of homes in Ramallah or Jenin, or the killing of numerous children and civilians, can only be taken up and interpreted as an act of hatred for Jews. If we imagine who is hearing, and who is hearing the former kinds of criticisms *as* anti-Semitic, that is, expressing hatred for Jews or calling for discriminatory action against Jews, then we are asked to conjure a listener who attributes intention to the speaker: "so and so" has made a public statement against the Israeli occupation of Palestinian territories, and this must mean that "so and so" actually hates Jews or is willing to fuel those who do. The criticism is thus not taken for its face value, but given a hidden meaning, one that is at odds with its explicit claim. In this way, the explicit claim does not have to be heard, since what one is hearing is the hidden claim made beneath the explicit one. The criticism against Israel that is levied is nothing more than a cloak for that hatred, or a cover for a call, transmuted in form, for discriminatory action against Jews.

So whereas Summers himself introduces a distinction between intentional and effective anti-Semitism, it would seem that effective anti-Semitism can be understood only by conjuring a seamless world of listeners and readers who take certain statements critical of Israel to be tacitly or overtly *intended* as anti-Semitic expression. The only way to understand *effective* anti-Semitism would be to presuppose *intentional* anti-Semitism. The effective anti-Semitism of any criticism of Israel will turn out to reside in the intention of the speaker as it is retrospectively attributed by the one who receives—listens to or reads—that criticism. The intention of a speech, then, does not belong to the one who speaks, but is attributed to that speaker later by the one who listens. The intention of the speech act is thus determined belatedly by the listener.

Now it may be that Summers has another point of view in mind, namely, that critical statements *will be used* by those who have anti-Semitic intent, that such statements will be exploited by those who want not only to see the destruction of Israel but the degradation or devaluation of Jewish people in general. In this case, it would seem that the discourse itself, if allowed into the public sphere, will be taken up by those who seek to use it, not only for a criticism of Israel, but as a way of doing harm to Jews, or expressing hatred for them. Indeed, there is always that risk, a risk that negative comments about the Israeli state will be misconstrued as negative comments about Jews. But to claim that the only meaning that such criticism can have is to be taken up as negative comments about Jews is to attribute to that particular interpretation an enormous power to monopolize the field of reception for that criticism. The argument against letting criticisms of Israel into the public sphere would be that it gives fodder to those with anti-Semitic intentions, and that those who have such intentions will successfully co-opt the criticisms made. Here again, the distinction between effective anti-Semitism and intended anti-Semitism folds, insofar as the only way a statement can become effectively anti-Semitic is if there is, somewhere, an intention to use the statement for anti-Semitic aims, an intention imagined as enormously effective in realizing its aims. Indeed, even if one did believe that criticisms of Israel are by and large heard as anti-Semitic (by Jews, by anti-Semites, by people who could be described as neither), it would then become the responsibility of all of us to change the conditions of reception so that the public might begin to learn a crucial political distinction between a criticism of Israel, on the one hand, and a hatred of Jews, on the other.

A further consideration has to take place here, since Summers himself is making a statement, a strong statement, as president of an institution that assumes its value in part as a symbol of academic prestige in the United States. In his statement, he is saying that he, as a listener, will take any criticism of Israel to be effectively anti-Semitic. Although in making his remarks he claimed that he was not speaking as president of the university, but as a "member of the community," his speech was a presidential address, and it carried weight in the press precisely because he exercised the symbolic authority of his office. And in this respect, he models the listener or reader we have been asked to conjure. If he is the one who is letting the public know that he will take any criticism of Israel to be anti-Semitic, that any criticism of Israel will have that effect *on him* and, so, will be "effectively" anti-Semitic, then he is saying that public discourse itself ought to be constrained in such a way that those critical statements are not uttered. If they are uttered, they will be taken up and interpreted in such a way that they will be considered anti-Semitic. The ones who make those arguments will be understood as engaging in anti-Semitic speech, even hate speech. But here it is important to distinguish between anti-Semitic speech that, say, produces a hostile and threatening environment for Jewish students, racist speech which any university administrator would be obligated to oppose and to regulate and speech that makes a student politically uncomfortable because it opposes a state or a set of state policies that any student may defend. The latter is a political debate, and if we say that the case of Israel is different because the very identity of the student is bound up with the state of Israel, so that any criticism of Israel is considered an attack on "Israelis" or, indeed, "Jews" in general, then we have "singled out" this form of political allegiance from all the other forms of political allegiance in the world that are open to public disputation, and engaged in the most outrageous form of silencing and "effective" censorship.[4]

Indeed, not only, it seems, will Summers regard such criticisms as anti-Semitic, but he is, by his example, and by the normative status of his utterance, recommending that others regard such utterances that way as well. He is setting a norm for legitimate interpretation. We do not know how he would rule on various cases if they were to reach his desk, but his current utterance gives symbolic authority to the claim that such utterances are impermissible, in the same way that racist utterances are. What is complicated, however, is that his understanding of what constitutes anti-Semitic rhetoric depends upon a very specific and very questionable reading of the field of reception for such speech. He seems, through his statement, to be describing a sociological condition under which speech acts occur and are interpreted, i.e., describing the fact that we are living in a world where, for better or worse, criticisms of Israel are simply heard as anti-Semitic. He is, however, also speaking as one who is doing that hearing, and so modeling the very hearing that he describes. In this sense, he is producing a prescription: he knows what effect such statements have, and he is telling us about that effect; they will be taken to be anti-Semitic; he takes them to be anti-Semitic; and in this way, rhetorically, he recommends that others take them to be so as well.

The point is not only that his distinction between effective and intentional anti-Semitism cannot hold, but that the way the distinction collapses in his formulation is precisely what produces the condition under which certain public

4. Robert Fisk writes, "The all-purpose slander of 'anti-Semitism' is now being used with ever-increasing promiscuity against people who condemn the wickedness of Palestinian suicide bombings every bit as much as they do the cruelty of Israel's repeated killing of children in an effort to shut [those people] up." "How to Shut Up Your Critics with a Single Word," *The Independent*, October 21, 2002.

views are taken to be hate speech, in effect if not in intent. One point Summers did not make is that anything that the Israeli state does in the name of its self-defense is fully legitimate and ought not to be questioned. I do not know whether he approves of all Israeli policies, but let us imagine, for the sake of argument, that he does not. And I do not know whether he has views about, for instance, the destruction of homes and the killings of children in Jenin which, last year, attracted the attention of the United Nations, but was not investigated as a human rights violation when Israel refused to let the UN survey the scene. Let us imagine that he objects to those actions and those killings, and that they are among the "foreign policy" issues that he believes ought to be "vigorously challenged." If that is the case, then he would be compelled, under his formulation, not to voice his disapproval, believing, as he does, that the voicing of that disapproval would be construed, effectively, as anti-Semitism. And if he thinks it is possible to voice that disapproval, he has not shown us how it might be voiced in such a way that the allegation of anti-Semitism might be averted.

If one were to decide not to voice a criticism of those killings, for fear that that criticism might be taken as critical of the Jews, say, as a people, or as stoking the fires of anti-Semitism elsewhere, one would be compelled to choose between exercising the right or, indeed, obligation to wage public criticism against forms of violent injustice, on the one hand, and fomenting anti-Semitic sentiment through the exercise of that right, on the other. If Summers did object to such policies, would he censor himself and ask that others do the same?

I do not have the answer to this question, but his logic suggests the following: one could conclude, on the basis of a desire to refrain from strengthening anti-Semitic sentiment and belief, that certain actions of the Israeli state—acts of violence and murder against children and civilians—must not be objected to, must go unremarked and unprotested, and that these acts of violence must be allowed to go on, unimpeded by public protest or outrage, for fear that any protest against them would be tantamount to anti-Semitism, if not anti-Semitism itself.

Now, it is surely possible to argue, as I would and do argue, that all forms of anti- Semitism must be opposed, but it would seem that now we have a serious set of confusions about what forms anti-Semitism takes. Indeed, the actual problem of anti-Semitism is elided here by the strategic way that the charge of anti-Semitism works, which means that when and if the charge ought to be made, it will have been made less robust by its use as a threatened interpellation. Indeed, if the charge of anti-Semitism is used to defend Israel at all costs, then the power of the charge to work against those who demean and discriminate against Jews, who do violence to synagogues in Europe, who wave Nazi flags and support anti-Semitic organizations is radically diluted. Indeed, many critics of Israel now dismiss all claims of anti-Semitism as "trumped up," after having been exposed to the use of the claim as a means to censor political speech, and this produces an insensitivity and refusal to acknowledge existing political realities that is worrisome at best. One reason, then, to oppose the use of the charge of anti-Semitism as a threat and as a means to quell political critique is that the charge must be kept alive as a crucial and effective instrument to combat existing and future anti-Semitism.

Summers, on the other hand, does not tell us why divestment campaigns or other forms of public protest *are* anti-Semitic, if they are. Rather, it seems that "anti-Semitism" functions here as a charge, one that does not correspond to a given kind of action or utterance, but one that is unilaterally conferred by those who fear the consequences of overt criticisms of Israel. According to Summers, there are some forms of anti-Semitism that are characterized retroactively by those who decide upon their status. This means that nothing should be said or done that will be taken to be anti-Semitic by others. But what if the others who are listening are wrong? If we take one form of anti-Semitism to be defined retroactively by those who listen to a certain set of speech acts, or witness a certain set of protests against Israel, then what is left of the possibility of legitimate protest against a given state, either by its own population or by those who live outside those borders? If we say that every time "Israel" is uttered, the speaker really means "Jews," then we have foreclosed in advance the possibility that the speaker really means "Israel."

If we distinguish between anti-Semitism and forms of protest against the Israeli state (or, indeed, right-wing settlers who sometimes act independently of the state), acknowledging that sometimes they do, disturbingly, work together, then we stand a chance of understanding that the Jewish population of the world does not conceive of itself as one with the Israeli state in its present form and practice, and that Jews *in Israel* do not conceive of themselves as one with the Israeli state. In other words, the possibility of a substantive Jewish peace movement depends upon (a) a productive and critical distance from the state of Israel (one that can be coupled with a profound investment in what future course it takes), and (b) a clear distinction between anti-Semitism, on the one hand, and forms of protest against the Israeli state based on that critical distance, on the other.

I take it that Summers' view, however, relies on the full and seamless identification of the Jewish people with the state of Israel, an "identification" that he makes, in coupling the two, but an "identification" that he assumed to be subjectively adopted by Jews themselves. His view seems to imply a further claim as well, namely, that any criticism of Israel is "anti-Israel" in the sense that the criticism is understood to challenge the right of Israel to exist.[5] I'll turn to the problem

5. Note in the full version of the statement offered as an epitaph to this essay how Summers couples anti-Semitism and anti-Israeli views: "Where anti-Semitism and views that are profoundly anti-Israel have traditionally been the primary reserve of poorly educated right-wing populists, profoundly anti-Israeli views are increasingly finding support in progressive intellectual communities." In this statement he begins by coupling anti-Semitism with anti-Israeli views, without precisely saying that they are the same. But by the end of the sentence, anti-Semitism is absorbed into and carried by the term "anti-Israeli" (rather than anti-*Israel*, as if it were the people who are opposed, rather than the state apparatus) so that we are given to understand not only that anti-Israeli positions but anti-Semitism itself is finding support among progressive intellectual communities.

of identification in a moment, but let's consider the latter claim for a moment. A criticism of Israel is not the same as a challenge to Israel's existence, and neither is it the same as an anti-Semitic act, though each could work in tandem with each of the other claims. There are conditions under which it would be possible to say that one leads to the next. A challenge to the right of Israel to exist can only be construed as a challenge to the existence of the Jewish people if one believes that Israel alone is what keeps the Jewish people alive or if one believes that all Jewish people have their sense of perpetuity invested in the state of Israel in its current or traditional forms. Only if we make one of these assumptions, it seems, does the very criticism of Israel function as a challenge to the very survival of the Jews. Of course, one could argue that criticism is essential to any democratic polity, and that those polities that safeguard criticism stand a better chance of surviving than those that do not. Let us imagine, for the sake of argument, that one set of criticisms do challenge the basic presuppositions of the Israeli state, ones that produce differential forms of citizenship, ones that secure the Right to Return for Jews, but not Palestinians, ones that maintain a religious basis for the state itself. For a criticism of Israel to be taken as a challenge to the survival of the Jews or Jewishness itself, we would have to assume not only that "Israel" cannot change in response to legitimate criticisms, but that a more radically democratic Israel would be bad for Jews or for Jewishness. According to this latter belief, criticism itself is not a Jewish value, and this clearly flies in the face not only of long traditions of Talmudic disputation, but of all the religious and cultural sources for openly objecting to injustice and illegitimate violence that have been part of Jewish life for centuries, prior to the formation of the contemporary state of Israel, and alongside it.

So it seems that the very meaning of what it is to be Jewish or, indeed, what "Jewishness" is, has undergone a certain reduction in the formulation that Summers provides. Summers has identified Jews with the state of Israel as if they were seamlessly the same, or he has assumed that, psychologically and sociologically, every Jew has such an identification, and that this identification is essential to Jewish identity, an identification without which that identity cannot exist. Only on the basis of such presumptions, then, does it follow that any criticism of Israel strikes against a primary identification that Jews are assumed to have with the state of Israel. But what are we to make of Jews who *dis*identify with Israel or, at least, with the Israeli state (which is not the same as every part of its culture)? Or Jews who identify with Israel (Israeli or not), but do not condone or identify with several of its practices? There is a huge range here: those who are silently ambivalent about how Israel handles itself now, those who are half-articulate about their doubts about the occupation, those who are very strongly opposed to the occupation, but within a Zionist framework, those who would like to see Zionism rethought or, indeed, abandoned, and either do or do not voice their views in public. There are Jews who may have any of the given opinions listed above, but voice them only to their family, or never voice them to their family, or only voice them to their friends, but never in public, or voice them in public, but cannot go home again. Given the extraordinary range of Jewish ambivalence on this topic, ought we not to be suspicious of *any* rhetorical effort to assume an equivalence between Jews and Israel? The argument that *all* Jews have a heartfelt investment in the state of Israel is simply untrue. Some have a heartfelt investment in corned beef sandwiches or in certain Talmudic tales, memories of their grandmother, the taste of borscht or the echoes of the Yiddish theater. Some have an investment in liturgy and ritual, historical and cultural archives from Eastern Europe or from the Shoah, or in forms of labor activism that are thoroughly secular, though "Jewish" in a substantively social sense. There are sources of American Jewish identification, for instance, in food, in religious ritual, in social service organizations, in diasporic communities, in civil rights and social justice struggles that may exist in relative independence from the question of the status of Israel.

What do we make of Jews, including myself, who are emotionally invested in the state of Israel, critical of its current form, and call for a radical restructuring of its economic and juridical basis precisely because one is invested? It is always possible to say that such Jews do not know their own best interest, that such Jews turn against other Jews, that such Jews turn against their own Jewishness. But what if one offers criticism of the Israeli state in the name of one's Jewishness, in the name of justice, precisely because, as it were, such criticisms seem "best for the Jews"? Why wouldn't it always be "best for the Jews" to embrace forms of radical democracy that extend what is "best" to everyone, Jewish or not? I signed one such petition, "Open Letter from American Jews" and there were finally 3,700 of us who, identifiably Jewish, opposed the Israeli occupation.[6] This was a limited criticism, since it did not call for the end of Zionism per se, or for the reallocation of arable land, for rethinking the Jewish right of return, or for the fair distribution of water and medicine to Palestinians, and it did not call for the reorganization of the Israeli state on a more radically egalitarian basis. But it was, nevertheless, an overt criticism of Israel. Let us assume that a vast number of those who signed that petition undergo something we might reasonably term *heartache* when taking a stand against Israeli policy in public, and that hands shook as they entered their names on that list. The heartache emerges from the thought that Israel, by subjecting 3.5 million Palestinians to a military occupation, represents the Jews in a way that these petitioners find not only objectionable, but truly terrible to endure, *as Jews*; it is precisely *as Jews*, even in the name of a different Jewish future, that they call for another way, that they assert their disidentification with that policy, they assert another path for Jewish politics, they seek to widen the rift between the state of Israel and the Jewish people to produce an alternative vision. This rift is crucial for opening up and sustaining a critical relation to the state of Israel, its military power, its differential forms of citizenship, its unmonitored practices of torture, its brutality at the borders, and its egregious nationalism.

6. One can see this letter and its signatories at www.peacemideast.org.

One could take the psychological view and say that these petitioners suffer from internalized anti-Semitism, but Summers, to be fair, does not make this statement, even if, *effectively*, the statement seems to follow logically from what he does say. If one calls for universities to divest from the state of Israel, as I, along with many others, have done, that is not the same as condoning the position that Israel should be "driven into the sea," and it is not, as a public speech act, tantamount to driving Israel into the sea. The speech act calls upon Israel to embody certain democratic principles, to end the occupation and, in some instances, to reject the Zionist basis of the current state in favor of a more egalitarian and democratic one. The petition exercises a democratic right to voice criticism, and it seeks to impose economic pressure on Israel by the United States and other countries, to implement rights for Palestinians otherwise deprived of basic conditions of self-determination. The criticisms of Israel can take several different forms, and they differ according to whether they are generated within the state or from the outside: some wish for the implementation of human rights; some wish for the end of the occupation; some call for an independent Palestinian state, and some call to reestablish the basis of the Israeli state itself without regard to religion so that a one-state solution would offer citizenship on an equal basis to all inhabitants of that land. According to this last call, Jewishness would no longer be the basis of the state, but would constitute one multivalent cultural and religious reality in that state, protected by the same laws that protect the rights of religious expression and cultural self-determination of all other people who have claims to that land.[7]

It is important to remember that the identification of Jewishness with Israel, implied by the formulation that maintains that to criticize Israel is effectively to engage in anti-Semitism, elides the reality of a small but dynamic peace movement in Israel itself. What do we make of those to the left of Peace Now, who belong to the small, but important post-Zionist movement in Israel, such as the philosophers Adi Ophir and Anat Biletzki; the professor of theater Avraham Oz; the sociologist Uri Ram; or the political critic Yitzhak Laor? Are we to say that Jews, nay, Israelis who are critical of Israeli policy or, indeed, call into question the structure and self-legitimating practices of the Israeli state are therefore self-hating Jews, or that they fail to be sensitive to the ways in which these criticisms can fan the flames of anti-Semitism? Could it be instead that these critics hold out a different path for the state of Israel, and that their politics, in fact, emerge from other sources of political vision, some clearly Jewish, than those that have currently been codified as Zionism? What are we to make of the new

---

7. See Adi Ophir's discussion of Uri Ram's vision of post-Zionism: ". . . for the post-Zionist, nationality should not determine citizenship, but vice-versa: citizenship should determine the boundaries of the Israeli nation. Judaism would then be regarded as a religion, a community affair, or a matter of a particular ethnicity, one among many" (186). See also Uri Ram's contribution along with other pieces in Laurence Silberstein, *The Postzionist Debates: Knowledge and Power in Israeli Culture*, New York: Routledge, 1999.

organization Brit Tzedek in the United States, numbering close to 20,000 members on last count, which seeks to offer an alternative American Jewish voice to AIPAC,[8] opposing the current military occupation, and struggling for a two-state solution?[9] And what about Jewish Voices for Peace, and Jews Against the Occupation, Jews for Peace in the Middle East, the Faculty for Israeli-Palestinian Peace,[10] Tikkun, Jews for Racial and Economic Justice, Women in Black or, indeed, the critical mission of Neve Shalom—Wahat Al-Salam, the only village collectively governed by both Jews and Arabs in the state of Israel, which also houses the School for Peace that offers instruction in conflict-resolution that opposes Israeli militaristic strategy.[11] What are we to make of the Israel/Palestine Center for Research and Information in Jerusalem?[12] And what do we make of B'Tselem, the Israeli human rights organization that monitors human rights abuses on the West Bank and in Gaza, or Gush Shalom,[13] the Israeli organization against the occupation, or Yesh Gvul,[14] the Israeli soldiers who refused to serve in the occupied territories? And finally, what do we make of Ta'ayush (which means "living together" in Arabic)? This last is a coalition that not only seeks peace in the region, but which, through Jewish-Arab collaborative actions, opposes state policies that lead to isolation, poor medical care, house arrest, the destruction of educational institutions, lack of water and food for Palestinians living under the occupation? Let me cite from one member's description of that group sent to me in the fall of 2002, a young literary critic named Catherine Rottenberg:

> It is a grassroots movement which emerged after the October 2000 events— the outbreak of the second intifada and the killing of 13 Arab citizens within Israel. The Israeli peace camp, particularly Peace Now, did nothing to bring people to the streets; in fact, there was barely a murmur of protest. It began when some professors at Tel Aviv University and Palestinian citizens of Israel from Kfar Kassem decided that a new and real Arab-Jewish movement was desperately needed. There were a dozen activists at the time. Now there are Ta'ayush branches all across Israel and about a thousand activists.
>
> Many of us were tired of going to protests to stand—once again—with a sign in our hand. We were thinking more of resistance than of protest.

8. AIPAC, the American Israel Public Affairs Committee, is the largest Jewish lobby in the United States and is almost always supportive of Israel in its current form and practices.
9. See *www.brittzedek.org.*
10. See *www.ffipp.org.*
11. See *http://oasisofpeace.org.*
12. See *www.ipcri.org.*
13. See *www.gush-shalom.org.*
14. See *www.shministim.org* for information on Yesh Gvul. See also Ronit Chacham, *Breaking Ranks: Refusing to Serve in the West Bank and Gaza,* New York: The Other Press, 2003.

Basically, we use non-violent civil disobedience to convey our message (which is similar to the one endorsed by the American Jewish academics [see "Open Letter . . ."]—but more radical). In Israel, we are probably best known for our food and solidarity convoys that defy the military siege, often breaking through physical barriers, not only the psychological ones. Jewish and Palestinian citizens of Israel travel in convoys made up of private cars (our last convoy included approximately a hundred cars) to West Bank villages where we establish—in advance—strong ties through months of dialogue. We try to break the walls—physical, psychological, and political—separating the two peoples and expose the brutality of the occupation. We bring humanitarian aid, but we use it more as a political tool to break the siege than as humanitarian relief. It doesn't look good in the international press when Israel prevents humanitarian aid from reaching the villages—although it does it all the time!

We usually manage to get some media attention. We have also helped organize many demonstrations; these are always in coalition with other organizations (like the Women's Coalition for a Just Peace).

Yesterday (August 10, 2002), Ta'ayush tried to reach Bethlehem—to break the curfew and to demonstrate with the residents against Israel's draconian policies. The police didn't let us enter the city, of course, and used tear gas and water hoses to disperse us. But we demonstrated anyway, near the checkpoint, calling our Palestinian partners (in Bethlehem) by cell phone so that they could speak to the crowd.

In the past few months, we have also worked within Israel, trying to expose and fight discrimination against the Palestinian population. Last week we organized a work camp at one of the many unrecognized villages in the North and next week a water convoy will go to unrecognized Bedouin villages that still do not have running water.

I have been an activist for many years, but Ta'ayush is something extraordinary. It has been an amazing learning experience—both in terms of democracy, as well as how to negotiate gender, class, sexuality and race in times of crisis. We all have different political agendas, but we have always managed somehow to maintain dialogue and work together. There is no office, no official positions; it is democracy at work and consequently we have hours and hours and hours of meetings. We have created a real community and as far as I can see, it is the only light (small that it is) at the moment.[15]

Such organizations are not only expressing notions of "Jewish" collectivity, but, like Neve Shalom, undercut a nationalist ethos in the interests of developing a new political basis for co-existence. They are, we might say, diasporic elements working with Israel itself to dislodge the pervasive assumption of na-

---

15. *http://taayush.tripod.com.* Citation quoted with the permission of the author.

tionalism. As Yitzhak Laor remarks, "a joint life means relinquishing parts of a national ethos."[16]

It seems crucial not only for the purposes of academic freedom, but surely for that as well, that we consider these issues carefully, since it will not do to equate Jews with Zionists or, indeed, Jewishness with Zionism. There were debates throughout the nineteenth century and the early twentieth, and indeed at the inception of Israel, among Jews whether Zionism was a legitimate political ideology, whether it ought to become the basis of a state, whether the Jews had any right, understood in a modern sense, to lay claim to that land, land inhabited by Palestinians for centuries, and what future lay ahead for a Jewish political project based upon the violent expropriation of the land of Palestinians, dispossession on a massive scale, slaughter, and the sustained suspension of fundamental rights for Palestinians. There were those who sought to make Zionism compatible with peaceful co-existence, and others who made use of it for military aggression, and still do. There were those who thought, and who still think, that Zionism is not a legitimate basis for a democratic state in a situation where it must be assumed that a diverse population practices different religions, and that no group, on the basis of their ethnic or religious views, ought to be excluded from any right accorded to citizens in general. And there are those who maintain that the violent appropriation of Palestinian lands, and the dislocation of 700,000 Palestinians at the time that Israel was founded, has produced a violent and dehumanizing basis for this particular state formation, one which repeats its founding gesture in the containment and dehumanization of Palestinians in occupied territories. Indeed, the new "wall" being built between Israel and the occupied territories threatens to leave 95,000 Palestinians homeless.

These are surely questions and issues to be asked about Zionism that should and must be asked in a public domain, and universities are surely one place where we might depend upon a critical reflection on Zionism to take place. But instead of understanding the topic of "Zionism" to be something worthy of critical and open debate, we are being asked, by Summers and by others, to treat any critical approach to Zionism as "effective anti-Semitism" and, hence, to rule it out as a topic for legitimate disagreement and discussion.

What better time, though, to ask after the history of Zionism, the implications of its implementation, the alternatives that were foreclosed when it took hold in 1948 and before, and what future, if any, it ought to have? A crucial history requires to be uncovered and opened to new debate: what were Hannah Arendt's objections to Zionism, and why did Martin Buber come to disavow its project? What were the movements critical of the Israeli state from its inception from within the community of Jews in Palestine: Brith Shalom, the Matzpen Movement? In the academy, we ask these questions about U.S. traditions of political belief and practice; we consider various forms of socialism critically and openly; and we consider in a wide variety of contexts the problematic nexus

16. Yitzhak Laor, "Will the Circle Be Unbroken? " *Ha'aretz*, August 2, 2002.

of religion and nationalism. What does it mean to paralyze our capacities for critical scrutiny and historical inquiry when this topic becomes the issue, fearing that we will become exposed to the charge of "anti-Semitism" if we utter our worries, our heartache, our objection, our outrage in a public form? To say, effectively, that anyone who utters their heartache and outrage out loud will be considered (belatedly, and by powerful "listeners") as anti-Semitic is to seek to control the kind of speech that circulated in the public sphere, to terrorize with the charge of anti-Semitism, and to produce a climate of fear through the tactical use of a heinous judgment with which no progressive person would want to identify. If we bury our criticism for fear of being labeled anti-Semitic, we give power to those who want to curtail the free expression of political beliefs. To live with the charge is, of course, terrible, but it is less terrible when you know that it is untrue, and one can only have this knowledge if there are others who are speaking with you, and who can help to support the sense of what you know.[17]

So many important distinctions are elided by the mainstream press when it assumes that there are only two positions on the Middle East, and that they can be adequately described by the terms "pro-Israel" and "pro-Palestinian." Vari-

17. When Daniel Pipes established "Campus Watch" in the fall of 2002, he produced a blacklist of scholars in Middle Eastern Studies who were, in his view, known to be critical of Israel and thus understood to be anti-Semitic or to be fomenting anti-Semitism. An e-mail campaign was begun by Mark Lance, a philosopher at Georgetown University, in which a number of us wrote in and complained about not being listed on the site. The point of the e-mail initiative was to undermine the power of "blacklisting" as a tactic reminiscent of McCarthyism. Most of us wrote in to say that if believing in Palestinian self-determination was adequate for membership on the list, we wished to be included as well. Although we were subsequently branded as "apologists" for anti-Semitism, and listed on the Web under this heading, there were no individuals who were part of this campaign who accepted the notion that to criticize Israel or to promote Palestianian self-determination were anti-Semitic acts. Indeed, when Tamar Lewin from *The New York Times* contacted me after my name was associated with the beginning of this campaign, she said she was doing a story on rising anti-Semitism on campus, implying that the opposition to the Daniel Pipes website was evidence of this rise. I explained to her that I was, like many others who wrote in, a progressive Jew (handling the discourse of identity politics for the moment), and that I rejected the notion that to support Palestinian self-determination was in itself an anti-Semitic act. I referred her to several Jewish organizations and petitions that held views such as my own, and suggested that this was not a story about anti-Semitism, but about how the charge of anti-Semitism plays to silence certain political viewpoints. Her story in *The New York Times*, "Web Site Fuels Debates on Campus Anti-Semitism" (9/27/02), skewed the issue significantly since it accepted the assumption that there were "pro-Israel" and "pro-Palestinian" positions that did not have any overlap, and it refused to name as Jewish several of us who opposed the Web site and its neo-McCarthyism. Indeed, the article managed to associate those who opposed Pipes with anti-Semitism itself, even though we had, in conversation with her, made clear our profound revulsion at anti-Semitism.

ous people are said to hold views that are one or the other, and the assumption is that these are discrete views, internally homogenous, non-overlapping. And the terms suggest that if one is "pro-Israel" then anything Israel does is all right, or if one is "pro-Palestinian" then anything Palestinians do is all right. But true views on the political spectrum do not fall easily into such extremes. So many complex formulations of political belief are erased from view. One can, for instance, be in favor of Palestinian self-determination, but condemn suicide bombings, and still differ with others who share both views on what form that self-determination ought to take. One can, for instance, be in favor of Israel's right to exist, but still ask, what is the most legitimate and democratic form that such an existence ought to take? If one questions the present form, is one therefore anti-Israel? If one holds out for a truly democratic Israel/Palestine, is one therefore anti-Israel? Or is one trying to find a better form for this polity, one that may well involve any number of possibilities: a revised version of Zionism, a post-Zionist Israel, a self-determining Palestine, or an amalgamation of Israel into a greater Israel/Palestine where all race- and religiously based qualifications on rights and entitlements would be eliminated? If one is against a present-day version of Zionism, and offers reasons, reasons that would eliminate all forms of racial discrimination, including all forms of anti-Semitism, then surely one is involved in a critique of Israel that does not immediately qualify as anti-Semitic.

This is not to say that there will not be those who seize upon the fact of critique to further their anti-Semitic aims. That may well take place, and it surely has taken place. I do not mean to dispute this possibility and this reality. But the fact that there are those who will exploit such a critique is not reason enough to silence the critique. If the possibility of that exploitation serves as a reason to quell political dissent, then one has effectively given the domain of public discourse over to those who accept and perpetrate the view that anti-Semitism is authorized by criticisms of Israel, including those who seek to perpetuate anti-Semitism through such criticisms and those who seek to quell such criticisms for fear that they perpetuate anti-Semitism. To remain silent for fear of a possible anti-Semitic appropriation is to keep the very equation of Zionism and Jewishness in tact, when it is precisely the separation between the two that guarantees the conditions for critical thinking on this issue. To remain silent for fear on an anti-Semitic appropriation that one deems to be certain is to give up on the possibility of combating anti-Semitism by other means.

What struck me as ironic here is that Summers himself makes the equation of Zionism with Jewishness and, so, it seems, of Zionists with Jews, even though this is the very tactic of anti-Semitism. At the same time that this was happening, I found myself on a listserve in which a number of individuals opposed to the current policies of the state of Israel and sometimes opposed to Zionism itself started to engage in this very slippage, sometimes opposing what they called "Zionism" and other times opposing what they called "Jewish" interests. Every time the latter equation took place on the serve, a number of us objected, and as a consequence several people took themselves off the listserve, unable to bear the slippage any longer.

The controversial academic in Manchester, England, Mona Baker, who dismissed two Israeli colleagues from the board of her translation studies journal in an effort to boycott Israeli institutions, offered a weak argument in defense of her act, claiming that there was no way to distinguish between individuals and institutions. In dismissing these individuals, she claimed, she was treating them as emblematic of the Israeli state, since they were citizens of that country. But citizens are not the same as states: the very possibility of significant dissent depends upon the difference between them. The presumption of a seamless continuity between Israeli citizens and the Israeli state not only made all Israelis equivalent to state interests, but makes it more difficult for academics outside of Israel to ally with dissidents inside who are taking strong and important stands against the occupation. Mona Baker's conflation of citizens with states was quickly followed, in her own discourse, by a collapse of "Israeli" interests with "Jewish" ones. Her response to the widespread criticism of the act in which she dismissed Israeli scholars from her board was to send around e-mails on the "academicsforjustice" listserve complaining about "Jewish" newspapers, labeling as "pressure" the opportunity that some such newspapers offered to discuss the issue in print with those she had dismissed. She refused such conversation. At that moment, it seemed, she was not only in a fight against current Israeli policy or, indeed, the structure and basis of legitimation of the Israeli state, but suddenly, now, with "Jews," identified as a lobby that pressures people, a lobby that pressures her. She not only engaged established anti-Semitic stereotypes, but she collapsed the important distinction between Jewishness and Zionism. The same criticism that I offered to Summers' view thus applies to Baker as well: it is one thing to oppose Israel in its current form and practices or, indeed, to have critical questions about Zionism itself, but it is quite another to oppose "Jews" or fear from "Jews" or assume that all "Jews" have the same view, that they are all in favor of Israel, identified with Israel or represented by Israel. Oddly, and painfully, it has to be said that at this point Mona Baker and Lawrence Summers agree: Jews are the same as Israel. In the one instance, the premise works in the service of an argument against anti-Semitism; in the second, it works as the effect of anti-Semitism itself. Indeed, it seems to me that one aspect of anti-Semitism or, indeed, of any form of racism is that an entire people is falsely and summarily equated with a given position, view, or disposition. To say that all Jews hold a given view on Israel or are adequately represented by Israel or, conversely, that the acts of Israel, the state, adequately stand for the acts of all Jews, is to conflate Jews with Israel and, therefore, to commit an anti-Semitic reduction of Jewishness. Unfortunately, Summers' argument against anti-Semitism makes use of this anti-Semitic premise. We see the anti-Semitism of the premise actively expressed in the remark that Mona Baker makes about the "Jewish" press that is presumptively identified with Israeli state interests.

In holding out for a distinction between Israel and Jews, I am calling for a space of critique and a condition of dissent for Jews and non-Jews who have criticisms of Israel to articulate, but I am also opposing anti-Semitic reductions of Jewishness to Israeli interests. The "Jew" is no more defined by Israel than by anti-Semitic diatribe. The "Jew" exceeds both determinations, and is to be found, substantively, as this diasporic excess, an historically and culturally changing identity that takes no single form and has no single telos. Once the distinction between Israel and Jews is made, an intellectual discussion of both Zionism and anti-Semitism can begin, since it will be as important to understand critically the legacy of Zionism and to debate its future as it will be to track and oppose anti-Semitism as it is promulgated throughout the globe. A progressive Jewish stance will pursue both directions, and will refuse to brand as anti-Semitic the critical impulse or to accept anti-Semitic discourse as a legitimate substitute for critique.

What is needed is a public space in which such issues might be thoughtfully debated, and for academics to support the commitment to academic freedom and intellectual inquiry that would support a thoughtful consideration of these issues. What we are up against here is not only the question of whether certain kinds of ideas and positions can be permitted in public space, but how public space is itself defined by certain kinds of exclusions, certain emerging patterns of censoriousness and censorship. I have considered the way in which the charge of anti-Semitism against those who voice opposition to Israeli policy or to its founding ideology seeks to discredit that point of view as hatred or, indeed, hate speech, and to put into question its permissibility as protected speech or, indeed, valued political commentary. If one cannot voice an objection to violence done by the Israeli state without attracting the charge of anti-Semitism, then the charge works to circumscribe the publicly acceptable domain of speech. It also works to immunize Israeli violence against critique by refusing to countenance the integrity of the claims made against that violence. One is threatened with the label, "anti-Semitic," in the same way that within the United States, to oppose the most recent U.S. wars earns one the label of "traitor," or "terrorist-sympathizer" or, indeed, "treasonous." These are threats with profound psychological consequence. They seek to control political behavior by imposing unbearable, stigmatized modes of identification which most people will want more than anything to avoid. Fearing the identification, they fail to speak out. But such threats of stigmatization can and must be weathered, and this can only be done with the support of other actors, others who speak in concert with you, and against the threat that seeks to silence political speech. The threat of being called "anti-Semitic" seeks to control, at the level of the subject, what one is willing to say out loud and, at the level of society in general, to circumscribe what can and cannot be permissibly spoken out loud in the public sphere. More dramatically, these are threats that *decide* the defining limits of the public sphere through setting limits on the speakable. The world of public discourse, in other words, will be that space and time from which those critical perspectives will be excluded. The exclusion of those criticisms will effectively establish the boundaries of the public itself, and the public will come to understand itself as one that does not speak out, critically, in the face of obvious and illegitimate violence—unless, of course, a certain collective courage takes hold.

Sharon, Le Pen, and Anti-Semitism

Naomi Klein

I knew from e-mail reports that something new was going on in Washington, D.C., last weekend. A demonstration against the World Bank and International Monetary Fund was joined by an antiwar march, as well as a demonstration against the Israeli occupation of Palestinian territory. In the end, all the marches joined together in what organizers described as the largest Palestinian solidarity demonstration in U.S. history, 75,000 people by police estimates.

On Sunday night, I turned on my television in the hopes of catching a glimpse of this historic protest. I saw something else instead: triumphant Jean-Marie Le Pen celebrating his newfound status as the second most popular political leader in France. Ever since, I've been wondering whether the new alliance displayed on the streets can also deal with this latest threat.

As a critic both of the Israeli occupation and of corporate-dictated globalization, it seems to me that the convergence that took place in Washington last weekend was long overdue. Despite easy labels like "anti-globalization," the trade-related protests of the past three years have all been about self-determination: the right of people everywhere to decide how best to organize their societies and economies, whether that means introducing land reform in Brazil, or producing generic AIDS drugs in India, or, indeed, resisting an occupying force in Palestine. When hundreds of globalization activists began flocking to Ramallah to act as "human shields" between Israeli tanks and Palestinians, the theory that has been developing outside trade summits was put into concrete action. Bringing that courageous spirit back to Washington, D.C., where so much Middle Eastern policy is made, was the next logical step.

But when I saw Le Pen beaming on TV, arms raised in triumph, some of my enthusiasm drained away. There is no connection whatsoever between French fascism and the "free Palestine" marchers in Washington (indeed, the only people Mr. Le Pen's supporters seem to dislike more than Jews are Arabs). And yet I couldn't help thinking about all the recent events I've been to where anti-Muslim violence was rightly condemned, Ariel Sharon deservedly blasted, but no mention was made of attacks on Jewish synagogues, cemeteries, and community centers. Or about the fact that every time I log on to activist news sites like Indymedia.org, which practice "open publishing," I'm confronted with a string of Jewish conspiracy theories about 9/11 and excerpts from the *Protocol of the Elders of Zion*.

The globalization movement isn't anti-Semitic; it just hasn't fully confronted the implications of diving into the Middle East conflict. Most people on the left are simply choosing sides and in the Middle East, where one side is under occupation and the other has the U.S. military behind it, the choice seems clear. But it is possible to criticize Israel while forcefully condemning the rise of anti-Semitism. And it is equally possible to be pro-Palestinian independence without adopting a simplistic "pro-Palestinian/anti-Israel" dichotomy, a mirror image of the good-versus-evil equations so beloved by President George W. Bush.

Why bother with such subtleties while bodies are still being pulled out of the rubble in Jenin? Because anyone interested in fighting Le Pen–style fascism or Sharon-style brutality has to deal with the reality of anti-Semitism head-on. The hatred of Jews is a potent political tool in the hands of both the right in Europe and in Israel. For Mr. Le Pen, anti-Semitism is a windfall, helping spike his support from 10 percent to 17 percent in a week. For Ariel Sharon, it is the fear of anti-Semitism, both real and imagined, that is the weapon. Mr. Sharon likes to say that he stands up to terrorists to show he is not afraid. In fact, his policies are driven by fear. His great talent is that he fully understands the depths of Jewish fear of another Holocaust. He knows how to draw parallels between Jewish anxieties about anti-Semitism and American fears of terrorism. And he is an expert at harnessing all of it for his political ends.

The primary, and familiar, fear that Mr. Sharon draws on, the one that allows him to claim all aggressive actions as defensive ones, is the fear that Israel's neighbors want to drive the Jews into the sea. The secondary fear Mr. Sharon manipulates is the fear among Jews in the Diaspora that they will eventually be driven to seek safe haven in Israel. This fear leads millions of Jews around the world, many of them sickened by Israeli aggression, to shut up and send their checks, a down payment on future sanctuary. The equation is simple: the more fearful Jews are, the more powerful Sharon is. Elected on a platform of "peace through security," Sharon's administration could barely hide its delight at Le Pen's ascendancy, immediately calling on French Jews to pack their bags and come to the promised land. For Sharon, Jewish fear is a guarantee that his power will go unchecked, granting him the impunity needed to do the unthinkable: send troops into the Palestinian Authority's education ministry to steal and destroy records; bury children alive in their homes; block ambulances from getting to the dying.

Jews outside Israel now find themselves in a tightening vice: the actions of the country that was supposed to ensure their future safety are making them less safe right now. Mr. Sharon is deliberately erasing distinctions between the terms "Jew" and "Israeli," claiming he is fighting not for Israeli territory but for the survival of the Jewish people. And when anti-Semitism rises at least partly as a result of his actions, it is Sharon who is positioned once again to collect the political dividends.

And it works. Most Jews are so frightened that they are now willing to do anything to defend Israeli policies. So at my neighborhood synagogue, where the humble façade was just badly scarred by a suspicious fire, the sign on the door doesn't say, "Thanks for nothing, Sharon." It says, "Support Israel. . . . Now more than ever."

There is a way out. Nothing is going to erase anti-Semitism, but Jews outside and inside Israel might be a little safer if there was a campaign to distinguish between diverse Jewish positions and the actions of the Israeli state. This is where an international movement can play a crucial role. Already, alliances are being made between globalization activists and Israeli "refuseniks," soldiers who refuse to serve their mandatory duty in the occupied territories. And the most powerful images from Saturday's protests were rabbis walking alongside Palestinians. But more needs to be done. It's easy for social justice activists to tell themselves that since Jews already have such powerful defenders in Washington and Jerusalem, anti-Semitism is one battle they don't need to fight. This is a deadly error. It is precisely because anti-Semitism is used by the likes of Mr. Sharon that the fight against it must be reclaimed.

When anti-Semitism is no longer treated as Jewish business, to be taken care of by Israel and the Zionist lobby, Mr. Sharon is robbed of his most effective weapon in the indefensible and increasingly brutal occupation. And as an extra bonus, whenever hatred of Jews diminishes, the likes of Jean-Marie Le Pen shrink right down with it.

Wall

C. K. Williams

1.
They're building a wall,
and tearing down houses.
They're erecting a high, cold concrete slab
that cuts across hill, valley, grove, village,
while monstrous bulldozers swarm
like demented insects
to raze houses.

These once houses, these slag heaps
of broken stone, smashed doors, raped windows,
where human beings lived
and where now only hatred,
only resentment,
only desire for vengeance flare;
does the wall run beside them,
or through them?

They are building a wall,
and razing houses.
What do they think they're doing?
What future they think they're effecting?

2.
I say, "They;"
mustn't I say "We?"
Hasn't it always been "We?"
Mustn't it be?

Yet how can I bring myself
to say "We" when the "We" I mean
I mistrust, find short-sighted,
self-destructive, blind to itself?

Can I ever not say it, though?
Can I ever say, "They,"
and believe I mean it?

They are building a wall.

How not believe it?

They are tearing down houses.

How not believe it?

3.
When I was there, my first evening I looked out and saw,
one after the other, those who come here, out of their history,
those who were born here, into a different history,
and though I had no plan to, I saw "We,"
and tears came to my eyes.

It was the time of peace, of hope, but the next day, in a park,
a class of children were having their outing: their teacher carried a rifle.
Watching the children, in their light, (though all children are light),
I was afraid for them, and I thought, though I had no plan to, "Mine,"
and tears came to my eyes.

And later, so many eons later, when the new Intifada began,
I saw the clip of the boy cowering next to his father, about to be shot,
about to die, I knew he would die, I'd already seen it in the paper,
but I kept thinking, "Don't let him die," and in my grief,
tears came to my eyes, and I thought, how could I not think,
"Isn't he mine?" Aren't all children mine, ours?
Aren't all children a portion of each "We"?
How can it be else?

To kill a child in error is to kill.
To kill a child inadvertently
is to kill.
To kill is to kill.

4.
They are building a wall.

Out of fear, reasonable fear, self-protection, they say,
to protect their homes and their lives.
Yes, but fear grows, fear cultivated
by those who seek power becomes swollen,
monstrous, bloated; it generates its own moral system,
its own cosmos of faith.

And cultivated fear finds in itself hatred,
and hatred finds in itself power,
the illusion of power,
the illusion of power over history, over fear.
And with the illusion of power
fear becomes arrogant, becomes pitiless,
becomes warrior, bigot,
becomes brute, becomes vile.

And in the cosmos in which fear is power,
and power becomes hatred, and hatred,
even reluctant, even blind, becomes all.
They are tearing down houses.

5.
They are building a wall
they say to protect them.
How deep in the earth will their wall go?
Deep enough so the rage it engenders
can't burrow beneath?

They are building a wall
to save lives:
how high in the air will their wall be?
Will it tower so high that the rage it provokes
won't slash down over it from above?

How long will the wall be?
Will it encircle the world?
Won't it have to?

Will it endure longer than rage?
Wouldn't it have to?
Is it eternal, immortal?
Will it last longer than history,
longer than existence?

6.

That other wall, before which they pray,
the wall they believe God put His seal on,
His sanction, His blessing;
that wall of cyclopean stone,
that ruin of memory,
do they think their new wall will enclose God,
will have God in it, too?

Shall the broken walls of a razed home
be less in the eyes of God
than the ruins of a temple?
Less beloved? Less sanctioned?
Who would the God be,
what would the God be,
who blessed a home
less than a temple?

7.

Sometimes I think they are building a wall
between "They" and "We."

Or might they be building a wall
in their own souls,
and in ours,
the soul of "They,"
and of "We"?

Or is it a wall between
"They" and "We"
and everyone else?

Is it the wall of history
that violates everything else?

8.

They are building a wall.

Have they forgotten the centuries of walls,
the epochs of walls
reared to isolate and contain them?

This is a wall of smooth, tempered concrete,
with electric sensors:
don't they remember the walls
of rough coarse blocks and coarse mortar,
erected around them, to cage them?

Coarse blocks, their surfaces rough,
as though with the pores of living skin.
Coarse mortar, rough
as though with fragments of bone,
as though with dried blood?

Don't they remember those walls
without reason?
Those walls without end?

Don't they remember the walls
of exclusion and death?
Why are they, why are we,
of all peoples
building a wall of exclusion and death.

They are building a wall.

9.
Can I still say,
of this anguish I feel,
this impotence and frustration,
"What are they doing to themselves?"
Mustn't "We" be there, too?
Mustn't we say,
"What are we permitting?
What are we condoning?"

10.
Where is there not wall?
Where will that place be
where no wall rises?

Where will no wall rise
between "They" and world,
between "We" and world?

What are we permitting?
What are we condoning?

Will there always be wall?
Will there always be fear?
Where there is fear,
won't there be wall?
Where there is wall,
won't there be fear?

What are we permitting?
What are we condoning?

Must we live always
with hatred?
Must fear condemn us
always to live
with hatred?

What are we permitting?
What are we condoning?

They are building a wall.
They are tearing down houses,
olive groves, villages, life;
they are tearing down life.

And building a wall.
They are building a wall.

The Fundamental Truth

Marge Piercy

The Christian right, Islamic Jihad,
the Jewish Right Bank settlers bringing
the Messiah down, the Japanese sects
who worship by bombing subways,
they all hate each other
but more they hate the mundane,
ordinary people who love living
more than dying in radiant glory,
who shuffle and sigh and break bread.

They need a planet of their own,
perhaps even a barren moon
with artificial atmosphere,
where they will surely be nearer
to their gods and their fiercest
enemies, where they can kill
to their heart's peace
kill to the last standing man
and leave the rest of us be.

Not mystics to whom the holy
comes in the core of a struggle
in a shimmer of blinding quiet,
not scholars haggling out the inner
meaning of gnarly ancient sentences.
No, the holy comes to these zealots

as a license to kill, for self-doubt
and humility have dried like mud
under their marching feet.

They have far more in common
with each other, these braggarts
of hatred, the iron hearted
in whose ear a voice spoke

once and left them deaf.
Their faith is founded on death
of others, and everyone is other
to them, whose Torah and Koran is splattered
in letters of blood.

Section Five

The Law of Return: A Forum

The Law of Return: A Forum

*W**ould you give up your access to the Law of Return (text below), which bestows upon Jews from around the world automatic citizenship in Israel, as a political statement to serve the cause of justice and peace in Israel/Palestine? Inspired by Melanie Kaye/Kantrowitz's idea for an action, we posed this question to a number of contributors to provoke reflections, arguments, and poetic ruminations on the Jewish Right of Return. Responses follow from: Melanie Kaye/Kantrowitz, Letty Cottin Pogrebin, Daniel Wolfe, E. M. Broner, Meg Barnette and Brad Lander, Susannah Heschel, and Lynne Tillman.*

The Law of Return

(passed unanimously by the Knesset on 5 July 1950)

1. Every Jew has the right to immigrate to the country.

2. (a) Immigration shall be on the basis of an immigrant's visa. (b) An immigrant's visa shall be granted to every Jew who has expressed his desire to settle in Israel, unless the minister of immigration is convinced that the applicant (1) is acting against the Jewish people, (2) is likely to endanger public health or the security of the state.

3. (a) A Jew who comes to Israel and after his arrival expresses his desire to settle there, is entitled, while he is still in Israel, to obtain an immigrant certificate. (b) The reservations detailed in section 2(b) will also be in force regarding the granting of an immigrant certificate, but a person will not be considered as endangering the public health as a result of an illness he contracted after his arrival in Israel.

4. Every Jew who has immigrated to Israel before this law entered into effect, and every Jew born in the country, whether before or after this law entered into effect, shall be considered as having immigrated according to this law.

5. The minister of immigration is responsible for the enforcement of this law, and he is empowered to enact regulations in all matters concerning its implementation as well as the granting of immigrant visas and immigrant papers to minors under the age of eighteen.

Returning the Law of Return
Melanie Kaye/Kantrowitz

In May 2001 a new formation called Jewish Unity for a Just Peace (JUNITY) convened an international conference in Chicago, attended by more than 175 activists from Israel, the United States, Canada and Brazil.[1] In a workshop focused on direct action, fifty-odd people tried to design an action that would help shift the center of Jewish peace activism leftward.

Some of us had worked in the movement to end the war against Vietnam. As we talked about our experience with different kinds of actions I flashed on the demonstration that had moved me most.[2] In 1971 Vietnam Veterans Against the War organized Operation Dewey Canyon,[3] "a limited incursion into the country of Congress," and two thousand soldiers marched on Washington to lobby, mourn, and indict. They came in wheelchairs and on crutches. Mothers of dead soldiers led the procession. The events culminated in nearly a thousand veterans hurling medals earned in combat fighting the Vietnamese onto the steps of the Capitol Building, soldier after soldier sobbing with rage and grief, throwing down their medals into a hated pile, shouting, "Here's my purple heart. Here's my silver star. They don't mean anything." Their sense of betrayal was raw and excruciating.

As I remembered the voices of those soldiers, I wondered what could we, Jews who oppose the occupation, give back that would communicate our rage at the Israeli government's violation of human rights, our grief at the protracted suffering, our sense of betrayal by those cynics who invoke Jewish survival—*our* survival—to justify brutality. That was the genesis of the idea of gathering at the Israeli consulate to give back our Jewish right to make *aliyah*: to return the right of return.

In the JUNITY workshop people found the idea powerful yet unnerving. Even for those like myself who never intended to make *aliyah,* just to imagine renouncing the right to do so felt scary. We agreed that this anxiety felt exactly right. The concept of renunciation touched a nerve. Many diaspora Jews stash an unexamined safety exit marked "Israel" somewhere in our gut. Some of us experience Israel like a crazy uncle[4]—Uncle Izzy, I've come to call him—someone over whom we have no control but whose behavior we're somehow responsible for. To publicly reject Izzy would expose our family's shame. For some, giving back the right of return felt like abandoning the Jews. The idea seemed to signal a profound confrontation with what have often been unconscious assumptions: *Is Israel a refuge? for whom? When does protection become privilege? Do we want the Palestinians to pay the price for our projected safety?*

1. Information on JUNITY can be found at *www.junity.org.*
2. Heard on KPFA/Pacifica radio.
3. Operation Dewey Canyon I and II were major military operations in Southeast Asia. For details on Operation Dewey Canyon III, the soldiers' demonstration (April 19–23, 1971), see: *http://www.geocities.com/Pentagon/Barracks/3853/journal.htm.*
4. The analogy is Larry Bush's.

How can we accept the concept of "aliyah" to a land that has made hundreds of thousands of Palestinians refugees?[5]

Responses to this idea were unpredictable, visceral. When it was announced in the plenary session's report-backs, people cheered. But later one woman told me she felt such shock and horror she was speechless and insisted that she personally would block such a demo from being listed on the JUNITY website. (She suggested we contact Al Awda—relegating the "return" to a Palestinian website, as if those who might choose to perform this action were no longer Jewish; exactly as the Jewish right tells those of us who criticize the Israeli government that we're not really Jews.) Someone wrote: "Finding symbols, not just words, to talk about 'two peoples, two states,' or 'both people's rights to self-determination and security' will be much more compelling than symbols of what we're against." Someone else argued that it would make more sense for large numbers of progressive Jews to use this right to make *aliyah* and struggle with Israeli politics. Others pointed out that many of our Jewish comrades have Jewish fathers and not mothers, and thus don't even have this right in the first place. Some challenged the whole notion of "return": *my people,* they said, *came from Vilna, Kiev, Salonika, Wasaw, Cordoba* . . . A friend said she wouldn't participate in the demonstration but she would watch and cheer on those who did. A rabbi said he wouldn't do it either but he would sponsor a discussion with his congregation. Most interesting to me was how the idea of returning the right to return brought up all our diverse Jewish histories, made people think about how and where we are positioned as Jews. A synagogue president I have known for a good ten years declared the idea brilliant and proceeded to talk about her Holocaust survivor father, about whom I'd never heard her speak.

In the end, although the idea of "returning the right of return" remained compelling for some of us, it seemed too divisive, too complicated for a demonstration with a goal of mobilizing massive Jewish opposition to the occupation. And then came the attacks of September 11, 2001, and the center of gravity shifted. Here, in the United States, we were going to have to fight the Israeli occupation in the light of greatly magnified American hatred of Arabs, overwhelming fear of terrorism, and increased identification with Israelis. For some of us, our role as Americans was nudging aside our role as Jews.

In the days before we'd decided against "return" as the demo focus, a friend[6] and I went to scope out the Israeli consulate as a site for the demo. The office

5. This does not mean I think Jewish refugees shouldn't go wherever they can, or that I'm sorry Jews in trouble have a place to go (any more than I'm sorry I have a place to live, even though it's horrible that some people don't). The issue is, does my house wipe out theirs?

6. Naomi Braine, activist with Jews Against the Occupation (JATO) and Women in Black.

is buried on the twenty-first floor of a building on Second Avenue. Security is tight. I claimed to be picking up information for my sister who wanted to make *aliyah.*

The surprise was the thick manila envelope I was handed. Inside I find a fat little *Aliyah Pocket Guide,* 7th edition: 168 pages; it opens with *Milestones on Your Road to Aliyah,* the first of which is:

> 1800 B.C.E. the patriarch Abraham leaves his native Ur and settles in the Land promised to him and his descendants by God. The beginning of the Jewish People's relationship with their homeland.[7]

The Milestones include (70 C.E.) the destruction of the Second Temple, (1932–5) the arrival in Eretz Israel of European Jews fleeing Hitler (never referred to as Palestine, despite the fact that many Jews who lived there at the time referred to themselves as Palestinians.) The list closes with:

> 199_ C.E.: I arrive in Israel.

I note how readily, instantaneously, any Jew can slip her/himself into this history of the Jewish People's relationship with the Land (albeit with an out-of-date date). The pocket guide abounds in complex detailed information, including items like: the Ministry of Immigrant Absorption will assist *olim* (immigrants) with:

> *arranging Hebrew study at an external *ulpan* and subsistence allowance during the study period
> *unemployment compensation or monthly income supplement; language instruction
> *assistance in paying nursery school tuition[8]

Also in the envelope: A twenty-eight-page pamphlet explains national insurance, including health insurance, old-age pension, unemployment, disability ... The only recognition of the occupation and of Palestinian legal inequality are two brief sections toward the end: *Compensation for Victims of Terrorist Acts,* and *Compensation for Prisoners of Zion* (explained as Jews taken prisoner in military attacks). A fifty-plus-page booklet explains in detail Health Services in Israel. A booklet on transportation explains how I'll get my driver's license, how to open a garage, how public transportation works. And a "Special Edition" of the *Information for Olim* newsletter focused on "government housing assistance to new immigrants," is packed with tables to help me calculate how many shekels housing allowance I would get depending on how many children and how

7. pp. 5–6.
8. p. 43.

many years in Israel. Assistance may take the form of monthly rent subsidies that last up to five years, or a special low-cost mortgage.[9]

Not only am I entitled to all this. Should I have grandchildren—as long as the mothers are Jews—they are entitled to all this, no matter how tenuous their connection with Jewishness, no matter their reason for exercising their right: They too can complete the list of Milestones with their year: *"I arrive in Israel."* Whereas because a Palestinian is Palestinian, no matter where born, even in the very house I might be able to purchase with my special low-cost mortgage or rent with my five years of rental subsidy: A Palestinian is entitled to nothing. Less than nothing.

Let us imagine the Palestinian envelope of disentitlements.

Disentitled to a secure home, any home at all. If someone from your family, or someone who knows someone from your family, or someone from your neighbor's family is suspected, only suspected, of terrorist activity, your house can be, is being, has been blown up.

Disentitled to adequate nutrition for your children. Estimates range from as high as more than 50 percent of children suffering from chronic or acute malnutrition, malnutrition severe enough to retard normal physical and intellectual development.

Disentitled to an education: Schools closed.

Disentitled to move freely, even—often enough—to step outside your house. Curfew, refusal of travel permits.

Disentitled to medical care. Curfew, checkpoints often mean desperately ill people, women giving birth, people having heart attacks, bleeding out, can't get to a doctor or hospital. How many have died, how many lives foreshortened?

Disentitled to work. Unemployment rate of 75 percent.

And most recently, disentitled to remain, never mind return. Transfer, expulsion, ethnic cleansing are already happening on a micro level, and being posed as serious options in Israel.

Let's face it. Disentitled to live. Are Jews supposed to feel proud or vindicated that Warsaw, Lodz, Vilna are the accurate analogies instead of Auschwitz? that genocide has not (yet?) accrued widespread open support?

Listen to an Israeli official defending the Law of Return. Shlomo Guberman, Deputy Attorney General, spoke at the World Conference against Racism, Racial Discrimination, Xenophobia and Related Intolerance, August 31 to September 7, 2001, in Durban, South Africa, to, I'm sure, a hostile audience:

> The State of Israel was established for the very purpose of repatriating the Jewish people from the Diaspora, to enable the "Ingathering of the Exiles," to give every Jew anywhere in the world an option to return to the land of

9. *Olim* not from English-speaking countries or Western Europe get extra assistance, called a *Sal Klita* (absorption basket).

his fathers [*sic*]. The State of Israel was established with the aim of implementing the Zionist solution of the "Jewish problem" . . . As such, the Law of Return is not a privilege set apart for members of the Jewish faith and denied to non-Jews . . .

Guberman continues:

The main criticism raised against the Law of Return is that it discriminates against Arabs and especially against Palestinian refugees who wish to return to their former homes in Israel. This argument has no basis; obviously there is no sense in inviting any Arab who so desires to immigrate at will to Israel, the Jewish State, which was established for the Jewish People in accordance with UN Resolution 181, and by virtue of the right of the Jewish People to self determination. Any gentile, be he Arab or from any other origin, who wishes to settle in Israel, may do so if he meets the requirements set forth in the Law of Entry to Israel (1952), regarding naturalization. These requirements are similar to those stated in the laws of most countries.[10] It is clear therefore, that this argument has no logic at all . . . . With regard to the Palestinian refugees—their plight must definitely be solved, but the solution to their problem has nothing to do with the Law of Return, which, as described above, is intended for the repatriation of the Jewish People to the Jewish State.[11]

Nothing to do with? Is Zionist intent, however generously interpreted,[12] the lone relevant factor? Do only Jewish need and suffering count? Is it plausible that rights enjoyed by Jews have nothing at all to do with lack of rights for Palestinians? Like describing whiteness in the United States without acknowledging the racism that makes of whiteness an entry into privilege. What of the practical reality of bringing many people to an area where land, water, housing, and jobs are scarce resources? The Law of Return rests on that old Zionist saw: a land without a people for a people without a land.

I know some of the things Jews will say in response. Indeed, some Jewish institutions are spending many thousands of dollars training Jewish students to say these things—as though a snappy retort were the point. Words like: *corrupt Palestinian Authority, Barak's generous offer, they don't care about life, push Israel into the sea, naturally violent, they have all those "regular" Arab countries* . . .

How can we understand our rights out of context with their *lack* of rights?

10. Guberman is correct. But most countries do not have a living, breathing, under siege, displaced population. (The United States, with our indigenous populations, however drastically reduced, is one exception.)

11. *http://www.mfa.gov.il/mfa/go.asp?MFAH0kdo0.*

12. See Tom Segev's devastating *The Seventh Million*, tracing Zionist cynicism, manipulation, indifference to actual Jewish life.

The idea of focusing on the right of return continues to intrigue me. What would it mean to return the envelope: expose the underbelly, unpack the privilege that hedges Zionism, see the tangle of our fate with theirs. To really absorb the words of the Palestinian feminist Rita Giacaman at Bir Zeit University on the West Bank in 1988: *I am very sympathetic to the suffering of the Jews in Europe, but I can never accept what was done to us to solve their problems.*[13]

Today I read in the *New York Times* a letter from a woman whose daughter has always planned to study in Israel and despite the terrorist attacks she intends to go because otherwise *they* will have won. *They* means Palestinians. No discussion of what it means that she, an American, can freely travel in and out of Israel, study, make it her home if she chooses, while Palestinians born within Greenline Israel or even the occupied territories cannot.

Meanwhile, the nation in which I am an actual, not genetically determined, citizen, the one I pay taxes and lend legitimacy to—is about to bomb the people of Iraq (again; or still?). Or maybe North Korea. Or Colombia. Or Venezuela, or Brazil, or the Philippines. Whom am I leaving out? In this context, the image of a "right to return" demo seems bizarre. What has this to do with reality?

Yet the concept still touches a nerve. And every so often someone who was at that JUNITY workshop, or participated in the early discussions of returning the right to return, raises it again. A group of forty-six British Jews printed a statement in *The Guardian* rejecting their right to *aliyah*.[14] I've thought about

---

13. Quoted in my essay "I've Been to Israel and to Palestine," in my essay collection, *The Issue Is Power: Essays on Women, Jews, Violence, and Resistance* (Aunt Lute Books, 1992).

14. "We Renounce Israel Rights," *The Guardian*, Thursday, 8 August 2002: "We are Jews, born and raised outside Israel, who, under Israel's 'law of return' have a legal right to Israeli residence and citizenship. (Real lives, G2, August 7). We wish to renounce this unsought 'right' because: 1) We regard it as morally wrong that this legal entitlement should be bestowed on us while the very people who should have most right to a genuine 'return,' having been forced or terrorised into fleeing, are excluded. 2) Israel's policies towards the Palestinians are barbaric—we do not wish to identify ourselves in any way with what Israel is doing. 3) We disagree with the notion that Zionist emigration to Israel is any kind of 'solution' for diaspora Jews, anti-Semitism or racism—no matter to what extent Jews have been or are victims of racism, they have no right to make anyone else victims. 4) We wish to express our solidarity with all those who are working for a time when Israel, the West Bank and Gaza Strip can be lived in by people without any restrictions based on so-called racial, cultural, or ethnic origins. We look forward to the day when all the peoples of the area are enabled to live in peace with each other on this basis of non-discrimination and mutual respect. Perhaps some of us would even wish to live there, but only if the rights of the Palestinians are respected. To those who consider Israel a 'safe haven' for Jews in the face of anti-Semitism, we say that there can be no safety in taking on the role of occupier and oppressor. We hope that the people of Israel and their leaders will come to realise this soon." (Signed) Michael Rosen; Ian Saville; Prof. Irene Breugel; Michael Kustow; Mike Marquess; Prof. Steven Rose; Leon Rosselson; and thirty-eight others. (Note: The full list of names was not printed in *The Guardian*.) *http://www.npaid.org/british_jews_renounce_israeli_citizenship.htm.*

street theater, maybe one person after another giving their names, their reasons, maybe burning the actual manila envelopes packed with guidebooks and newsletters. Here is what I imagine myself saying:

My name is Melanie Kaye/Kantrowitz. I was born in Brooklyn in 1945 just after the war. I have lived all over the United States and have sometimes experienced discrimination and hatred because I am a Jew. But I do not believe the solution to anti-Semitism is the creation of another hated minority so that I can enjoy the privileges of majority. Far from feeling protected by Israel, I feel exposed to danger by the actions of the Israeli state. Because of our legacy of Holocaust, it still frightens me to say I will never avail myself of *aliyah* as long as Palestinians are in unwilling diaspora. But in recognizing how little identity politics protect or even describe me, I see the irrational nature of my fear. What am I sacrificing?

I am declaring another way to be Jewish. I separate myself from Baruch Goldstein—the U.S.-born Israeli settler who massacred twenty-nine Muslims as they prayed at the tomb of Abraham in Hebron. I separate myself from the rabbi who eulogized him thus: "One million Arab lives are not worth one Jewish fingernail." I separate myself from those who would dangle the promise of protection founded on such an inequation.

I identify with those people who cherish life and believe that each of us is worth exactly the same. With Nurit Peled-Elhanan, the mother of thirteen-year-old Smadar, who was killed by a suicide bomber in Jerusalem in September 1997. Nurit said:

"When my little girl was killed a reporter asked me how I was willing to accept condolences from the other side. I replied without hesitation that I refuse it: When representatives of Netanyahu's government came to offer their condolences, I took my leave and would not sit with them. For me, the other side, the enemy, is not the Palestinian people. For me the struggle is not between Palestinians and Israelis, between Jews and Arabs. The fight is between those who seek peace and those who seek war. My people are those who seek peace. My sisters are the bereaved mothers, Israeli and Palestinian, who live in Israel and in Gaza and in the refugee camps. My brothers are the fathers who try to defend their children from the cruel occupation, and are, as I was, unsuccessful in doing so."

In accordance with Nurit's vision, I declare my separation from the envelope of benefits. Since these benefits rest on the back of wrongs done to Palestinians, I renounce my right to return. I ask others, in their own ways, searching for effective venues, to renounce theirs, too, and, along with me, to commit to the hard road of making peace between Israel and Palestine. Here in the United States that may mean fighting U.S. aid to Israel. It may mean bringing our bodies to the occupied territories in solidarity. It may mean bringing the voices of Nurit, of the Israeli refuseniks, of the women's peace movement here, to Jews in the United States who must, at last, acknowledge Palestinian rights.

In Defense of the Law of Return
Letty Cottin Pogrebin

Israel was established as a democratic Jewish state. While reasonable people may differ as to whether it is "too Jewish," or how well it has fulfilled its promise of equal rights for all, few would dispute that the Law of Return is on its face antithetical to the core principles of democracy. Passed on July 5, 1950, the anniversary of Theodor Herzl's death, it guarantees every Jew automatic entrance and immediate citizenship. Members of other ethnic and religious groups may be accepted as immigrants or refugees but Jews who "make *aliyah*" instantly acquire the right to vote, receive financial benefits, even run for the Knesset. Since the Law privileges Jews and only Jews, its perils are obvious:

1) It codifies a double standard. In contravention of the Declaration of Independence of 1948, which ensures "complete equality of social and political rights to all its inhabitants," the law grants one group a superior legal entitlement, creating a hierarchy of human worth based on religious identity and setting the stage for other asymmetrical privileges.

2) It nullifies and supersedes legitimate property rights. Jews with no claim to residence (aside from biblical assurances or messianic eschatology) are welcomed with open arms while Palestinians who hold keys to particular homes or deeds to particular property are denied entry.

3) It serves hegemonic goals. Many who proselytize for privileged Jewish immigration espouse a not-so-hidden agenda. They want Jewish citizens to outnumber Arab citizens in order to control the Jewishness of the state and concentrate power in Jewish hands. (And the Jews they want are usually Greater Israel triumphalists, not members of Brit Tzedek, B'nai Jeshurun, or your local lesbian-feminist *havurah*.)

Recognizing these problems, how can I, a civil libertarian and longtime critic of Israel's discriminatory policies toward its Palestinian/Arab citizens, defend the Law of Return?

Because in this case, I believe history trumps ideology and politics. The Jewish right to instant citizenship strikes me as a factually warranted, compensatory response to the truth of Jewish experience. In David Ben Gurion's words, "this right is inherent in every Jew by virtue of his being a Jew." Since being a Jew has been enough in some places to mark one for persecution or death, at least on one spot on the globe it should be a ticket to safety. However—and this is where I part company with many Zionists—Jews should be entitled to no other prerogatives, claims, immunities, or indulgences. Immigration is the only policy arena that merits diluting the purity of democracy with the poison of privilege.

Put simply, I view the Law of Return as the affirmative action program of the Jewish people. It's a legal accommodation that has been earned in the same way that preferential educational and employment policies in the United States were earned by of people of color: through suffering. If four centuries of slavery and institutionalized racism can justify affirmative action programs for American blacks whether or not they themselves were brought here in chains, then surely twenty centuries of oppression and annihilation—think Crusades, Inquisition, forced conversions, pogroms, the Gulag, the Holocaust—justify similarly discrepant favoritism for Jews in Israel.

Bias in favor of an "affected class" is an acknowledgment of the continuing vulnerability of individuals who belong to a disadvantaged group. Much as we Jews might yearn to be a people like any other, the events of three millennia attest that we tend instead to be universal pariahs, perennial exiles, the boat people of the world. I'm mindful of the arrogance of asserting national uniqueness—and of citing Jewish weakness in the face of Israeli military strength—but the fact remains that in every era of recorded time, someone, somewhere had it in for the Jews. Egypt, Rome, Babylonia, Cyprus, Spain, France, Germany, Poland, Lithuania, Italy, Russia, Syria, Iraq, the former Soviet Union, Turkey, Yemen, Ethiopia—all have produced horrific tyrants and run-of-the-mill tormentors who have excoriated, demonized, humiliated, scapegoated, blood-libeled, ghettoized, banished, or slaughtered Jews.

The Law of Return is a remedy for that past and a guarantor of future asylum. As one friend, the child of Holocaust survivors, confessed, "It's my security blanket." One needn't be Simon Wiesenthal to notice the scary things happening to Jews around the world right now: In Paris, a group of Muslim youths forced a woman to swallow her Star of David necklace; a cinema refused to allow a showing of *Harry Potter* to 800 Jewish children because of threats of violence; the words "dirty Jews" were painted on the statue of Alfred Dreyfus. In Berlin, visiting American rabbis were given a police escort for their own safety and warned not to wear their yarmulkes in public. In Brussels, two synagogues were firebombed, a third sprayed by automatic weapons. A yeshiva student in Orthodox attire was stabbed twenty-seven times on a London bus. A woman in Russia was maimed when she tried to remove an anti-Semitic billboard that was booby-trapped with explosives.

According to a 2002 ADL poll, 30 percent of respondents in England, Germany, France, Denmark, and Belgium expressed "strong" anti-Semitic feelings, as did more than one in five respondents in Italy, Spain, Austria, Switzerland and the Netherlands. Measured by swastika graffiti and cemetery or synagogue vandalism, anti-Semitism in the United States rose eight percent last year, averaging four incidents per day.

Other chilling developments: Rumors that "the Jews" masterminded the bombing of the World Trade Center or were warned in advance to stay home from work on 9/11 have entered respectable public discourse on web sites and in communities where the notion of "Jewish power" is buttressed by the *Protocols of the Elders of Zion*.

On some American campuses, anti-Israel rhetoric has been conflated with flagrantly anti-Semitic slogans, like "Hitler should have finished the job." Such verbal abuse, often accompanied by physical harassment, can be so traumatizing as to make Jews wonder if they should leave the country before it's déjà vu all over again. (For the left to ignore attacks on Jews as Jews is as morally execrable as criticism of Sharon's government is morally obligatory.)

Recently the specter of "dual loyalties," long a trigger of anti-Semitic bigotry, was raised when Patrick Buchanan, the ultra-right commentator and former presidential candidate, cast aspersions on those who "harbor a passionate attachment to a nation not our own." Rep. James Moran of Virginia stirred up another incendiary canard—Jewish influence—by attributing America's war with Iraq to "the strong support of the Jewish community," though polls showed Jewish attitudes toward military action precisely matched the national sentiment.

In the 1970s, during Jimmy Carter's oil crisis, I pulled into a service station behind a car with a bumper sticker that read, "If you're waiting in line for gas, blame the Jews." Now, it seems the Jews are responsible for the Iraq war, Islamic terrorism, oil shortages, the AIDS epidemic, and international anti-Americanism. The culprits are not Richard Perle, Paul Wolfowitz, Elliott Abrams, or Douglas Feith, but "the Jews." (I've yet to hear someone blame the Methodists for George Bush and Dick Cheney, or the blacks for Condi Rice and Colin Powell.)

Given rising anti-Semitic vitriol and the recurrent habit, especially in hard times, of attributing to Jews nefarious motives and conspiratorial power, there is new resonance to the old joke—"Even paranoids have enemies." I've begun to wonder how many more Americans—ordinary working people cowed by accusations of "class warfare" and unwilling to trace their economic and social discontents to globalization, tax cuts for the rich, corporate malfeasance, or cowboy leadership—might start looking for someone to blame. And whether, to assuage a disgruntled populace or achieve an ideological or political purpose, those in power might dump on "the Jews" to the point where we are once again at risk. And whether any nation, based on its track record, can be trusted to guarantee Jewish safety. And why, after all we've been through, Jews should have to justify the existence of a haven, a place where, in Robert Frost's words, "when you have to go there, they have to take you in."

For me, the reason to maintain the Law of Return is Rescue. Every country formulates its immigration policy to suit its perceived national self-interest. The United States maintains quotas, deports "undesirables," welcomes Cuban defectors while denying asylum to Nigerians escaping worse persecution. Israel takes in Jews. Mideast harmony does not require world Jewry to renounce this lifeline. Were the Knesset to rescind the Jewish right of return tomorrow it would not by itself reignite the peace process. What would advance the cause, however, would be Israel's acknowledgment of the Palestinian right of return. While it is not feasible to absorb millions of Palestinian refugees inside the Green Line, it is possible, in lieu of physical return for Israel to pay reparations and help the Palestinian State absorb some of its own diaspora within its own borders. It is possible for Israel to admit that the displacement of another people was a by-product of establishment of the Jewish State, to address the pain of that expulsion diplomatically and economically, and find a compromise that honors Palestinians' parallel passion for this beleaguered land.

Were Israel as committed to justice as to Jewishness, her internal democracy would not be threatened by the Law of Return because, beyond instant citizenship, Jews would enjoy no special rights. Jewish institutions would not receive disproportionate resources. Jewish neighborhoods would not be better served by public utilities and government agencies. The Jewish National Fund would not have the power to deny non-Jews the right to live, work, or run a business on "State lands." Jewish votes would not count more than the votes of other citizens in the psychology of electoral legitimacy. Jewish officials would be held accountable for the impact of their policies on non-Jews. Orthodox political parties would not be permitted to hijack the political process for the exclusive advantage of their own communities. The rabbinate would not control the laws of "personal status" that affect every citizen.

But then, some might ask, what would make the Jewish State Jewish? Culture. Historical markers. Educational priorities. Hebrew as the official language. Jewish holidays. If Christmas and Easter qualify as national holidays in our democracy, why not Chanukah and Purim in Israel? If Thanksgiving and July 4 can be celebrated by all Americans, including those without the remotest connection to the Pilgrims or the Founding Fathers, why can't Yom Ha'atzmaut or Tisha B'av be official commemorations in Israel? If "bombs bursting in air" can be glorified in our national anthem, "*nefesh Yehudi*" (the Jewish spirit) can be tolerated in Hatikva. If Sunday remains the preeminent day of rest here with shuttered liquor stores to prove it, Israeli banks can be closed on Shabbat.

Just as American history takes precedence in our school curricula, Jewish history can hold pride of place in Israel. If American teachers can struggle with competing narratives—about cowboys and Indians, or the McCarthy era, or the Confederate flag—Israeli educators can haggle over conflicting perspectives on the British Mandate, the War of Independence, or the Zionist dream.

More than anything else, Jews can make the state Jewish by acting Jewishly. This is *tachlis*, not tautology. Israel needs more Jews who are willing to pay for the privilege of citizenship with the practice of justice. Jews who actualize Jewish values in their everyday life rather than merely speak the right words in synagogue. Jews who do not oppress the stranger, do not treat the Other as they would not wish to be treated, and never forget that each human being was created in God's image. Jews who seek peace and pursue it.

Roadblocks of the Soul

Daniel Wolfe

Next year in Jerusalem, we say every year at Seder, though I don't mean it anymore. The people at the table are my homeland. We have studied together, marched together, prayed and feasted together. We have helped each other to say "we" as Jews. But not next year in Jerusalem, not really, not even with "in peace" or any of those qualifiers. Until the occupation ends, Israel is not fit for visiting, and Jerusalem must be less a city and more a state of mind. Hear, O Israel. There is another law of return: the Karmic one. Do right, it says, and right comes back to you.

It is suspiciously easy for me to contemplate relinquishing my right of return in protest. Return to what? Even all those visits to Israel later, I was never really there. I would not choose to live where freedom comes so clearly from the army's boot on someone else's neck. Perhaps because I learned Arabic before I knew a word of Hebrew, I feel oddly split in Israel, like a dog summoned by a whistle most humans don't hear. The Knesset wrangles over whom precisely the law of return enfolds—the Carmelite priest, the Ethiopian Falasha, the Manipuri claiming descent from a lost tribe—but is deaf to the Palestinian claims that most need tending. Hear, O Israel? You do not need Arabic to know how it feels to wait for four hours at checkpoints on your way to work, or to see every third man in your family taken at night by soldiers. You do not need to ask if the people who planted those orange trees in Yaffa miss them.

I am complicit, not superior. In 1981, going by bus from Cairo over the newly returned Sinai, a border guard pulls me aside after she hears me tell someone where the bathroom is in Arabic. She is beautiful, her flowing, vaguely electric hair a flock of goats streaming down Gilead. You will miss the bus, she tells me coldly. "I'm a Jew, from Long Island," I protest in response to questions like "do you sleep with Arabs?" or "do you have Arab friends?" and then flush with gratitude when she lets me pass.

Ten years later, I go with a Jewish friend to a refugee camp. The Israelis claim this is Jerusalem proper, not the occupied territories, though the people sing the same laments—the checkpoints, the daily humiliations, the land taken, the martyrs. Not fifty feet from us a stone-throwing boy is killed by soldiers, and the camp trembles with grief and rage. As the men rush to pull on ski masks and set fire to tires in the streets, our host hustles us away. "You must go back," he says, leading us up over a hill of gravel while shots whistle around us. "We will be under curfew here for days." As one, my friend and I raise our arms—to hail a cab to a Jerusalem restaurant. Rubber bullets have steel centers. The rice pudding was delicious.

The Jerusalem of my imagination is burnished gold, glowing with prayer and the light of a million Shabbat candles kindled in unison. The Jerusalem of the world? I can no longer even visit.

Israel is a lover who breathes promises in your ear, but at the same time slips a heavy stone in your pocket.

Utopia: An English Professor's Answer

E. M. Broner

"Home!" E.T. pointed a bony finger at his planet.

"Home!" I cried after recuperating from an illness in Orange County and being forced to read *The Orange County Register* instead of being on Planet Upper West Side with the *Times*.

"This is home!" said my Russian cousins living nearby in Santa Monica. In Kiev they shared an apartment and kitchen with several other families. Not only the living quarters, but the state was inhospitable to Jews. Here the American daughter has her own room, her digital camera, and, without worry about quotas, is applying to colleges.

Home is expansion.

When I taught in Israel at Haifa University in 1975, my Israeli Palestinian students invited me to their homes. One, an older man in a literature survey class, was grateful to have the opportunity for education and showed us his land, the view of the Haifa hills, the apricot trees from which he made brandy.

"We share the same view," he said.

Another young man, Mr. Khoury, in a poetry workshop, invited us to his home in Nazareth. He was feeling kindly toward his professor and the class because one of his favorite poets was invited to lecture on his latest poetry, "The Wandering Arab." The reading was followed by discussion, disputation and general excitement. Hence the invitation.

After the abundant repast, our host showed me the limited space in which he was allowed to live, for the Army would not let the city expand. Mr. Khoury wondered whether to leave the land and let himself expand, or stay and try to settle things there.

"What do you think, my professor?" he asked.

"Leave," I said sadly.

That was 1975, a year I spent teaching at the university, which had a good representation of its Arab/Palestinian citizens. Graduation was a great honor. It made them friendlier to this country, their home.

Since then the time of struggle has bitterly increased. The name of "Israel" itself means struggle, Jacob wrestling with the angel, emerging limping from the encounter. But those decades ago we were optimistic.

I wish now that I had added Etymology when I lectured in the English department, for words are directional signals.

For instance, the root of "nation" is "gene." Related derivatives are: gentle, kin, generative, genuine, native, genetic, gender. If we had remembered that we occupants of the land are "kin," who, before the state, both defined ourselves as Palestinian, would we have treated each other more gently? Would our agreements be genuinely signed and our genders respected for we have the same DNA?

I would have taught Mr. Khoury's class that to "settle" is to put in order, to fix. Since we were all settlers in the land, those who claimed special rights, protection as a result of their wrongful definition of the word, would have had to leave those "settlements" which they turned into unsettling, dangerous places.

I would teach about symbols: the anthem, the flag. "Symbol" is a word whose root is almost alive, like quicksilver. Its derivatives are: parable, parliament, problem. The anthem, if in a shared state, could be antiphonal, one voice answered by another. We would sing: "O Palestine! O Israel! You're mine!"

Its parliament, Knesset, Hebrew for "entrance way," would be an entrance for all the peoples.

As for "religion," I would inform the students that "religion" is derived from "religare," to tie fast. Religion tethers us, fastens us so tightly we have no flexibility of movement. Would a state be more likely to succeed if it were secular?

Would I have to have Israel as home, to be granted citizenship? My Russian cousins may have needed America. Those fleeing during and after the Holocaust may have needed a place of haven. But American Jews do not need another home, a suburban, country home. Would I give up citizen for peace? Easily. After all, "citizen" is merely "one from the city" and there are many cities for urban people. If we give up the flag and the anthem and citizenship, would it do away with the tanks and the bombings of houses, or with antiphonal suicide bombings?

Language is both fluid and exact. If we are clear in what we say, then we can see the view together from the top of the mountain. "Utopia" means "No Place," but I was shown, long ago, by one of my students, that Utopia is fact.

To Our Son, Marek Alexander Barnette, on the Occasion of His Naming

Meg Barnette and Brad Lander

Marek, we inscribe you today into the Jewish covenant. We are imposing upon you a set of overlapping identities, inscribing you with a name of our choosing and with the ritual violence of circumcision. We do not pretend that these are the best identities, and we know they contain many contradictions. But we have found much to celebrate in them. If this is a kind of violence, it is also a profound gift, deeply rooted in our love for you.

We hope that you will learn to embrace this gift without thinking that you are better than others, or that your identity ought to endow you with special privileges. In particular, we are thrilled to pronounce you a Jew without the Right of Return. Your name contains our deep hope that you will explore and celebrate your Jewish identity without confusing it with nationalism.

Your last name is your mother's—a non-Jewish one—by fact of which you are ineligible for the nationalist privilege of automatic Israeli citizenship under the Law of Return. We believe that law confuses the wonderful and painful inheritance of identity with unearned advantages—legal, political, and financial—granted by a militarized state over other people, including so many whom it oppresses daily.

Your first name is after Marek Edelman, a Bundist (secular Jewish socialist) and a leader of the Warsaw Ghetto Uprising against the Nazis in 1943. One of the few who survived, he chose to remain in Poland, where he became a cardiologist, and later an activist with the Solidarity movement. More recently, he earned the ire of many Jews for writing to Palestinians in tactical and moral terms—though he was encouraging them to cease suicide attacks on civilians—because he was implicitly comparing their struggle with his own.

We wish for you his courage, and the good fortune never to need it. We hope you will be inspired by his socialist ideals, and blessed with a better chance to help make them real. And we pray that you will come to celebrate the Yiddish concept of *doikeyt*, of here-ness; that like Marek Edelman, you will express your Jewish identity in social justice struggles where you live, and not be tempted by the too-easy answers of nationalism. Those answers provide solace and consistency, but they are sources of so much violence, hatred, and suffering on our planet.

We pray fervently that by the time you read this, the Israeli occupation of the West Bank and Gaza, the settlements, the house demolitions, the violence will be history. But even then, we hope you will appreciate this absence of nationalist privilege in your inscribed identity. We hope you will work for a world where identity is explored, nurtured, critiqued, celebrated, and protected—but not the basis for privilege, for discrimination, for money, for power.

We hope you will find meaning in being part of communities rooted in values and engaged in the struggle for justice. Communities with a sense of obligation, of *mitzvah*, but also with passionate debate, critical inquiry, and a celebration of difference.

We hope you will develop an appreciation of the cultures being handed down to you, along with a willingness to challenge traditions that seem oppressive, even things that we hold dear.

We hope you will find inspiration, love, and safety from the people in your communities, the people gathered around you today. We hope they will be for you, as they are for us, mentors, friends, and comrades. By being here today, they are promising to be there for you on the many inevitable occasions when you find us impossible to communicate with.

We hope you will come to find yourself within this covenant as a wonderful paradox—a fabulous, unique individual with all our love; and an intersection of communities and traditions that have existed long before you, and that will exist for many generations to come.

Should Jews Relinquish the Right of Return? No!

Susannah Heschel

Those of us who grew up in the Diaspora as children of survivors or of refugees from Europe looked to Zionism as our safety net. The terrors of our nightmares were calmed by our parents' reassurance that a Jewish state would defend us, that we could always pack our bags and move there. Zionism was also an imaginative place of spirit, of young, vibrant enthusiasm for being Jewish, redeeming us from the plaintive, somber quality of our religious Judaism.

Somewhere along the line, the State of Israel destroyed our Zionism. The Jewish fundamentalism of the Diaspora hijacked its principles and substituted a fanatical claim to the land rooted in a profound racism toward Palestinians. Israel became not simply a vulnerable target of hatred, but an occupying force destroying the economy, social fabric, and the lives of Palestinians under its control.

Conscience is left no breathing room when racism takes over a society, and support for Israel has become rooted in a horrific Jewish racism toward Palestinians, just as so many Palestinian leaders have paralyzed their political interests with anti-Semitism. For many Jews, all Arabs are terrorists, and defense of Palestinian interests is too often viewed as treason of the Jewish community.

Withdrawing my support from Israeli politics by renouncing my right of return is one kind of protest, yet I ask, what will it accomplish? It reminds me of the Germans who claimed to go into "internal exile" while living in the Third Reich, or of the Vietnam War protesters who went to jail, claiming their conscience did not permit them to live freely in a United States at war.

We Jews have created the State of Israel, and we are the only ones able to transform the force of oppression that it has become into the idealistic Zionist state we dreamed about years ago. The issue today is not alleviating the angst of my conscience, unwilling to be complicit with a state violating human rights, but bringing an end to the destruction of Palestinian society. This, now, is the great obligation that devolves upon every Jew.

Many Palestinians are our enemy, to be sure, and wish our death and destruction—all of us, Diaspora Jews as well as Israelis. Only a fool would fail to recognize that. Yet in Israel and elsewhere we also hear about Palestinians as Amalek—the incorrigible enemy whom we are obligated to wipe off the face of the earth. What an irony, if it were not so painful, that we spent fifty years after the end of World War II calling the attention of the world to the Nazi racism and genocide against us, and now it is we who must attend to the racism of our own community.

We Jews cannot walk away from Israeli policies and simply say we abjure the country. Ours is the duty to revolutionize the State of Israel and its Diaspora supporters. This is a moral obligation that will haunt us for generations to come.

Nothing Is Good for the Jews

Lynne Tillman

Like humans you're related to and don't like, exasperating questions about Jewish identity make their appearance and persist. In a Delmore Schwartz story, one character tells of a Polish girl who's asked her religion. She says: I'm an antagonist.

I am, too. Let's say I assert: I'm an American, a nonhyphenated one, since in "American" resides a reality or abstraction or right, something maybe solely of possibility, that I might fight for. It's as an American that I object to Israel's occupation of the territories and to its shocking abuses of Palestinians.

Suicide serves Sharon, like vengeance serves Ashcroft. With it, they can execute death for others.

What did the Taliban and Bush do first? Limit women's lives. "As a woman,"

I'm threatened as much if not more by fundamentalists than I am "as a Jewish American." With what should I identify? And why?

I could pin the name tag on my chest and stamp my foot: I refuse to live my life as if "it" were going to happen again, with "never again" and "is it good for the Jews?" the dour cheerleader's background chants. Rationality speaks, but it's power and irrationality that rule.

At the turn of the last century, a German intellectual said he was Jewish because of anti-Semitism. For a while I thought that's how I'm Jewish, since I'm an athiest, never have had a religious or spiritual practice, and dislike religions generally. Nationalism, too, which lacks spirituality's consolations for death. But without the nation-state, as Hannah Arendt seems to indicate, where would protection come from? There is also civil death.

I'm an assimilated American, though maybe that's redundant because America is an assimilation. I like the American experiment, I'm part of it, worried about where it's broken, scared it can't be fixed. I'm fortunate to have the freedoms I do, and I want to use them, though I'm regularly inadequate to their uneasy, exacting demands.

Am I a "progressive" Jewish-American? Don't know what that is, really. But just who does she think she is? you might ask. In a funny way, I'm more interested in what I do and can't do than am. Call me existentialist, that was an antagonistic philosophy, born of war.

I'm not proud to be an American, female, Caucasian, heterosexual, Jewish, etc.; I'm not ashamed, either. These are conditions of existence, birthrights, birthwrongs. Pride and shame, self-satisfaction and self-disgust foment emotional stations on Identity Road—they're not safe houses, but restive ones. And, after thirty years of intense claims for it, identity can be ripped off. What's in a name? Just a name, and our fin de siècle's most bitter irony. Maybe once identity is found or fixed, it can become lost or, at least, unfixed.

We Americans who were born Jewish were spared the terrible fate that fundamentally overturned Western civilization's notions of itself. The Holocaust was the fatal dissolution of Western chauvinism. The logic of the unconscious trumped humanism, since it really didn't matter that you were educated, rational, or enlightened, you could be barbaric; actually, because you loved music and literature and despaired they would be destroyed by others, you could be fiercely racist, anti-Semitic.

Should the right to return be used like a debit card, when all else fails? A last resort is just that. Oscar Levant quipped, in *The Bandwagon,* "I can stand anything except failure." It would be a failure to rely on a last resort, and, needing its guarantee, to justify Israel's wrongdoings. The terror of future persecution shouldn't determine present action. An ethical response, to my way of thinking, can't be guided by fear; it has to wrestle with it. Fear makes blind attachments to identity fraudulent.

Atavisms are plagues. Nothing is good for the Jews. Nothing is bad for the Jews. Tribal thinking isn't good for the tribe.

Borders

Ruth Knafo Setton

For Eran Riklis

In Oslo and D.C., fat fingers trace
a line that shaves your face in half, slices
brothers into enemies, and tears
through a house: you sleep
in Palestine but stumble
barefoot to piss in Israel.
Your front door, a barbed wire fence:
"Before, we were at war, and I roamed—
Park Place to Oriental Avenue.
Now we're at peace, I follow
the laws: wait in Jail for my turn."
The Druze bride, engaged

to a Syrian soap star,
says goodbye to mother, father, sisters.
Israel stamps her passport,
but Syria won't let her through:
the stamp reads Golan,
and Golan is ours. I'll erase it, says
the young Israeli guard, touched
by the bride in dusty white, her hair
a tissue-stuffed pyramid. We have to send
to Assad, says Syria. No! wails the groom,
fingers tangled in the wire. The bride sits
on a folding chair, her cone of hair dipping

between two countries. Red tape,
like red sky, scorches her eyes.
A mother grips the great wall and cries
to Lebanon: What have you done
with my son? He had eyes as green
as the Black Sea, he loved

Elvis—who will give him his milk now?
Her tears water the desert.
On your side grows parsley, on mine, mint.
I lick the leaves, dare them to flower
and tornado the wall. Meanwhile I lift
weights and eat yogurt: wasn't Samson

a woman and Delilah the man
who cut her hair? Watch how I make the tea
on my little fire. Crush green leaves from Sinai,
mud from the Dead Sea, blood from my heart.
Let steep.
Like my Moroccan grandfather, pour
from on high, down to my parched throat.
I splash the tea—dark and orange-
scented—through the barbed holes, glimpse
you crouching to catch
the drops—one by one—
on your Jewish-Arab tongue.

Section Six

Trips to the Holy Land

Intifada Diptych

Alisa Solomon

1. Withdrawing from Lebanon

It's in the *Lebanon Star*—an English-language daily published in Beirut—that I first read about the suicide bombing of a Tel Aviv discotheque on June 1, 2001, that kills twenty-one Israelis, almost all of them teenagers. I study the paper, drinking thick, sweet coffee in a cafe overlooking the glinting Mediterranean in a northern coastal city of Lebanon called Tripoli, where I have come to cover a two-week workshop the Living Theater is conducting with some forty theater students from the University of Beirut. I imagine the site of the attack—the Dolphinarium—whose own Mediterranean shore I sat gazing at exactly a year earlier.

I had been in Tel Aviv for an academic theater conference in June 2000— my only trip of half a dozen to Israel so far when I haven't been on assignment as a journalist. So, for a change, I was not racing from the Negev to the Galilee, finding my way around the West Bank and Gaza Strip, nor turning every conversation with a friend, relative, shopkeeper, waiter, peace activist or cabdriver into a pesky interview. I marveled—guiltily, of course—at how relaxed I felt, at how much I could actually enjoy the place. Having been to Israel previously to cover crises—the first intifada in 1988, the Gulf War in '91, the period after the Rabin assassination in '95—I had always arrived at Ben Gurion in one unshakable way like the American Zionist I was raised to be: with a mission. Never mind that my politics had long swerved away from the milk-and-honey homilies of Hebrew school (in part, precisely because I had visited the territories and seen the occupation in all its demoralizing and destructive detail); I had absorbed well the principle that I was to go to Israel not for fun or careerism (if that's what academic conferences represent), but with a sense of obligation.

But there I was, in a sparkling spring, enjoying grilled fish by the sea, arguing aesthetics till all hours in friends' apartments, even going to the beach. I had harbored few illusions about the Oslo accords. I had been at Manger Square on *erev*-Christmas in 1995, when IDF troops were redeploying from Bethlehem, the red-and-green pennants festooning the plaza doing both national and yuletide duty. Amid the celebrations, a young man named Khaled told me: "It's impossible not to be excited here. Usually Christmas means curfews and Israeli soldiers keeping us away. It's never been like this before that we could come out and sing and dance in our own city. But that doesn't mean the Oslo agreement is good. The problem of refugees isn't even mentioned. The Israelis still control our roads and electricity and water. Tonight feels like freedom, but tomorrow the people will be stopped at a roadblock and wake up." A joke going around the West Bank at the time held that Palestinians had made an exclusive deal with Japanese automakers to produce special cars for the checkpoint-laden roads: no fourth gear. I knew very well that land expropriation and settlement building had accelerated since '93, especially under Ehud Barak. Still, June 2000 felt like a hopeful, largely trouble-free time. My partner and I asked a friend to take us for a day's drive through the Golan, actually figuring it might be our only chance to see the Banyas waterfalls or eat kanafe in Majdal Shams without a Syrian visa.

For the first time I'd felt in Israel the mood I had been well-trained to expect there: the promise of new possibility. And, though more guarded, such eagerness was palpable in Palestine, too. Take my little scholarly precinct, for example: an actor we met, a Palestinian citizen of Israel, invited us to the opening of a play about the experiences of the 1948 refugees, which he was starring in at a new theater in Ramallah; the production as well as the new facility and all its vibrant activity, he beamed, was evidence of the ever-growing vitality of inquiry and creativity in Palestine. Just a few weeks before we arrived, a Tel Aviv friend, a Jewish director, had staged a project with Jews and Palestinians that used testimonies from court cases and journalistic reports, presented by actors as well as actually aggrieved people, as a model truth and reconciliation commission. Both endeavors, because of their footing on frank recognition of the past, looked hopefully, and not naively, toward the future.

Most heartening, right before our arrival that spring, Israel withdrew from southern Lebanon after eighteen years, with wide public support spearheaded by an anti-war group called the Four Mothers. At around the same time, the Israeli courts ruled that a lesbian couple could jointly adopt a child. *Ha'aretz* celebrated the forward-looking spirit occasioned by both developments with a charming cartoon: A child tells an IDF soldier, "I have two mommies." The soldier replies, "So what? I have four." How beautiful it was that June, a cool constant breeze softening the sun's harsh edge.

Now, in June 2001, the same sea breeze is wafting over me in Tripoli, Lebanon. But the climate has changed radically.

The Lebanese have just finished celebrating the anniversary of Israel's withdrawal from their territory, but the Palestinians have had no such cause for rejoicing. It's been eleven months since the Camp David talks collapsed, nine since Ariel Sharon strode to Haram al Sharif/Temple Mount backed by a huge police force to boast that a Jew has the right to go anywhere in Jerusalem he wants, four since escalating violence swept him into office (though not on the landslide the American media reported. Sharon won votes from some 35 percent of the electorate; so many Israelis either submitted blank ballots—"none of the above"—or declined to vote that the old warrior was elected with *fewer* votes than Netanyahu had garnered when he'd *lost* to Barak in the prior election). Despite the heady feeling of the previous summer, the collapse of the "peace process" could not have been a surprise to anyone who had noticed the continued construction of Jewish-only bypass roads chopping the West Bank up into disconnected cantons, the relentless rise of yet more settlements, the persistent Israeli control of the movement of water, capital, labor, and plain folks. As Jeff Halper, the Israeli anthropologist who heads the Committee Against House Demolitions there, puts it, prisoners might be granted 95 percent of a penitentiary's grounds—cells, mess hall, recreation area—but as long as someone else determines where they can go and when, they are not free, independent, autonomous, self-determining. Only the prevailing myth that "Barak made the most generous offer and the Palestinians answered with violence because they just don't want peace" could cloud the fact that the Aqsa intifada was an effort to resist an occupation that wasn't going away. The myth prevailed all the same, egged on by a massive Israeli PR campaign in the United States—and, no less, by the rise in Palestinian extremists' attacks on civilians inside the green line.

Ruchama Marton, president of Israel's Physicians for Human Rights, says that for Israeli Jews, history always begins with the latest trauma. Thus Palestinian violence is detached from context, never recognized as being a reaction—as well as prod—to any assassinations or bombings or house demolitions or civilian casualties Israel might have inflicted. The Dolphinarium bombing—disgusting, deplorable, indefensible, do I need to say?—is quickly pointed to as "proof" of preternatural Palestinian Jew-hatred, of Palestinian insistence on "pushing Jews into the sea," of justification for any collective punishment by the IDF. And collective punishment does come, swiftly and mercilessly. Israel's military commander for the West Bank tells the Israeli press in the summer of 2001 that strangling the Palestinian economy, bulldozing houses, and restricting people's movement *produces* rather than *prevents* suicide bombers. And a year later, defense minister Benjamin Ben-Eliezer makes the same assertion about the IDF incursions said to root out terrorism: ". . . the operations themselves become a hothouse that produces more and more new suicide bombers. The military actions kindle the frustration, hatred and despair and are the incubator for the terror to come." Since June 2001, the spiral has tightened and gathered speed, sucking ever more innocent people into the vortex of violence.

Urging people to swim out of the relentless undertow of vengeance has been a central aim of the Living Theater since its establishment in 1948. In Lebanon in 2001, the lefty, international, boho, anarchist-pacifist, experimental theater company founded by rootless cosmopolitans is trying to create a show with several dozen diverse Lebanese students who are just old enough to have real memories of their fifteen-year civil war, which claimed nearly 200,000 lives and displaced two-thirds of the population of 4 million. Here, the news of the Dolphinarium bombing becomes a flashpoint for exposing the wide rifts in perception not only between the American/European artists and the Arab college kids, but within the Living Theater (LT) and among the students themselves. The crash of reactions splinters something in me as well.

That very day the LT holds an emergency meeting in response to bad news they've just had from their trip organizer, Habiba. In addition to presenting their anti–death penalty play, *Not in My Name*, in Tripoli, the group plans to perform in Khiam—the site of the former notorious prison where fighters against Israeli occupation, as well as their relatives, neighbors, and many other innocent bystanders, were detained and tortured, mostly by troops in the South Lebanese Army, Israel's proxy militia. Word has just come that the work must be approved by censors from Hizbullah, the militant Shi'ite faction that controls southern Lebanon and the museum/memorial that Khiam has become.

A gray-haired, gray-suited apparatchik of Hizbullah turns up in Tripoli to have an advance look at the script. Though skeptical, he's held off somewhat when he's told that there isn't one—the LT is using the method of collective creation to develop a piece with the students and the workshops are only a couple of days old. But his demand riles up some members of the LT.

The two Germans in the company in particular object to having to be declared kosher by "terrorists." One of them holds up the day's front-page story about the disco bombing from the *Herald Tribune*—and a German film crew making a documentary about the LT that happens to be along on the trip zooms in on the tears streaming down her face and the photo of the carnage in the paper. No matter that Lebanon's Hizbullah had nothing to do with the bombing at the Dolphinarium. Such instantaneous terro-porn graphs all attacks on Israel—violence against civilians, assaults on occupying soldiers (Hizbullah's primary target), even verbal critique—onto a continuum whose endpoint is Jewish extermination, and then collapses it all into a single undifferentiated mass, unavailable for analysis.

Two of the Jews in the company—artistic directors Judith Malina and Hanon Reznikov—are the ones to point out that the LT has frequently performed under despicable governments, precisely to bring their defiant message to regimes where it's seldom heard. "We went to Milosevic's Belgrade. And we went there to object to the violence, the same as here. I'll go and say 'peace' anywhere," Malina asserts. Another actor responds, "As a German I just don't want to be linked to a regime that wants to destroy the Jewish state." Replies Malina: "Was it okay to be linked to a regime that destroys Bosnian Muslims? What's the difference?"

Jewish history, of course, though no one says so, least of all the Germans. I'm both touched and disturbed by their reaction, knowing too well how the casting of Jews as eternal, innocent victims, first of all, conflates Jew and Israeli (or, more precisely, the Jewish People and the Israeli State), and second, constructs us as incapable of committing atrocity except, perhaps, in the justifiable case of self-defense. While Nazis and their enablers may have fantasized about Jewish control of media, finance, and eventually the entire world, no Jewish army ever invaded Berlin. Hizbullah came into existence precisely to resist Israeli military incursion.

Not that Hizbullah doesn't give me the creeps, but more because they are fundamentalists than that they hate Israel, which from their perspective stands to reason, even if I object to their tactics and views. In telling us about the censor's demands, Habiba has also mentioned that the Jews among us—one of the LT actors in addition to Reznikov, Malina, and myself—might not be allowed into the south; the rest of the LT would have to take the students there while we would wait behind (or maybe go east to tour the spectacular ruins of Baalbeck, I'm already thinking). But a policy of no-Jews-allowed turns out to be Habiba's paranoid invention—the gray apparatchik never mentioned it. Still, the day of discussion around this possibility stirs my own formidable queer/Jewish panic, and it bubbles up like yeast from its always-fermenting place in my breast as I contemplate entering Hizbullah territory with my American passport, butch haircut and a name that might as well be a neon implant in my forehead, flashing "*yahoud, yahoud.*" Before the falseness of the policy is exposed, Habiba recommends some strategies: Can any of us pass for Russian or something? *Reznikov* doesn't necessarily ring Hebrew in Arab ears, she tells us. Even more cheerfully, she assures us that *Malina* sounds Italian, or maybe Spanish. Besides, we can all assert that we reject Zionism and if Hizbullah isn't satisfied in my case, they can go to the *Village Voice* website and read my stories that expose the brutality of the occupation.

I am not relieved. In fact, I become indignant. In my years of anti-occupation and anti-racist activism in New York, I have always bristled when I have sensed that I was being embraced as an Acceptable Jew and now, in Lebanon, I feel the shiver under my skin that tells me that a primal nerve has been hit: I refuse to submit to a test that would determine whether I could step "beyond" my Jewishness and acquire honorary status as an ordinary human being. And though it's not that long ago that my mother—a Hebrew school principal, no less—was mortified to hear me say that I am not a Zionist, I cannot say, especially not in a command performance for this audience, and certainly not without a long disquisition on what we mean by the terms, that I am an anti-Zionist.

A different anger—at myself for feeling flattered and vaguely pleased—flushes my cheeks when Sasseen, one of the students in the workshop with whom I have been enjoying lengthy political and theatrical discussions, tells me, "I'm proud you are the first Jew I have met. I hope when I meet my first Israeli, I will also not be disappointed." Like the other students in the workshop, he's impressively well-read, urbane, trilingual. All of them are politically aware and interested—and they are amused that an American professor would find such student engagement astounding. But at twenty-two, Sasseen seems more driven than the others to dive into some direct means of making the world right. Like me, he's obsessed with what's happening in Israel and Palestine; like me, he's marginalized in his community—Maronite Christians—because he supports Palestinian freedom. He asks me to send him some books about Zionism when I get back home—they are not for sale in Lebanon—and he shows me a scrap of an Israeli soccer magazine that he has taken as a souvenir from an abandoned IDF post. (His friends, he says, preferred to collect bullet shells and other military detritus.) He is astonished to learn that Hebrew, too, runs from right to left.

Sasseen also tells me, that day after the Dolphinarium bombing, "I hope I am not shocking you, but I was delighted when I heard the news." Moral arguments can't dampen his vicarious craving for retribution. "It's not even one for one," he reasons, "but one for a hundred." And tactical arguments fare worse.

"It's revolutionary violence that drove Israel out of Lebanon. What else do the Palestinians have?"

Little surprise that a few days later, he's one of the dozen students who don't show up for rehearsals. They have decided, they explain in an evening meeting when they read us their hastily drafted manifesto, that they cannot participate in *Not in My Name* because it advocates pacifism and they do not want to be misunderstood as not having supported the resistance to the occupation. Though the Khiam play is not yet finished, they fear that the LT's thorough opposition to violence will seep out no matter what they create collectively, and especially in Khiam, they don't want to be perceived as rejecting Hizbullah's victory. These students leave the project, expressing friendship and respect for the LT, but rejecting their ideology as utopian and naive—and debating the point vociferously with the majority of the students who stay. There might be room for dreams of nonviolence in the privileged West, the defectors say, but in the face of occupation, such fantasies are death.

So it's a smaller group that finally makes the trip south. The drive takes several hours, racing perilously along the coast into Beirut, then winding through severe hills. Greenish from a distance, they're all scruff and scorched scrabble up close, the almond orchards that once shaded the earth long decimated in bombing raids. Portraits of resistance fighters flap from lampposts along the roads with exhortatory slogans (alongside others that urge, visit this cafe, buy that skin cream). The faces are young, always male, the portraits medieval in their use of light and upcast eyes: saintly. Small versions can be purchased in the Khiam museum—posters, key chains, stickers. I retreat from my impulse to buy what I can only regard as Hizbullah kitsch: the horror of the site won't let me make a joke even of these tchotchkes.

I could hardly stand to be at Khiam. It wasn't that the small cement cells were punier or harsher than those at other prisons I'd seen. Or that the guard tower looming over the grounds still seemed threatening. Or even that a guide displayed torture devices with expert narration. The "death to Israel" slogans scrawled all over the place sickened me—because it was unavoidably obvious why they are there. *We did this.* Shame and sorrow swept through me like nausea. Many times over the last fifteen years I had listened to Palestinians in the West Bank and Gaza describe in harrowing detail the abuses and humiliations they'd suffered at Israel's hands. I'd reacted with sorrow, of course, but never with shame, for I'd never felt that Israel acted on my behalf or represented me—how could it, given my wholeheartedly diasporic posture? On the rocky pathways of Khiam distance fails. I am ambushed by the inescapability of my bound-up Jewish fate.

As for many progressive Jews of my generation, it was Israel's invasion of Lebanon in 1982 that first punctured my romance with our putative homeland. I hadn't yet visited, but my brother moved to a kibbutz as a teenager in the mid-'70s and stayed, on and off, half-a-dozen years. Years earlier, a first cousin had made *aliyah,* married a sabra, and was raising a family near Ber Sheva. More distant cousins had arrived directly from smoldering Europe.

Despite my years in Hebrew school and in the Zionist youth movement Habonim, I was not burning to make the summer roots-trip that so many of my suburban cohorts made (in part, because even then I had an inchoate sense that my roots, though violently dug up, were in Vilna and Kraków), but as I come from a long line of Hebrew educators, talk of the wonder of Israel, along with debate over the perpetual crisis of Jewish continuity, dominated dinner-table discourse in our liberal Midwestern home. I accepted that somehow Israel belonged to me, and I to it, the way I might acknowledge that I had relatives, say, in Argentina whom I'd never met: attached, alluring, yet an abstraction.

But my unperturbed sense of Jewishness came from other places: holidays, rituals, Marx Brothers movies, my grandmother's recipes, the harangues of the Prophets, the Gershwin Preludes my sister practiced endlessly, Wise Men of Chelm stories, Shabbos, table-thumping debate. As I began to get politically engaged as an undergraduate in Ann Arbor in the mid-'70s, Israel seldom came into the picture. Stirrings of pro-Palestinian activism on campus, and the infamous Zionism = Racism resolution passed by the UN in 1975, made me nervous, just as Sadat's visit to Jerusalem in 1977 gave me a thrill, but none of it gripped or unsettled me.

The massacres at Sabra and Shatila did—for all the same reasons the war in Lebanon was the first to divide Jewish Israeli citizens and to spark a mass peace movement and a refusal movement among reservists there. And this split, in turn, created an opening for dissent within Jewish America's unqualified support for Israel, which had coalesced during the 1967 war. Now, twenty years later, in the heat of the Aqsa intifada, the Jewish establishment in the United States has, with haste and hostility, reassembled the old consensus. Like George Bush *fils*, they are drawing lines: You are with us or against us.

Outraged by Israel's siege of Beirut, the great civil rights and anti–death penalty activist Henry Schwarzschild, who had fled Germany shortly after his post-Kristallnacht closet bar mitzvah, wrote a provocative and passionate editorial in *The Nation* in 1982. "The price of a Jewish state is, to me, Jewishly unacceptable," he charged, "and the existence of this (or any similar) Jewish ethnic-religious nation-state is a Jewish—i.e. a human and moral—disaster and violates every remaining value for which Judaism and Jews might exist in history."

I came across this writing only years later, after I had come to know Henry (*olevasholem*) as a mentor in the fledgling years of the New York grassroots group Jews for Racial and Economic Justice. Though the Lebanon war shifted my paradigms, there's no particular moment when I stopped being an American Zionist (which I qualify to mark a distinction from Israeli patriotism and nineteenth-century European Zionism, both quite different creatures). I didn't experience a sudden epiphany, a brutal rupture, or a political conversion that has propelled me to evangelize. It's been, rather, a gradual grinding down, the sad wasting away of idealism and hope and faith that justice was being served. This dissolution has paralleled, of course, the emptying out of the very term "Zionist"—except, perhaps, in its very American meaning: not just the religion of American Jews, but a wellspring of that invigorating admixture of Jewish power and vulnerability. But this erosion has not in the slightest eaten away at my sense of, or even pleasure in, being Jewish. That is no doubt why I have come to think that Henry could be right. And to yearn for his own prophetic harangues in these perilous times.

2. Selling Our Birthright

In preparing for my trip to Lebanon, I had read some histories of the civil war as well as some personal accounts of the siege of Beirut. Mahmoud Darwish's motif of morning coffee in *Memory for Forgetfulness: August, Beirut, 1982*—the systematic search for water, the careful method of moving the pot on and off the fire, his assessments of people based on the scent of the coffee they make, his stubborn insistence on the normality of the daily ritual even in the middle of bombing raids—still rushes into my imagination any morning I wake to the aroma of java brewing. Darwish writes with a terrible beauty of the relentless attacks: "The sky hugs the earth with a smoky embrace. It hangs down, heavy with molten lead, a dark gray whose nothingness can only be penetrated by the orange leaked from jets whose silver flashes to a blazing whiteness. Graceful airplanes, slender, riding securely the furrowed air." And he reflects on exile, the poet's responsibility to the resistance, the function—and distortions—of collective memory.

In *Beirut Fragments: A War Memoir*, Jean Said Makdishi also recounts the ravages of the civil war and of the Israeli invasion, chronicling the narrowing of physical movement and imagination wrought by the violence, as well as the war's corruption of language. Both works are elegiac, reflective, literary, and thus easy to enter, lovely to read despite their dreadful tales.

Now, in 2002, one more June later, from the breezeless heat of still-wounded New York, I read a less mediated genre of memoir: the blurted chronicles of trauma that arrive by e-mail every day from Nablus, Jenin, Ramallah, sometimes forwarded by Israeli peace activists in Tel Aviv, Haifa, Jerusalem. Unlike the measured prose of Darwish or Makdishi, pleading for us to remember a disaster in danger of being forgotten before being understood or redressed, the missives that pour into my inbox, some dozen each day, are raw appeals for simple recognition, a detailed and desperate sort of electronic graffiti: We are here.

We are here, where our living rooms are trashed by IDF soldiers—bookshelves heaved to the floor, drawers dumped out, family portraits smashed. Where women give birth and patients die at checkpoints because soldiers won't let them continue on to a hospital. Where children are shot on their way to the store, and crops rot on the vines because farmers cannot go out to harvest.

These testimonies share space in my inbox with the panicky postings of relatives and friends in Israel, explaining how they have rerouted their daily patterns to avoid public squares or crowded markets, stopped going to cafes or to the theater, can hardly bear to send their kids off to soccer practice.

I check my e-mail each morning to find Jewish terror and Palestinian horror meeting in a virtual chorus of discordant despair. Often I break down at the computer.

I go religiously to the *Ha'aretz* website. And I keep up my subscriptions to the *Jerusalem Report* and the *Forward* and god-knows-how-many left-Israeli newsletters and bulletins. And I scan the websites of Palestinian NGOs and publications. In part, I have fallen for the Internet-induced illusion that staring into a screen is a means of engagement; in part I am like a neurotic who can't interrupt a pattern of masochistic relationships.

As I have never acceded to the now hegemonic principle that all Jewish identity must emanate from an Israeli center, why can't I proclaim my Bundist affiliations, curl up with a volume of Rokhl Korn or Nathan Englander, blare the Klezmatics on my Walkperson, and learn to look away from Zion?

Not simply because Israel claims to speak in my name and on my behalf, an assertion that carries as much weight with me as, say, Bush's promise to protect my security by running roughshod over the Constitution. Nor because my visits to Israel—not hitting just the UJA high points, but also the development towns that never developed, the unrecognized Palestinian-Israeli villages, the foreign worker neighborhoods, the gay bars—have made the place too concrete to function as a free-floating metaphor for my Jewish self-invention.

More important, Palestinians have become concrete—specific, individual, diverse—because, quite simply, I have talked to some, visited their homes, shared meals. What ought to be a most unremarkable fact contains a fundamental rebuke to American Zionism, which requires that Palestinians be a fantasy: an unaccountably enraged population fueled by anti-Semitic passions. Such absolutes are required because to "love Israel" as an American Zionist is not at all the same sort of experience as to love, say, Italy.

One can have a fulfilling, even mature, romance with Italy—and who doesn't?—without ever being asked to declare her position on Berlusconi (much less on the history of Mussolini) because loving Italy has to do with art, food, landscape, opera—features that endure and define the culture even if there's a corporate despot in office, or a fascist resurgence in the north. Denounce Berlusconi, rail against the anti-immigrant secessionists in the Veneto, complain about the motorini or the catcalling men: your affections are not compromised.

In contrast, I am crazy about the architecture of the Hebrew language (though I speak it execrably), the light in Jerusalem, the hills of Haifa, the cafe culture of Tel Aviv. But that's not what is being asked of me when I'm expected to declare my devotion to Israel. On the contrary, it's the state qua state that is supposed to make me swoon, even if there's a war criminal in office or a fundamentalist movement colonizing the West Bank with full governmental support. Denounce, rail, complain: you're a self-hating Jew.

Arrested adolescent adoration means, of course, that the love object must be idealized. American Zionism grants the favor—along with millions of dollars in annual donations—as a down payment for some imagined future when another anti-Semitic calamity would require the Jewish state to take us in. Despite our success in America, Jewish fear persists—the *pintele yid* in its twisted essence: Harboring such fear may be the only way some Americans remain Jewish. And it leaves no psychic room for recognizing a terrible contradiction: that Israel is not making Jews safe. With its vast military might and American backing, there is little chance that Israel's existence as a state can be threatened; individual Israelis, however, are acutely endangered by the current hostilities. But to sustain the just-in-case availability of Israel as a refuge, American Zionism cannot allow that Israel might share any responsibility for the brutal conflict. The violence must be entirely the fault of the Palestinians.

The deep seepage of the doctrine of demonization into Jewish American Zionism roared notoriously to the surface at the pro-Israel rally in Washington in April 2002, when hawkish Paul Wolfowitz got viciously booed by the crowd for daring to mention—along with asserting his unqualified support for Israel— that Palestinians have suffered, too. No Jewish leader reprimanded the protesters from the stage.

I saw the syndrome reveal itself more insidiously when I spoke on a panel a few weeks later at a conference for Jewish college-student reporters on the theme of covering Israel. I offered a few anecdotes, trying to explain how I position myself as an alternative journalist (lacking the infrastructure, access, and cash of mass media's local bureaus) to look for the stories that the mainstream media neglect. During the first intifada, I told them, I wanted to move away from the daily clash stories and try to get at how the uprising was lived day-to-day by Palestinians and Israelis, so chose to build a collage of profiles. I described, too, how in my most recent trip—most of August 2001, just two months after my visit to Lebanon—I decided to do one of my three stories about the ongoing occupation, a situation largely lost on American readers, so went to Gaza and the West Bank to interview farmers whose crops had been uprooted by the IDF, villagers whose water was repeatedly turned off by nearby Jewish settlers, and so on.

Their responses astonished me. Far from all, but many of the students who spoke up went on the attack: If I have interviewed Palestinians who say they have been victims of human rights violations, have I interviewed the relatives of Israelis killed in suicide bombings? I tried to explain that although I have talked to such families, they are covered extensively in the mass media—which I can't compete with in any case—and that I'm trying to strike a balance on a larger scale. In principle, they took issue with my willingness to give voice to Palestinian experience, but they were polite, congratulating me on my courage: how dangerous they imagined it must have been for me to sit with a Palestinian in her kitchen in Ramallah, or to hang out in a family's living room in a Gaza refugee camp. I appealed to their duty as journalists, insisting that they must at least be willing to hear a narrative, and accept it as the teller's own, even if they don't agree with it. But they had been well counseled precisely in how not to hear any Palestinian narrative. They rebutted me by stressing that as Jewish journalists, their first obligation is to report on Israeli experience, and by asserting (like Ehud Barak not long before) that Palestinians lie by nature, and thus are unworthy sources for their stories.

Mainstream Jewish-American organizations have made a priority of shoring up such self-righteous Zionism among college kids: Hillel sent hundreds to Israel to "improve their Israel advocacy skills" that spring, and AIPAC has hundreds of college affiliates. The organizational response to the rise of pro-Palestine activism on campuses—as any number of panicky op-eds in Jewish papers around the country have baldly stated—has been to defend: not to provide a place where Jewish students of all perspectives and with many questions might be exposed to a range of views (even if it were only a range of Israeli views), learn something, grapple toward their own conclusions, and maybe even engage in genuine dialogue with their apparent activist foes. Rather, the institutions have moved in to indoctrinate. And to circle the wagons. At many universities, a Jewish kid with misgivings about the occupation has nowhere to be Jewish on campus. I fear that she might just stop being Jewish at all.

Increasingly, the self-proclaimed guardians of the Jewish-American future are constructing Jewish identity on the negation of another people and the wrong that has been done to them in the name of Jewish survival: Their land was taken, their homes destroyed, their lives constrained, their dreams deferred. Jewish life has no moral future if we do not own up to these incontrovertible facts. Whether Palestinians really want a uni-national state in all of historic Palestine is not the point. Negotiations and fixed borders and security arrangements presided over by one of the world's most powerful armies can guarantee that even if Palestinians will it, it will remain a dream. (Though some of us may wish for a genuine binational democracy, respecting and advancing both cultures, expecting that outcome in the present context is, sadly and simply, preposterous.)

Acknowledging Jewish responsibility for the dispossession of Palestinians in 1948 does not have to mean the dismantlement of Israel, as the state's supporters always fear whenever the Palestinian catastrophe is even mentioned. But we cannot persist in building Jewish identity around the hollow core of disavowed knowledge. It's just plain wrong. And also, ultimately, very bad for the Jews.

The lengths to which American Zionist leaders will go to sustain the foundational lie is staggering, imperiling the fundamental character of American Jewish culture: its liberalism, flexibility, and openness to—indeed, fostering of—dissent.

Institutional leaders have embraced the Christian fundamentalist right—the only group that gives more support to Israel than American Jews. Never mind that their motive is ultimately anti-Semitic—the second coming requires the return to Zion of all the Jews, who will not be invited to the post-apocalypse party. As long as Billy Graham and Tom DeLay and Ralph Reed and Dick Armey and Family Research Council spokesperson Janet Parshall and a cadre of other high-up end-timers will shill for Sharon's hard line, they are being welcomed into the Zionist fold. In exchange, Jewish organizations are already showing a willingness to abandon long-standing support for environmental protections and even for immigrant rights.

Meanwhile, what a friend who works in a New York Jewish agency has been calling "Jewish communal McCarthyism" has chilled even the most measured critiques of the occupation. Members of the synagogue I belong to were spit on and kicked for carrying pro-peace signs at the April rally in Washington; a friend who was invited to submit an article to a journal suggesting what should be done with excess Nazi reparation money was told he'd risk his job in a Jewish organization if he published his idea that it should be used for Palestinian nation-building; a Hebrew school principal told me that if she simply neglected to send busloads of kids to her local annual pro-Israel parade—much less, made a statement opposing it—she'd be forever ostracized from her professional community.

Whatever happened to: two Jews, three opinions? To the essential, shaping fact that Abraham argues with God? To the very idea of the Talmudic tradition? To good old Jewish disputatiousness?

In my darkest hours, I fear that the rightward-rushing, dissent-killing, tribe-narrowing proponents of a fortress American Zionism will shrink American Jewishness to a mean and little space. Those who don't toe the right-wing Zionist line will be so unwelcome in Jewish places as to abandon them altogether, leaving the right to define and delimit Jewish American aspirations and expressions. They will make a culture that will continue to produce its Podhoretzes, Kristols, and Morton Kleins, but not its Tony Kushners, Marshall Meyers, Marcia Falks, or Judith Malinas.

According to Zionist creed, in addition to being a safe haven, Israel was supposed to be the place where Jews could most assuredly live full Jewish lives, neither crushed by bigotry nor attenuated by assimilation. It's debatable whether that purpose has been fulfilled in Israel for anyone other than the ultra-Orthodox—and arguably their choosing to keep one foot in the eighteenth century rather restricts the fullness of their Jewishness. My Ber Sheva cousin's children, now adults, don't primarily think of themselves as Jewish. They are *Israeli*, one of them insisted when she visited me in New York a couple of years ago. She couldn't understand why I recommended a visit to the Jewish Museum and was genuinely baffled that my partner would host a weekly radio program on Jewish affairs or that I would learn Yiddish or ever set foot inside a synagogue. These were quaint and pointless endeavors as far as she was concerned, harmless maybe, but passé, even embarrassing.

Perhaps she's not representative of her generation of sabras—though I've encountered the attitude among many of her peers—so it's best not to conclude that Jewish life has shrunk rather than expanded in Israel. In any case, there is no question but that Jews in America—at least those who have wanted to—have been able to build Jewish lives of infinite variety, matching the American imperative of self-invention with the ur-performativity of Jewish identity.

But today, American Zionism is doing nothing less than diminishing the polymorphous, exuberant and myriad ways of being Jewish in America. Quite deliberately, it is weeding out the tribe. As Henry Siegman, once the head of the American Jewish Congress, lamented in an interview with the *New York Times* in June 2002, nowadays, according to the *macher* organizations, "If you do not support the government of Israel then your Jewishness, not your political judgment, is in question."

If that is so—if, after all these millennia, the Conference of Presidents really gets away with instituting a kind of Jewish excommunication over its rapturous rallying behind Sharon—then Zionism will forever distort, and even threaten to destroy, the creativity, the diversity, the genius of American Jewishness. Zionism, *khas v'kholile*, will turn out to be the greatest peril Jewish America has ever faced.

Next Year Where?

Jonathan Safran Foer

I didn't exactly have a choice. My girlfriend's grandparents, who live in Jerusalem, have been aging a few weeks every day. Her grandfather has suffered two major strokes, and her grandmother's Alzheimer's is quickly becoming her defining characteristic. Like the country in which they've made their second lives—he came by way of London, she Nuremberg—they are a mix-up of time. Because of their failing memories, what is familiar is entirely new: their children, the pictures that surround them, even their beloved vase. And as one of those strange, heartbreaking side effects of dementia, they have begun to act childlike. Nicole and I had talked for months about paying them a visit before it was too late.

It was a difficult moment to make a trip to Israel, both personally and globally. I was feeling frazzled by recent traveling, and by my inability to get any writing done. I felt scattered, dispersed, unable to make decisions. America was once again on high alert, and there were a few more reasons—reasonable or not—to be anxious about air travel. In the previous month there had been three major suicide bombings in Israel—two in the vicinity of where we would be spending most of our time.

But it's always been a difficult moment. For more than ten years I'd been putting off a trip to Israel, waiting for some better situation, here and there. In that meantime, I'd been to the Ukraine, rural Mexico, southern Brazil, and several other places that are far more logistically difficult to travel to. What makes the trip to Israel so seemingly impossible has to do with more than time, money, or even safety. There is an imposed distance.

I'm thinking of the generation of Jews who, after fleeing slavery in Egypt, were forced to wander in the desert for forty years. God required that a generation pass, so that the Holy Land wouldn't be "defiled" by those who had known slavery. Not even Moses, the liberator and leader, was allowed in, but instead had to view Jerusalem, as he took his last breaths, from a bordering hillside. The story resonates within me, although all of the roles are mixed up. Who imposes the distance? Who are slaves, and who are the masters? Which generation must pass? Is it the land we are trying to save, or ourselves? And if ourselves, from what?

The Tower

After dropping off our things at the hotel, we went to see Nicole's grandparents. Their apartment is in one of the towers that overlook the Knesset, and from the fifteenth floor, you can see everything. It's an amazingly small and large city from up there, like one of those clown cars at the circus that holds comically more than its size could ever allow. It was the first time I'd ever seen Jerusalem from above—the white of the Jerusalem stone sent the sun back at me like a mirror—and I wanted to take in everything. My eyes were drawn to the Palestinian sections of the city: the clotheslines, the broken windows. I was overcome with that same shameful curiosity that compels me to stare at fistfights. I didn't want to look, but I wanted to look.

Nicole's grandfather was davening when we came in, and when we left, and the entire time we were there. His trembling accentuated the eccentricity and precision of the rituals he fulfilled. He hasn't left the apartment—hasn't been to the ground—in many months. He said he was very pleased to meet me several times, as he opened and closed the prayer book he'd used since his bar mitzvah. He was obviously unsure of where he was in his prayers, and occasionally tried to hide his confusion. More often, though, it seemed that knowing that he was somewhere in them was enough.

Nicole's grandmother's face was the ruin of a beautiful face. She wore too much makeup, and fingered her pearl earrings, drawing attention to them. She loved to talk about how popular she'd once been. "All of the boys," she kept saying, over and over, touching her collar. She didn't recognize Nicole at first.

"And what do you do?" she asked, turning to me.

"I'm a writer."

"He wrote that book," Nicole said, pointing to my novel, which was displayed on their coffee table. The sight of it—that articulation of that past self—made me feel all the more disconnected from my present self. (What do I have to do with that person I once was? Am I bound to the person I will be when we return to New York?) Nicole picked up the book and showed her grandmother my photo on the inside of the dust jacket.

"Oh, yes," Nicole's grandmother said, extending the yes like a hand. "I will tell you, I tried to read that book many times, but each time I got stuck in the beginning."

"Others have had that problem," I told her, trying to extend a hand.

"Each time I got stuck."

The Tunnel

We spent our second morning in Jerusalem going through the series of caves that trace the Western Wall. They had precipitated bloody riots—which commonly mark the start of the second intifada—when Palestinians claimed that the Israeli archeologists were digging under the Temple Mount. (They weren't, but it's easy to understand why Israel's initial secrecy, and ultimate brazenness about the project, might stir up some seriously bad feelings.) What I found most strange about the story was that the excavating had been going on for decades— more or less since the end of the Six-Day War. It wasn't until a second exit was dug, which surfaced in the Palestinian quarter so that visitors wouldn't have to double back, that the situation was a situation at all. For all of those years, the Palestinians didn't know about what was happening beneath their basements, and sometimes on the other sides of their walls.

Once, I learned, the archeologists had accidentally excavated into a Palestinian home. Fortunately, it was the middle of the day, and the place was empty. The archeologists sealed up the hole, and repainted the wall. The owner of the house never knew any better—unless, perhaps, he wondered just what it was about his house that looked so new. Everyone on the tour laughed. It was a contagious, violent laughter. I was absolutely disgusted by it, and I laughed, too.

The striations of civilization were breathtaking: so many Jerusalems, one atop the other. It was impossible not to imagine what Jerusalem might one day cover the Jerusalem presently above us. I thought of *Had Gadya,* the song my family always ends the Seder with: a cat chasing the kid, a dog chasing the cat, a stick beating the dog, a fire burning the stick, and water, and an ox, a slaughterer and the angel of death . . .

The more I thought about it, the less sense it made to me. How could they have repainted the wall from the other side of it? Mustn't you be in the room, thereby painting yourself out of the tunnel from which you came? That, too, resonates within me.

I went to Hebrew school as a child, and was given—through stories with morals—an unquestioning, pre-conscious love for Israel. I remember singing Hatikvah, without knowing what I was singing. I remember being able to read and write with the Hebrew alphabet, without knowing what the words meant. (In class, my Jewish friends and I would send each other notes written in transliterated English.) I loved Israel like I loved my parents.

It wasn't until I was in my early teens that I knew that there were Arabs in Israel. I learned about them casually—a reference on the news, an article in the paper. In high school, and to a much greater extent in college, I learned more, and trusted my upbringing less. I began to see things that I couldn't love: denials of basic rights to Palestinians; the withholding of everything from utilities to education; deliberate humiliations. I remember the first time I heard the word *intifada,* the first pictures I saw of my Palestinian counterparts throwing stones, and being shot at with rubber bullets, the first Edward Said essay I'd read (it's hard, as a teenager, not to be smothered by his rhetoric), and when, during a seminar at college, a graduate student used the word "rape" in the context of the occupation.

I wasn't so naïve as to believe that the Palestinians were blameless. And I appreciated the complexity of ensuring safety—ensuring existence—when surrounded by such hostile enemies. But I couldn't forgive Israel. Or I couldn't forgive myself for my unquestioning love of Israel. (I was never good at distinguishing Israel from my love for Israel.) I turned on the country, much more strongly than I intended to, or should have.

And now, so many years and books and pictures later, I'm afraid of sealing off the way from which I came. I want to be sufficiently critical; I want to be guided by reason, to help those who need help, and take the taskmasters to task. But I know there's something else . . . it's embarrassing even to gesture at.

The Vase

There was a vase on the table. Nicole's mother had bought it—red with purple stripes—for the live-in helper to fill with fresh flowers every week. It was all that they could talk about. "What an absolutely beautiful vase," Nicole's grandmother kept saying to me, delighting in it newly, endlessly. She had lost everyone and everything from her childhood, and I hoped that her Alzheimer's was generous enough to erase that, too. "I am truly lucky. I look around my apartment, and I see all of the photos, and that beautiful vase, and I feel so lucky. I was born in Nuremberg. Can you believe it? Do you know about Nuremberg? And now, from the window of my beautiful apartment I can see all of Jerusalem. Who would have thought, when I was a little girl in Nuremberg, that I would have such a beautiful apartment in Jerusalem?"

Nicole's grandfather noticed things about the vase that he had noticed only a moment before, he touched it hesitantly, tenderly, as if for the first time. "It really is amazing," he kept saying, opening and closing his prayer book. He, too, had lost. "What did we ever do to deserve such a beautiful thing?"

The Skirt, the Songs

Why do people go to Jerusalem? Why do they leave? Nicole's grandparents came to save their lives. They never left because the place gave their lives meaning. Others come to fulfill what they believe to be God's commandment to make *aliyah*. Others come to spend money. Others leave to make money. Others come and leave for other reasons.

I've never felt like a tourist, although that's certainly the best way to describe my status. And I've never been a citizen, although as a Jew, I've always had the right of return. I don't pray, in Israel or elsewhere. And yet I've never felt entirely secular in Israel, either. I've never been forced to go to Israel, but I've never felt that I had a choice in going—there's always been some immediate cause for the trip.

We spent our fourth afternoon walking through neighborhoods we'd never before visited. We decided to go for a walk through Me'ah She'arim, one of the oldest, most religious communities in Jerusalem. There was a banner hanging above the main street, asking, among many other things, that women wear skirts and long sleeves. Knowing that a certain amount of a certain kind of humility was expected, Nicole had worn pants and long sleeves. A group of young men stopped us, as we were about to cross the threshold of the neighborhood. One of them stabbed his finger in the direction of the banner. "Skirt," he said. In large block letters the banner read, "IT GREATLY OFFENDS OUR RESIDENTS."

My first response was to feel embarrassed and apologetic. My second—which came at the same time, actually, and with equal force—was anger and repulsion.

What if you greatly offend me? I wondered. Why is tolerance unidirectional? You find it offensive that a woman would wear pants, and I find it offensive, I find it morally repugnant, that women in your communities are trapped as they are, with no means to educate themselves, or free themselves economically. Your wigs greatly offend me.

And then I was embarrassed and apologetic again.

Part of me wanted to please them, to be included. Part of me—it's almost impossible to write—actually loved them.

That night were the festivities marking the anniversary of the "liberation" of Jerusalem, the culmination of the Six-Day War. Thousands of young, healthy-looking Israelis paraded through the streets, waving flags, hollering anthems. I saw the secular counterparts to the boys in Me'ah She'arim, and again I was divided. Part of me was terrified by that other kind of fanaticism—in part because such fervent patriotism was so foreign to me, and in part because what I could understand of the songs they were singing was downright scary. There's nothing more frightening than the unity of voices, the steady flow of bodies, the syncopated clapping of young hands . . .

But again, part of me wanted to be included. Part of me was deeply moved by the allegiance. I told Nicole, "If my mother were here, this would bring tears to her eyes." I hated them, and I was envious of them, and I wished they didn't exist, and I wished I were one of them. What is my song?

Next Year

I have heard the story of the Exodus from Egypt every year of my life. I've been told, again and again, about our enslavement, and the plagues, and the parting of the Red Sea. I've dipped my finger in the wine, and transferred a portion of the sweetness to my plate, in memory of all of those throughout history who have had to suffer so that Jews wouldn't have to. Next year in Jerusalem, I can hear in my grandfather's voice, and in my father's. Next year in Jerusalem, I've said, again and again and again. That central trope of the Passover Seder, the moral of the story, has always fascinated me, in large part because I'm not sure what it means to me.

Of course there have been times—the times of our bondage—when Jerusalem was a logistical impossibility. But I proved that now it takes a little less than a thousand bucks, and a little more than ten hours on a plane. If we wanted to have our Seders in Jerusalem, if we wanted to live in Jerusalem, no more would be required than our efforts. This year in Jerusalem.

Perhaps the Jerusalem of next year isn't a place but an idea—an idealized place. Next year among that future generation of Jews—the Sauls, who are allowed to build the Temple, rather than the Davids, the Warrior Kings, who are forbidden from doing so. Next year in a perfect world.

The problem, though, is that the better place of next year is personalized to each of us. It would be impossible for us to coexist, next year, in the Jerusalem of next year, because our visions are different, and competing.

To the ultra-Orthodox—those who we greatly offended, those who are, ten at a time, on their way to constituting the majority of Jews in Israel—the Jerusalem of next year would look like a place without Arabs, and without secular Jews, a place whose borders extend well into Egypt, Syria and Jordan, a place reawakened by the Messiah.

To those marching through the streets, Jerusalem would be a safe place, at any cost. It would be a Jewish place, the capital of a Jewish State.

Others have other Jerusalems.

We visited my cousin, Nadav, one evening, in his home. He lives in a gated community, that, save for the Jerusalem stone, resembles an American suburb. He owns a mini-market and a dress shop, plays basketball every day, and is obsessed with the newest gadgets. The television wasn't off while we were there, just as Nicole's grandfather's prayers had no beginning or end. "We're tired of war," he said. "We want a good economy." His Jerusalem would look a lot like New York.

The maids in the hotel have Jerusalems.

Sharon has a Jerusalem, as does Arafat.

The Arab-Israeli selling fruit has a Jerusalem. The man checking bags for bombs. The children too young to know the difference between an Arab and a Palestinian and a Jew.

While the Jerusalem of "next year" is symbolic, the Jerusalem of next year is anything but. The future of Israel, and of world Jewry, and of the world, will be determined by competing visions of Jerusalem—the force with which those visions are articulated, and the extent to which they are realized.

When I say, Next year in Jerusalem, to what place am I referring? What does it have to do with the grid that I saw from the tower, and the striations of civilization that I saw in the tunnel? And what about that banner, stating great offense? And what about the songs? Is there a place where my revulsion and love can coexist?

The Mountain

I was quite moved by the Mount of Olives, being in the presence of the bodies that match up with the myths, as if to confirm them. In a few cases, I was sur-

prised that the stories, which I'd grown to think of as being entirely mythological, had referents in the physical world.

I grew up on Genesis and Exodus, which probably explains why, despite my
efforts, my writing always returns to them. As a child, I took the stories literally, unquestioningly. I remember when my father explained to me that the Red
Sea didn't actually part. The story was a metaphor.

"What about the plagues?" I asked. "Are they for real?"

"They point at something real," my father said.

"What about Moses?"

"There was a person named Moses. We know that. And he was a leader of
the Jews. But he didn't see a burning bush, or talk to God."

"What about God?"

It wasn't the betrayal of the myth that confused and hurt me, but the ambi-
guity. The plagues pointed at something real. There was a person named Moses,
but he wasn't the Moses of the story. Myth and history intersected, but weren't
continuous. It was my problem then, and it's my problem now. And it's Jerusalem's
problem. Where does the world end and the otherworldly begin? Where are
the intersections between the Jerusalem of "next year" and the Jerusalem of
next year? Are there intersections?

Dinner with Nadav

Nadav is two years older than I, but has had several more lives of experiences.
After his time in the army, he got married, had a child, opened a mini-market
and a dress shop. For much of the night, I grilled Nadav about his experience
in the army. I'm ashamed of myself, in retrospect, but I couldn't stop asking
questions. Nadav told us that he had been an engineer.

"What kind of engineer?"

"I drove a bulldozer. American-built."

"What did you bulldoze?"

"Houses."

"Palestinian houses?"

"Of course."

"Did you ever bulldoze a house with someone still in it?"

He nodded.

"What do you think about the peace process?"

"People are tired of war," he said. "We want a good economy."

"You would give back land for peace?"

"Certainly."

"Jerusalem?"

"If Jerusalem were a UN city, and there were peace, I would be happy with that."

"Do you feel any spiritual connection to the land?"

"My daughter lives here. That is my spiritual connection."

"But no religious resonance?"

"I am a Jew. This is the Jewish homeland."

"Nothing biblical?"

He laughed.

As we ate dessert, Nadav and his wife had a small quarrel in Hebrew in the kitchen. When he came back he explained, "I have to go to Toronto next week. For business. But my wife doesn't want me to go."

"Why not?"

"She doesn't think it's safe."

"Toronto?"

"SARS."

Black Mud

We spent our last morning in Israel at Mineral Beach, on the Dead Sea. We relaxed—if that's the right word—in Sulfur Pools, crowded in with overweight Russian immigrants, who floated like buoys, or mines. When we couldn't stand it any longer, we went down to the sea itself. Following the lead of the other beach-goers, we covered our bodies in the thick, black mud, which is supposed to open and replenish the pores. So many different kinds of Jews: Polish survivors, air-lifted Ethiopians, Jews from South America and Australia and Iraq, Sephardim and Ashkenazim, Jews of varying levels of observance and pride and patriotism—we were covered, all of us and equally, in black. And all of my disconnected selves were covered in black, too, unified under the mud, or hidden.

I felt, at the center of my being, a reflexive core. It wasn't the residue of Hebrew school indoctrination, and it wasn't any sort of intellectual peace I'd come to. It was angry, and ashamed, and relentless, and fundamental to me. Leaving, I then realized, would be as difficult as coming had been. The distance surrounds me. The wall divides me. I am entirely confused, in the deepest part of me. And it's not a good confusion. It's not a beautiful, sustaining argument. It's painful.

And it's a confusion that I absolutely must face. Because if I don't, the Jerusalem of next year will be left to those who aren't confused, those with the loudest voices. Liberalism is inherently questioning, while fundamentalism is inherently absolute. And as in America, the right in Israel is much more active than the left, more observably passionate, and far more politically successful. Which makes silence unacceptable.

My Jerusalem . . .

My Jerusalem . . .

My Jerusalem would be a tolerant but passionate place, modern and historic. That much I know.

My Jerusalem wouldn't be absent of religion—those who envision such a world do so at their own risk, like those who can imagine a world without art. But it would be without fundamentalists. And without settlements. And with a healthy

Palestinian State, which receives large amounts of American and Israeli aid, and thrives in economic and cultural cooperation with Israel.

If I had my way, Jerusalem wouldn't even be in Jerusalem. Or rather, not exclusively in Jerusalem. Israel has become a golden calf, the greatest false idol of them all. It is treated as the final purpose, to which all other considerations are subject. Which it is not. It is a holy place, of course—because it has been a holy place to so many for so long. It is a profoundly beautiful place, physically and historically. It is spiritual, by just about any definition. But it is subject to the same contingencies as everything else. My Jerusalem would not be an imperative, but a choice.

My Jerusalem...

The Vase

After showering, we went back to Nicole's grandparents for the last time. They were on the sofa when we came in. Her grandfather was folding his tallis. Her grandmother was staring at the vase.

"I will tell you," she said to me, after I'd reintroduced myself. "I tried to read that book many times, but each time I got stuck in the beginning."

"Oh," I said. "That's too bad."

"Yes," she said. "I tried many times, but each time I got stuck."

"Hm."

"So let me ask you something," she said.

"Yes?"

"What is it that you think you did wrong?"

Nicole went through the stacks of photo albums, hoping to have her grandparents' help in identifying the people in the pictures, before they dissolved into unknowability. (As it turned out, many of the people were her grandparents.) I looked out the window. It's an amazing feeling to look at something for what you think might be the last time. You are consumed with the desire to absorb every last detail: the slogans on the blowing banners, the immensity of the cranes, the bigness, the smallness, even the color of the frame of the window. It's a beautiful feeling, because it's desperate.

It was time to say good-bye for the final time. I doubted I ever would see Nicole's grandparents again, and I wonder what occasion would bring me back to Israel. I looked over my shoulder as we were about to leave. Nicole's grandmother was on the sofa with her husband, who was opening and closing his prayer book. They looked—despite their late place in life, despite the ancient surroundings outside of their windows—like young lovers. They were young lovers. She smiled at me, somehow knowingly, then signaled for me to come over. I went to her. She gestured for me to bring my ear to her lips. (Her lips were pursed and pale. Her blouse had silver buttons. The vase was red with purple stripes.) She gave a subtle nod toward her husband, then whispered: "He wants to know who you are."

Ruins, Mounting toward Jerusalem

Jonathan Boyarin

Where national memories are concerned, griefs are of more value than triumphs, for they impose duties, and require a common effort.

Ernest Renan (1990: 19)

Certainty may be a need for a man, but in itself, it is only a vacant reply to a penultimate question, with the ultimate left in suspense . . . vacant like a lot on which no building will ever rise because it would immediately tumble to ruins.

Edmond Jabès (1989: 17; ellipsis in original)

My primary concern here is with the heritage of Palestinian dispossession—a history that constitutes an unmasterable past (see Maier 1988), for Israeli Jews and for all Jews, insofar as they identify with the State of Israel. This past that is not yet mastered is not over. It is still happening. It is meant therefore that my text be less than masterful. I will not conceal the fact that my "activity is one of arranging" (Benjamin 1977: 179). Any such presentation is nothing more or less than a fragment of a continuing discussion.

I begin then not with the destruction of the Second Temple in Jerusalem, not with the book of Lamentations, which mourns that destruction, but with a striking passage of metadiscourse contained in Eichah Rabbah, the rabbinic midrashic commentary on Lamentations, composed in Palestine roughly between the fifth and seventh centuries C.E. The midrash informs us as follows:

> Rabbi used to expound the verse "The Lord laid waste without pity" in twenty-four ways. R[eb] Yohanan could expound it in sixty. Could it be that R. Yohanan was greater than Rabbi! Rather, because Rabbi was closer in time to the Destruction of the Temple he would remember as he expounded and stop to weep and console himself; he would begin again only to weep, console himself, and halt. R. Yohanan, because he was not close in time to the Destruction of the Temple, was able to continue to expound without pause. (Solomon Buber edition, 1899, p. 100, translated by Mintz 1984: 50)

We, of course, are much further in time from that destruction than even Reb Yohanan was. We can compensate for that somewhat and move immediately very close to the destruction in space. Not, surely, onto the Temple Mount itself, as some contemporary Jewish zealots would like, since that is now a Muslim holy site. We can in any case approach that venerated outer wall somewhat

inaccurately referred to as the Western Wall of the Temple. Let us imagine ourselves there. We have made *aliya!* We have, in the words of the biblical phrase
that is the source of the current Israeli Hebrew term for immigration to Israel,
"gone up" to Jerusalem, to the pinnacle of Jewish pilgrimage, to Judaism's highest
ruin.

That this relic is visitable at all by Jews or by visitors to Israel is itself, of course,
a mark of Israel victorious in the 1967 war. I first visited the Wall as a child,
coming to Israel for the first time, only a few days after the end of that war. I
remember hardly anything except a large, dusty, raw plaza. Indeed, as I try to
recall that early memory, it is twice overlaid: first, by the image of the stone-
paved courtyard, the paved entranceway and the security checks that stand in
front of the Wall today; second, by the phantoms of the Arab houses that, I have
since been told, were destroyed to make space for that very plaza.

During the months I spent in Jerusalem in 1991, I had the nagging sense
that I should have visited the Wall more, knowing that it, and the Dome of the
Rock that lies behind and above it, are the very epicenters of the contest between Jews and Arabs for memory and territory. Yet it confused and repelled
me in a way that I will not detail further now—except to say that I feel there
none of the "concentrated holiness" that attracts so many other Jews to the spot.
I visited the Wall only twice during that year, in fact: once for a generally failed
attempt by Israeli peace activists to organize a ritual commemoration of the massacre of Palestinian worshipers on the Temple Mount on October 8, 1990; the
second time for my nephew's swearing-in as a member of the elite paratroopers' unit of the Israeli Defense Forces, held at the Wall partly because it was
the paratroopers who captured the area around the Wall in 1967.[1]

I could find more to say about the wall here. But if—as I began just now—
we ignore the journey from Ben-Gurion Airport and begin by facing the West-

---

1. Don Handelman has provided us with an exhaustive ethnographic description of
a similar ceremony, emphasizing that this monument serves as an effective prop for in-
culcating a sense of unity among Israeli citizens: "Throughout the [remembrance] ceremony [at the Wall] there is the decisive symbolic equation between 'oneness' and unity.
Therefore there is little or no recognition of horizontal variation within categories of
persons or symbols. . . . The version of moral and social order that is presented through
this ceremony is marked by a sparseness and singularity of roles and symbols, by a ho-
mogeneity of membership, by a single-mindedness of intention, and by a oneness of being—
of everything in its place, in a continuous hierarchy of heritage and legacy. An extremely
holistic unity, in which each component imparts its sense of purpose to the one beneath,
with little strain, competition, or conflict" (Handelman 1991: 210–11). The Wall did not
suddenly become a political focus with the victory in 1967 or even with its loss to Jewish
access in 1948. For the Wall as a site of political contention within the Jewish community
of Jerusalem in the nineteenth century, see Halper 1991: 104, 136; for its role in inter-
ethnic politics at the same period, see ibid: 35. For an indication of the potent symbolism of pilgrimage and restoration of the Temple in Israeli popular culture, listen to the
song "Hilloula" on the best-selling tape *Masala,* by the group bearing the name Ethnix.

ern Wall, we thereby reinforce the obfuscation of another set of ruins available to the perceptive viewer from the highway leading up from Tel Aviv to Jerusalem. Where the most famous Jewish ruins in Israel—the Western Wall and Masada— are monumental relics of ancient Jewish state power, these Palestinian ruins, which easily blend into the landscape, stand as witness to domesticity and to local communal life (see Shammas 1989). This difference between national-monumental ruins and communal-domestic ones is compounded by the fact that the former are ancient, the latter virtually contemporary by comparison. The contest between these two different landscapes of commemoration is especially dramatic where they constitute chronotopes in collision. Thus the Dome of the Rock, still physically intact and in use, can nevertheless be spoken of as a relic of the long period of Muslim Arab hegemony. It sits on top of the site, and therefore presumably above the very ruins, of the Second Temple—excavation of which many Jews would consider sacrilege.

As the midrash suggests, some of the sting of loss represented by ruins may be diminished over the years. Nevertheless, although physical erosion takes place, old ruins don't just fade away; there is no external force called "time" that heals all wounds or effaces every trace. On the contrary, the rhetoric of ruins is a perfect example of the way destruction and loss are created. This is evidenced not by a "reversibility" in the process of creation and destruction but rather by a multiplicity of frames and effects that confounds the linearity that is still our first, unreflective assumption. Thus ancient ruins are subject in different ways to participatory immersion. This was brought home to me at a site called Hirbat Madras, a partially excavated Jewish settlement dating from the period of the disastrous Bar-Kokhba revolt against the Romans. In preparation for the rebellion, a honeycomb of narrow tunnels was dug out, enabling the residents of the town to slip out at night and conduct guerrilla—or should I say "terrorist"—attacks against the occupiers. Venturesome tourists visiting the site today can crawl through a portion of these tunnels themselves, experiencing the constriction of siege if not the desperate desire to shake off the oppressor. Thus the ancient ruins of Hirbat Madras envelop or incorporate the intrepid visitor.

More commonly the remains of former inhabitants—whether ancient or recent—are themselves incorporated within new architectures.[2] They need not of course be ruins. Thus the village of 'Ein Karem, outside Jerusalem, is now a lush and expensive center for tourists and artists. So is the former Arab village of 'Ein Hod south of Haifa, distinctive because descendants of some of the former residents of the village now live just two hills over, in a new village with the same name that has yet to be recognized by the Israeli government. The wealthy Jerusalem neighborhood of Baka'a, before 1948 ethnically mixed but predominantly Arab, is now a desirable address for Jewish Jerusalemites from Western countries. Buildings of Deir Yassin near 'Ein Karem, the site of a famous mas-

2. For a discussion of the incorporation of Tenochtitlan into Mexico City, see Rabasa 1990.

sacre by Menahem Begin's forces in 1948, are now incorporated into a mental hospital. It is easy to imagine some Palestinian version of *One Flew over the Cuckoo's Nest* set in Deir Yassin.

Ancient ruins incorporating tourists who arrive by jet. Relics of medieval empire on top of ruins of an ancient commonwealth, the site of murderous struggles today. Abandoned, evacuated houses left intact, coming into the hands of new residents from far away. All these reminders work against the tendency to assume that if, as Walter Benjamin wrote early in his career, "in the ruin history has physically merged into the setting" (Benjamin 1977: 177–78, cited in Crapanzano 1991), then this merging must be a "natural" process. The process that Benjamin notes is not only confirmed but aesthetically and morally endorsed in an essay by Georg Simmel, who assumes a priori an absolute dichotomy between nature and spirit. When a building becomes a ruin,

> the balance between nature and spirit, which the building manifested, shifts in favor of nature. This shift becomes a cosmic tragedy which, so we feel, makes every ruin an object infused with our nostalgia; for now the decay appears as nature's revenge for the spirit's having violated it by making a form in its own image. . . . For this reason, a good many Roman ruins, however interesting they may be otherwise, lack the specific fascination of the ruin—to the extent, that is, to which one notices in them the destruction *by man*; for this contradicts the contrast between human work and the effect of *nature* on which rests the significance of the ruin as such. (Simmel 1959)

Simmel insists that violence contradicts the meaning of the ruin—whereas it is almost always either overt violence, the imperiousness of a politico-economic system, or a disastrous shift in the resource base that initiates the process of ruination. This tendency to naturalize the process of ruination can and often does serve the state, as I will discuss at the end. It is hard to resist rhetorically, and I will indulge it at first, only to break with it partially at the end of this text.

So if I focus further on the ruins of pre-1948 Palestinian life in Israel, it is partly to confront the legacy of violence that ruins safeguard. But I am wary lest such a move smack of a too-easy appropriation of the mantle of the Other or the authoritative voice *for* (not of) the oppressed. The shift to a discussion of Palestinian ruins carries its own rhetorical dangers of naturalization, as does my framing of this discussion within a Jewish hermeneutic, rather than an autonomous Palestinian, Muslim, or Arab tradition of commemoration. These thoughts take shape within the context of a larger study of the critical challenge posed to Jewish collective identity by the formation and persistence of Palestinian collective identity. Hence, despite brief references to Palestinian colleagues toward the end, my main strategy is to record my own growing critical awareness. My attention to Palestinian ruins is both an extension of my work on Jewish memory and an attempt to assure myself that my own ambivalence toward the Jewish state is not just a phantasmatic personal quirk.

Is the dialogic model of ethnographic fieldwork appropriate to an encounter with such ruins? Is a "dialogue" with ruins possible at all? Even my idea that the stone remains of prewar Palestinian life can be made to speak is a reference back to a Jewish source: a volume of photographs of synagogues and Jewish cemeteries in Poland published after World War II and titled in Yiddish *Shteyner dertseyln*—Stones re-tell (Gostynsky 1973). To the extent that we confront the Other only in relics, we are cast back even more on our own codes than in conversation with another living person. Which cannot gainsay the *desire* at least for autonomous communication reflected in a painful recognition of ruins.

We engage such theoretical aporiae best when we allow them to sharpen our work, to make us approach if not overcome the communicative barriers identified in theory and in personal encounters. Rather than "settle" the question of dialogue with ruins, it may be helpful to document a series of such encounters with ruins of pre-1948 Palestinian life that are visible from the modern Tel Aviv–Jerusalem Highway, thereby making explicit the notion of recursive difference implicit in my title. I hope thereby to suggest something about the way in which ruins either remain part of the background or alternatively come to the forefront of consciousness—a coming to consciousness that is always incomplete and to which the best response might be a straightforward acknowledgment of provisionality, against the comprehension and closure still expected of scholarly criticism.

The stretch I will be visiting and revisiting here begins at the place called in Arabic Bab-el-Wad and in Hebrew Sha'ar ha-Gay, both meaning "the gate to the valley." From this spot the new four-lane highway winds upward for perhaps fifteen miles before reaching the edge of Jerusalem, the first several miles through a narrow and steep pass. Again, of my first visit to Israel in 1967, all I remember is what was doubtless pointed out to me: the hulks of armored cars on the side of the highway, relics of the battle for access to Jerusalem during the 1948 war. In several trips during the past years, I have noticed that these wrecks are periodically painted with rust-free paint, precisely to prevent their merging back into the landscape.

On later visits, I began to discern the remains of agricultural terracing on the dry, steep slopes of the wadi. Toward these I experienced an inchoate, doubtless romanticized nostalgia—precisely the kind of response to ruins evoked by Simmel, but already mixed with a vague need to distinguish them from the landscape. Then, during my extended stay in 1991, as I took the bus back and forth between Tel Aviv and Jerusalem, these terraces began to come into sharper focus for me. On July 26 I wrote in my journal:

The more times I travel back and forth along the Jerusalem–Tel Aviv Highway, the more clearly I see the traces of the artificial . . . terracing on the hillsides—places where there are just the ruins of stone walls, places where the terraces are intact but the fields are not in use, a few places where the terraced fields are still in use. . . . In at least one place where the natural striation of the rock was relatively stable, it has humanly produced rock walls on top of it, so there the distinction that worried me the day I first came up, about which was natural and which was a trace of Palestinian settlement (which, in fact, reflected my worry about my own biases—I didn't want to sound like a jerk talking about abandoned Palestinian fields which were actually just "undeveloped" mountainsides), was dissolved. Presumably if there were places where the natural striation was adequate to provide terracing, then they just used that.

Here the problem is fairly straightforward: the built terraces had originally been inspired by, and served to extend and reinforce, limestone striations that themselves formed a kind of terracing. Until I understood that, I constantly worried whether I was looking at a geological formation and reading into it a history of settlement and expulsion that was not proper to it—or whether I was looking at the ruins of a humanly produced landscape and seeing it as ahistorical, as a pile of rock devoid of human agency. When I understood better the relation among the stone structure of the mountain, the effort that had gone into making its slopes tillable, and the deterioration resulting from the absence of those who had once kept the terraces in order, my guilty consciousness was relieved; but the horror itself was none the less.

Terraced hillsides are not the only remains of earlier settlement that can be seen from the Jerusalem–Tel Aviv Highway. Just outside of Jerusalem the hills fall away to the north, and I was always struck by the steep slopes descending both right next to the road and in front to the left, as if protecting the entrance to the new city. I wondered as well for years at the few houses hugging the slope hard by the highway, which are inhabited but obviously predate the Israeli state. It was not until I began my formal fieldwork in 1991—already looking out for traces in the landscape—that I realized these few houses were only the uppermost of a large number of gray, empty houses scattered along those two slopes. I couldn't understand why they were left there, empty, like a memorial to the vanished Palestinians at the entrance to the Jewish city. Why had they been neither destroyed nor renovated?

The place is called Lifta (Ignatius 1982; Khalidi, ed., 1992). At the time it had not yet been incorporated into Jerusalem, cut off as it is by two highways from the rest of the city. I finally visited there in the beginning of November, only several days before I was to return to New York City and my family. I was first amazed by how wealthy the village had evidently been. These were not the monochrome-gray hovels they appeared to be from the highway, but substantial homes, several with large upper rooms covered by high, vaulted ceilings, lower levels, and storage basements, all open to the mountainside. Most of them had once had the magnificent tile floors that characterize Arab homes in this region. Many of the floor tiles had been stolen. Those that were covered in dust revealed none of their brilliance. Only those floors that lay under shallow pools of water from recent rains shone proudly. One reason for the wealth of the village was evident even before descending toward the houses: a spring that runs constantly out of the mountainside, at the intersection of the two slopes along which Lifta was built. A small pool at the mouth of the spring appears to have been restored rather recently, and traces of the irrigation system that led from the spring to the pool remain.

My companion/guide—also an American Jew—and I scrambled all through the abandoned village, wondering at a deer that betrayed its presence by sneezing and at the evidently young almond trees that, as I learned later, propagate themselves once they've been planted at a certain spot. The interiors of several of the houses revealed that squatters had lived there recently: there were fireplaces at the center of former living rooms and storm candles in window frames. My companion told me stories about wild parties thrown at Lifta by Argentinean immigrant hippies, and later I learned that members of the so-called Jewish underground had hidden out there from the Israeli police. We sat for a while on a cast-iron balcony, thirty feet above ground, until we realized the danger of sudden collapse. We heard the sounds of a construction crew, evidently working on restoring one of the houses highest up, closest to the Jewish city.

Why has Lifta been left alone for so long? Perhaps not many Israelis or tourists have the same kind of troubled curiosity about such a place as does the anthropologist searching for the presence of memory in the landscape. And people elsewhere have little trouble conducting their everyday lives in and among the remains of much greater horrors.[3] We might speculate that some remains might be left precisely to indicate Palestinian guilt: as Alan Mintz suggests, "There is something in us that resists the spectacle of a destruction that is not in some sense a punishment" (1984: 18).

Such speculation is not in order, however. Answers to the mystery of Lifta are available, though I have only begun to collect them. The answers are mostly prosaic: Lifta and its lands turn out to be a scarce resource, the object of a competition that has yet to be fully resolved. Much of the village's land was sold to Jews before the State of Israel was established. Many of the houses in the village were destroyed in recent years to make room for the building of the highway to the massive Jewish suburb of Ramot. The elegant restaurant at the top of the hill—called May Neftoach after the Hebrew name for Lifta's spring—belongs to a friend of Ariel Sharon.[4] In short, it seems that Lifta as a whole remains outside Jerusalem because there is no single controlling plan as to how it should be incorporated into the victorious city.

One of the uses of this site is the rhetorical use to which I am putting it. However mundane the reasons for it, the simultaneous persistence and near-invisibility of a site like Lifta challenge us to refine the statement by Vincent Crapanzano

3. See James Young (1992b) on Polish residents of Oswiecim picnicking on the grounds of Auschwitz-Birkenau.
4. Jeff Halper, personal communication.

that the ruins that Benjamin and Simmel described as merging with nature have "been replaced by . . . the trace, [which] becomes at once an emblem of a past evacuated of history . . . and a signal of the artifice of any such account, any history" (1991: 431). A bit later in the same essay, Crapanzano admits that "the post of postcolonialism is not subject to the same play, not yet at least, as the post of postmodernism. . . . The past of postcolonialism . . . cannot be reduced to a trace" (434). 1 would argue that at a site like Lifta, the difference between a ruin (which need not be monumental in any case) and a trace is a highly unstable one. Apparently, for the vast majority of travelers on the highway entering Jerusalem, what they see when they look at Lifta is a trace, at best; and yet this certainly does not mean that the site has "really" been evacuated of history. Depending precisely on the optic of the observer—anamnestic, naturalizing, or, perhaps inevitably, a troubled and confused combination of the two—Lifta is a subtle and picturesque relic of traditional habitation, a conundrum for the symbolic ethnography of the state, or an agonizing reminder of the violent erasure of life in this place not long ago at all.

The last appearance in Benjamin's work of the figure of piling up of ruins is, of course, in *The Theses on the Philosophy of History*: the Angel of History is forever blown away from paradise, toward which he stares back "while the pile of debris before him grows skyward. This storm is what we call progress" (Benjamin 1969: 258). The earlier moral and aesthetic rescue of the Baroque, the rehabilitation of the fragment, and the renunciation of the ultimate goal have here become a mortally urgent critique of the ideology of progress. In the discussion of Baroque ruins, Benjamin was already free of the very evacuation of historical pain that seems to characterize Simmel's essay. Here Benjamin would seem to say more directly that ruins are in fact nothing if not markers of past violence in the present.

As thus as metacritics, we heap our interpretations on top of interpretations. The expositions mount, and the ruins themselves do not cease to pile up. Not always through destruction, but sometimes indeed through a "restoration" that distorts them beyond recognition of their original, lived-in outline. The Israeli journalist Danny Rubinstein records the following incident that took place in the village of Sataf near Jerusalem, restored by the Israelis as "a model of mountain agriculture." As a result of the Israeli conquest in 1967, refugees from Sataf are sometimes able to visit the homes they were completely barred from between 1948 and 1967:[5]

> One summer day in 1988, when the site was filled with Israeli visitors, shouts were suddenly heard from an elderly woman in traditional Palestinian village dress. She was ranting against the Israelis at the top of her lungs, in

5. Compare the accounts of visits to their old homes by ethnic Greeks from Turkey now living in Crete and by former Cretan Muslims now living in Turkey, in Herzfeld 1991.

the rural dialect of Arabic characteristic of the area. It turned out that the woman was a native of Sataf who now lived in a refugee camp near the West Bank city of Ramallah. One of her sons, who was living in Kuwait, had brought his family for a visit, and she took them all to her native village—a custom widespread among refugees. The woman's ire had been kindled by an error in the restoration. She discovered, to her outrage, that the wall rebuilt next to the well should not have reached as far as the mulberry tree. "It's a lie," the old woman shouted. She recalled that her little sister had once fallen there, so there couldn't have been a wall. (Rubinstein 1991: 12)

Whether through restoration or obliteration—and even where, as in the case of the martyred village of Oradour in France or the Israeli armored cars from the 1948 war, an attempt is made to preserve ruins in their pristine ruined state— the physical remains taken for the rock of memory often prove slippery. The double character of ruins—better, the double perspective with which we approach them—is captured in the prosaic title of an encyclopedia of destroyed Palestinian villages: *All That Remains* (Khalidi, ed., 1992). These stones, we hear at first, are the only things that persist; this is all that remains. And yet also the very possibility of an encyclopedia implies a plenitude: *all that* remains . . . in our memory. Both memorial books and physical ruins can constitute sites of memory. The existence of Palestinian ruins within an Israeli landscape bears witness to a collective struggle for control of space. Can that struggle be overcome in memory? Is there a possibility of commensuration within a shared ethos of memory as constituting particular yet nonexclusive humanity—not, that is, the monumental commemoration of triumph but a ruinous commemoration "under the sign of mourning" (Koshar 1991: 57; J. Boyarin 1992, chap. 7)?

The midrash with which I started can serve as a guide here. Doubtless the Palestinian memorial literature, too, is already huge. It is not, to my knowledge, grounded in the same ancient experiences of loss to which the Western Wall attests, nor in the depth of interpretive and expositive tradition begun with the book of Lamentations. Does this mean that we can measure Palestinian loss against Jewish loss and declare one greater, one lesser? The midrash asks in astonishment: "Could it be that R. Yohanan was greater than Rabbi!" No: he who was further in time from his loss could articulate, could expound it more; he who remembered the loss directly must weep, console himself, and halt. Certainly the later master was not more "progressive" than the earlier one! Here too, the wall of the Temple courtyard is not to be measured against the lost well in Lifta. Nor should the Palestinians' more recent "exposition"—their uncertain and tortured search for the very language in which to communicate their loss—be taken as a sign that those with the more recent loss are themselves "lesser," or their loss diminished. Rather this midrashic reminder should direct us back to a greater concern with the different situations of loss and construction of self in, through, and with ruins.

That's the first ending, and rather sentimental at that. I mentioned toward the beginning that the temptation to reproduce in my own account the allegorical relation between geography and memory is a strong one, and until now I've indulged it: the narrow passage through the dangerous valley of theory and ethnography has led us upward toward an idealized "New Jerusalem" of empathic mutual memory.

I want to question that indulgence now, by shifting briefly to a very different and equally compelling site of competing Jewish and Palestinian ruins. Yes, I'm piling up fragments, but don't worry: I won't do so ceaselessly, and this coda will be free of theoretical detours. The place we are moving to now is a hilltop in the northern Galilee, close to the Lebanese border. Until 1948, it was inhabited by Maronite Christian Arabs. They were forcefully evacuated from their homes during the 1948 war, and, although they remained within Israel and have struggled ceaselessly to be permitted to return to their homes, they never have been allowed to move back (Chacour and Hazard 1984; Chacour 1990). During the early 1950s, their homes were destroyed by the Israeli army, so that even though there was no massacre, the place is reminiscent of some unkempt Oradour.

The village is called Bir'im in Arabic. It is an ancient settlement—so old that it is mentioned in the Talmud—and it is also an archaeological site called Biram on Israeli maps. This slight change: Bir'im, Biram, is an unusually literal example of *differance*. The place with an *i* as its second vowel is the ruin of an Arab village. The place with an *a* is, at least for the Israeli government, the site of an ancient synagogue. It must be added that many Israeli Jews—both individuals and political parties—have disagreed with that government, arguing alongside the villagers that their right to return home must be honored.[6]

Unlike at Lifta, which most Israelis or tourists would only see from a distance—from the highway or at best from the restaurant at the top of the hill—the visitor to the excavated and partially restored ancient synagogue at Biram is surrounded by the ruins of Bir'im. The site has obviously been landscaped and designed so as to encourage visitors to walk straight to the synagogue site and then to return to their cars without examining too closely the destroyed Arab houses. Thus one sign at the parking lot informs us, in Hebrew and in English, of the significance of the place:

6. "It has been more than six months since the plenary session of the Knesset authorized, by majority vote, the proposal to recognize the right of the exiles from Ikrit and Biram to return to their villages from which they were 'distanced' for two weeks by order of the IDF in 1948. Two months ago a committee of ministers was appointed to discuss their demand. However, during the meeting of the ministerial committee this week, the *Shabak* (General Security Services) said 'no!' According to the *Shabak* the implementation of the return of the Ikrit/Biram exiles to their villages would set a precedent for demands by Palestinian citizens of Israel who since the 1948 war have yet to be authorized to return to their villages. This would also weaken Israel's opposition to the Palestinians' right of return" (Anonymous 1994).

Site of one of the many Jewish settlements in Upper Galilee during the period of the Second Temple. Remains of the beautiful third century (C.E.) synagogue reflect the high standard of religious and cultural life maintained by the Jews of the region, even after the destruction of the Temple. The work of restoration and landscaping was carried out by the Department for Landscaping Improvement and Development of Historical Sites of the prime minister's office.

The didactic point is not lost on anyone familiar with the politics of settlement and land control in the Galilee since the establishment of the State of Israel. The "Judaization" of the north has been a fairly constant priority. The excavated synagogue (which is indeed quite beautiful) is not only a tourist attraction but a mark of the Jewish claim to this area and of the persistence of Jewish habitation in Palestine after the end of the second Jewish commonwealth.

Another sign cautions:

National parks contain antiquities, natural sites, and hazardous terrain. Visitors are therefore advised to be careful during their stay on the grounds.

"Antiquities" presumably are things visitors should be careful not to harm by stepping on them. "Hazardous terrain" is a place visitors should avoid for their own safety. But why should anyone be cautioned about avoiding "natural sites"? The copula that joins "landscaping improvement" and "development of historical sites" in one bureaucratic slot gives us a clue here: these natural sites are freshly planted. The state is trying to grow ruins into the landscape. Please don't interfere by looking at them too closely.[7]

This visitor and his companions—one a Palestinian professor of anthropology at Bir Zeit University, the other a Palestinian-American graduate student doing fieldwork on the role of archaeology in Israeli national culture—ignored the warnings about hazardous terrain, examining closely the ruined houses, the still-intact church (used occasionally for weddings and the like), and the graveyard, where by court order the people of Bir'im are allowed to bury their dead. On the wall of perhaps the most impressive house in the village, a cross carved into the lintel had been destroyed by vandals; the date the house was built was partially legible: 19 . . . but the last two digits had been obliterated.

The professor from Bir Zeit—himself a native of the Galilee—further broke the spell of nature cast on the ruins by the landscaping department by engag-

7. In his account of the Palestinian exodus, the Israeli historian Benny Morris no doubt unwittingly colludes in this obfuscation of the ruins of Bir'im: "Within months, Bir'im's lands were distributed among Jewish settlements and, in the early 1950s, the village itself was levelled" (Morris 1987: 239). Unfortunately perhaps for Biram the historical site, the village itself was not—quite—leveled. For a more general account of "the politics of seeing" (see Buck-Morss 1989).

ing with the Druze gatekeeper in a detailed conversation, reminiscing about the fates and present whereabouts of various former residents of the area who were all mutual acquaintances of theirs. Doubtless there cannot be a dialogue *with* ruins: stones speak only in our metaphors. But it seems there can indeed be dialogue *around* ruins.

On the back wall of the church at Bir'im, there are graffiti in three languages: *"Biram ahuva"*—"Beloved Biram," in Hebrew; *"Hona bakun,"* "Here I will be," in Arabic; "Biram forever," in English; most poignantly ironic of all, and also in English: "Let my people return." It is interesting to note that not only do the residents— or more likely, their children—express their longing to go home in Hebrew and in English but that when they do so, they now call their home Biram.

Clearly the site of the Arab village of Bir'im/Biram is not only a ruin. It also functions as a memorial. But it remains a place of contention, so clearly it does not serve the same healing and unifying function as the usual state memorial. It is tempting to think of the destroyed village with its graffiti as a *Gegendenkmal,* an "antimonument," like the monument against fascism in Harburg, Germany, which is lowered periodically into the ground as its base is covered with graffiti. Norbert Radermacher, the designer of the antimonument, "suggests that the site alone cannot remember, that it is the projection of memory by visitors into a space that makes it a memorial" (Young 1992a). Different memories are projected by different visitors to this site in the Galilee, with and against the connivance of the state. Perhaps the destroyed modern village surrounding the restored ancient synagogue serves as a sort of antimonument for at least some Israeli visitors and as a memorial for the villagers of Bir'im who have become visitors to Biram. But in any case the ruins of the village are in no way an allegory or a prototype for all the ruined Palestinian villages. This is evidenced by the particular circumstances in which the people of the village still find themselves—refugees of a sort and Israeli citizens at the same time.

In the larger sense, unlike the double destruction of the Temple in Jerusalem that has become the prototype for all Jewish experiences of catastrophe, there is no prototypical ruined Palestinian village. They were lost, to borrow a phrase, "one by one by one." Any attempt to understand the persistence of Palestinian nationalism will have to face that loss and the ruins that testify to it; any genuine reconciliation between Israeli Jews and Palestinian Arabs will have to make room for the different modalities of the losses and commemorations that are at the heart of their respective national identities. At Biram, the attempt to impose a sense of the place as uniquely and properly Jewish is effectively undercut by the remains of an Arab village. Through their periodic returns to their homes, the villagers and their descendants ensure that this is more than a passive effect. They *make* their stones tell a story against the story told by the Department for Landscaping Improvement and Development of Historical Sites of the prime minister's office. In parody of the little booth with the lonely Druze gatekeeper inside guarding the way from the parking lot to the synagogue site, one house near the church has a single word, painted in English over its empty doorway: "Information."

Works Cited

Anonymous, "Palestinians Inside Israel: The *Shabak* vs Ikrit and Baram," *The Other Front* 258 (February 2, 1994): 4

Walter Benjamin, *Illuminations* (New York: Schocken, 1969)

_____ *The Origins of German Tragic Drama* (London: New Left, 1977)

Jonathan Boyarin, *Storm from Paradise: The Politics of Jewish Memory* (Minneapolis: University of Minnesota Press, 1992)

Susan Buck-Morss, *The Dialectics of Seeing: Walter Benjamin and the Arcades Project* (Cambridge, MA: MIT Press, 1989)

Elias Chacour, *We Belong to the Land* (San Francisco: HarperSanFrancisco, 1990)

Elias Chacour and David Hazard, *Blood Brothers* (Grand Rapids: Chosen Books, 1984)

Vincent Crapanzano, "The Postmodern Crisis: Discourse, Memory, Parody," *Cultural Anthropology* 6/4, 1991: 431–46

_____, "Discussion of Boyarin," *Found Object* 3, 1994: 49–54

Zalman Gostynsky, *Shteyner dertseyln*, Paris, 1973

Jeff Halper, *Between Redemption and Revival: The Jewish Yishuv of Jerusalem in the Nineteenth Century* (Boulder: Westview, 1991)

Don Handelman, *Models and Mirrors: Toward an Anthropology of Public Events* (New York: Cambridge University Press, 1991)

Michael Herzfeld, *A Place in History: Social and Monumental Time in a Cretan Town* (Princeton, NJ: Princeton University Press, 1991)

David Ignatius, "Palestinians Carve Out Lives in Distant Lands but Hunger for 'Home'," *The Wall Street Journal*, September 13, 1982

Edmond Jabès, *The Book of Shares*, trans. Rosmarie Waldrop (Chicago: University of Chicago Press, 1989)

Walid Khalidi, ed., *All That Remains: The Palestinian Villages Occupied and Depopulated by Israel in 1948* (Washington, DC: Institute for Palestine Studies, 1992)

Rudy Koshar, "Altar, State and City: Historic Preservation and Urban Meaning in Nazi Germany," *History and Memory* 3/1, 1991: 30–59

Charles S. Maier, *The Unmasterable Past: History, Holocaust, and German National Identity* (Cambridge, MA: Harvard University Press, 1988)

Alan Mintz, *Hurban: Responses to Catastrophe in Hebrew Literature* (New York: Columbia University Press, 1984)

Benny Morris, *The Birth of the Palestinian Refugee Problem, 1947–1949* (New York: Cambridge University Press, 1987)

José Rabasa, "Dialogue as Conquest: Mapping Spaces for Counter-discourse," *The Nature and Context of Minority Discourse*, ed. Abdul R. JanMohamed and David Lloyd (New York: Oxford University Press, 1990): 187–215

Ernest Renan, "What Is a Nation?" *Nation and Narration*, ed. Homi Bhabha (New York: Routledge, 1990): 8–22

Danny Rubinstein, *The People of Nowhere: The Palestinian Vision of Home* (New York: Times Books, 1991)

Anton Shammas, "The Two-Language Solution," paper read at Modern Languages Association convention, Washington, DC, 1989

Georg Simmel, "The Ruin," *Georg Simmel 1858–1919: A Collection of Essays, with Translations and a Bibliography*, ed. Kurt H. Wolff (Columbus: Ohio State University Press, 1959): 259–266

James Young, "The Counter-monument: Memory against Itself in Germany Today," *Critical Inquiry* 18/2, 1992: 267–296.

—————, *The Texture of Memory* (New Haven: Yale University Press, 1992)

Prayer

Grace Schulman

For Agha Shahid Ali

Yom Kippur: wearing a bride's dress bought in Jerusalem,
I peer through swamp reeds, my thought in Jerusalem.

Velvet on grass. Odd, but I learned young to keep this day
just as I can, if not as I ought, in Jerusalem.

Like sleep or love, prayer may surprise the woman
who laughs by a stream, or the child distraught in Jerusalem.

My Arab dress has blue-green-yellow threads
the shades of mosaics hand-wrought in Jerusalem

that both peoples prize, like the blue-yellow Dome of the Rock,
like strung beads-and-cloves, said to ward off the drought in Jerusalem.

Both savor things that grow wild—coreopsis in April,
the rose that buds late, like an afterthought, in Jerusalem.

While car bombs flared, an Arab poet translated
Hebrew verses whose flame caught in Jerusalem.

And you, Shahid, sail Judah Halevi's sea as I,
on Ghalib's, course like an Argonaut in Jerusalem.

Stone lions pace the sultan's gate while almonds bloom
into images, Hebrew and Arabic, wrought in Jerusalem.

No words, no metaphors, for knives that gore flesh
on streets where the people have fought in Jerusalem.

As this spider weaves a web in silence,
may Hebrew and Arabic be woven taut in Jerusalem.

Here at the bay, I see my face in the shallows
and plumb for the true self our Abraham sought in Jerusalem.

Open the gates to rainbow-colored words
of outlanders, their sounds untaught in Jerusalem.

My name is Grace, Chana in Hebrew—and in Arabic.
May its meaning, "God's love," at last be taught in Jerusalem.

Section Seven

Resistance and Activism

On the Refusniks

Robert Jay Lifton

I had this exchange with Chris Hedges while working feverishly on a book dealing with Islamist terrorism and the American response, which I call "Superpower Syndrome." All along I had been struck by the sad parallels between Israel and the United States. Both countries have justified brutal behavior as part of a "war on terrorism." Both end up responding to Islamist apocalyptic violence with a version of their own. Yet both also possess noble democratic traditions which can be called upon for more humane and compassionate approaches to the world. The members of Courage to Refuse, as discussed in the interview, have done just that.

A Profile of Dr. Robert Jay Lifton

Chris Hedges

Dr. Robert Jay Lifton has spent his life studying people in extreme situations. He has written about Japanese survivors in Hiroshima, Vietnam veterans, Nazi doctors and members of terrorist cults. But he has also spent a lifetime as an activist, involved in the Vietnam antiwar movement and the antinuclear movement. The two activities, scholarship and activism, are for him intertwined. All of his work is infused with the struggle to live the moral life.

He and a number of colleagues have organized support in the United States for some 500 Israeli soldiers who have banded together in an organization called Courage to Refuse. These soldiers will not serve in the Israeli-occupied territories, saying they will no longer "dominate, expel, starve and humiliate an entire people."

The group Dr. Lifton helped found, Friends of Courage to Refuse, is made up mostly of American Jews. It has pitted itself against the powerful array of pro-Israeli groups in the United States, most of which have what Dr. Lifton calls "an uncritical endorsement of Israel's aggressive policies against the Palestinians." He and some 230 supporters across the country have raised $5,000 to take out an ad this week in the Israeli newspaper *Ha'aretz* backing the Israeli resisters. And in this move, as in other grass-roots campaigns of the past, Dr. Lifton sees the kernel of a potent opposition "which could have considerable influence beyond its numbers."

"When I worked with Vietnam veterans, I found them to have been placed in atrocity-producing situations," he said. "Soldiers found themselves in environments where the structure of the conflict led them to commit atrocities.

"They were not bad people, not worse than you or me, but they were terrified. They were frustrated at not being able to find and destroy the enemy, at having their own men killed. They developed an impulse to strike back at old men, children, women, laborers in a rice field, under the illusion that everyone, even those who were not armed, was the enemy. This can happen when you combat a hostile population, when you fight an elusive opponent. It is what I see happening in the occupied territories."

As a psychiatrist, he views such conflicts as disastrous, not only for individuals but societies. Ordinary men, he said, "can all too readily be socialized to atrocity."

"These killing projects are never described as such," he said. "They are put in terms of the necessity of improving the world, of political and spiritual renewal. You cannot kill large numbers of people without a claim to virtue. Our own campaign to rid the world of terror is expressed this way, as if once we destroy all terrorists we destroy evil."

Dr. Lifton, 76, is a distinguished professor emeritus from the City University of New York. He is now a visiting professor at Harvard Medical School. He spoke Sunday afternoon at the Harvard Club in Manhattan, his shock of unruly white hair combed down over his ears.

He is married to the psychologist and writer Betty Jean Lifton and is the father of two grown children. He grew up in Brooklyn. He was deeply influenced by his father, a politically progressive businessman who was a fervent atheist. As a teenager, Dr. Lifton was drawn to books about contemporary history, and most of his work, he said, has been concerned with "history and the historical process."

He said that the fundamentalist Israelis and Palestinians, and most avid supporters of "the war on terror" in the United States, combine to further "the growing impulse toward apocalyptic violence."

"Apocalyptic violence is aimed at large-scale destruction to renew the world spiritually," he said. "You have this on the Israeli side with these religious groups that were fundamental in shaping the mind of the assassin of Prime Minister Yitzhak Rabin. You have this among the Islamist fundamentalist groups like Hamas. But you also have this here in the United States among those who use the threat of terror to justify world domination militarily."

Dr. Lifton said such groups "act in concert," and "even though they denounce each other they contribute to the growth and power of their opponents."

"The mutual violence propels these apocalyptic groups to the center of their societies," he said, "and those that urge peaceful methods to solve conflicts are relegated to the fringes. The interaction of violent groups comes to dominate relations between opposing societies. Voices of restraint are increasingly excluded."

It is this drive for wholesale slaughter, made possible by the tools of modern industrial warfare, that he ultimately says he is fighting to thwart. And it is why he gives importance to Courage to Refuse. These groups, he says, are a bulwark that can stop a slide into self-annihilation.

"Our own bellicosity is part of our effort to compensate for the weakness and vulnerability that came out of our defeat in Vietnam," he said. "We have built an alliance with Israeli leaders who share our vision. This has become a unifying principle.

"A war on terror, without limits on time or place, brings us one step closer to the use of apocalyptic violence. Our technology, our nuclear weapons, has made all this a lot easier. These weapons are apocalyptic in essence and bring this vision to the people who possess them. Islamist terrorists hunger for these weapons, maybe all the more so because we continue to embrace them."

On Courage, Truth, and Resistance

Susan Sontag

The keynote address given at the Rothko Chapel in Houston on March 30, 2003, on the occasion of the presentation of the Oscar Romero Award to Ishai Menuchin, chairman of Yesh Gvul ("There is a Limit"), the Israeli soldiers' movement for selective refusal to serve in the occupied territories.

Allow me to invoke not one but two, only two, who were heroes—among millions of heroes. Who were victims—among tens of millions of victims.

The first: Oscar Arnulfo Romero, Archbishop of San Salvador, murdered in his vestments, while saying mass in the cathedral on March 24, 1980—twenty-three years ago—because he had become "a vocal advocate of a just peace, and had openly opposed the forces of violence and oppression." (I am quoting from the description of the Oscar Romero Award, being given today to Ishai Menuchin.)

The second: Rachel Corrie, a twenty-three-year-old college student from Olympia, Washington, murdered in the bright neon-orange jacket with Day-Glo striping that "human shields" wear to make themselves quite visible, and possibly safer, while trying to stop one of the almost daily house demolitions by Israeli forces in Rafah, a town in the southern Gaza Strip (where Gaza abuts the Egyptian border), on March 16, 2003. Standing in front of a Palestinian physician's house that had been targeted for demolition, Corrie, one of eight young American and British human-shield volunteers in Rafah, had been waving and shouting at the driver of an oncoming armored D-9 bulldozer through her megaphone, then dropped to her knees in the path of the supersized bulldozer . . . which did not slow down.

Two emblematic figures of sacrifice, killed by the forces of violence and oppression to which they were offering nonviolent, principled, dangerous opposition.

Let's start with risk. The risk of being punished. The risk of being isolated. The risk of being injured or killed. The risk of being scorned. We are all conscripts in one sense or another. For all of us, it is hard to break ranks; to incur the disapproval, the censure, the violence of an offended majority with a different idea of loyalty. We shelter under banner words like justice, peace and reconciliation that enroll us in new, if much smaller and relatively powerless, communities of the like-minded. That mobilize us for the demonstration, the protest and the public performance of acts of civil disobedience—not for the parade ground and the battlefield.

To fall out of step with one's tribe; to step beyond one's tribe into a world that is larger mentally but smaller numerically—if alienation or dissidence is not your habitual or gratifying posture, this is a complex, difficult process. It is hard to defy the wisdom of the tribe, the wisdom that values the lives of members of the tribe above all others. It will always be unpopular—it will always be deemed unpatriotic—to say that the lives of the members of the other tribe are as valuable as one's own. It is easier to give one's allegiance to those we know, to those we see, to those with whom we are embedded, to those with whom we share—as we may—a community of fear.

Let's not underestimate the force of what we oppose. Let's not underestimate the retaliation that may be visited on those who dare to dissent from the brutalities and repressions thought justified by the fears of the majority. We are flesh. We can be punctured by a bayonet, torn apart by a suicide bomber. We can be crushed by a bulldozer, gunned down in a cathedral. Fear binds people together. And fear disperses them. Courage inspires communities: the courage of an example—for courage is as contagious as fear. But courage, certain kinds of courage, can also isolate the brave.

The perennial destiny of principles: While everyone professes to have them, they are likely to be sacrificed when they become inconveniencing. Generally a moral principle is something that puts one at variance with accepted practice. And that variance has consequences, sometimes unpleasant consequences, as the community takes its revenge on those who challenge its contradictions—who want a society actually to uphold the principles it professes to defend.

The standard that a society should actually embody its own professed principles is a utopian one, in the sense that moral principles contradict the way things really are—and always will be. How things really are—and always will be—is neither all evil nor all good but deficient, inconsistent, inferior. Principles invite us to do something about the morass of contradictions in which we function morally. Principles invite us to clean up our act, to become intolerant of moral laxity and compromise and cowardice and the turning away from what is upsetting: that secret gnawing of the heart that tells us that what we are doing is not right, and so counsels us that we'd be better off just not thinking about it.

The cry of the anti-principled: "I'm doing the best I can." The best given the circumstances, of course.

Let's say, the principle is: It's wrong to oppress and humiliate a whole people. To deprive them systematically of lodging and proper nutrition; to destroy their habitations, means of livelihood, access to education and medical care, and ability to consort with one another. That these practices are wrong, whatever the provocation. And there is provocation. That, too, should not be denied.

At the center of our moral life and our moral imagination are the great models of resistance: the great stories of those who have said no. No, I will not serve. What models, what stories? A Mormon may resist the outlawing of polygamy. An antiabortion militant may resist the law that has made abortion legal. They, too, will invoke the claims of religion (or faith) and morality against the edicts of civil society. Appeal to the existence of a higher law that authorizes us to defy the laws of the state can be used to justify criminal transgression as well as the noblest struggle for justice.

Courage has no moral value in itself, for courage is not, in itself, a moral virtue. Vicious scoundrels, murderers, terrorists may be brave. To describe courage as a virtue, we need an adjective: We speak of "moral courage"—because there is such a thing as amoral courage, too. And resistance has no value in itself. It is the content of the resistance that determines its merit, its moral necessity. Let's say: resistance to a criminal war. Let's say: resistance to the occupation and annexation of another people's land.

Again: There is nothing inherently superior about resistance. All our claims for the righteousness of resistance rest on the rightness of the claim that the resisters are acting in the name of justice. And the justice of the cause does not depend on, and is not enhanced by, the virtue of those who make the assertion. It depends first and last on the truth of a description of a state of affairs that is, truly, unjust and unnecessary.

Here is what I believe to be a truthful description of a state of affairs that has taken me many years of uncertainty, ignorance and anguish to acknowledge.

A wounded and fearful country, Israel, is going through the greatest crisis of its turbulent history, brought about by the policy of steadily increasing and reinforcing settlements on the territories won after its victory in the Arab-Israeli war of 1967. The decision of successive Israeli governments to retain control over the West Bank and Gaza, thereby denying their Palestinian neighbors a state of their own, is a catastrophe—moral, human and political—for both peoples. The Palestinians need a sovereign state. Israel needs a sovereign Palestinian state. Those of us abroad who wish for Israel to survive cannot, should not, wish it to survive no matter what, no matter how. We owe a particular debt of gratitude to courageous Israeli Jewish witnesses, journalists, architects, poets, novelists, professors—among others—who have described and documented and protested and militated against the sufferings of the Palestinians living under the increasingly cruel terms of Israeli military subjugation and settler annexation.

Our greatest admiration must go to the brave Israeli soldiers, represented here by Ishai Menuchin, who refuse to serve beyond the 1967 borders. These soldiers know that all settlements are bound to be evacuated in the end. These soldiers, who are Jews, take seriously the principle put forward at the Nuremberg trials in 1945–46: namely, that a soldier is not obliged to obey unjust orders, orders that contravene the laws of war—indeed, one has an obligation to disobey them.

The Israeli soldiers who are resisting service in the occupied territories are not refusing a particular order. They are refusing to enter the space where illegitimate orders are bound to be given—that is, where it is more than probable that they will be ordered to perform actions that continue the oppression and humiliation of Palestinian civilians. Houses are demolished, groves are uprooted, the stalls of a village market are bulldozed, a cultural center is looted; and now, nearly every day, civilians of all ages are fired on and killed. There can be no disputing the mounting cruelty of the Israeli occupation of the 22 percent of the former territory of British Palestine on which a Palestinian state will be erected. These soldiers believe, as I do, that there should be an unconditional withdrawal from the occupied territories. They have declared collectively that they will not continue to fight beyond the 1967 borders "in order to dominate, expel, starve and humiliate an entire people."

What the refuseniks have done—there are now more than 1,000 of them, more than 250 of whom have gone to prison—does not contribute to telling us how the Israelis and Palestinians can make peace, beyond the irrevocable demand that the settlements be disbanded. The actions of this heroic minority cannot contribute to the much-needed reform and democratization of the Palestinian Authority. Their stand will not lessen the grip of religious bigotry and racism in Israeli society or reduce the dissemination of virulent anti-Semitic propaganda in the aggrieved Arab world. It will not stop the suicide bombers.

It simply declares: enough. Or: there is a limit. *Yesh gvul.* It provides a model of resistance. Of disobedience. For which there will always be penalties.

None of us have yet to endure anything like what these brave conscripts are enduring, many of whom have gone to jail. To speak for peace at this moment in this country is merely to be jeered (as in the recent Academy Awards ceremony), harassed, blacklisted (the banning by one powerful chain of radio stations of the Dixie Chicks); in short, to be reviled as unpatriotic.

Our "United We Stand" or "Winner Takes All" ethos: The United States is a country that has made patriotism equivalent to consensus. Tocqueville, still the greatest observer of the United States, remarked on an unprecedented degree of conformity in the then-new country, and 168 more years have only confirmed his observation.

Sometimes, given the new, radical turn in American foreign policy, it seems as if it was inevitable that the national consensus on the greatness of America, which may be activated to an extraordinary pitch of triumphalist national self-regard, was bound eventually to find expression in wars like the present one, which are assented to by a majority of the population, who have been persuaded that America has the right—even the duty—to dominate the world.

The usual way of heralding people who act on principle is to say that they are the vanguard of an eventually triumphant revolt against injustice. But what if they're not? What if the evil is really unstoppable? At least in the short run. And that short run may be—is going to be—very long indeed.

My admiration for the soldiers who are resisting service in the occupied territories is as fierce as my belief that it will be a long time before their view prevails. But what haunts me at this moment—for obvious reasons—is acting on principle when it isn't going to alter the obvious distribution of force, the rank injustice and murderousness of a government policy that claims to be acting in the name not of peace but of security.

The force of arms has its own logic. If you commit an aggression and others resist, it is easy to convince the home front that the fighting must continue.

Once the troops are there, they must be supported. It becomes irrelevant to question why the troops are there in the first place.

The soldiers are there because "we" are being attacked or menaced. Never mind that we may have attacked them first. They are now attacking back, causing casualties. Behaving in ways that defy the "proper" conduct of war. Behaving like "savages," as people in our part of the world like to call people in that part of the world. And their "savage" or "unlawful" actions give new justification to new aggressions. And new impetus to repress or censor or persecute citizens who oppose the aggression the government has undertaken.

Let's not underestimate the force of what we are opposing. The world is, for almost everyone, that over which we have virtually no control. Common sense and the sense of self-protectiveness tell us to accommodate to what we cannot change.

It's not hard to see how some of us might be persuaded of the justice, the necessity of a war. Especially of a war that is formulated as a small, limited military action that will actually contribute to peace or improve security; of an aggression that announces itself as a campaign of disarmament—admittedly, disarmament of the enemy; and, regrettably, requiring the application of overpowering force. An invasion that calls itself, officially, a liberation.

Every violence in war has been justified as a retaliation. We are threatened. We are defending ourselves. The others, they want to kill us. We must stop them. And from there: We must stop them before they have a chance to carry out their plans. And since those who would attack us are sheltering behind noncombatants, no aspect of civil life can be immune to our depredations.

Never mind the disparity of forces, of wealth, of firepower—or simply of population. How many Americans know that the population of Iraq is 24 million, half of whom are children? (The population of the United States, as you will remember, is 290 million.) Not to support those who are coming under fire from the enemy seems like treason.

It may be that, in some cases, the threat is real. In such circumstances, the bearer of the moral principle seems like someone running alongside a moving train, yelling "Stop! Stop!" Can the train be stopped? No, it can't. At least, not now. Will other people on the train be moved to jump off and join those on the ground? Maybe some will, but most won't. (At least, not until they have a whole new panoply of fears.)

The dramaturgy of "acting on principle" tells us that we don't have to think about whether acting on principle is expedient, or whether we can count on the eventual success of the actions we have undertaken. Acting on principle is, we're told, a good in itself. But it is still a political act, in the sense that you're not doing it for yourself. You don't do it just to be in the right, or to appease your own conscience; much less because you are confident your action will achieve its aim. You resist as an act of solidarity. With communities of the principled and the disobedient: here, elsewhere. In the present. In the future.

Thoreau's going to prison in 1846 for refusing to pay the poll tax in protest against the American war on Mexico hardly stopped the war. But the resonance of that most unpunishing and briefest spell of imprisonment (famously, a single night in jail) has not ceased to inspire principled resistance to injustice through the second half of the twentieth century and into our new era. The movement in the late 1980s to shut down the Nevada Test Site, a key location for the nuclear arms race, failed in its goal; the operations of the test site were unaffected by the protests. But it led directly to the formation of a movement of protesters in faraway Alma Ata, who eventually succeeded in shutting down the main Soviet test site in Kazakhstan, citing the Nevada antinuclear activists as their inspiration and expressing solidarity with the Native Americans on whose land the Nevada Test Site had been located.

The likelihood that your acts of resistance cannot stop the injustice does not exempt you from acting in what you sincerely and reflectively hold to be the best interests of your community.

Thus: It is not in the best interests of Israel to be an oppressor. Thus: It is not in the best interests of the United States to be a hyperpower, capable of imposing its will on any country in the world, as it chooses.

What is in the true interests of a modern community is justice.

It cannot be right to systematically oppress and confine a neighboring people. It is surely false to think that murder, expulsion, annexations, the building of walls—all that has contributed to reducing a whole people to dependence, penury and despair—will bring security and peace to the oppressors. It cannot be right that a president of the United States seems to believe that he has a mandate to be president of the planet—and announces that those who are not with America are with "the terrorists."

Those brave Israeli Jews who, in fervent and active opposition to the policies of the present government of their country, have spoken up on behalf of the plight and the rights of Palestinians are defending the true interests of Israel. Those of us who are opposed to the plans of the present government of the United States for global hegemony are patriots speaking for the best interests of the United States.

Beyond these struggles, which are worthy of our passionate adherence, it is important to remember that in programs of political resistance the relation of cause and effect is convoluted, and often indirect. All struggle, all resistance is—must be—concrete. And all struggle has a global resonance.

If not here, then there. If not now, then soon. Elsewhere as well as here.

To Archbishop Oscar Arnulfo Romero. To Rachel Corrie. And to Ishai Menuchin and his comrades.

Doing Activism, Working for Peace:
A Roundtable Discussion

Naomi Braine, Steven Feuerstein,
Marcia Freedman, Irena Klepfisz, Joel Kovel,
Rabbi Michael Lerner, Rabbi Ellen Lippmann,
Mitchell Plitnick

The following roundtable discussion among Jewish activists took place on March 9, 2003.

ALISA SOLOMON: Please introduce yourself and say something about the work you're doing on the Israeli-Palestinian conflict as an activist and briefly how you came to do this work.

JOEL KOVEL: I teach at Bard College in upstate New York. My principal work in this is contributing prose, I guess. I'm not immediately involved with any activist group on this subject, though I've written some and I've been very active over the years in many groups, including the Green Party and journals and general intellectual life on the left.

MITCHELL PLITNICK: I'm director of administration and communication for A Jewish Voice for Peace in the Bay Area. I've been involved with this activism for about four years now. Lately we've been focusing on educational efforts, trying to gather in particular a lot of Jews around the country who feel very disaffected. We've had a lot of success with offering people a Jewish group that they could go to and work with on this issue and also been providing community for Jews who have felt alienated from what they have perceived as the Jewish community.

We've made a lot of educational efforts. We're doing a lot of media activism and have also been involved in the recent antiwar effort.

MARCIA FREEDMAN: I have been involved with this issue since the early 1970s—Oh, God help me! I'm both Israeli and American. I'm a former member of the Israeli Knesset. I've been very active with the Women's Peace Movement in Israel. And just this past year here in the States, I'm president of Brit Tzedek v'Shalom, the Jewish Alliance for Justice and Peace. And what we're trying to do is to establish a mass membership, chapter-based organization of mainstream American Jews who are very uncomfortable with the government's policies but are pro-Israel.

MICHAEL LERNER: I'm editor of *Tikkun* magazine and rabbi of Beyt Tikkun Synagogue in San Francisco and co-chair of the Tikkun Community, which is a national organization with chapters around the country of both Jews and non-Jews who are seeking a middle path—a progressive middle path, both pro-Israel and pro-Palestinian.

I've been involved in these issues since, well, it's hard to say. In 1967, I was president of Berkeley's Students for Democratic Society and the '67 war started, and I suddenly found many of my Jewish colleagues denouncing Israel and Zionism. From that point, I began to realize that there was a need for a progressive voice that also understood the legitimacy of the national liberation struggles of Jewish people.

STEVEN FEUERSTEIN: I'm sort of like the little baby in terms of my level of involvement in this work. I've been active on Israel/Palestine peace issues since about September 29 of 2000 when the latest round of conflict exploded. And after a decade or fifteen years of various progressive work like Central American solidarity and antiapartheid work, I finally found myself confronted with the ongoing devastation and the failure of the peace process and felt personally, individually compelled to speak out, just to say loudly that what Israel was doing was not being done in my name as a Jew.

And that developed into an organization called Not In My Name here in Chicago. We worked on developing the national Jewish Unity for a Just Peace Network. I've been involved in a number of initiatives lately. I'm spending the majority of my time on this issue and in my life on the Refusenik Solidarity Network, of which I'm currently the coordinator. It's an effort to create a clearinghouse, an international and somewhat institutionalized organizational framework through which we can provide ongoing support to the Refusenik Movement in Israel, which we think is strategically important in terms of providing a partnership with Jewish peace activists to seek a way to raise concerns about Israel more effectively by joining with the voices of soldiers and conscripts who are refusing to serve.

IRENA KLEPFISZ: I started Middle East peace work in about 1980 or '81. It was a feminist group called Di Vilde Khayes—the wild beasts.

And after that, about ten years later, I was involved with the Jewish Women's Committee to End the Occupation, here in New York. I was executive director of New Jewish Agenda for a couple of years. And now I'm active in Brit Tzedek. I've also written a lot about the Middle East.

ELLEN LIPPMANN: I'm the rabbi of a congregation in the Holy City of Brooklyn called Kolot Chayeinu. Just being a rabbi of a Jewish congregation in these days, you have to be thinking about Israel and saying something about Israel. It was probably in connection with a sermon that I gave on the High Holidays several years ago that I kind of jumped with both feet into action about Israel. Because after the sermon—actually it might have been before—I said that during the afternoon anyone who wanted to could gather and we would talk about what we might want to do as a community.

We at Kolot Chayeinu had a vigil that got a whole lot more media attention than we might ever have imagined because it took place on the same day as an enormous pro-Israel rally at the UN. We were apparently the only Jewish voice out there saying anything different that day.

Since then we have continued to be not the only but among a few Jewish congregational voices that are out there at various times saying things critical of Israel publicly. And that's a difficult thing, I think, for Jews in congregations to do.

I'm also now on the advisory boards of Brit Tzedek v'Shalom and Rabbis for Human Rights–North America and a number of other groups. At Kolot Chayeinu we have continued to hold educational programs and other events about Israel/Palestine.

NAOMI BRAINE: I was somewhat involved in Middle East–related work during the first intifada in the late '80s in the Midwest, but in a relatively distant way. I spent much of the '80s focusing on antimilitarism and work around Central America and much of the '90s doing AIDS activism.

But at some point, about 1994 or '95, I began to get involved in Jews for Racial and Economic Justice in New York, in order to do activist work from a specifically Jewish perspective.

In September 2000, when this current intifada began, I found myself suddenly becoming very active—first with a new organization, Jews Against the Occupation (JATO), in New York and more recently also with the Women in Black Vigil here in New York.

Through JATO I've also had some involvement with a group known as the Palestine Activist Forum, which is an explicit effort to bring together Jewish and Palestinian American activists in New York to do work together.

ALISA SOLOMON: All of you are working in Jewish contexts in some respect—some of you specifically trying to reach a Jewish audience and some of you looking more broadly than that. What audience are you trying to reach and why? What's gained and lost in the approach you choose?

MARCIA FREEDMAN: For me, this has been a very, very conscious strategic decision over the past two years. When I came back from Israel two years ago, several months after the start of the second intifada and with the images of F-16s and Apache helicopters raining bombs on Gaza and the West Bank and Ramallah and so forth, I was just crazed and outraged and began speaking within the Jewish community from that point. I found very quickly that I was being totally ineffective, that I was being called "Jeremiah," that I was not being listened to in the slightest, that nobody could hear these things that I thought needed to be said from a very strong moral point of view, which I thought was of course a very Jewish point of view.

My decision was to really try to find a way to tailor a message to ordinary liberal Jews who have been involved in social justice issues forever and have never really had an interest in Israel, who are now finding themselves very, very upset. I know that there are hundreds of thousands, if not millions, of such Jews in this country, who agree with us.

We are trying to mobilize that body of opinion and to get them onboard in a way that everybody can easily be counted. The idea is hopefully within a year's time to get to tens of thousands of members and supporters and, through that, to begin to have an influence within the Jewish community and through that to begin to influence U.S. foreign policy, which I am totally convinced is the key to any future of what's going to happen between Israel and Palestine. If we can't do that, then it's really a lost cause for many decades to come.

ALISA SOLOMON: Do others agree that trying to influence U.S. foreign policy is the primary target?

MITCHELL PLITNICK: That's certainly fundamental to what A Jewish Voice for Peace (JVP) does. The idea that we operate from is that our strength as American Jews is not to influence what Israel does or what the Palestinians do surely, but rather what the U.S. government does. In my view, the U.S. government is the primary actor in preventing a resolution to this conflict because of its particular policies in the Middle East that just perpetuate Israeli hubris and Palestinian rage and that fuels the entire cycle.

So, our strategy has generally been to try and gather in Jews who feel very cut off from the community. It's a somewhat different target audience than the one Marcia described. It's also a priority for us to give license and some guidance to non-Jewish groups who are reluctant to speak out on this for fear of being labeled anti-Semitic and at the same time to be able to provide some leadership to what's hopefully a growing American movement against the occupation that can steer it away particularly from the growing sort of Jewish conspiracy theory around it, which is this idea that the Jews or the Zionists or the Israelis—whatever label people put on it—have taken control of U.S. foreign policy, which in my view is an absurdity, but a view that's gaining a bit more purchase throughout the movement. I think it's only going to be Jews who can stem that.

And so for that purpose, the idea for JVP is to reach into two different directions—both mainstream America and what I'd call nonaligned Jews.

JOEL KOVEL: I think that this is one of those very difficult moments. Certainly one would not say that Jews have "taken control of U.S. foreign policy," but it's certainly the case—and I think a very ominous case—that the Bush administration, to a much greater degree than any previous administration, has people in it who are ardent right-wing Zionists and who have actually been advisors in upper echelons of government. We don't want to talk about "The Jews." But I think it is important to talk about people with a very strong militant imperialist sort of Zionist mentality.

The fact of the matter is that these people are substantially more powerful in this administration than they have been in any other. These are also the same people who are leading the United States into a kind of preemptive mode, which is so appalling and terrifying to the whole world.

I disagree with what Mitchell just said on that subject. I think we have to learn ways to speak about the actualities of Zionism without falling into the abyss of anti-Semitism. That's a very, very difficult question. It's something that's inhibited critique of Israel for many, many years. We have to be very forthright and say that this kind of rational critique of the Zionist project is really necessary. It's necessary in order to prevent anti-Semitism, among other things.

MITCHELL PLITNICK: What I think is an important point is that these people that you're identifying—the Richard Perles and Paul Wolfowitzes and several others that we can talk about—are the same architects of U.S. policy who also wrote their rather infamous paper for Netanyahu back in '96. It's kind of a chicken-or-egg question, but an important question to try and pursue.

The aims of Israel since 1967 have been increasingly intertwined with the aims of the United States. It's impossible to try and distinguish where the viewpoint of an individual, who may be in government making decisions, begins and ends as far as Israel is concerned. But what is clear is that it's U.S. global interests that are at the heart of both Israeli and American policies in these regards, as far as the Perles and Wolfowitzes are concerned.

It's a mistake to characterize them as Zionists as if they are primarily motivated by whatever they perceive as Israel's interests. They perceive Israel's interests as being servile to the United States. That's the key point that has to be brought out.

MARCIA FREEDMAN: I want to stress what Joel said about right-wing Zionists and make the point that there's a very broad spectrum of Zionism since before the establishment of the State until this very day. These are right-wing Zionists who, like Netanyahu and Begin, are the descendants of Jabotinsky, who was extremely militant. This was a strain within Zionism prior to the establishment of the State. It was a very small minority voice that has grown in this century, and probably over the last twenty years really, to become a very dominant voice. That is a major shift in what Zionism is and how we can understand it. But still, I really want to make a distinction between right-wing Zionism and Zionism per se.

ALISA SOLOMON: Let's talk a little more about that. The label "Zionist" is one of the most fraught terms in this work right now. Some of the groups many of you are working with explicitly label yourselves as Zionists or talk about your love for Israel; others of you don't. I'd like to explore why that is and what it means.

NAOMI BRAINE: I'll jump in on that. JATO has taken a great deal of heat at times for the fact that while we don't call ourselves a non-Zionist organization, in all honesty, that is a reasonable description of us. Being a Jewish organization that is not only critical of Zionism but really takes non-Zionist positions and does a lot of work in coalition with Palestinians, we have often borne the brunt of a certain kind of hostility within the Jewish community. Saying in public that there are Jews who will speak out on these issues who are not Zionists is a very controversial thing. We are essentially accused of not being Jews, as if the definition of a Jew is a Zionist. We have had to really fight to stake our claim to be a Jewish voice, an admittedly marginal one. We did not found ourselves to be a big-tent Jewish organization but to stake out a position.

We do try to speak to the Jewish community as well as to larger coalitions. Part of the way we see our role in relation to Jewish communities is to remind

U.S. Jews that there is a progressive Jewish history, a leftist Jewish history specifically, that was never Zionist, and that was not that long ago, that exists within living memory.

The most controversial things we have done are when we're primarily addressing Jewish audiences, as we do, for example, on almost every holiday. We have taken an enormous amount of heat during some of those actions: "How dare you use Jewish symbols and Jewish holidays and Jewish events to give voice to a perspective that is unpopular?" Yet we are committed to being that presence that will have an anti-occupation *sukkah* with pictures of destroyed Palestinian buildings and adapt other rituals in certain ways.

ELLEN LIPPMANN: From the sort of liberal-to-left religious place, we've gotten some of the same kinds of criticism for saying things somewhat differently. It's been really important in our context to say that we are always criticizing Israel because of our love for Israel and our deep concern for Israel to survive morally as well as physically.

And yet, we are saying things that are critical of Israel and often at holiday times and using holiday symbols. We have gotten a certain amount of the same kind of criticism.

I have tended to stay away from uses of the word "Zionism" partly because it raises certain kinds of hackles that I'm not sure have been useful, at least in our conversations. I think it's been much more useful to say we have a range of opinions in a community about Israel. Most people support Israel's existence, and many, many people have affection or suffer love for Israel.

IRENA KLEPFISZ: I want to disagree a little bit with Marcia. My perception of the way Zionism is being used is that the distinctions among different kinds of Zionism have collapsed. There is very little nuance. Even though I know there's leftist Zionism and so on, the fact is that everything becomes a pro and con in the Jewish community to the point even that saying you're a non-Zionist can no longer be distinguished from saying you're an anti-Zionist, as once was possible, though there is a big difference. For example, you could be supporting two states without necessarily adhering to the Zionist vision of homeland and Diaspora. That distinction is no longer possible.

I think it's symptomatic of a lot of problems around language and linguistics. The problem in the Jewish community is not just with words like "Zionism." It's also with words like "occupation." People do not grasp what that means on a real day-to-day basis.

We have real problems with terminology within the Jewish community. One of the most difficult issues for activists is to find the rhetoric through which we can say what we feel and have the Jewish community be able to listen to us. We're almost talking different languages. It's very disturbing to see. It doesn't enable dialogue.

We're not a nuanced community anymore. It's all either/or. I feel my identity is so bound up with it. I feel I'm trying to save myself. If I lose Jewish community, I'll lose myself.

TONY KUSHNER: Do you think this is something specific to the struggles of the Jewish community at this point or is it just part of a general political problem of the vulgarization of language?

IRENA KLEPFISZ: Certainly it's in the larger society. I mean, I can't even turn on the TV because I can't listen to the language that I hear there on the news.

We talk about Jews' loyalty to Israel and Zionism. We don't talk about Jewish loyalty to the American government. I think that's really converged now. I'm not sure I know of an instance where American Jews have really opposed very loudly American policy as a group.

MARCIA FREEDMAN: I don't think that's correct. If you think of the civil rights movement and the anti–Vietnam War movement, the Jewish voice was very strong.

IRENA KLEPFISZ: That's true. But right now in the American Jewish community, who among us can imagine Jews going to the American government and saying "We don't like what you're doing"?

ELLEN LIPPMANN: An example is what just happened at the Jewish Council for Public Affairs where the Reform movement tried to come with a resolution about settlements. It seemed like a fairly innocuous resolution they tried to put forward. They weren't even able to bring it forward until they watered it down. And then it was defeated because it was seen as much too far to the left for what a group of American Jewish organizations could bring to the American government, though it was pretty mild compared to what I think many of us would want them to say.

MARCIA FREEDMAN: It was just about freezing settlement building. It was a nothing statement. It supported a two-state solution. But I think to understand better what happened there, you have to understand that that organization is the umbrella organization for the Jewish Community Relations Councils, which are part of the organized Jewish community and therefore part of the organized Jewish voice that's being directed out of the Israeli Foreign Ministry and AIPAC. This was not anything that represents the Jews. It represents a certain section of the Jewish population that is "the organized" population.

I want to return just for a second to the language issue because I think it's really crucial. I don't think there's a vulgarization of language that's taking place. I think there's an ongoing—and always is—politicization of language.

In the 1970s, to talk about the establishment of an independent state of Palestine and to be an Israeli or a Jew was to be called an anti-Zionist, a self-hating Jew and an Arab-lover. To use the word "Palestinian" was absolutely beyond the pale. So was "occupation."

And now what we're seeing coming back is this right wing—the right wing in Israel and the right wing within the Jewish community here—trying to once again make this word "occupation" into a dirty word, and they're talking about "disputed" territories. Not about "settlements" but about "communities" and so forth.

There's a battle over language going on that reflects itself in the word "Zionism," which is the granddaddy of all of these political words in this context. For many years—really decades—I've made a conscious decision never even to use that word because it means too many different things no matter who's waving it in the air. On the extreme right, it's almost jingoistic terminology and on the extreme left, it's anathema, a dirty word.

But I do think there is a point in talking about whether or not one agrees with the right of the State of Israel to exist as a Jewish state. I think there's a legitimate argument and a difficult argument. But I wouldn't like to muddy that one up with the words, "Are you a Zionist or not?"

JOEL KOVEL: But that's what Zionism is.

MARCIA FREEDMAN: That's one meaning of the word.

JOEL KOVEL: Yeah, but I think if you abandon that then we lose any sense of history.

MARCIA FREEDMAN: You don't have to abandon it. But you have to contextualize.

JOEL KOVEL: But you said you don't use it. I don't think we have to fight. I think we have to define it very clearly. But I think it's essential that we recognize there are profound contradictions inherent in that term, which people have not been willing to spin out.

Suppose I said here that Zionism is equivalent to a form of racism. Now people would get very outraged about that. But that's exactly how most of the world feels, and there's an inherent logic about that because it's a belief system that's guided the formation of Israel from the beginning and inherently contains the seeds of its own internal right-wing and more imperial shift.

MARCIA FREEDMAN: As do all nationalisms.

JOEL KOVEL: Well, this is not just nationalism. This is the Jewish homeland at the expense of another people. And that's what it's about. And that's what the rest of the world knows it's about.

MARCIA FREEDMAN: I can't go along with the idea that it's necessarily at the expense of another people. There are many brands of Zionism—

JOEL KOVEL: Well, that's the history of Israel.

MARCIA FREEDMAN:—calling for a binational state as well as for anarchism, et cetera.

MITCHELL PLITNICK: I think that this—this argument that's going on right here between Joel and Marcia—is indicative of exactly what Irena was talking about. It's a question of how Zionism is defined. There's a common use of "Zionism" that is extremely simplified and simply means backing Israel no matter what Israel does. I think that's what it's come to mean in the minds of many, many people.

Most of us, if not all of us in this conversation, would oppose that idea. But Zionism has in the past meant many different things. I would disagree, I guess, with Marcia just in the differentiation she made earlier between the right wing and the sort of mainstream of Zionism, particularly in the '20s, '30s, '40s, and

'50s. Jabotinsky ended up influencing the Labor leaders quite a bit. Ben Gurion adopted a lot of his ideas.

The key is to go back even further and recognize the strain in Zionism that was not even talking about a state, but about Jewish cultural attachments to that area of the world. At the time they were very important and today they have also a great deal of importance. That's very different from state politics. If we're breaking the word down into its myriad different meanings, that could be very helpful.

At the same time, in many people's minds the only solution to anti-Semitism and to the problems Jews have faced historically is a state. I disagree with that. I don't think that having a state has necessarily served us well in those terms. I don't think it's going to.

So there are a number of different places we can go and different ways we can think about it. It behooves us to think about those different ways and not try to narrow the definition of Jewish liberation. Even calling it "national liberation" is problematic; there are a lot of problems with defining Jews as a nation. But in any event, whatever Jewish liberation struggles we may have, there's only danger in limiting it to a statist and *realpolitik* view about how to go about it.

NAOMI BRAINE: One way to get around some of these conflicts over how Zionism is defined and what it has come to symbolize and represent, often even more than the technical definition, is to talk about the components of the situation rather than some of the buzzwords that have become attached to it. I said JATO could probably be considered a non-Zionist organization, but we don't have a position on Zionism one way or the other. We don't mention it anywhere in our statement of principle.

What we do talk about is self-determination, and we talk about a Palestinian right of return, which is how we're often classified. We also talk about Jewish self-determination. We talk about the rights of refugees. We talk about human rights.

We don't take a position on how many states should exist in any part of the world. We live in the United States. We can't dictate other people's state formations. But we put on the table some of the most volatile issues without getting bogged down in terms that have very different meanings and have become very culturally loaded.

IRENA KLEPFISZ: I don't totally agree. I think you have to talk about two states—or one state or whatever number of states. You're talking to the Jewish community and they want to know whether at least one—their state—is going to continue existing. I don't think you can have a conversation without the number of states coming up at some point. It's just impossible at present.

But the other thing I think about that is almost new to me and has to do with the Zionism issue is whether we need to focus on history. I used to think you had to really study history. I'm beginning to think that history is screwing us totally up!

[LAUGHTER]

What we really need to do is to look at what's going on, what's the situation right now? Who is where? There are people who have been exiled; they're in exile. There are people who are in what we call "Israel." There are people who are in a place we call "Palestine." And that's the thing that we should address. I used to want to just teach everybody the history. Now I'm sort of thinking: forget the history. Because all the who-did-what-when, who-started-what-how gets in the way of dealing with the present. You can almost get rid of the whole issue about Zionism and the history of Zionism and whether it contained the seeds of its own self-destruction—I'm not sure any of that actually helps our dialogue with the community.

The dialogue with the community should be about the present and existing situation and exactly what it is. Our vocabulary has to include "occupation" and "settlement" and what that really means.

JOEL KOVEL: I don't want to get into a big argument. But I just want to register that I couldn't disagree more. Human beings are historical creatures. That's who we are. And that's what people are fighting over. I just don't think one can or should evade that. I think then our arguments become incoherent and we have no sense of what our values are. You cannot ignore history. It's very painful. It's very difficult. There's good history. There's bad history. But without history, we don't exist as human beings.

MARCIA FREEDMAN: I want to make a distinction. Because I think Irena was talking about effective ways of speaking about the situation today to try to bring about change. I think that's a very different subject from what is the relevance of history to the—

JOEL KOVEL: I agree. But she said you shouldn't take history into account.

MARCIA FREEDMAN: It's not the place to start from. And I think from my experience, that's pretty right.

ALISA SOLOMON: I want to see if we can talk more about strategies for activism. That certainly relates to these questions. It also marks some of the difference between where Joel's coming from and where Irena's coming from in terms of bringing the activism to the streets or into community forums and so on.

When you're taking up some of the sticky issues, what are you organizing for specifically? What are you calling for? I know there's division among you over the question of whether we should be calling for an end to U.S. military aid or economic aid to Israel or a linking of that aid or not saying anything about the aid. What about the question that Naomi already raised of Palestinian refugees?

STEVEN FEUERSTEIN: One of the biggest weaknesses of our entire movement, however you want to define what that is, has been the inability to fashion a clear strategy and an objective as to what we actually want to accomplish over some period of time.

For example, Not In My Name and many other groups are focused on the essential slogan or goal of ending the occupation, so we stand around saying, "End the occupation," as if that's going to do it. To me, fundamentally the only thing that will really affect Israeli policy is going to be a challenge to U.S. aid of one form or another.

And that's not going to happen. There's no political will or power for that to happen for years given the current situation. So, to me, the question shouldn't be so much "Do you oppose military aid? Do you oppose all aid? What's your position?" But doing an analysis of where we need to get, what kind of power we need to assemble in order to have some kind of effect. And then moving backward from there to map out how we get there.

In my experience, among just about any of the peace activists I work with, there's no effort or maybe even real ability to fashion out that road map. We need a road map, and we're not even talking about that.

MARCIA FREEDMAN: For me, the question about strategy is what community, what population are you trying to influence? Where are you trying to work? It's very, very different if you're trying to influence American public opinion on these issues or if you're trying to influence American Jewish public opinion or if you're trying to influence alienated Jews, as JVP is doing. There are different strategies for different populations.

STEVEN FEUERSTEIN: Marcia, here's my question, if you don't mind my asking. Let's suppose Brit Tzedek is incredibly successful—and I hope it is, and I'm a member and helped found it. So we've got 10,000 members in a year and 25,000 members the year after that. What is Brit Tzedek going to call on the United States to do or Israel to do to actually make a difference?

MARCIA FREEDMAN: I think what we need to do is call on the United States to exercise its power and influence in the Middle East in a way that's just and fair to both sides. It's not rocket science. We need to advocate. I don't think that if the United States decides that it needs to use aid as a club or a threat to the Palestinians or to the Israelis, I'm not going to say no, but I'm not going to call for the United States to do that. I don't need to tell the United States how to do what it needs to do. They know perfectly well.

STEVEN FEUERSTEIN: So how do we—

MARCIA FREEDMAN: The idea of numbers, and numbers that are really countable because they've paid their dues and they're in the database, is that we have influence politically, that we can go to our congresspeople, particularly the Jewish congresspeople, and say, "Okay here in your district you've got 5,000 supporters of Brit Tzedek who are potentially voters for you who are not going to vote for you if you don't do XY and Z." When we've talked to Congress people over this past year, we have been told again, and again, and again: "We support your position but we cannot speak out. You have to bring us the grassroots. We don't have any grassroots support out there that we can feel." From my point of view, at least in terms of what I'm trying to do, that is the mission. That is the endgame.

MITCHELL PLITNICK: Marcia, I really agree with that strategy. I think though—and, again, we at JVP speak to a different audience than Brit Tzedek does—that part of bringing that political force to bear is having particular things that people can support. I think if we just say "Change the policy, be more fair," and we speak in such generalities, we have a harder time marshaling the real support that we need.

I think AIPAC positions—I hate to say the "pro-Israel" side because that can be a loaded term, we know who I'm talking about—have enormous numbers and most of those numbers are not Jewish. There just aren't enough Jews in this country to wield that power in terms of the grassroots. There aren't enough Jews in the world to do that.

So, the question is, how do we marshal those numbers for ourselves? Part of the answer is having a specific political platform. I think that where we can focus that on Congress is around the aid issue and saying that basically what American governments have occasionally—when they've really been motivated to—said in the past is that aid is tied to Israel doing certain things like freezing settlements, and then we can push that to dismantling them or abandoning them, whichever is possible.

MARCIA FREEDMAN: That's quite right, if what you're trying to do is organize American public opinion or alienated Jewish opinion. Going after the mainstream Jewish community and beginning with "stop aid"—you're dead in the water.

MITCHELL PLITNICK: Agreed.

MARCIA FREEDMAN: Might as well not bother.

MICHAEL LERNER: I haven't brought much up till now, but want to return to the question of strategies. The Tikkun Community is aimed at both Jews and non-Jews. And the reason for that is close to what Mitchell just talked about: namely that our desire to end the occupation and to protect the well-being of the Jewish people and of the Palestinian people requires a change in American policy that cannot be achieved by Jews alone. And that would not be achieved if we depended upon the Jewish world to become the vanguard of a progressive or a humane policy with regard to Palestinians. It's extremely implausible that it's achievable in anything like the next ten years.

From our standpoint, we want to transform the debate on this issue and to change American policy and build an organization both for Jews and for non-Jews. Of course that creates some issues and tensions. One of the things holding people in place in the current policy is that many, many decent Christians feel intimidated to speak out on these issues. They, as well as Jews, need a great deal of support to speak out because of the fear that they will be labeled anti-Semitic. It's a well-founded fear, given the actual discourse that exists in the organized Jewish community if they were to articulate a strong critique of Israeli policy. Creating an organization for Jews and non-Jews, I believe, is politically a necessary part of any strategy to change the policy.

So that's who we're trying to speak to. What's the strategy for that? There are two parts of our strategy in the short-run. Actually one long-term and one short-term but in our view they go hand in hand. So, long-term strategy, which I believe to be indispensable to actually changing the American policy either with regard to Israel or with regard to anything else for that matter, is to re-credit and restrengthen one of the following two paradigms. You'll know immediately which one. One paradigm says that the world, America, Israel can achieve safety and security through power and domination and control over others. And the other paradigm says, the way the world, the United States and Israel can achieve security is through cooperation, generosity and caring for each other.

Now this may sound very abstract, but far from it. I believe it's the center of what a politics has to be about in this period. The reason it's impossible to move policies in a progressive direction, either in Israel or in the United States, is because of the increasing triumph of the view that the only way to achieve safety for anyone is through the domination and control over others.

Consequently, if you want to provide safety for Israel and security for Israel, in my view, you need to relegitimate another paradigm. That's part of another aspect of the Tikkun view, which is that there is no individual solution for Israel. That Israel will never be safe and secure unless there's safety and security for all people on the planet. Although that sounds utopian and far away, in fact articulating that kind of politic is the most practical way of building the kind of movement in this country that could actually change American policy with regard to Israel. So that's the larger frame.

The more immediate frame is that we're focused on trying to bring people, both Jews and non-Jews, to Washington each year starting this year in June— and we hope to do this every year—for a conference and lobbying effort that is meant to legitimate a comprehensive vision of what a peace settlement could be because many, many people have used the word "peace." Now even Ariel Sharon is talking about a Palestinian state. But what is meant by these words quickly vitiated.

In our view, the strongest way to build support is to put forward a concrete vision of what that would be about. So we've articulated a plan that calls for an end to the occupation, a return of Israel to the pre-'67 borders with minor border modifications so that the Jewish parts of Jerusalem could become part of Israel and reparations for the Palestinian people, security for the State of Israel and for the Palestinian state, some form of military arrangement to provide security for both sides, reparations also for Jews who fled Arab lands and a few other points that together constitute a vision of what it could look like to be a just solution and to put that forward into public discourse to try to get local city councils to endorse it, to try to get local groups to put this on the ballot and to generate a public debate—not just in the Jewish community, but in the society as a whole about what it is that we're talking about when we're talking about a just solution for the Middle East.

ALISA SOLOMON: Michael, Marcia, Irena and others of you have been doing activism on this issue for a very long time. How has the climate changed? What's different about doing this work now from how it was fifteen years ago during the first intifada or during the '70s or earlier? And what lessons do those differences have for the kind of work that needs to be done now?

MARCIA FREEDMAN: There are lots of answers to that question. If I look back and say, "What was it like to be saying what I'm saying today?" which is fairly mainstream—two-state solution, roughly along the '67 borders, et cetera—to say that thirty years ago literally was considered to be traitorous within the Jewish community and certainly within the State of Israel and the society of Israel. Today, even Ariel Sharon talks about the establishment of a Palestinian state. There's a way in which we have won that argument.

But the way that it hasn't changed is that the resistance to giving up this territory has been so persistent from '67 on. There's been such stubborn resistance to it. The expansionist strain within Zionism, like the right wing in the United States, has great patience. It refuses to go away and it multiplies.

MICHAEL LERNER: I disagree with you, Marcia. I don't believe we've won anything. I think that the change in discourse—maybe this is just a semantic difference because I think you probably agree with some of this—has been only a change in discourse, not a change in substance. In fact, the liberal and progressive forces are in worse shape today than they've been in the organized Jewish community. The Reform movement, for example, or those who work specifically in the Jewish world, find themselves more intimidated rather than less intimidated today to articulate a humanistic view of the Palestinian people and their rights. People who express that in the Jewish world are more on the defensive today than they have been almost at any time, even though you're certainly right to say that the language has changed because now people say, "Oh, yeah, Palestinian state and so forth" in one breath and then in the next breath go right back to the extreme chauvinism and rejection of human rights and insensitivity to the pain and suffering of the Palestinian people. That's a reflection of the bankruptcy of the particular strategies engineered in part by Peace Now, in part by the Labor Party, that thought that the solution to these problems would come, that we would get people signing on to it a particular agreement or set of words rather than dealing with the fundamentals, which in my view include a recognition that every single human being is created in the image of God. Or, if you don't like religious language, then that Jews and non-Jews are fundamentally equally valuable, that Palestinian life is just as important as Jewish life.

Because we haven't waged the struggle on that, but have instead thought we would be more practical by confining ourselves to a language that seemed more realistic, we've ended up not addressing the fundamental core issue that is at the center of this, which is the humanity of the other and our ability to acknowledge that and to say that our needs as human beings can only be fulfilled through the fulfillment of everyone's needs.

JOEL KOVEL: I completely agree with what Michael just said, but would add that we have to also talk about territories not just life. When you talk about that, you're entering a very, very difficult area because to assert that Palestinians have as much right to the territory as Israelis and Jews is of course a huge issue.

MICHAEL LERNER: Yes, I meant to include that but thank you, Joel, for clarifying it.

JOEL KOVEL: In terms of what Michael said about not really winning anything, I think that we have to be very concrete here and talk about the precise state of affairs, not just sort of generalities about whether we're going to have a two-state or one-state solution, but what is in fact looming in the occupied territories. It's talked about in the Israeli press itself: an ongoing process there, namely the expulsion of the Palestinians, the destruction of Palestinian society. Things have gotten very much worse.

There was a story in the press the other day about the tripling of the poverty rate in the Palestinian community over the last six months. What we're seeing under the cover of business as usual and the press keeping all of this hidden and the whole discourse being very muddled is a situation in which apartheid, which is the sort of normal situation, has been expanded to ethnic cleansing. We really have to deal with this.

When we're talking about organizing, I don't think we can just organize for the future. There's an immediate disaster looming that could actually blow up as soon as Bush invades Iraq, which could provide the conditions under which the actual ethnic cleansing or expulsion of Palestinians could take place. In any event, their lives are being rendered unsupportable. So right now—what are we going to do here, what are we going to do now, to deal with the impending disaster?

MITCHELL PLITNICK: Personally I doubt there's going to be a mass expulsion. I think too many people know about it and the Iraq war wouldn't actually provide cover for it.

But the question that Joel's raising speaks to a more fundamental issue, which is, let's say we all got together and came up with a brilliant plan of how to stop it. How would we implement it? This is a universal problem among progressive movements and certainly has been one on this question: We see the suffering. We see horrible things going on, happening to both Israelis and Palestinians. We see the bombing in Haifa. We see the daily attacks on Palestinians and the numbers killed constantly escalating. We want to stop it now. And that's right and good and we should want to stop it now. But we have to have the means. We have not over the years been able to coalesce those means. Now, especially since the beginning of the latest intifada, there are a lot more resources out there for us to try and gather together.

But it's a time-consuming and painstaking process. And it hurts because while that time is being consumed and that painstaking effort is being pursued, more people are dying, more people are losing their homes, more people are getting blown up on buses. It hurts to sit by and watch it. But I don't see that we have any other choice. I think we have to marshal the forces together to really have an impact rather than see how we can respond in a small way that won't fundamentally change anything about the latest horrifying news out of Israel and the occupied territories.

NAOMI BRAINE: I agree with Mitchell. I know that there are Jews in Israel who are advocating transfer. But I think the major and most immediate danger is already happening and is going to intensify if there's a war, and is going to continue on after the war. It's Sharon's vision of setting up eight Palestinian enclaves, crowding people into them, fencing them off from one another, and calling this a Palestinian state. That is the danger. The real danger, from where we're sitting here as American Jews, is that he'll be able to sell that vision to the Bush administration. If we're looking for where we have to be putting our energy right now, it's to prevent that from being able to happen in any way that we possibly can. Mitchell's right: it's going to take a lot of hard work on the ground of marshaling forces.

IRENA KLEPFISZ: Just to go back two steps to the question of what it's like to be doing this work now as opposed to before. I think it's just incredibly harder. One of the things we're dealing with in the Jewish community, which I've encountered over and over again, is that there was a slippage. There were people who were with us during the first intifada who are no longer with us. I remember when people were very moved—Jews were very moved by seeing kids throwing rocks at tanks during the first intifada. This second intifada has shifted that.

They say, "Oh, we tried the peace process. They turned it down." This is much worse. Someone who has been there and rejected empathy is a much harder person to convince. That's partly what we're facing.

Also, we haven't mentioned one of the worst things now to have to deal with: to discuss suicide bombing. How do you deal with suicide bombings in the Jewish community? It was one thing when settlers in the first intifada were the ones being attacked. As long as it was outside of the green line, it was tolerated because it was understood that settlers had a choice.

But once the suicide bombing started within the green line, the Jewish community here became paralyzed with fear, with that anxiety that you might be minimizing the threat to Israelis in speaking from a progressive perspective. It's a very difficult thing to address. Some of it is psychological, and people don't—are just—they're scared!

Now it may be their fears are out of proportion. We can all point to the numbers—for every Israeli killed, there may be six or ten Palestinians killed. But those kinds of numbers just don't go over.

We have on our hands a community that's psychologically really messed up. I don't know how to say it any other way. But when you talk about strategy, you're talking about sort of a logical progression of things. And I don't think we're dealing with a terrain that allows for that kind of linear progression. It terrifies me. I'm worried about transfer. I'm worried even not about transfer but about people who leave voluntarily because of the untenable circumstances. So they don't even have to do official transfer.

From everything I see, I think it will take a very, very long time to change people's minds, move them, humanize the Palestinians. It's a very long-term thing. And we have this immediate crisis.

ELLEN LIPPMANN: I agree. I remember the point at which the Israeli government first prevented Arafat from going to Bethlehem at Christmas. And he said, "I'm going to go to Bethlehem if I have to walk." And everybody I knew here said, "Do it! Millions of people will walk with you. We will be for you." People began to imagine a huge possible shift, I think, because there was that chance of a nonviolent kind of gathering response.

Irena's absolutely right. Every time there's a bus bombing—especially buses because everybody rides them and all of us who've been in Israel have ridden them and can imagine that experience—people turn off a little bit more. Here in New York, September 11 complicated that kind of response. It mushes it all together. People are fearful in a kind of unnamed mushy way.

The last time I was in Israel was in 2000. I was convinced with all the groups that we met with, which included Palestinian peace groups and Israeli women peace groups, that there was going to be a two-state solution at any moment. The issue in Israel at that time was whether they were going to give back the Golan to Syria. And all over the country were banners saying, "Don't give back the Golan to Syria." It's stunning to think that was only three years ago. People have reminded me, of course, that among Palestinians it wasn't so clear that there would be a two-state solution at that time.

I remember we met with a city council woman in the West Bank, who showed us a map and said, "Here's where we are, and here's where we're staying." We saw essentially the same map at the Palestinian Center for Peace and Democracy. And they said, "This whole territory is ours, and it's going to be Jew-free, if we have our way." It was the same map. And I started to remember that we had both of those visits, and that essentially that intransigence is now where things are—they both have their maps.

NAOMI BRAINE: I agree that doing this work now is infinitely harder than it was fifteen years ago. That story of the two maps, in a sense, captures a piece of it in that I've found in trying to talk with Jews about what's happening now, the history I feel I need to teach people is not going back to 1948 but to 1998 and what was actually happening in the territories. I find that so many people don't allow themselves to really grasp that during the so-called "peace process," the settlements were expanding, the bypass roads were going in. Life in the territories took a nosedive. Those were the seeds of the current intifada.

But very few Jews know that, very few Jews were aware—even in Israel never mind the United States—of what Palestinian reality between 1995 and 2000 was. We're fighting this idea that Barak made a generous offer of peace and they turned it down.

There's a genuine ignorance. But I also think it's about the control of information. And about how hard you have to work in order to get certain information.

We need to think in both long-term and short-term now. There's not likely to be a radical shift within the Jewish community in the immediate future for all the reasons we've all been talking about and Irena summarized very well. But the issue of U.S. foreign policy is not just a Jewish issue. It's important for those of us who work outside the Jewish community to talk about this as an issue that doesn't affect only Jewish America. One strength of anti-occupation activism right now is that we have different groups addressing different communities. Everybody doesn't have to do the same thing. I respect people who are working in the mainstream Jewish community, and in all honesty, I don't think I would be capable of it.

I really think that we have to think about what's going on now as a form of ethnic cleansing. I was in the territories over the summer when every city was under twenty-four-hour curfew, essentially seven days a week, and movement was almost impossible. I don't know that there will be mass transfer. But everything short of that is already taking place.

Those people who can leave, if not quite everyone, have left. And the people who are there—there's such an enormous level of cultural destruction. There are no institutions left. The universities have been closed and sealed. There are attacks on students and faculty. They're even worse than they were during the last intifada. There is such systematic destruction at this point of Palestinian cultural institutions that the population that remains is really struggling just to survive, to eat, to feed their children. The malnutrition is astounding. We really have to be honest with ourselves and say that in and of itself that is a form of ethnic cleansing.

ELLEN LIPPMANN: I thought I'd go back to Irena's point about not remembering history. Because one of the things we come up against all the time in the Jewish community is the question of Jews being the victim. It's one of the things that blinds people to being able to see other people as victims—or that we are victimizers. That is, we can't possibly be victimizers because we're the victim. This is a horrible way to put it, but one of the results of the suicide bombings is that we truly are victims, yet also thus continue that cycle of seeing ourselves only as victims. It's an enormous psychological reality.

IRENA KLEPFISZ: One of the most telling things about American Jewry intellectually and psychologically you can find in a bookstore. Look into a Judaica section. It's 45 percent Holocaust, 45 percent Zionism and Israel, and 10 percent whatever's left over. That is a real reflection of where American Jews are and it's very, very appalling.

Or if you go to a university and ask them, "What Jewish Studies courses are you giving?" "Well, we have a course on the Holocaust. We have a course on Zionism and Israel." Do you even give a course on pre-1939 Jewry in Europe? Does anybody know where the Jews who died came from? Who they were?

This is the part of me that wants people to know history, but at the same time to be able to recognize what does a victim look like at a particular moment. That you can be a victim and also a victimizer.

We had to learn this in the women's movement and in the lesbian feminist movement—that the movement could be racist as much as it could be fighting homophobia. It could be anti-Semitic. There could be lesbian violence. Somehow the Jewish community has never faced this.

MITCHELL PLITNICK: It's important to bring the whole question of the Jewish position in today's times into focus here. It strikes me as profoundly tragic that most Jews don't recognize what a relative high point this is in our history. There haven't been a whole lot of times in Jewish history that Jews have done as well on any level, in any place as we have particularly in the United States, but also in Canada and Great Britain, and have—at whatever cost—a flowering society in Israel.

At the same time our position in the global politics around the Middle East and these perceptions of Jewish power in American politics replicate a lot of the danger times that Jews have faced in the past. Some of our greatest tragedies have also come after some of our periods of greatest prosperity. We need, as Jews, to worry about this—I don't think anyone else necessarily can be made to worry about it. We need to address the fact that if the Middle East situation blows up sufficiently, it's Israel and indeed the Jews that get blamed. That concerns me a great deal.

So I would point us in the direction of looking at the dynamic that's being set up and looking at the position we're in and recognizing that our leadership, as has happened all too often in the past, is putting us collectively in a pretty dangerous position. And acting in ways that are really anathema to most of our ethics. It's up to us—people like us, Jews like us—to confront that without these fears of attacking other Jews or being too disruptive to unity or any of that sort of thing. Not that I think any of you folks are particularly concerned about that sort of thing on that level. But we have to bring together a Jewish community that really does critically examine all of our actions and all of our place in society. So I think that is a big part of our work on Israel and Palestine as well.

ALISA SOLOMON: You've all outlined an incredibly urgent and depressing situation. Those of you who have been doing this work for a long time have talked about how much harder, more tragic and more impossible the work has become. So my question is, where do you get the energy? Where do you find a sense of hope? How do you get up in the morning and have the commitment to keep doing this work?

MARCIA FREEDMAN: It's something very fundamental: I can't live without it. I would crash in despair and probably not give a shit about my own personal life at all if I couldn't find someplace to put my energy that said, "Okay, here's the steps that I can take that may lead to something that may be better and different." For me it's congenital, temperamental. It's not rational at all.

MITCHELL PLITNICK: I guess there are a few things that I try to remind myself of. One is that conflicts end eventually. The Hundred Years' War went for 100 years, but it did end. [LAUGHTER]

Look at Europe. Europe was at each other's throats in the most bloody fashion for century after century. And most of the biggest combatants there are now at peace and working together. Conflicts do end. And groups of people, however we organize ourselves—by culture, by nationality, by ethnicity—do progress, and they do grow. And in many cases, at least, they do survive. Certainly as Jews, we've seen our ability to survive lots and lots of different things. This period is actually one of our toughest tests.

So, to me the future is not at all written. In ten years, in five years, things happen that we can't predict. For me, the hope lies in the idea of doing what I think is in the best interest of the world, the best interest of the Jews, the best interest of everyone the Jews are dealing with around this issue, and being ready for something good to come along to help us: Being and doing the best we can until then and being ready to capitalize on circumstances which I think inevitably will come, just as negative circumstances come.

STEVEN FEUERSTEIN: I gain a lot of strength—and I don't even know if it's optimism but just energy and will to keep going—through my contacts and work with Israeli and Palestinian peace activists. One of the most exciting things for me around doing this work is the amount of contact I've had and the ability to actually strategize and learn from people who are in the midst of the conflict. I'm very much a solidarity person. One of the ways you sustain solidarity is through the person-to-person linkages, particularly with the people who are in the fire and have really been tested and proven by it. I have a lot to learn from them.

JOEL KOVEL: One thing that gives me hope is that we happen to be in the midst of a worldwide transformation of the peace movement that I have never seen in forty years of struggling. And that transformation has incalculable results. I see my students coming alive in ways intellectually and politically that has not been the case since the Vietnam years, and even in a much more hopeful way.

NAOMI BRAINE: For me action wards off despair. If I didn't do anything, I would find it much harder to get out of bed and would feel much more overwhelmed. Taking action is a way to deal with the enormity of the mess at an emotional level as well as a political level.

I also think that the people I work with are a lot of what keeps me going. That's certainly true for my Jewish colleagues and co-workers. It's also true in terms of the alliances I've developed here in New York with Palestinian American activists and the processes I've been through in creating real coalition work between Jewish Americans and Palestinian Americans, which has not always been easy. But there is something very hopeful and very inspiring coming out of some of those meetings and having been in a room with people who are committed to creating a shared space, and not just in that room at that moment, but creating a demonstration, for example, where there will be both Jews and Palestinians. And talking about what will it take to do that and thinking strategically together about creating shared space in public spaces. And then doing our best, as a team—a team of both Jews and Palestinians—to go about enacting it.

It doesn't always work. But that process with each other and our commitment to creating shared public space is very important.

ELLEN LIPPMANN: I want to put in a word for prayer. And for the existence of Shabbat and to say to some extent having a day off regularly is not a bad way to get new energy. But also to say that I get to come together every week with a group of mostly like-minded people or at least people who are willing to talk together and think together. One of the ways we put some energy into maybe the edges of this issue is working on those prayers that Jews have said for centuries and which we are working to change in various ways, either wrestling together with traditional words or working on changing traditional words so that we can pray in a new way and not be thinking so Jewishly exclusively, and not so focused on Israel that we're not looking at the rest of the world as well. There are certainly other places that are doing that work too, but I think we shouldn't ignore the ways in which changed prayer can have an influence on Jewish thinking.

Certainly centuries of Jews yearning for Jerusalem has had an effect on Jewish thinking. And the ways in which we can lead to new centuries of other kinds of thinking will have some effect.

IRENA KLEPFISZ: I'll echo what others have said about working with others. Not working is not an option because it just seems impossible not to do anything. And I work very hard on this issue.

But I'm going to put in a note of pessimism. While I also believe that things change, there's a part of me that's very despairing about what's going on because it's so unnecessary. Whatever hurt and damage is done now, whoever is killed, whoever's maimed, whoever's exiled—if you have peace ten years from now, even six months from now, they're not going to be healed. They're not going to come to life. In the end it's going to come out anyway with a peace because it has to. Then why can't it happen now? I feel like I operate on these two levels—one that acts and the other one that's despairing and then kind of pushes it aside and gets up and keeps going.

MICHAEL LERNER: I draw my hope from belief in God and understanding the Jewish concept of Yud Hey Vav Hey—YHVH—as the conception of the force of healing and transformation in the universe that makes it possible to transform that which is into that which ought to be. That force has been with us for a long time and is getting closer and closer. Recognizing who the God of the universe is, is a source of sustenance for me.

The Jewish people have been screwed up from the beginning and our tradition has been one of making that very explicit, from Abraham's outrageous treatment of his wives and almost killing his son to the people making the golden calf right after to the massacres of people.

And so, prophets and others in the Jewish tradition have come along over and over and over again and said the same thing: "Hey, you guys are all screwed up. You've forgotten everything about what the core vision is here. And you've got to make repentance or transformation, go back to the highest ideals." Well, this has been going on for a very long time. And what keeps me hopeful is that there is this force in the universe that manifests through the people like the people in this conversation, in this group and many, many others—both Jews and non-Jews—who are fighting for a world that manifests the fullest possibilities of love and kindness and generosity.

Contributors' Biographies

SETH ACKERMAN is a contributing writer to FAIR, the national media watch-group. His articles have appeared in *Harper's, In These Times, Left Business Observer,* and the *Washington Times.* He lives in Brooklyn, New York.

AMMIEL ALCALAY's books include *from the warring factions* (2002), *Memories of Our Future* (1999); *After Jews and Arabs* (1993), and *the cairo noteboooks* (1993); his translations include *Keys to the Garden: New Israeli Writing* (1996), and two books by Bosnian poet Semezdin Mehmedinovic, *Sarajevo Blues* (1998) and *Nine Alexandrias* (2003).

MEG BARNETTE is the director of member services and counsel for the Community Development Venture Capital Alliance. BRAD LANDER is the director of the Fifth Avenue Committee, a community development group in Brooklyn, and a board member and former co-chair of Jews for Racial and Economic Justice. They live in Brooklyn with their son Marek and daughter Rosa.

JOEL BEININ has taught Middle East history at Stanford University since 1983. His most recent book is *Workers and Peasants in the Modern Middle East* (Cambridge University Press, 2001). He has a long association with the Middle East Research and Information Project and has been a member of Jewish Voice for Peace for the last three years.

PHYLLIS BENNIS is a Fellow of the Institute for Policy Studies in Washington. Her books include *Before & After: U.S. Foreign Policy and the War on Terrorism* (Interlink, 2002) and *Calling the Shots: How Washington Dominates Today's UN* (Interlink, 2000). She is also author of *The Palestine-Israeli Crisis: A Primer,* published by TARI (2003).

DANIEL BOYARIN, Taubman Professor of Talmudic Culture and Rhetoric at the University of California, Berkeley, is the author, among other books, of *Intertextuality and the Reading of Midrash* (1990) and *Unheroic Conduct: The Rise of Heterosexuality and the Invention of the Jewish Man* (1997). *Border Lines: The Partition of Judaeo-Christianity* is forthcoming in 2004. He received the 1994 Crompton Noll Award from the Gay and Lesbian Caucus of the MLA.

JONATHAN BOYARIN is a lawyer and anthropologist who lives on the Lower East Side of New York City. His first book was *From a Ruined Garden: The Memorial Books of Polish Jewry* (with Jack Kugelmass), and his most recent is *Powers of*

Diaspora (with Daniel Boyarin). In between he has written and edited several books on his own, including *Palestine and Jewish History*.

NAOMI BRAINE is a sociologist and community activist. In addition to her work on the Middle East, she has been active in feminist, antimilitarist, and AIDS movements. She is a member of Jews Against the Occupation and on the Board of Directors of Jews for Racial and Economic Justice.

E. M. BRONER, Ph.D., Prof. Emerita, has written ten books, among them the novel *A Weave of Women,* and is co-author of *The Women's Haggadah.* She has been leading The Women's Seder for twenty-eight years. She has won two National Endowment for the Arts Awards and a Wonder Woman Award. Broner taught at Wayne State University, Sarah Lawrence College, Haifa University (Israel), and UCLA. She has been active politically since she was six years old.

JUDITH BUTLER is Maxine Elliot Professor of Rhetoric and Comparative Literature at the University of California, Berkeley. Her books include *Antigone's Claim: Kinship Between Life and Death* (Columbia University Press, 2000), *Gender Trouble: Feminism and the Subversion of Identity* (Routledge, 1990), and *The Psychic Life of Power: Theories of Subjection* (Stanford University Press, 1997). Forthcoming books include *Undoing Gender* (Routledge) and *Precarious Life* (Verso).

BLANCHE WIESEN COOK is distinguished Professor of History and Women's Studies at the John Jay College and Graduate Center of the City University of New York. Her most recent book, best-seller *Eleanor Roosevelt: Volume Two,* was published in 1999. *Volume One* was published in 1992 and she is currently working on the third and final volume.

MARC H. ELLIS is University Professor of American and Jewish Studies and Director of the Center for American and Jewish Studies at Baylor University in Waco, Texas. Professor Ellis has lectured around the world and has published books and essays relating to the question of Jewish identity in light of the Holocaust and the ongoing crisis in the Middle East. He has published more than twenty books, including *Toward a Jewish Theology of Liberation* and *Israel and Palestine: Out of the Ashes; The Search for Jewish Identity in the 21st Century.*

MARCIA FALK's poems, translations, and essays have appeared widely in the United States and abroad. Her books include *The Book of Blessings*, a re-creation of Jewish prayer from an inclusive, nonhierarchical perspective; *The Song of Songs: A New Translation;* and a forthcoming translation of the poems of the Hebrew poet Zelda. Her website is *www.marciafalk.com.*

STEVEN FEUERSTEIN is an author and trainer on the computer programming language Oracle PL/SQL. He helped found and organize Not In My Name, Jewish

Unity for a Just Peace (JUNITY), Brit Tzedek v'Shalom, and the Refuser Solidarity Network, which he now coordinates. He was active in the antiapartheid movement and the Committee in Solidarity with the People of El Salvador (CISPES) in the 1980s.

JONATHAN SAFRAN FOER is the author of the novel *Everything Is Illuminated* and the editor of *A Convergence of Birds,* a collection of writing inspired by the bird boxes of Joseph Cornell. He lives in Brooklyn, New York.

MARCIA FREEDMAN was one of the founders and leaders of the feminist movement in Israel and served in the Israeli Knesset from 1973 to 1977. She has been an activist for Middle East peace for more than thirty years. She is currently president of Brit Tzedek v'Shalom, the Jewish Alliance for Justice and Peace.

RICHARD GOLDSTEIN is the executive editor of the *Village Voice,* where he has written about the intersection of politics, culture, and sexuality for the past thirty-five years. He is the author, most recently, of *Homocons: The Rise of the Gay Right* (Verso) and is currently at work on a book about neo-macho in contemporary American life.

PHILIP GREEN, Visiting Professor of Political Science at the New School University Graduate Faculty and a member of the Editorial Board of *The Nation,* is the author of, among other works, *The Pursuit of Inequality; Retrieving Democracy: In Search of Civic Equality;* and *Equality and Democracy* (The New Press, 1998).

MARILYN HACKER is the author of nine books, including the just-published *Desesperanto; Winter Numbers,* which received a Lambda Literary Award and the Lenore Marshall Award of *The Nation* magazine and the Academy of American Poets in 1995; and *Selected Poems,* which was awarded the Poets' Prize in 1996. She lives in New York and Paris, and teaches at the City College of New York.

SUSANNAH HESCHEL is the Eli Black Associate Professor of Jewish Studies at Dartmouth College. She is the author of several books, including *Abraham Geiger and the Jewish Jesus,* and co-editor of *Insider/Outsider: American Jews and Multiculturalism.* She serves as co-chair, with Michael Lerner and Cornel West, of the Tikkun Community.

ESTHER KAPLAN is a Brooklyn-based journalist and a community activist. A former editor at *The Nation, POZ,* and the *Village Voice,* she is now a radio producer for WNYE and co-host on WBAI of a program on Jewish culture and politics. She is on the board of directors of Jews for Racial and Economic Justice and the workers' rights board of New York Jobs with Justice.

MELANIE KAYE/KANTROWITZ, an activist since the early 1960s and the first director of Jews for Racial and Economic Justice, is author of *The Issue Is Power: Essays on Women, Jews, Violence, and Resistance; My Jewish Face & Other Stories*, and a new book, *The Color of Jews*, to appear in 2004. She holds a doctorate in Comparative Literature and directs the Queens College/CUNY Worker Education Extension Center.

NAOMI KLEIN is an award-winning journalist and author of the international best-selling books, *No Logo: Taking Aim at the Brand Bullies* and *Fences and Windows: Dispatches from the Front Lines of the Globalization Debate*. She writes internationally syndicated monthly columns for *The Globe and Mail* newspaper and *The Nation*.

IRENA KLEPFISZ, born in Warsaw in 1941, has taught English, creative writing, Women's Studies, and Yiddish at Columbia University, YIVO, and elsewhere. An activist in the lesbian/feminist and Jewish communities, her books include *A Few Words in the Mother Tongue, Poems Selected and New (1971–1990)* and *Dreams of an Insomniac: Jewish Feminist Essays, Speeches and Diatribes* (1990).

JOEL KOVEL's most recent book is *The Enemy of Nature* (Zed, 2002). In recent articles in *Tikkun* magazine (available on *www.joelkovel.org*) and in a book he is now preparing, Kovel is exploring the possibilities of a post-Zionist Israel.

TONY KUSHNER's plays include *Angels In America: A Gay Fantasia on National Themes, Hydriotaphia, A Bright Room Called Day, Slavs!: Thinking About the Longstanding Problems of Virtue and Happiness, Homebody/Kabul,* the musical *Caroline or Change* and several adaptations. He is the recipient of a Pulitzer Prize, two Tony Awards, and a lifetime achievement award from the National Foundation for Jewish Culture.

DANIEL LAZARE is the author of *The Frozen Republic: How the Constitution Is Paralyzing Democracy* (Harcourt Brace, 1996) and *The Velvet Coup: The Constitution, the Supreme Court, and the Decline of American Democracy* (Verso, 2001). He lives in Manhattan.

MICHAEL LERNER is Rabbi of Beyt Tikkun Synagogue in San Francisco, editor of *Tikkun*, national chair of the Tikkun Community, and author of nine books including *The Socialism of Fools: Anti-Semitism on the Left, The Politics of Meaning, Jewish Renewal,* and most recently *Healing Israel/Palestine* (North Atlantic Books, 2003) *www.tikkun.org*

ROBERT JAY LIFTON is Visiting Professor of Psychiatry at Harvard Medical School. His books include *Death in Life: Survivors of Hiroshima* (which won a National Book Award), *The Nazis Doctors: Medical Killing and the Psychology of Genocide,* and (most recently) *Superpower Syndrome: America's Apocalyptic Confrontation with the World.*

ELLEN LIPPMANN is founder and rabbi of Kolot Chayeinu/Voices of Our Lives, a progressive congregation in Brooklyn. She serves on the rabbinic boards of the Hannah Senesh School and the New Israel Fund, and on the advisory boards of Rabbis for Human Rights–North America and Brit Tzedek v'Shalom. Her essays and midrashim appear in *The Women's Torah Commentary* and in other publications.

MICHAEL MASSING is a New York writer and a regular contributor to such publications as *The New York Times, The New York Review of Books, The Nation,* and *The American Prospect.* He is the author of *The Fix,* a critical study of the U.S. war on drugs.

ARTHUR MILLER was born in New York City in 1915 and studied at the University of Michigan. His plays include *All My Sons, Death of a Salesman, The Crucible, The Price, The Ride Down Mt. Morgan,* and *Broken Glass.* His most recent play, *Resurrection Blues,* opened in 2002.

AURORA LEVINS MORALES is a poet, historian, and essayist of Russian Jewish and Puerto Rican heritage. Her most recent books are *Remedios: Stories of Earth and Iron from the History of Puertorriqueñas, Medicine Stories,* and *Telling to Live: Latina Feminist Testimonios by the Latina Feminist Group,* of which she is a member.

MARILYN KLEINBERG NEIMARK co-hosts (with Esther Kaplan) "Beyond the Pale: The Progressive Jewish Radio Hour" on WBAI in New York City. She is a co-founder (with Donna Nevel) and board member of Jews for Racial and Economic Justice, a grassroots activist organization. She is Professor of Accountancy at Baruch College, The City University of New York.

GRACE PALEY is a writer and a teacher, a feminist and an activist. Her books include *Just As I Thought,* a collection of her personal and political essays and articles; *Begin Again,* her collected poems; *The Collected Stories,* which was a finalist for the National Book Award; and *Long Walk and Intimate Talks* (Feminist Press), illustrated by Vera Williams. She lives in New York City and Vermont, where she is the Poet Laureate.

MARGE PIERCY's memoir is *Sleeping with Cats* (Perennial). Knopf published *The Art of Blessing the Day: Poems with a Jewish Theme* (paperback 2001) and *Colors Passing Through Us* this spring, her sixteenth poetry book. Her most recent novel, *Three Women; The Third Child,* is due in November from HarperCollins.

ROBERT PINSKY's newest books are *Democracy, Culture and the Voice of Poetry* (Princeton University Press, 2002) and the forthcoming anthology *Invitation to Poetry* (W.W. Norton, 2004). He is the author of six books of poetry, most recently *Jersey Rain,* and translator of *The Inferno of Dante.* He teaches in the graduate writing program at Boston University.

MITCHELL PLITNICK is the Director of Administration and Policy of Jewish Voice for Peace. He was a key organizer in growing JVP into the largest Jewish peace organization of its kind in the United States. He has had numerous articles published in *Znet, Jewish Currents, Source Point,* the *San Francisco Chronicle, The UN Observer,* and *Israel Insider.*

LETTY COTTIN POGREBIN, a founding editor of *Ms.* magazine and the author of nine books, is a writer and activist focusing on women's equality and Israeli-Palestinian peace. Her best-known titles include *Deborah, Golda, and Me: Being Female and Jewish in America,* and the novel *Three Daughters.* She is a past president of the Authors Guild and a past chair of Americans for Peace Now.

ADRIENNE RICH's most recent books of poetry are *Midnight Salvage* and *Fox. Arts of the Possible: Essays and Conversations* was published in 2001. She has been a recipient of the Brandeis Medal in the Arts, the Lannan Foundation Lifetime Achievement Award, the Lambda Book Award, the Lenore Marshall/*Nation* Prize, the Bollingen Prize in Poetry, and the 2003 Literary Award from the National Foundation for Jewish Culture.

SARA ROY is a senior research scholar at the Center for Middle Eastern Studies, Harvard University. She has written extensively on the Palestinian-Israeli conflict with a focus on Gaza. Her books include *The Gaza Strip: The Political Economy of Dedevelopment* (now in its second edition) and *From Extremism to Civism and Back: The Palestinian Islamic Movement in Transition* (forthcoming).

DOUGLAS RUSHKOFF is the author of nine best-selling books, including *Media Virus, Coercion, Ecstasy Club,* and *Exit Strategy.* His commentaries appear on NPR and *CBS Sunday Morning,* as well as in *Time* and *The New York Times.* His latest book, *Nothing Sacred: The Truth About Judaism,* has generated new conversations across America about Torah, faith, and Zionism.

GRACE SCHULMAN's recent poetry collections are *The Paintings of Our Lives* and *Days of Wonder: New and Selected Poems.* Awards include The Aiken Taylor Award for Modern Poetry; the Delmore Schwartz Award for Poetry; and the Distinguished Alumna Award from New York University's Graduate School of Arts and Sciences.

RUTH KNAFO SETTON is the author of the novel *The Road to Fez* (Counterpoint Press). She is the writer-in-residence for the Berman Center for Jewish Studies at Lehigh University, a faculty member of the MFA program at Georgia College & State University, and the fiction editor of *Arts & Letters: A Journal of Contemporary Culture*.

ELLA HABIBA SHOHAT, Professor of Cultural Studies at New York University, has lectured and published extensively on the intersection of gender, post/colonialism, and multiculturalism as well as on Zionist discourse, the Arab-Jewish and Mizrahi question. Her books, among others, include *Israeli Cinema: East/West and the Politics of Representation* (University of Texas Press, 1989) and *Forbidden Reminiscences* (Bimat Kedem LeSifrut Publishing, Tel Aviv, 2001, Hebrew).

HENRY SIEGMAN, Senior Fellow and Director of the U.S./Middle East Project of the Council on Foreign Relations, was executive director of the American Jewish Congress (1978–94) and director of the American Association for Middle East Studies and editor of its quarterly publication, *Middle East Studies* (1958–63). His books include *Strengthening Palestinian Public Institutions* (1999) and *U.S. Middle East Policy and the Peace Process* (1997).

ALISA SOLOMON has been covering Israel/Palestine since the mid-1980s as a staff writer at the *Village Voice*. She is also a Professor of English/Journalism at Baruch College–City University of New York, and of English and Theater at the CUNY Graduate Center. She is the author of *Re-Dressing the Canon: Essays on Theater and Gender*.

SUSAN SONTAG has written novels, stories, essays, and plays; written and directed films; and worked as a theater director in the United States and Europe. Her novel *In America* won the National Book Award for fiction in 2000. In 2001 she was awarded the Jerusalem Prize for the body of her work, and in 2003 she received the Friedenspreis (Peace Prize) of the German Association of Publishers and Booksellers.

MICHAEL E. STAUB is the author, most recently, of *Torn at the Roots: The Crisis of Jewish Liberalism in Postwar America*. His work analyzes the rise of Jewish neo-conservatism and charts how liberal, radical, and feminist Jews revitalized Jewish life in the 1960s and 1970s. He lives in Ann Arbor, Michigan.

LYNNE TILLMAN's novels are *Haunted Houses, Cast in Doubt, Motion Sickness,* and *No Lease on Life* (a finalist for the National Book Critics Circle Award, 1998). Her story collections are *The Madame Realism Complex, Absence Makes the Heart,* and, most recently, *This Is Not It*.

ARTHUR WASKOW is the director of The Shalom Center (www.shalomctr. org) and the author of many books on Judaism, spirituality, and social change, including *Godwrestling—Round 2.*

C. K. WILLIAMS's most recent books of poetry are *The Vigil* and *Repair,* which won the Pulitzer Prize, and a collection of his poems on love, *Love About Love.* A book of essays, *Poetry and Consciousness,* appeared in 1998, and a book of autobiographical meditation, *Misgivings,* in 2000. His new book of poems, *The Singing,* will be published in fall 2003.

ELLEN WILLIS directs the Cultural Reporting and Criticism program in the Department of Journalism at New York University. She is the author of three books of cultural and political commentary and contributes to *The Nation, Dissent, Salon,* and other publications. Her essays on various aspects of the Jewish condition include "The Myth of the Powerful Jew," "Next Year in Jerusalem," and "Exile on Main Street: What the Pollard Case Means to Jews."

DANIEL WOLFE is a community scholar at Columbia University's School of Public Health, and the author of the *Our Bodies, Ourselves*-inspired *Men Like Us: The GMHC Complete Guide to Gay Men's Sexual, Physical, and Emotional Well-Being* (Ballantine Books). He is the author of several books on the Middle East, and his writing has appeared in publications including *The New York Times Book Review, The Guardian, POZ, The Advocate,* and the *Village Voice.*

Birkat Shalom, Blessing of Peace
From *The Book of Blessings*
Marcia Falk

נִשְׁאַל מֵעֵין הַשָּׁלוֹם:
יִזַּל כַּטַּל,
יַעֲרֹף כַּמְטַר הַשָּׁלוֹם,
וְתִמְלָא הָאָרֶץ שָׁלוֹם
כַּמַּיִם לַיָּם מְכַסִּים.

Nish'al mey'eyn hashalom:
Yizal katal,
ya'arof kamatar hashalom,
v'timla ha'áretz shalom
kamáyim layam m'khasim

Eternal wellspring of peace—
may we be drenched with the longing for peace
that we may give ourselves over
as the earth to the rain, to the dew,
until peace overflows our lives
as living waters overflow the seas.